M
inc
Bi
mc
an

-
-
-
-

W
th
th
rel

A
R
au
of

BRENT LIBRARIES

Please return/renew this item
by the last date shown.
Books may also be renewed by
phone or online.
Tel: 0115 929 3388
On-line www.brent.gov.uk/libraryservice

ALSO AVAILABLE FROM ROUTLEDGE

The Bible: The Basics
John Barton
978-0-415-41136-3

Screening the Afterlife: Theology, Eschatology, and Film
Christopher Deacy
978-0-415-57259-0

**Theology Goes to the Movies: An Introduction
to Critical Christian Thinking**
Clive Marsh
978-0-415-38012-6

The Routledge Companion to Religion and Film
John Lyden
978-0-415-60187-0

The Religion and Film Reader
Jolyon Mitchell, S. Brent Plate
978-0-415-40495-2

CONTENTS

ALPHABETICAL LIST OF
ENTRIES

CHRONOLOGICAL LIST
OF ENTRIES

CLASSIFIED LIST OF ENTRIES

THE BIBLE ON FILM

Ben-Hur (1959)
David and Bathsheba (1951)
From the Manger to the Cross (1912)
Godspell (1973)
Gospel According to St. Matthew, The (1964)
Greatest Story Ever Told, The (1965)
Green Pastures, The (1936)
Intolerance: Love's Struggle through the Ages (1916)
Jesus Christ Superstar (1973)
Jesus of Montreal (1989)
Jesus of Nazareth (1977)
King of Kings (1961)
King of Kings, The (1927)
Last Temptation of Christ, The (1988)
Life of Moses (1909–1910)
Monty Python's Life of Brian (1979)
Passion of the Christ, The (2004)
Prince of Egypt, The (1998)
Robe, The (1953)
Salome (1923, 1953)
Samson and Delilah (1949)
Son of Man (2006)
Ten Commandments, The (1956)

THE BIBLE *IN* FILM

2001: A Space Odyssey (1968)
Aguirre: The Wrath of God (1972)

CONTRIBUTORS

George Aichele, Emeritus Professor of Philosophy and Religion, Adrian College, Adrian, Michigan, USA

Tom Aitken, Gladstone's Library, Hawarden, North Wales, UK

Roy M. Anker, English, Calvin College, Grand Rapids, Michigan, USA

Richard S. Ascough, School of Religion, Queen's University, Kingston, Ontario, Canada

Alice Bach, Religious Studies, Case Western Reserve University, Cleveland, OH, USA

Lloyd Baugh, Theology and Film, the Pontificia Università Gregoriana, Rome, Italy

Mary Ann Beavis, Religion and Culture, St. Thomas More College, Saskatoon, SK, Canada

Rhonda Burnette-Bletsch, Religion, Greensboro College, Greensboro, NC, USA

Jaime Clark-Soles, New Testament, Perkins School of Theology, Southern Methodist University, Dallas, TX, USA

Laura T. Copier, Media and Culture, University of Amsterdam, Amsterdam, The Netherlands

Christopher Deacy, Theology and Religious Studies, University of Kent, Canterbury, UK

J. Cheryl Exum, Biblical Studies, University of Sheffield, Sheffield, UK

Peter Francis, Gladstone's Library, Hawarden, North Wales, UK

Susan R. Garrett, New Testament, Louisville Presbyterian Seminary, Louisville, KY, USA

S. D. Giere, Homiletics and Biblical Interpretation, Wartburg Theological Seminary, Dubuque, IA, USA

Pamela Grace, Brooklyn College, City College of New York, New York, NY, USA

Arnfríður Guðmundsdóttir, Theology and Religious Studies, University of Iceland, Reykjavik, Iceland

Anton Karl Kozlovic, Screen and Media, Flinders University, Adelaide, Australia

Ross S. Kraemer, Religious Studies and Judaic Studies, Brown University, Providence, RI, USA

Larry J. Kreitzer, New Testament, Regent's Park College, The University of Oxford, Oxford, UK

Tina Pippin, Religious Studies, Agnes Scott College, Decatur, GA, USA

Adele Reinhartz, Classics and Religious Studies, University of Ottawa, Ottawa, ON, Canada

Matthew S. Rindge, Religious Studies, Gonzaga University, Spokane, WA, USA

P. Jennifer Rohrer-Walsh, English, Methodist University, Fayetteville, NC, USA

Mark Roncace, Religious Studies, Wingate University, Monroe, NC, USA

Erin Runions, Religious Studies, Pomona College, Claremont, CA, USA

Susanne Scholz, Old Testament, Perkins School of Theology, Southern Methodist University, Dallas, TX, USA

Robert Paul Seesengood, Religious Studies, Albright College, Reading, PA, USA

David Shepherd, Theology and Religious Studies, University of Chester, Chester, UK

Thomas Slater, English, Indiana University of Pennsylvania, Indiana, PA, USA

Jon Solomon, Classics, University of Illinois at Urbana-Champaign, Urbana, IL, USA

Jeffrey L. Staley, Theology and Religious Studies, Seattle University, Seattle, WA, USA

W. Barnes Tatum, Religion and Philosophy, Greensboro College, Greensboro, NC, USA

William R. Telford, Theology and Religion, Durham University, Durham, UK

Richard Walsh, Religion, Methodist University, Fayetteville, NC, USA

Sze-kar Wan, New Testament, Perkins School of Theology, Southern Methodist University, Dallas, TX, USA

Jane S. Webster, Religious Studies, Barton College, Wilson, NC, USA

Reinhold Zwick, Institut für Katholische Theologie und ihre Didaktik, Westfälische Wilhelms-Universität Münster, Münster, Germany

ACKNOWLEDGEMENTS

Thanks to the good people at Routledge, principally Andy Humphries, Rebecca Shillabeer, and Emma Hudson, for steering this project from conception to publication. It has been a pleasure to work with you all. Thank you to Kim Shier for superb proofreading assistance and to Shoshana Walfish for help with the indexes. My profound appreciation also to the Institute for Advanced Study, Princeton, NJ, where I edited and compiled the book, and to the Hetty Goldman Membership Fund for the generous support that made my year at the Institute possible. Most of all, I wish to thank the thirty-seven contributors to this volume for their interest in the project, their superb essays, and their adherence to the deadlines that made it possible for this book to appear on schedule. I know that the readers of this book will appreciate your insights and interpretations as much as I do.

INTRODUCTION

The Bible has been a star of the silver screen since the birth of cinema. Among the very first films to win popular acclaim was *The Horitz Passion Play*, which premiered in Philadelphia in November of 1897; the flow of Bible and Bible-related movies has continued unabated ever since. The term 'Bible movie' most often conjures up the grand epics such as Cecil B. DeMille's *The Ten Commandments* (1956) or George Stevens' *The Greatest Story Ever Told* (1965). But the Bible, Bible stories, Bible characters, Bible verses and Bibles themselves appear in countless films made in Hollywood and in many other national cinemas, in virtually every genre including epics, romantic comedies, action films, disaster films, superhero films, children's animations, boxing movies, prison escape movies, spy movies, war movies, horror movies, science fiction, end-of-the-world movies, and numerous spoofs of the above.

This book presents fifty essays on fifty movies in which the Bible or aspects thereof figure in significant ways. Its goal is simple: to enhance our understanding and appreciation of film by looking at a broad range of examples in which one particular staple of the full-length feature film – the Bible – plays a significant role.

How to choose fifty key films from a large and diverse cinematic corpus that spans approximately 115 years and counting? With great difficulty, as it turns out, and by keeping in mind the intended audiences for this book – general readers who are interested in film, the Bible, or both; students in formal or informal courses on Bible and film; and college, university, divinity school or adult education instructors in need of resources for their courses in this area, or perhaps seeking to add movies to their courses in biblical studies.

A number of general principles guided the selection. The first is availability. The list contains only films that are readily available on VHS, DVD, or by legal digital download (e.g., iTunes, Amazon). This in itself tends to foreground American films, which are distributed more broadly than those of any other national cinema. Nevertheless, the list includes a significant number of international films from countries such as Canada, France, Germany, Japan, and South Africa. The second is breadth, from the very familiar, such as *Ben-Hur* (1959), to the relatively unfamiliar, such as *The Green Pastures* (1936), and from the early silent era, such as *The Life of Moses* (1909–1910) and *Intolerance* (1916) to relatively recent movies such as *Gran Torino* (2008) and *A Serious Man* (2009). The third is variety with regard to the films' use of the Bible. The filmography distinguishes between 'Bible movies' that take the main outline of their plot, their ancient setting, and their main characters from the Bible, and fictional feature films that quote the Bible, make paradigmatic use of its plot and characters, and/or use the Bible as a prop on the screen but do not claim to retell a biblical story as such. In doing so, the book considers movies from many different film genres.

These factors helped to guide the selection, but the book by no means claims to have created a 'canon' – a list of *the* fifty key films in which the Bible figures. Rather, it examines fifty of what could easily have been a list of 100, 200, or many more key films. Readers may well find that some of their personal favourites have been omitted while other films of less interest to them are included. And because everyone, including those of us that research and write about film, has their favourites, their less-than-favourites, and a good many films they have not viewed and do not plan to view, the list here may omit entire categories – for example, horror films, exorcism films, vampire films – that may include the use of Bible but which I cannot bring myself to watch.

There was no attempt to impose uniformity of approach or focus among the fifty essays included here, beyond the simple and obvious request that each essay address explicitly the film's use of the Bible. As a result, the essays collectively reflect a broad range of theoretical approaches, such as auteur criticism, which situates a film in the context of the director's larger oeuvre; cultural criticism, which considers the ways in which the film does or does not reflect, shape, or otherwise address the historical, social and cultural contexts within which it was made; film history, which situates the film in the context of the technical, economic, social and other factors that affect the production and distribution of movies; and reception history, which addresses the responses that the film evokes from different audience groups. Some essays even challenge the very enterprise in which they are engaged by questioning the value of identifying and analysing biblical characters and references when there are so many other important themes to discuss. Finally, all of the essays draw attention to the cinematic elements of the film, such as setting, casting, costuming, colour, music, camera angles and shots, editing, as well as the ways in which many of these Bible-related films draw very explicitly upon other Bible-related films. One example is the opening of *The Ten Commandments* (1956) which likely draws upon the much earlier film *The Life of Moses* (1909–1910), and, in turn, informs the more recent animated film, *The Prince of Egypt* (1998).

The pervasive use of the Bible in film, and, indeed, in other cultural products such as art music, literature, and television, should underscore the ongoing importance of biblical literacy, not only for those who situate themselves within the communities of faith for whom the Bible – whether in its Jewish, Protestant, Catholic, Orthodox Christian, or other versions – are considered holy scripture, but for anyone who participates in contemporary culture and society in North America, Europe, and indeed – given the increasingly interconnected world we inhabit – also globally. Knowing something about the Bible, its role in history, society and culture, and familiarity with its stories, characters, and idioms, will help to deepen our knowledge and understanding, not only of film, but of the world, of others, of ourselves, and of the movies that we enjoy.

Each essay concludes with a short list of further reading, for those who are interested in reading other analyses of these films, or in exploring the numerous issues that the essays address. Quotations from the Bible are from the New Revised Standard Version, unless otherwise indicated. Film dialogue, where included, is transcribed from the films themselves, unless otherwise noted.

It is my hope that readers will enjoy and learn from these essays, and that they will be enticed to seek out some of the films with which they are not yet familiar or to re-view those that they have already seen. Most of all, I hope that they will take away a heightened sensitivity to and appreciation of the varied use of the Bible in film that will enhance their viewing pleasure for many years to come.

Further reading

George Aichele and Richard G. Walsh (2002) *Screening Scripture: Intertextual Connections between Scripture and Film*. Harrisburg, PA: Trinity Press International.

Bruce Babington and Peter William Evans (1993) *Biblical Epics: Sacred Narrative in the Hollywood Cinema*. Manchester: Manchester University Press.

Alice Bach (ed.) (1996) *Biblical Glamour and Hollywood Glitz*. Semeia 74. Atlanta, GA: Society of Biblical Literature.

Lloyd Baugh (1997) *Imaging the Divine: Jesus and Christ-Figures in Film*. Communication, Culture & Theology. Kansas City, MO: Sheed & Ward.

William L. Blizek (ed.) (2009) *The Continuum Companion to Religion and Film*. London; New York, NY: Continuum.

David Bordwell (1985) *Narration in the Fiction Film*. Madison, Wis.: University of Wisconsin Press.

Eric S. Christianson, Peter Francis, and William Telford (2005) *Cinéma Divinité : Religion, Theology and the Bible in Film*. London: SCM Press.

Christopher Deacy (2001) *Screen Christologies: Redemption and the Medium of Film*. Religion, Culture, and Society. Cardiff: University of Wales Press.

Craig Detweiler (2008) *Into the Dark: Seeing the Sacred in the Top Films of the 21st Century*. Grand Rapids, MI: Baker Academic.

J. Cheryl Exum (ed.) (2006) *The Bible in Film – and the Bible and Film*. Leiden: Brill.

Gerald Eugene Forshey (1992) *American Religious and Biblical Spectaculars*. Media and Society Series. Westport, CN: Praeger.

Pamela Grace (2009) *The Religious Film: Christianity and the Hagiopic*. New Approaches to Film Genre. Chichester; Malden, Mass.: Wiley-Blackwell.

Geert Hallbäck and Annika Hvithamar (2008) *Recent Releases: The Bible in Contemporary Cinema*. The Bible in the Modern World. Sheffield: Sheffield Phoenix Press.

Robert Jewett (1993) *Saint Paul at the Movies: The Apostle's Dialogue with American Culture*. 1st ed. Louisville, Ky.: Westminster John Knox Press.

——(1999) *Saint Paul Returns to the Movies: Triumph over Shame*. Grand Rapids, Mich.: William B. Eerdmans.

Larry J. Kreitzer (1993) *The New Testament in Fiction and Film: On Reversing the Hermeneutical Flow*. The Biblical Seminar; 17. Sheffield: JSOT Press.

——(1994) *The Old Testament in Fiction and Film: On Reversing the Hermeneutical Flow*. The Biblical Seminar. Sheffield: Sheffield Academic Press.

John C. Lyden (ed.) (2009) *The Routledge Companion of Religion and Film*. London: Routledge.

Peter Malone (1990) *Movie Christs and Antichrists*. New York, NY: Crossroad.

Clive Marsh (2007) *Theology Goes to the Movies: An Introduction to Critical Christian Thinking*. London; New York, NY: Routledge.

Joel W. Martin and Conrad Eugene Ostwalt (1995) *Screening the Sacred: Religion, Myth, and Ideology in Popular American Film*. Boulder, CO: Westview Press.

Margaret R. Miles (1996) *Seeing and Believing: Religion and Values in the Movies*. Boston, MA: Beacon Press.

Jolyon P. Mitchell, and S. Brent Plate (2007) *The Religion and Film Reader*. New York, NY; London: Routledge.

Adele Reinhartz (2003) *Scripture on the Silver Screen*. Louisville, Ky.: Westminster John Knox Press.

——(2007) *Jesus of Hollywood*. New York, NY: Oxford University Press.

——(2013) *Bible and Cinema: An Introduction*. London: Routledge.

Mark Roncace and Patrick Gray (2007) *Teaching the Bible through Popular Culture and the Arts*. Society of Biblical Literature Resources for Biblical Study. Leiden; Boston, MA: Brill.

Erin Runions (2003) *How Hysterical: Identification and Resistance in the Bible and Film*. New York: Palgrave Macmillan.

Jon Solomon (2001) *The Ancient World in the Cinema*. Rev. and expanded ed. New Haven, CN: Yale University Press.

Jeffrey L. Staley and Richard G. Walsh (2007) *Jesus, the Gospels, and Cinematic Imagination: A Handbook to Jesus on DVD*. Louisville, KY: Westminster John Knox Press.

W. Barnes Tatum (2004) *Jesus at the Movies: A Guide to the First Hundred Years*. Rev. and expanded ed. Santa Rosa, Calif.: Polebridge Press.

Richard G. Walsh (2003) *Reading the Gospels in the Dark: Portrayals of Jesus in Film*. Harrisburg, PA: Trinity Press International.

——(2005) *Finding St. Paul in Film*. New York, NY: T & T Clark International.

Melanie Jane Wright (2007) *Religion and Film: An Introduction*. London: I.B. Tauris.

Maria Wyke (1997) *Projecting the Past: Ancient Rome, Cinema, and History*. New Ancient World. New York, NY: Routledge.

Reinhold Zwick (1997) *Evangelienrezeption Im Jesusfilm: Ein Beitrag Zur Intermedialen Wirkungsgeschichte Des Neuen Testaments*. Studien Zur Theologie Und Praxis Der Seelsorge 25. Wèurzburg: Seelsorge-Echter.

BIBLE AND CINEMA: FIFTY KEY FILMS

2001: A SPACE ODYSSEY (1968)

[Producer and Director: Stanley Kubrick. Screenplay: Stanley Kubrick and Arthur C. Clarke. Cinematography: Geoffrey Unsworth. Art Director: John Hoesli. Cast: Daniel Richter (Moon-Watcher), William Sylvester (Heywood Floyd), Keir Dullea (David Bowman), Gary Lockwood (Frank Poole), Douglas Rain (voice of HAL 9000).]

Stanley Kubrick's *2001: A Space Odyssey* opened in 1968 as an immediate box office success. While some spectators admittedly left theaters in confusion, others eulogized the film as a life changing, almost spiritual experience. This was especially the case with young counter-culture audiences that tended to view the film repeatedly. Critical reception of *2001* was also largely positive despite some early negative reviews following the New York premiere. Renata Adler of the *New York Times*, for example, judged the film to be 'somewhere between hypnotic and immensely boring' (Schwam 2000: 147). Yet, by the early 1970s, *2001* was widely recognized by film critics as an extraordinary cinematic achievement (Krämer 2010: 93).

Such wide-ranging responses to *2001* were enabled by Kubrick's persistent refusal to explain the film. As he said early in his career, 'I think for a movie or a play to say anything really truthful about life, it has to do so very obliquely, so as to avoid all pat conclusions and neatly tied-up ideas' (Nelson 2000: 9). He deliberately constructed *2001* as an open narrative that would require spectators to fill in gaps as they subjectively react to the interplay between image and sound. Thus, it is designed to provoke and sustain countless interpretations.

The film avoids the expository style of the novel by the same title that was produced concurrently by Kubrick's co-writer, Arthur C. Clarke. Kubrick omitted an extensive voiceover narration that had been intended for the film, as well as a ten-minute prologue in which scientists and religious leaders discussed the origins of life, the future prospects of humanity, and the implications of extra-terrestrials and machine intelligence. Questions that the novel explains – such as the origin and purpose of monoliths – the film leaves unanswered.

Thwarting accepted conventions of Hollywood storytelling, Kubrick's film calls attention to elements of form that are usually hidden. *2001* leaps over time and space to follow three disparate storylines without providing explicit connections. Kubrick tests the patience of his audience by lingering over shots that do not contribute to narrative progression. The film provides no clear protagonist(s) with whom audiences may identify. Dialogue is extremely curtailed. So little attention is paid to character development that the film's most human character is a computer.

All of these very deliberate choices advance the artistic vision of a director known for meticulous attention to the smallest details. Kubrick's intention was to create a nonverbal cinematic experience that – much like a monolith – might subconsciously exert a transformative effect on its viewers (Krämer 2010: 50–52). To that end, his film places in conversation motifs drawn from the Bible, Nietzschean philosophy, Darwinian evolution, Homeric mythology, and science fiction speculation about extra-terrestrial life.

The film's opening sequences evoke the Bible's first creation story (Gen. 1:1–2:4a). Against the 'formless void' of a dark screen, György Ligeti's *Atmosphères* provides an eerie three-minute overture, which fades into a silent darkness interrupted only briefly by the MGM logo. With the first bars of *Also Sprach Zarathustra* (Richard Strauss's 1896 musical homage to Nietzsche's epic of the same title), we look from the barren surface of the moon toward the rising earth, which in turn is capped and illuminated by a rising sun. This alignment of celestial bodies suggests form and order within the cosmos. The subjective camera angle in this scene directs our attention to what we will soon learn is the beginning of life on earth. Whose perspective this camera has adopted is left unexplained. Are we observing earth through the eyes of a heavenly Creator? This visual suggestion is undercut by the musical reference to Nietzsche's poem, which challenges and redefines onscreen images by proclaiming the death of God.

In the next sequence, rather pretentiously entitled 'The Dawn of Man', we see another sunrise – this time viewed from a more familiar earth-bound perspective. In several successive shots, we encounter the sound of wind, dry land, and an absence of vegetation that might suggest the beginning of the third day of creation (Gen. 1:9–13). But that notion is again disrupted by a distant birdcall and the presence of bleached bones (animal and hominid) that introduce an element of potential danger.

Blending biblical and Darwinian accounts of origins, Kubrick introduces a tribe of ape-like hominids grazing the barren landscape, falling prey to a leopard, and vying unsuccessfully with another tribe over rights to a small waterhole. High-angle shots diminish the hominids in relation to their environment and convey their vulnerability. Huddling together in a rocky hollow during the night, they apprehensively track the sounds of a leopard prowling in the darkness. Primitive humanity clearly does not hold dominion over this creation (cf. Gen. 1:26), nor can such a barren and hostile environment be described as a paradisiacal garden (cf. Gen. 2–3).

At sunrise, we hear the otherworldly strains of Ligeti's *Requiem* and watch the wakening hominids react in fear to something outside of the camera's frame. A sudden wide-angle shot reveals a rectangular black monolith, whose geometric perfection marks it as wholly 'Other', at odds with the irregularities of otherwise natural surroundings. Whereas Clarke's novel explains monoliths as machines created by an advanced alien species to guide human evolution, Kubrick's film allows multiple interpretations. Viewers can choose to understand monoliths as alien machines, the presence of God, or visual metaphors for human inspiration.

As the music swells to drown out the screeching hominids, their leader (named Moon-Watcher in Clarke's novel) overcomes his fear sufficiently to extend a hand and touch the monolith in an iconic image echoing Michelangelo's 'Creation of Adam' (1511; ceiling of the Sistine Chapel at the Vatican). This impulse to touch recurs throughout the film in each monolith encounter. A reverential low-angle shot directs our attention to another magical alignment directly above the monolith as the sun rises beneath a crescent moon.

This event later inspires an evolutionary leap forward as Moon-Watcher crouches amidst tapir bones. After a subliminal shot recalling sunrise over the monolith, the hominid tilts his head in a universal thinking pose as again we hear the first strains of *Also Sprach Zarathustra*. At first awkwardly, Moon-Watcher uses a long bone to strike the skeleton. As the hominid gains confidence and the music crescendos, Kubrick adopts an extreme low-angle shot to capture a hairy arm wielding the bone in slow motion. Subsequent low-angle shots show Moon-Watcher enthusiastically smashing a skull as he imagines killing tapirs for meat.

The monolith has functioned as a tree of knowledge (Gen. 2:16–17; 3), transforming primitive humans into tool-wielding carnivores. Like the biblical Garden of Eden story, this acquisition of knowledge may be read as both a fall and an ascent. Primitive humanity gains godlike creative potential that soon reveals a capacity for violence, when their tool becomes a weapon in the struggle for waterhole rights. Moon-Watcher leads his tribe in the bludgeoning murder of another hominid in a scene strongly reminiscent of Cain's murder of Abel (Gen. 4). The camera tracks the tool/weapon as it is flung jubilantly into the heavens by an unrepentant Cain/Moon-Watcher.

A match-cut replaces the falling bone with a nuclear weapon orbiting Earth, visually equating these two human tools and their destructive

potential. The absence of a new title suggests that this space-age segment is still 'The Dawn of Man'. Surprisingly, not much has changed
in several million years despite humanity's obvious technological
advances. Like their hominid ancestors, twenty-first-century humans
eat, sleep, and use the toilet with the added complication of zero
gravity. Diplomatic posturing between American and Russian scientists at the Hilton Space Station recalls posturing over waterhole rights
by rival hominid tribes. Although humans have developed speech, it
is employed only in banal small talk and deception. In this way,
Kubrick suggests that human evolution is essentially stalled in the
early chapters of Genesis.

Wide-angle interior shots of the spacecraft *Orion* (and later the Clavius
briefing room) create a sense of artificial enclosure, while contrasting
exterior shots draw attention to the immeasurable vistas of space as
ships and celestial bodies dance gracefully to Johann Strauss's *Blue
Danube* waltz (1866). We eventually learn that the *Orion*'s sole passenger,
Dr Heywood Floyd, is traveling to the American lunar colony to
investigate the top-secret discovery of another monolith. Like Moon-
Watcher, Floyd is compelled to touch this mysterious object; as
celestial bodies align, it emits a high-frequency signal.

The next segment begins abruptly with the title 'Jupiter Mission:
18 Months Later'. Kubrick again contrasts the vastness of space with
the enclosed interior of the spaceship *Discovery*. And again human
characters (David Bowman and Frank Poole) follow daily routines of
exercising, eating, and sleeping without emotion or meaningful social
interaction. They are nearly as insensible as the *Discovery*'s hibernating
crewmembers. The most human character is ironically the HAL 9000
computer, which controls every aspect of the Jupiter mission.

HAL is presented as the ultimate tool, supposedly 'foolproof and
incapable of error'. Kubrick leaves open the question of whether the
computer is actually sentient or simply following his programming.
Likewise, when HAL begins to behave erratically and turns on
Discovery's crew, we do not know if this is due to a mechanical error
or a psychological breakdown. It is tempting to read this segment of
the film as another creation story – this time with humanity cast in the
role of Creator. Like Moon-Watcher, human technology has reached
a new evolutionary stage embodied by HAL. Created 'in our image'
(Gen. 1:26–27), HAL shares humanity's godlike potential (indeed,
he is essentially omnipotent and omniscient aboard the *Discovery*) but
also exhibits our flaws. HAL, like Moon-Watcher, reacts to a
perceived threat with Cain-like violence in the murder of Frank
Poole and the hibernating astronauts. Bowman is forced to abort

humanity's technological creation, like Frankenstein's misbegotten monster.

HAL's 'death' (or, more accurately, his forced devolution) inadvertently triggers a prerecorded message by Heywood Floyd that reveals the true reason for the Jupiter mission: the lunar monolith's signal has been traced to Jupiter space. Following an intermission, we jump abruptly to the film's final segment entitled 'To Jupiter and Beyond the Infinite'. Again celestial bodies align, as a monolith drifts through space to Ligeti's *Requiem*. Perhaps unintentionally, the monolith passes through this alignment at a perpendicular angle producing a cross-shape that lingers onscreen for several seconds.

Bowman leaves *Discovery* in a space pod to be swept up into a star gate indicated by a rush of colours and patterns. He reacts viscerally to this journey, suffering an apparent seizure, as the camera focuses increasingly on the colours reflected in his eye. The trip ends unexpectedly in a neoclassical bedroom where he lives out the rest of his days in a matter of minutes. Soon an extremely aged Bowman is confronted by another monolith that appears at the foot of his bed. Reaching a shaky finger toward it like Michelangelo's Adam, he is transformed into the Star-child as the opening bars of *Also Sprach Zarathustra* sound once more. The film ends as the Star-child, floating freely in a transparent bubble, returns to earth completing the film's Homeric odyssey.

This last segment is perhaps the most confusing part of the film. Clarke explains the bedroom as an observation tank where the godlike extra-terrestrials guiding human evolution use Bowman to initiate its next stage. In the novel, the Star-child returns to Earth in order to detonate orbiting nuclear weapons in an act of cosmic purification. But Kubrick, as usual, leaves open our interpretive options. We might read Bowman's character in the final segment of the film as an inverted Christ figure whose passion in the stargate is followed by a lonely last supper and a transfiguration. However, given the film's three-fold repetition of *Also Sprach Zarathustra*, it may be that Bowman (representing humanity) is merely an evolutionary bridge between ape and *Übermensch*. Recurrent birth imagery (birthdays, Bowman's airless re-entry into the *Discovery* in a fetal position through a tunnel, the severed umbilical cord that trails from Poole's body, and finally the Star-child) also reinforces the theme that semi-civilized humanity must now be reborn as something more to avoid the imminent threat of self-annihilation.

This threat was very apparent to Kubrick and his audiences in the midst of the Cold War and had recently been underlined by the

Cuban Missile Crisis of 1962. Kubrick's gift as a director was his ability to translate the major cultural concerns of his day into commercially successful and critically acclaimed films. Like his previous release, *Dr. Strangelove* (1964), *2001* addressed the imminent danger of nuclear devastation. In both films, Kubrick expressed modern fears that humans will lose control of our technology or that our Cain-like bent toward violence will inevitably turn science toward destructive ends. However, *2001* also visually celebrates the technology that would enable a manned moon landing only a year after the film's release. In contrast to the unrelenting satire of *Dr. Strangelove*, which ends with nuclear detonation, *2001* articulates a hopeful vision of human transformation. Moreover, it affirms the possibility of a guiding force behind human evolution though not necessarily the god of traditional religion.

Rhonda Burnette-Bletsch

Further reading

R. Kolker, (ed.) (2006) *Stanley Kubrick's 2001: A Space Odyssey*. Oxford: Oxford University Press.
P. Krämer (2010) *2001: A Space Odyssey*. BFI Film Classics. London: Palgrave Macmillan.
T. A. Nelson (2000) *Kubrick: Inside a Film Artist's Maze*. Bloomington: Indiana University Press.
E. Nordern (2001) '*Playboy* Interview: Stanley Kubrick (1968)', in Gene D. Phillips (ed.) *Stanley Kubrick Interviews*. Jackson: University Press of Mississippi. pp. 47–74.
S. Schwam (2000) *The Making of 2001: A Space Odyssey*. New York: Modern Library.

AGUIRRE: THE WRATH OF GOD (AGUIRRE: DER ZORN GOTTES) (1972)

[Production Companies: Werner Herzog Filmproduktion and Hessischer Rundfunk, 1972. Director: Werner Herzog. Screenplay: Werner Herzog. Cinematography: Thomas Mauch. Music: Florian Fricke (Popol Vuh). Cast: Klaus Kinski (Don Lope de Aguirre), Helena Rojo (Inez), Del Negro (Gasper de Carvajal), Ruy Guerra (Don Pedro de Ursúa). Language: German.]

Werner Herzog begins his *Aguirre: the Wrath of God*, with a long shot of the majestic but menacing slopes shrouded in mist from high up in the Andes. The scene is accompanied by a chorus. The music, by Florian Fricke of the German band Popol Vuh, is played on what Herzog calls a 'choir-organ'. It has three dozen tapes running in parallel and a keyboard, and one could play the tapes as one would an organ. The result is hauntingly beautiful but also eerily artificial (Ebert 1999). *Popol Vuh,* literally 'Book of the People', is an ancient creation myth of the Quiché Kingdom in the Guatemalan western highlands. Herzog has a narrator reading passages from it in his 1971 film *Fata Morgana* to suggest the world's emptiness before creation. The combination of image and music in the opening sequence of *Aguirre* also evokes creation but this time, it is its chaotic savagery that is in focus.

As the camera zooms in and pans downward we see a long line of barely discernible figures snaking down the treacherous slopes. Conquistadores in heavy armour carrying sabres and muskets plod their way down a mountain path, slipping and sliding, looking anything but fit for battle. Downhill they roll cast-iron cannons, impossibly heavy-looking contraptions on steel-studded wheels, over muddy tracks strewn with rocks and boulders. When they are stuck, which is often, the soldiers whip their chained-up Indian slaves, who then extricate them. Astoundingly, the Indian slaves are also hauling two ornate velvety sedan chairs, each bearing a courtly Spanish lady. One is Inez, the wife of the general Don Pedro de Ursúa, leader of the expedition. The other is Flores, the fifteen-year-old daughter of Don Lope de Aguirre, the second in command. Their finery stands in jarring contrast to the splattered surroundings and the human detritus as the Indian slaves drop one by one from diseases brought on by the Europeans. A voiceover explains that the expedition 'descended through the clouds' into the jungle, on Christmas Day 1560, looking for the legendary Eldorado and to bring the word of God to the heathens. The voice belongs to Brother Gasper de Carvajal, whose diary is the only surviving witness of the ill-fated journey.

Herzog immediately introduces the film's two central characters, invisible because of their ubiquity: the narrator and the jungle. Because Brother Carvajal writes his diary as a member of the expedition, he is not the usual omniscient narrator – contrast Joe Gillis in *Sunset Blvd.* (1950), who can divine even motives because he is already dead – but he is subject to the same doubts, weakness, and limitations as the other characters. Omniscience belongs to the audience, because they know from the opening credits that Eldorado is an Indian invention to throw off the conquistadores, and that all have perished. Aguirre, the title character, through treachery and murder, wrests control of the expedition from Ursúa but will lead his followers, including his own daughter, to their deaths. The audience are therefore asked not to suspend their disbelief but to form judgement on the characters as they follow the diary.

The other central character of the film is the jungle and the Amazon River that runs through it. As Aguirre and company flow down the river, they realize that the jungle gives life but also takes it away. When the Indians attack, they do so as part of the jungle. Herzog never shows the shooters as the deadly arrows fly; they come from behind thickets, camouflaging themselves against the foliage, and melt back into the background afterwards. A soldier is ensnared by a lift-trap and he dies off-screen, voiceless and clueless. On the raft Aguirre's daughter Flores is mortally shot while facing a brush. Her death happens in silent stillness, 'with no pain, no gore or blood' (Cronin 2002: 80). The deaths of Ursúa and his wife Inez are depicted as quiet absorption into the jungle. He is executed with no struggle, no protest, and no emotion; she walks alone into the jungle in her finest dress and disappears. The river and the jungle are where 'God never finished His creation', as an Indian and his wife say to the Europeans.

It is tempting to see the downward trek into the jungle as descent into hell, but it may be more illuminating to see it as an allusion to the incarnation, the birth of a messiah. The descent takes place on Christmas Day. Aguirre is proclaimed leader of the expedition by his disciples while detractors are ruthlessly and silently eliminated. He is a messianic figure who attempts through his single-mindedness to lead his people to the promised land. On the raft flowing down the river, he seldom sits but stalks about in an awkward gait as if he were walking on water. He has the power of life and death, and controls the thoughts and speech of his men. At one point he cuts off the head of a man for dreaming about escape, and pontificates:

> If I, Aguirre, want the birds to drop dead from the trees, the birds will drop dead from the trees. I am the Wrath of God. The earth I walk upon sees me and quakes. But whoever follows me and the river will win untold riches. But whoever deserts ...

Aguirre is the Wrath of God, because, as Matthew (10:29) intimates, 'Are not two sparrows sold for a penny? Yet not one of them will fall to the ground apart from your Father.'

Aguirre's megalomania brings his company to ruin, but that is precisely what many messianic figures have wrought in history. Born during the war, Herzog himself lived through the messianic reign of Hitler and the aftermath of its defeat. Though Herzog disavows that connection (Cronin 2002: 93), it is hard to dismiss signs of death and the 'rebellion against an inevitable and catastrophic defeat' so pervasive in *Aguirre* and similar films as unrelated to the destruction of Nazi Germany (Nagib 2011: 82–83).

At the end of the film, Aguirre, the lone figure on the raft of death, still dreams of finding Eldorado, taking Trinidad from the Spanish crown and Mexico from Cortez. His daughter dead at his feet, he delivers a trancelike soliloquy: 'I, the Wrath of God, will marry my own daughter and with her I will found the purest dynasty the earth has ever seen. Together, we shall rule this entire continent.' This is of course a reference to the drunken Lot with whom his daughters commit incest to ensure progeny (Gen. 19:30–38). He continues: 'We will endure. I am the Wrath of God. Who else is with me?' The tragedy is that his question solicits only silence. He has been absorbed by the jungle.

Aguirre's final loneliness calls to mind a biblical tragedy, the Gospel of Mark. Though the resurrection of Jesus is predicted, the narrative ends not in glorious vindication of an executed criminal, as in the other three canonical Gospels that are dependent on Mark at least in part, but in the utter loneliness of Jesus. Throughout Mark, Jesus' single-mindedness is roundly misunderstood, even rejected by his followers. Peter is ready to proclaim Jesus Messiah and King (8:29), but he cannot accept his leader's suffering and defeat in death (8:31–33).

The loneliness of Jesus intensifies in the passion narrative. Between the chief priests and scribes plotting to kill Jesus (14:1–2) and Judas Iscariot's decision to betray him (14:10–11), Mark inserts a story of an anonymous woman anointing Jesus in Bethany (14:3–9). Far from a tribute to the woman's supposed virtue and devotion to Jesus, the story in fact depicts how utterly misunderstood and alone Jesus is in his messianic quest. None present understand the significance of the anointing. Their concerns with the high cost of the ointment (14:5) have blinded them to the gathering storm outside their dinner party. They are after all impoverished guests of a social outcast, a leper (14:3), and 300 denarii is a great deal of money to them. But even the woman who initiates the commotion misunderstands Jesus. While she intends to crown Jesus as King by anointing his head, Jesus corrects her: 'she has anointed my body beforehand for its *burial*' (14:8; emphasis added). Jesus chooses a path that no one will follow. He stands alone at his trial and execution save a few brave women, his disciples having long scattered. At last, before the empty tomb, even the women fled, 'for terror and amazement had seized them; and they said nothing to anyone, for they were afraid' (16:8). Mark's script ends as abruptly as *Aguirre*.

Like Aguirre, Jesus is a traitor. To the high priests and other officials who rely on the Romans for patronage and who control the
Jerusalem temple, Jesus' 'cleansing' (11:15–17) is the act of a terrorist
aimed at destroying the economic lifeblood of the city. That is what
seals his fate, as the powers that be are now determined to eliminate
him (11:18). And just as Aguirre at the end is swallowed up by the
jungle and the chaotic creation it represents, the empty tomb signals
that Jesus, too, is absorbed into the chaotic world.

It is with these similarities between Jesus and Aguirre in mind that we
can also appreciate the stark difference between them. While Aguirre
rules his people through intimidation and tyranny, the Markan
Jesus fulfils his mission through suffering. After an initial reluctance
('remove this cup from me'), he accepts his demise with meekness
and obedience ('yet, not what I want, but what you want', 14:36).
While Aguirre operates through violence, Jesus accomplishes his
quest by enduring violence. While Aguirre thinks of only wealth
and power for himself, Jesus renounces his ego in a supreme act
of self-sacrifice. But if Aguirre's fate is well deserved, Jesus' death
as an innocent victim makes the Gospel of Mark that much more
tragic.

In one other respect does *Aguirre* recall the Gospel of Mark: audience
participation. Werner Herzog is fond of saying that he does not distinguish between making a fictional film and making a documentary.
The making of the film is as integral to the final product as the
narrative. That is amply evident in *Aguirre*. Shots of rapids held for an
extended time, water vapours and droplets on the lens, a butterfly sitting
on a finger, characters relaxing in silence, long passages of an Indian's
reedy music, and so on, all contribute to the feel of a 'making-of'
documentary. Soldiers make their descent in heavy armor, but the
audience see actors labouring through unforgiving terrains in their
cumbersome costumes. We are witnessing not a dramatic enactment
of a long-forgotten expedition but the real struggle of a megalomaniac
(Herzog himself) making a film with actors struggling in real, hostile
terrains. The fictive divide between character and actor is thus rendered invisible, so that the audience are destabilized to the point
of questioning whether they are seeing the performance of a script or
a documentary on the performance. 'The main purpose, in *Aguirre*',
in the words of film scholar Lúcia Nagib, 'was to abolish the divide
between representational and real worlds, and for this reason the
entire crew and cast were submitted to the torments of location
shooting in the Andes and the Amazon jungle and rivers' (Nagib
2011: 115). The audience cannot relegate themselves to the role of

detached observers; they must take part in passing value judgement on the proceedings, for the audience is omniscient. A similar demand is made on the audience of the Gospel of Mark. The abrupt ending demands that hearers pass judgement on the cowardly disciples and other followers who utterly fail Jesus. In so doing, however, the audience must pass judgement upon themselves as well: How will they act in face of adversity? Inasmuch as Aguirre attains cinematic resurrection through a reenactment of a surviving diary and the audience's participation in its reading, Jesus will attain resurrection only to the extent that his audience will participate in the retelling of his life and the reenactment of the Gospel of Mark.

Sze-kar Wan

Further reading

Dana Benelli (1986) 'The Cosmos and its Discontents', in T. Corrigan (ed.) *The Films of Werner Herzog: Between Mirage and History*. New York and London: Methuen. pp. 89–103.
Paul Cronin (ed.) (2002) *Herzog on Herzog*. London: Faber and Faber.
Roger Ebert (1999) 'Aguirre, the Wrath of God', available online at: http://rogerebert.suntimes.com/apps/pbcs.dll/article?AID=/19990404/REVIEWS08/904040301/1023 (accessed 14 October 2011).
Lúcia Nagib (2011) *World Cinema and the Ethics of Realism*. New York: Continuum.
Brad Prager (2007) *The Cinema of Werner Herzog: Aesthetic Ecstasy and Truth*. London and New York: Wallflower Press.

Further viewing

Fata Morgana (Herzog, 1971)
Fitzcarraldo (Herzog, 1982)
Cobra Verde (Herzog, 1987)

APOCALYPSE NOW (1979)

[Production Company: Omni Zoetrope. Director: Francis Ford Coppola. Screenplay: John Milius, Francis Ford Coppola, and Michael Herr, based on *Heart of Darkness* by Joseph Conrad. Cinematography: Vittorio Storaro. Cast: Marlon Brando (Colonel Walter E. Kurtz), Martin Sheen (Captain Benjamin L. Willard), Robert Duvall (Lieutenant Colonel Bill Kilgore), Albert Hall (Chief Phillips), Laurence Fishburne (Tyrone 'Clean' Miller), G. D. Spradlin

(General Corman), Harrison Ford (Colonel Lucas), Dennis Hopper (Photojournalist).]

Hailed as a masterpiece of film-making and recognized by numerous accolades and awards, *Apocalypse Now* sets the classical tale of human struggle between good and evil in the jungles of Indochina in 1968–69 during the American war with North Vietnam (an extended 'director's cut' was released in 2001 as *Apocalypse Now Redux*). The plot, based loosely on Joseph Conrad's *Heart of Darkness*, follows Captain Willard as he travels in a river patrol boat (PBR) along the Nung River from Vietnam into Cambodia on a mission to find and kill a rogue American Colonel. Along the way, Coppola uses stunning visual imagery and a jarring soundtrack to create a surrealist impression of the chaos and confusion for which the American presence in Vietnam has become justly known.

The title aptly reflects the film's dual connection with the Bible in that 'apocalypse' both conjures images of fiery conflagrations and end-of-the-world cataclysms and also invokes the revealing of previously hidden aspects of the human condition. Both elements are seen most extensively in the biblical Book of Revelation, which also bears the title Apocalypse in some English versions of the Bible. Just as the biblical Revelation had in its background the moral failings of the Roman empire, *Apocalypse Now* reveals how the American psyche irrevocably changed through involvement in the Vietnam War. Social commentators before and after the film have noted the shift that occurred in the United States not only as a result of participation in a war whose outcome was at best ambiguous and at worst a loss, but also through the revelation of human atrocities carried out by American soldiers in Vietnam and beyond. Unlike so many films produced after World War II, *Apocalypse Now* does not valorize the war or its American combatants. Rather, it reveals their military flaws, their strategic mistakes, and their human moral failings at every level, from the leadership down to the soldiers on the ground. While Scott is not incorrect that the *Now* of the title underlines the point that once hell is unleashed on earth it is inescapable (1994: 199), the *Now* also invites viewers to recognize that this 'apocalypse' is a revelation to viewers, as individuals and collectively, concerning human capacity for moral turpitude.

In the opening sequence, the haunting melody of The Doors' song 'The End' (1967) aurally dominants depictions of the obliteration of the lush jungle in a conflagration that evokes images of the fiery end of the world depicted in the biblical Book of Revelation (e.g. Rev.

9:18). Meanwhile the intermittent appearance of low-flying Huey helicopters and the whoosh of their rotor blades suggest the horsemen of the apocalypse, who unleash judgement on the earth (Rev. 6: 2–8). Such cataclysmic scenarios are commonly assumed when the word 'apocalypse' is employed in popular culture, and are used to good effect in the film. At the same time, the core aspect of the biblical use of 'apocalypse', which indicates an 'uncovering', is by no means lost in the film. Within the plot itself there is revelation to Willard, not only as he slowly understands the inner psyche of Kurtz during the river journey, but also through his own growing self-understanding as events reveal to him what he is and is not capable of doing.

The film also invites viewers to experience a revelation. In the opening sequence, intercut scenes of Willard staring bleakly into space and then trashing his hotel room (an unscripted scene in which Sheen was actually as drunk as portrayed) introduce the viewer to the narrator. The narrator is the one who will not only himself become the recipient of the revelation, but also who will guide the viewer through the images of the 'other-worldly' journey, a common feature of the 'apocalyptic' literary genre. The film asks viewers to consider whether they would act any differently than Willard or than Kurtz, given similar circumstances. The moral challenge to Willard and to the viewer is offered early in the film, during the meeting in which Willard receives his orders from his superior officer. General Corman declaims,

> Well, you see, Willard, in this war, things get confused out there. Power, ideals, the old morality, and practical military necessity. But out there with these natives, it must be a temptation to be God. Because there's a conflict in every human heart, between the rational and irrational, between good and evil. And good does not always triumph. Sometimes, the dark side overcomes what Lincoln called the better angels of our nature. Every man has a breaking point. You and I have 'em. Walt Krutz has reached his and very obviously he has gone insane.

In carrying out his mission, Willard is pushed to his own breaking point, faced with the temptation to become a god.

As he travels along the river en route to Kurtz, Willard breaks open the seals on seven sets of classified documents detailing Kurtz's life, colleagues (Capt. Colby), and exploits through letters, photos, records, and clippings (listed in Cowie 2001: 22). Each of the seven sets provides the impetus for much of the voiceover narration in which Willard reflects on the effects of the war on various combatants. The symbolic significance of the number seven will not be lost on readers of Revelation, within which there is also the breaking open of seven sealed documents (Rev. 6:1–9:21), each one revealing something more about the impending global cataclysm that God will unleash. The seventh and final document is the most horrific in detailing plagues and disasters that will fall upon the entire earth, destroying much of it along with its inhabitants (Rev. 8:1–9:21). Likewise, in the film the seventh document Willard opens provides the order and codes to unleash an airborne fire-strike on Kurtz's compound that will obliterate all traces of it. Although some earlier releases on VHS included an alternate ending in which Willard does call in the airstrike, both the original theatrical release and *Apocalypse Now Redux* end with him silently drawing away from the riverbank. It is an ambiguous ending, 'with Willard apparently either trapped for ever by the spirit of Kurtz, or sailing downstream to salvation' (Cowie 2001: 117). In this way, the ending reflects the quotation from T. S. Eliot's 'The Hollow Men', recited by the photojournalist: 'This is the Way the world Ends, Not with a Bang but a Whimper' (cf. Scott 1994: 180).

In the film's climactic scene, Willard eerily arises from the river water just offshore from Kurtz's encampment, as though he has just been baptized. As after a baptism, his status is transformed, demarcated by his appearance – he is now covered in camouflage grease paint – but also by the decision to carry out his assignment to terminate Kurtz's command 'with extreme prejudice'. The ritualized killing of Kurtz, in a scene that is again dominated by the haunting music of The Doors' 'The End', is intercut with scenes of the ritual slaughter of a *carabao* (water buffalo). When it is over, Willard has an opportunity to replace Kurtz as leader of the compound. Like Jesus standing on the pinnacle of the Jerusalem temple and being offered the earthly power and glory in exchange for denying his mission (Matt. 4:1–11; Luke 4:1–13), Willard stands atop the Buddhist temple gazing down god-like on Kurtz's 'children' (the *montagnards*) gathered below. After a pregnant pause, these former devotees of Kurtz kneel before Willard. As Willard descends the stone steps and throws down his machete, the others lay down their weapons in deference as he passes. They are willing to follow him as a god if he will give into the temptation and take the mantel. Yet, having reached the breaking point, in the end, Willard, like Jesus, does not succumb.

Other intersections with the Bible occur, whether intentionally or simply as a result of the rich textures of the film. For example, as Willard's boat approaches Kurtz's camp the way is dotted with empty crosses. The photojournalist there tells Willard that members of the compound 'are Kurtz's children' who 'worship Kurtz like a god', evoking the idolatry so often condemned in the Hebrew Bible (e.g. Exod. 20:4–5; Hos. 1–2). Earlier, we learn that a successful, albeit unauthorized, mission undertaken by Kurtz was codenamed 'Archangel', for which Kurtz was promoted to his rank as Colonel. It also marks the peak of Kurtz's career, after which he begins his slow drift into his oligarchic reign, suggesting he has become the 'fallen angel'. The codename given to Willard for calling in the final airstrike is 'Almighty', an attribute of the biblical God, subtly suggesting that it is God (the American military?) who will strike down the fallen angel (those who do not fall into line with policy?).

A subtle juncture with biblical imagery can also be found in the scene in which Lt. Col. Kilgore's air cavalry helicopters depart in the breaking dawn for the aerial attack on Vin Din Drop. A bugler sounds the frontal attack call, summoning for the biblically literate the trumpet that will sound at the return of Jesus (Matt. 24:31; 1 Thess. 4:16; 1 Cor. 15:52) or, more likely, the trumpets in Revelation 8:7–11:19, which successively announce disasters upon the earth. Likewise, the metaphoric use of the boat as a place of safety resonates with the safety offered to biblical characters such as Noah or Jonah, who were safe on their respective boats. After coming face to face with a tiger in the mango groves and sprinting back to the boat, a breathless Chef pants 'Stay on the boat … never get out of the boat.' Yet even the boat does not provide the physical safety desired in war; both Clean and the Chief are killed on the boat, as, eventually, is Chef. Nor does the boat remain a place of moral safety. In the narration, Willard contrasts Chef's comment with Kurtz, who 'got out of the boat'. In a later scene when Willard is in Kurtz's compound, Kurtz asks Willard 'How far are you from the river?' Literally, the river is not far away, but is unreachable. Metaphorically, Kurtz is asking how far Willard has strayed from the path of safety and sanity – from the boat. Yet, the earlier scene in which Willard's companions massacre the occupants of a small Vietnamese vessel belies the 'boat' as a place of moral neutrality.

The one explicit visual reference to the Bible in the film occurs in one of the final scenes as the camera pans over Kurtz's private library. Among his books are James Frazer's *The Golden Bough* and Jessie Weston's *From Ritual to Romance*, both of which deal with the study of religion and are inter-textually linked to the poetry of T. S. Eliot and, through Eliot to the film itself (see Cowie 2001: 156–57). The book that first appears dominant in the frame, however, is a black leather-bound Holy Bible (which Cowie fails to mention in his otherwise insightful analysis of the scene), which stands upright and dominant in the shot, suggesting that interspersed visual and auditory intersections of *Apocalypse Now* with the Apocalypse of the Bible are by no means accidental.

Scott (1994: 181) rightly notes that the discordant soundtrack and images and the 'interweaving of real and surreal' are constant throughout the film. In this regard, the film is very much like the ancient literary genre for which it is named, especially the Book of Revelation. Here we find the interweaving of real and surreal. Images blend together as the writer seeks to employ metaphor to explain his vision of heaven and hell and everything in between, limited by an imagination that is of necessity locked into the writer's own cultural context. For Coppola, American military engagement in Vietnam provides the imaginative discourse necessary to convey a vision of hell, although unlike the Book of Revelation, there is no countervailing vision of heaven. It is a descent into madness and moral ambiguity, a descent into the human heart of darkness.

Richard S. Ascough

Further reading

Peter Cowie (2001) *The Apocalypse Now Book*. New York: Da Capo Press.
Bernard Brandon Scott (1994) *Hollywood Dreams and Biblical Stories*. Minneapolis: Fortress. pp. 175–81.

BABETTE'S FEAST (1987)

[Released in Denmark as *Babettes Gæstebud*. Production Companies: Panorama Film A/S, Det Danske Filminstitut, Nordisk Film, and Rungstedlundfonden. Director: Gabriel Axel. Screenplay adapted by Gabriel Axel from short story 'Babette's Feast' by Isak Dinesen/Karen Blixen. Cinematography: Henning Kristiansen. Cast: Stéphane Audran (Babette Hersant), Jarl Kulle (General Lorens Löwenhielm), Jean Philippe LaFont (Achille Papin), Bodil Kjer (Filippa), and Birgitte Federspiel (Martine).]

Set against the windswept landscape of the northernmost portion of Denmark's Jutland peninsula, *Babette's Feast* is director Gabriel Axel's retelling of the short story of the same name by Danish author Karen Blixen (Isak Dinesen). Here the lives, piety, and day-to-day cuisine of the characters mimic their austere surroundings, with the hymns of the film serving as a descant invoking something beyond.

In terms of genre, *Babette's Feast* is both Christ-figure film (Stone 2000: 160–62) and an ecclesial vision (Anker 2004: 191–214; see also *Så som i himmelen*, 2004). The primary tension in the film lies between piety and beauty. The pietism of this small and isolated community requires that its faithfulness remain untainted by the potentially sinful tastes of the world. They abstain (at least outwardly) from the joys of the flesh in favor of purity in the present and the promise of heavenly joy.

This is illustrated by a comic scene early in the film. The beauty of the minister's two daughters, Martine and Filippa, is well known by the young men of the area. Since the daughters do not attend social functions, the young men have to go to church in order to see them. As the camera pans the congregation, the worship of the young men is clearly more directed toward the minister's daughters than God, even as they all sing:

> Oh, Lord, allow thy kingdom
> To descend upon us here,
> So that the spirit of mercy
> May wipe out all trace of sin.
> Then we shall know in our hearts
> That God lives here with us,
> And that Thou art dwelling
> With those that trust in Thee.

The hymn captures the piety of the minister, his daughters, and the community – a faith that starves the desires (and suitors!) of this world in favor of the promises of the next. It is only when the life and piety of the community is intersected by outsiders that the community's eyes are opened to participation in beauty and grace this side of death.

The film nods toward the Danish Lutheran context of its setting. The names of the minister's daughters evoke the Protestant Reformation; Martine is named for Martin Luther (1483–1546), and Filippa, for Luther's student and fellow reformer, Philipp Melanchthon (1497–1560). Their father, the minister, serves a parish church that is part of the Lutheran state church of Denmark, the *Folkekirken*. In addition, he also tends a smaller flock that meets in his home. This smaller gathering of the faithful is akin to the *Indre Mission* or Inner Mission, a pietistic movement within the *Folkekirken* characteristically focusing on conversion, personal faith, and holy living (Tolderlund-Hansen 1964: 75–9).

The unlikely Christ-figure of the film is the outsider, Babette Hersant, who first appears on the doorstep of the sisters, when they are both 'past the first flush of their youth'. In order to understand Babette's entry into the story, however, we must first attend to the stories of two other outsiders: Lorens Löwenhielm and Achille Papin.

Löwenhielm, a young lieutenant in Denmark's Hussars, is from a family of means and influence but has himself fallen into debt and disrepute. In an attempt to get his head on straight, Lt. Löwenhielm's father, much to the younger man's chagrin, temporarily exiles him to the manor of his elderly aunt in Jutland in the minister's parish.

As Lt. Löwenhielm rides his horse through the parish, he is smitten with beautiful Martine. With the assistance of his pious aunt, he gains access to the minister's smaller flock in order to pursue Martine. However, as the Lieutenant participates in these gatherings, he quickly realizes that his efforts are in vain. With young Löwenhielm beside Martine at table, the minister quotes Psalm 85:11, a psalm of restoration and the key biblical text in the film: 'Righteousness and peace shall kiss one another'. Shortly thereafter the lieutenant makes his first exit from the film. Out in the entryway he says to Martine, 'I am going away forever, and I shall never see you again. For I have learned here that life is hard and cruel and that in this world there are things that are impossible.' The Lieutenant's pursuit of beauty has led him into a pious cul-de-sac where righteousness and peace do not kiss one another in this life.

The second outsider is Achille Papin, a Parisian, a 'papist', and a star of European opera. In search of solitude Papin visits the coast of Jutland. Enchanted by the voice of Filippa rising above the singing of the congregation, he enters the small Lutheran church, as the congregation sings:

> Lord, our God, Thy name and glory
> Should be sung throughout the world.
> And every soul, Thy humble subjects,
> And every wayfarer shall sing aloud Thy praises ...

Papin, the wayfarer, is not without piety as he sits in the congregation. Hearing Filippa sing, he prays, 'Almighty God, Thy mercy ascends to the heavens and Thy righteousness reaches to the ocean's depths. Here is a diva. She will have Paris at her feet.'

Papin receives the minister's permission to work with Filippa. From Mozart's *Don Giovanni*, they sing the sensual duet (*Là ci darem la mano*) between Zerlina and Don Giovanni, wherein Don Giovanni is attempting to seduce Zerlina away from her betrothed, Masseto. Here the lines between *Don Giovanni* and *Babette's Feast* are blurred but for the fact that Papin attempts to seduce Filippa away from her piety and the piety of her father, the minister. With Papin engrossed in the duet, Filippa's unease grows as she sings with Zerlina, 'I'm afraid of my own joy ... My soul weakens already.' As the duet concludes, Papin embracing her, they sing together, 'Love will unite us.' Papin has fallen head over heels. Filippa, however, has decided to end the lessons and with them the relationship, breaking Papin's heart.

The intersection of the stories of these outsiders anticipates the third and primary outsider, the Christ-figure. Thirty-five years after Papin's brokenhearted departure, Babette appears on the sisters' doorstep, their father now long dead. As Martine and Filippa welcome the stranger into their home, she hands them a letter from Papin. Babette has fled the 1871 Communard uprising in Paris. Her husband and son are dead, and she herself has barely escaped the sword of General Galliffet. Papin has sent her to the sisters for refuge, telling them that she 'knows how to cook'. The sisters, assuming the refugee to be a housekeeper, tell her that they cannot afford to employ her. She begs them to let her stay, saying, 'If you won't let me serve you, I will simply die.' The sisters relent, and Babette stays, serves, and learns the simple life and cuisine of the sisters and their community, all the while subtly expanding their tastes with her cooking and disposition.

As the community ages, the relationships among the pietists who meet in the minister's house gradually sour. While the sisters speak of forgiveness and God's heavenly kingdom, disagreements, grudges, shames, and betrayals fester just below pious veneers.

The story turns when, years later, Babette wins ten thousand francs in the Paris lottery. She begs permission to prepare a true French dinner on the occasion of the minister's hundredth birthday, and the sisters reluctantly agree. Yet, as the foreign fixings for the feast arrive, the community is shaken by the mysterious crates, live quail, and even a turtle. Responding to their hushed, pious concerns, Martine says, 'We had no idea where it might lead. And now we have exposed ourselves to dangerous, or maybe even evil, powers.' The community agrees to eat the meal as promised but to say and enjoy nothing. For fear of evil, they withhold all comment. As one of the men says, 'It will be as if we never had the sense of taste.' To ward off their fear, they sing:

> Jerusalem, my heart's true home,
> Your name is forever dear to me,
> Your kindness is second to none,
> You keep us clothed and fed,

> Never would you give a stone
> To the child who begs for bread.

As preparations for the feast begin, there comes news that now *General* Lorens Löwenhielm will attend the anniversary dinner with his now very old aunt. This makes the number of guests for dinner twelve, no accidental allusion to Jesus' disciples.

As the feast begins, the faithful dutifully hold their tongues. Yet, delighted and in awe, Löwenhielm cannot help but break the determined silence with compliments and exclamations as he savours the beauty of the tasteful feast. Course after course, wine after wine, the faithful watch and learn from the General. Stories begin to flow. Together they recall the teachings of and stories about the minister. In spite of their pious pact, fellowship breaks in.

With the service of quail (*Caille en Sarcophage*), the General bites into the quail's skull and sucks out the brain, raising the eyebrows of the faithful. He recalls a meal hosted by General Galliffet at the Café Anglais in Paris where the chef, a woman, served this same signature dish. He muses, that this chef 'had the ability to transform a dinner into a kind of love affair. A love affair that made no distinction between bodily appetite and spiritual appetite'. Further unwrapping the irony of the many intersecting stories, Löwenhielm recalls how General Galliffet had said that the only woman in Paris for whom he would shed his own blood was the chef at the Café Anglais. The chef is later confirmed to be Babette herself, who left Paris with Galliffet seeking her blood.

The theological and biblical climax of the film comes with the General's speech:

> There comes a time when your eyes are opened. And we come to realize that mercy is infinite. We need only await it with confidence and receive it with gratitude. Mercy imposes no conditions. And, lo!, everything we have chosen has been granted to us. And everything we rejected has also been granted. Yes, we even get back what we rejected. For mercy and truth are met together. And righteousness and bliss shall kiss one another.

Here *General* Löwenhielm brings Psalm 85:11 back into focus, the same verse that the minister had quoted when then *Lieutenant* Löwenhielm sat at this same table. The General's 'sermon' interprets Babette's 'genuinely eucharistic' (Anker 2004: 214) feast as a means of grace by which the participants are transformed into a community of forgiveness and mercy despite their own resistance.

The dénouement to the feast comes as the dinner guests retire to the parlor where Filippa begins to play the piano and sing. To the tune 'Wer Nur den Lieben Gott' by Georg Neumark (1621–81) she sings the words of Danish bishop and hymn writer Thomas Kingo (1634–1703):

> Oh watch the day once again hurry off,
> And the sun bathes itself in water.
> The time for us to rest approaches.
> O God, Who dwelleth in heavenly light,
> Who reigns above in heaven's hall,
> Be for us our infinite Light in the valley of night.
> The sand in our hourglass will soon run out.
> The day is conquered by the night.
> The glories of the world are ending,
> So brief their day, so swift their night.
> God, let Thy brightness ever shine.
> Admit us Thy mercy divine.

As if recognizing the folly of withholding forgiveness and abstaining from joy, the faithful listen to Filippa's song. Old disagreements, grudges, shames, and betrayals that have festered are addressed with honesty and mercy.

Again in the entryway, where they stood so many years before, Martine and Lorens Löwenhielm bid farewell. With the transformation of the sacramental meal, Lorens' vision of the world has been transformed as well, ' … this evening I have learned, my dear, that in this beautiful world of ours all things are possible'.

In light of the meal, the community has experienced and can now see the beauty of the world. Babette, the Christ-figure, has given her all: the whole of her winnings are spent on the meal. All is not lost, however, for in the fullness of her giving she has become more fully the artist who she is, and her initially resistant guests have become more fully who they are. The feast is not an end in itself but an event of God's mercy whereby the community becomes fully human. The hope of heaven does not disappear, yet salvation and beauty are no longer isolated in the by-and-by. In the meal, the Christ-figure, Babette fulfills the promise of Psalm 85:11:

> Mercy and truth have met together.
> Righteousness and bliss shall kiss one another.

S. D. Giere

Further reading

Roy M. Anker (2004) *Catching Light: Looking for God in the Movies.* Grand Rapids: Eerdmans.

Isak Dinesen (1993) 'Babette's Feast', in *Anecdotes of Destiny and Ehrengard.* New York: Vintage International. pp. 19–59. (Initially published in English in *The Ladies Home Journal*, 1950.)

Bryan P. Stone (2000) *Faith and Film: Theological Themes at the Cinema.* St Louis: Chalice.

G. Tolderlund-Hansen (1964) 'History of the Danish Church', in Poul Hartling (ed.) *The Danish Church.* Trans. Sigurd Mammen. Copenhagen: Det danske Selskab.

Further viewing

Så som i himmelen / As It Is In Heaven (Kay Pollak, 2004)
DeUsynlige / Troubled Water (Erik Poppe, 2008)
Des hommes et des dieux / Of Gods and Men (Xavier Beauvois, 2010)

BAGDAD CAFE (1987)

[Original Title: *Out of Rosenheim.* Production Company: Bayerischer Rundfunk. Director: Percy Adlon. Screenplay: Percy and Eleonore Adlon. Cinematography: Bernd Heinl. Cast: Marianne Sägebrecht (Jasmin Münchgstettner), C C H Pounder (Brenda), Jack Palance (Rudi Cox).]

Bagdad Cafe is an off-beat, original film-parable of redemption in the Christian pattern. In spite of its whimsical, eclectic blend of elements of the western, psychological drama, musical comedy and love-story, Adlon's film packs a serious moral-spiritual point. Set in the wasteland of the California desert, in a rundown truck-stop-motel, the film represents a world in need of redemption: the inhabitants of the Bagdad Gas and Oil Cafe, a gathering of misfits, live in conflict with one another; the new highway has bypassed the Cafe; it has lost most of its clients and is doomed to a lethargic, 'no-exit' existence.

In that dusty, desperate world, the film represents the need for redemption on two levels. Using classical categories of moral theology, the community of the Cafe is afflicted by an original sin, most evident in the hopeless disharmony of life there – and for which no single person seems responsible – a situation of collective moral paralysis. More significantly, each member of the community has their own personal disharmony or sinfulness, a situation that afflicts them and contributes to the general moral disorder.

Into this moral disorder, Adlon introduces a mysterious outsider: a German woman-tourist, abandoned by her husband, who shows up at the Cafe and determines to stay for a while. Though her looks, dress, heavy accent and eccentric behaviour set her apart from the locals, her vulnerability, quiet presence and gracious ways gradually break down moral barriers and ultimately bring about fundamental conversion in individuals and the redemption of the community.

Adlon creates three main characters, who carry the brunt of the moral dynamics in the film. Brenda, a thirtyish African-American woman, is the strong-willed, matriarchal, owner of the Cafe. Abandoned by her husband, saddled with two irresponsible teenaged children and a grandchild, she is stressed-out, angry, aggressive with her children and the Native-American barman. Brenda screams a lot and is clearly a woman-on-the-edge. Brenda's counterpart is the German tourist Jasmin: full-faced, full-figured, approaching middle-age, and dressed in Bavarian classic garb. The woman's appearance, her unlikely arrival on foot at the Cafe and her insistence on paying with travelers cheques and staying indefinitely, incur the suspicion and verbal abuse of Brenda: 'She shows up outa nowhere, without a car, without a man ... It don't make no sense at all.' Jasmin is a well-balanced and patient person, and reacts only with courtesy and acceptance to Brenda and to all.

The third main character is Rudi Cox, a seventyish retired Hollywood set-designer and sometimes painter, who lives on a trailer on the grounds of the motel. Played by the archetypal villain of Hollywood Westerns and melodramas, Jack Palance, here outrageously transformed by colourful silk shirts, silk-bandanas and peacock feathers, the ever-polite Rudi functions at the limits of the Brenda–Jasmin dynamic, as a choric-figure, chronicler and interpreter of the soteriological events he witnesses.

Clearly, the principal beneficiary of Jasmin's redemptive presence and activity is Brenda. When her strong, persistent resistance to this mysterious newcomer are met with only polite generosity and acceptance, and particularly when Jasmin reveals her own vulnerability, Brenda undergoes a powerful transformation: she begins to speak and behave calmly and patiently, and with a radiant smile she resumes her responsibilities as head of the Bagdad Cafe community.

Others, more quickly receptive to Jasmin, precede Brenda in the experience of redemption, and in each case, it is because of their contact with Jasmin: Brenda's daughter Phyllis puts an end to her partying with truckers; her son Salomo overcomes his depressive lethargy and plays the piano flawlessly; the barman Cayahuenga learns to use the German coffee machine; and Rudi, clearly inspired by Jasmin, begins again to paint.

Even the physical reality of the Cafe responds to Jasmin and undergoes a redemptive change: neat order replaces the chaos of the motel office; the broken coffee machine is replaced; the buildings and grounds overcome their dusty decay. A trickle of returning truckers and tourists becomes, in the film's conclusion, a flood of happy, enthusiastic people.

The redemption experience offered by Jasmin through her alliance with Brenda is available to all, even a ninth hour arrival on the scene, Brenda's repentant husband. But, as in the Gospel the film is evoking, the grace of redemption can be refused: two people exclude themselves from the redemptive harmony that Jasmin offers: the woman's brutish husband and Debbie, the motel's resident tattoo artist and sometime prostitute. The latter offers a telling motivation for moving out: since Jasmin has arrived, there is 'too much harmony' at the Cafe.

Though it is mainly in the film's narrative – its intradiegetical structure – that Adlon generates the powerful meaning of his moral parable, it is clear that he supports and modulates this meaning with a variety of extradiegetical or film-stylistic strategies. Foremost among these is the music of the film, beginning with the haunting theme song, 'A desert road from Vegas to nowhere', which announces the need for redemption in this disordered world: 'a coffee machine that needs some fixin'. The same song proclaims the advent of that redemption – 'A change is comin', just around the bend … sweet relief' – just as Jasmin meets Brenda for the first time. Another piece of music used with virtuoso effect by Adlon is Bach's composition, 'Prelude in C Major from The Well-Tempered Clavier'. Through the first part of the film, Salomo attempts to play it, but weighed down by the disharmony of the Cafe, he never gets beyond the first bars. Towards the end of the film, and liberated by his association with Jasmin, he plays the entire piece without interruption: it is a sublime expression of new life and hope, of the power of grace.

Adlon also uses a variety of cinematographic effects to highlight his themes. In the opening of the film, for example, he represents bizarre details of the desert landscape in disconcerting oblique angles and fragmented compositions. These images, accompanied by violent sounds and voices, clearly suggest an unbalanced world in need of redemption. Later, as Jasmin, in real time, cleans Brenda's office, Adlon edits in three shots, surrealistic in composition and lighting, that suggest the timeless, transcendental reach of Jasmin's redemptive action. Later, Adlon elaborates complex shifts in lighting in an otherwise static scene of Jasmin listening to the redeemed Salomo play the Bach Prelude, which manifestly underlines the ecstatic quality of the moment.

In *Bagdad Cafe*, a wide range of symbols and leitmotifs are another powerful strategy for proposing the moral-spiritual meaning of the film. Repeated images of billowing desert sand and dust, for example, represent the dusty moral state of the people of the Cafe. The magic tricks learned and performed by Jasmin are evocations of the spiritual wonders, redemptive miracles, already in act in the community. The German coffee machine that comes to occupy a place of honour in the Cafe, offering a new and different way to make 'real' coffee, is a transparent symbol of the presence and power of Jasmin, offering a new, different and 'real' way of living to the community. Perhaps the most unusual symbol in the film is a boomerang, provided by an Australian backpacker: it swings harmoniously over the motel, its shape and its sound evoking a hovering dove, a spirit of peace and harmony in this redeemed world.

Finally, Adlon invents a powerfully-expressive structural device in the frame he constructs around the main narrative of the film, consisting of a prologue and an epilogue. The former, the opening scene of the film already discussed, represents the state of moral imbalance and disorder that holds hostage the people of Bagdad Cafe, and the advent of the redeemer who will end that siege. The latter, beginning after the resurrection-return of Jasmin, represents the great celebration of song, dance, magic and harmony that ushers in the new reality of a redeemed Bagdad Cafe. Clearly echoing the eschatological banquet of Revelation 19, it is the polar opposite of the prologue in content, tone and meaning. The time of desert, disharmony and death is over; joy, hope, harmony and love reign supreme.

Beyond the overall theme of redemption that functions as the principal moral dynamic of the film, two other dimensions of *Bagdad Cafe* make it a particularly interesting text: first, though without explicit references to the Gospel, the film submits easily and fully to a reading as a classical Christ-figure film, with Jasmin functioning as the Christ-figure; second, the film is a strong, uncompromising feminist text.

The overall dynamic of redemption, effected through and by Jasmin, already suggests her identity as a Christ-figure, in a direct line of descent from her namesake, Gelsomina, the splendid Christ-figure in Fellini's classical film, *La Strada* (1954). In Jasmin, Adlon embodies some essential christological elements: incarnation – she enters fully and irrevocably into the world in need of redemption; kenosis – she empties herself of all power and privilege and makes herself utterly vulnerable; selfless ministry – she seeks only to serve and help others.

Adlon gives Jasmin a privileged relationship with children; he has her perform wondrous magic tricks that transform people's lives, transparent metaphors of the miracles of Jesus; he even has her undergo a mysterious transfiguration experience. Further reflecting the saving mission of Jesus, Jasmin's offer of liberating grace is gentle, discreet, respectful and absolutely unconditional; she affirms and inspires the best in others, leaving them free to respond to her or not.

In the end, and by way of rendering definitive the redemptive experience of the community, Adlon has Jasmin run into trouble with the law, undergo rejection and a kind of death experience, from which she then returns, transformed, dressed in brilliant resurrection white. A highly original christological element in the film is the role of Rudi Cox as little less than a painterly evangelist of the gospel in Jasmin: he, more than anyone else, witnesses her revelation, he is present, and on his knees, at her transfiguration, and, in a series of icon-like portraits of Jasmin (in one, she assumes a Pantocrator pose), he generates a visual tradition-*kerygma* of this transcendent figure.

A number of elements signals *Bagdad Cafe* as a classical and powerful feminist text, much more so than two other feminist-coded Christ-figure films, *Babette's Feast* (1987) and *Chocolat* (2000). The feminist reach of the film is highlighted in its opening, by the theme song of the film, 'I am calling you', a vocation-redemption calling to Brenda sung by a woman, and then by the epiphanic first encounter between Jasmin and Brenda, marked by a flash of blinding sunlight. Redeemer and about-to-be-redeemed, both are women without men. The antagonism between the two women is the main dynamic of the first part of the film; their protagonism, their rapprochement, and the redemption of the community that it announces and effects, are the main dynamic of the second part.

The climax of the film, the moral turning point and victory, is the dramatically and humanly poignant confrontation scene in which Jasmin makes herself totally vulnerable to Brenda on an issue exclusive to women, child-bearing; she confesses sadly that she has no children. And it is on that issue that Brenda is touched, moved, and reconciled to Jasmin. Immediately after this moment of Jasmin's greatest kenosis, and clearly not by chance, Adlon represents the two women happily helping each other serve in the cafe. Redemption has come to Bagdad Cafe thanks to this fruitful encounter of two women. Their embrace towards the end of the film after the resurrection-return of Jasmin – a kind of reverse, unisex 'Noli me tangere' – is perhaps the most satisfying and reassuring spiritual moment of the film.

If the women in this film are primary, strong and compactly united – Brenda's daughter happily gives up her 'extracurriculars' to serve with her mother and Jasmin – the men are secondary and weak. Both husbands are sidelined early on in the film; Salomo and Cayahuenga receive salvation from the women. Rudi Cox is certainly not weak, but neither is he strongly masculine. In the dramatic economy of the film, Rudi is a passive observer rather than an active participant: his presence has absolutely no effect on the dynamic of the narrative nor on its outcome.

In the tradition of film magic shows, the magicians are usually men dressed in formal tuxedos and assisted by women. In *Bagdad Cafe*, the roles are reversed: presiding at the concluding celebration, a rousing Eschatological feast, are Brenda and Jasmin, dressed in baby-blue silk tuxedos, and singing, dancing and performing magic tricks together, in a kind of ecstatic 'Lord of the Dance' show. They are assisted by men: Salomo provides the music and Rudi guides the spotlight.

At the very end of the film, concluding its epilogue, Adlon edits in a brief scene in which Rudi pays a private visit to Jasmin. Ever the gentleman, he offers her a bouquet of flowers, and then, shyly, awkwardly, proposes marriage to her, explaining that this would be a way to obtain an immigration permit and thus to stay at Bagdad Cafe forever. Jasmin, a serious expression on her face, says: 'I'll talk it over with Brenda.' Clearly, this reply has a feminist dimension: Jasmin's allegiance now, as it has been throughout the film, is to Brenda; sealed by a rainbow, the relationship of these two women is an alliance of biblical proportions. Still, as with the alliance of God with the Patriarch Noah (Gen. 9), in and through Brenda, the Matriarch of the community, Jasmin is offering redemptive harmony to all the members of the community and beyond. For Jasmin, that redemptive mission and alliance has absolute priority over any personal and sentimental considerations.

Lloyd Baugh

Further reading

Laurence Alster (1988) 'Review of Bagdad Café', *Films and Filming*. 409 (October): 30.

Lloyd Baugh (1997) 'The Woman as Christ Figure', in Lloyd Baugh, *Imaging the Divine: Jesus and Christ-Figures in Film*. Kansas City, MO: Sheed and Ward. pp. 130–56.

Giuliana Mercorio (1988) 'A Bavarian in Bagdad', *Films and Filming*. 409 (October): 12–14.

Tom Milne (1988) 'Review of *Out of Rosenheim* (*Bagdad Café*)', *The Monthly Film Bulletin*. 55/657 (October): 307–9.

BEING THERE (1979)

[Production Company: Warner Brothers. Director: Hal Ashby. Screenplay: Jerzy Kosinski. Cinematography: Caleb Deschanel. Cast: Peter Sellers (Chance), Shirley MacLaine (Eve Rand), Jack Warden (President 'Bobby'), Melvyn Douglas (Benjamin Rand), Richard Dysart (Dr. Robert Allenby), Richard Baseheart (Vladimir Skrapinov).]

In 1970, the first children to be raised in front of a television were coming of age. What would they know about the world? How would they spend their days? What kind of citizens might they be? Jerzy Kosinski's novella, *Being There*, explores the possibilities in a disturbing story of a secluded, middle-aged man who does little else but watch TV and work in an enclosed garden (on the theme of 'watching' in the film, see Meyrowitz 2009: 32–48). When he is released into the world, he quickly and easily moves into a world of privilege and power. According to Kosinski, 'watching' may have been an advantage. Peter Sellers (of *Pink Panther* fame) was so intrigued by the novel that he sent a note to the author offering his services as a gardener. Not long after – 1979 – the film went into production, but the director Hal Ashbury took the film in a completely new direction.

The film begins in a beautiful old house in Washington, DC. Chance, played by Sellers, moves about the house shifting his attention from one television screen to the next as he gets up in the morning, eats his meals, putters in the garden, and retires at night. When Louise (Ruth Attaway), the maid, informs him that Old Man Jennings is dead, Chance goes to look at him, and then returns to the gentle rhythm of watching TV. The next day, attorneys arrive to close the house, and finding no documents or photos that explain why Chance is there – except, says Chance, 'You have me. I'm here,' and have lived here 'ever since I can remember' – they ask if he 'would make a claim'. Misunderstanding, Chance claims that 'the garden is a healthy one'. Thus begins a long series of similar misunderstandings.

The attorneys asked him to leave the house the next day. Chance seems unperturbed as he wanders from room to garage to shed to garden watching TV, catching glimpses of the symphony, cartoons, *Sesame Street*, talk shows, weather reports, and mimicking the handshake and hat tipping of the characters on the screen. All of the furniture is covered with dust cloths; the shades are drawn. The old life of Chance begins to shut down.

As Chance leaves his house through the front door for the first time, leaving behind his meticulous garden, with its raked gravel and carefully groomed plants, Eumir Deodato's jazz/funk arrangement of the opening fanfare from *Also Sprach Zarathustra* (Opus 30) by Richard Strauss heralds the dawn of a new age. The stark reality of the world outside seems destitute. Chance wanders the siren-filled streets in his Magritte-Charlie Chaplin top hat and umbrella; he watches street people chatting around a trash can fire, walks past graffiti-marked walls and stripped-down car frames, steps around trash and garbage, and peers into dirty windows selling stereos. He asks street kids where he can find a garden so he can plant some seeds, and they threaten him with a knife. Chance pulls the TV remote from his pocket 'to change channels', but is perplexed when nothing happens. The gloomy street scenes are framed with glimpses of the Washington Memorial and Capitol in the distance. Throughout, Chance does not react; he just watches, detached.

Mesmerized by his own projected image on a TV in a shop window, Chance walks backward for a full-length view right into the bumper of a limousine. As 'chance' would have it, Eve, played by Shirley MacLaine, emerges from the car; she too worries that he might 'make a claim', and she takes him to her glorious mansion in DC for medical care. When she asks his name, she misunderstands and calls him 'Chauncey Gardiner'. Chance does not correct her. He meets Eve's husband, Ben (Melvyn Douglas), an invalid shrouded in newspapers. Because Eve and Ben misconstrue his discarded, old-fashioned but elegant clothes as signs of wealth, Chance enters seamlessly into their lives of power and privilege; he even meets the president of the United States and offers 'economic' advice: 'First there is fall and winter, and then there is spring and summer'. The president misunderstands Chance's gardening advice as a metaphor for the economy, and enthusiastically mentions his name to the press referring to Chance as 'a top advisor'. This sets off a flurry of unsuccessful investigations into Chance's identity. Meanwhile, anticipating his imminent death, Ben 'gives Eve' to Chance, and Eve 'gives herself' to Chance, but instead of engaging physically with Eve, Chance says, 'I like to watch.' Eve misunderstands so she performs for him, but Chance watches TV oblivious to her gyrations on the floor. Later,

Chance gives a television interview, meets foreign ambassadors, and generally impresses everyone he meets with his prosaic agricultural metaphors, and by, well, just 'being there'.

In the final scenes of the film, as power brokers identify him as a candidate for the presidency, Chance wanders off alone to the edge of a spring pond. Chance walks out upon the pond, stopping to insert his umbrella deep into the water to 'prove' he stands atop it. By including this major departure from the novel, Ashby throws the whole film into a new genre. Instead of a film that examines the role of the media or the institutions of power, this film enters the 'Christ-figure film genre'.

The ironic humour in the film arises because viewers are led to believe that they 'know' the truth about Chance and that they perceive how other characters in the story misunderstand him. The viewer knows, for instance, that Chance is not a savvy economic advisor to the president but an illiterate gardener; he is not a wealthy businessman, but a man of no resources; he likes to watch TV, not sex. With each new character that misunderstands Chance's identity, the viewer gets more and more self-satisfied about knowing the truth. But with the final scene, the director makes the viewer a fool: unlike the characters, the viewer missed the clues that Chance is really Jesus-in-disguise. Time to take another look.

True, like Jesus, Chance's origins are unclear. No one in the Old Man's house knows where he comes from or why he is there. Like Jesus who pre-exists creation (John 1:1) and says, 'Before Abraham was, I am' (John 8:57), Chance says, 'You have me. I am here ... I have always been here'. Like Jesus who comes from an otherworldly Edenic place – heaven (John 3:13) – and 'dwells among the people' (John 1:14), Chance resides in an 'otherworldly place' – a protected house and garden – and then comes to the real world of crime-ridden and dangerous streets. Like Jesus, Chance seems to be a (holy) innocent, unassuming man. Like Jesus, Chance's presence provokes questions of identity: 'Who is he!?' But unlike Jesus who is ultimately rejected by the rich and powerful, Chance is drawn right into the center of wealth and power.

Chance is also similar to Jesus in that he speaks in agricultural parables. As a wisdom teacher, Jesus speaks of the labourers in the vineyard (Matt. 20:1–16), the weeds among the wheat (Matt. 13:24–30), and the size of the mustard seed (Mark 4:31–32). He tells one parable in particular that resembles Chance's language:

> The kingdom of God is as if someone would scatter seed on the
> ground, and would sleep and rise night and day, and the seed

would sprout and grow, he does not know how. The earth produces of itself, first the stalk, then the head, then the full grain in the head. But when the grain is ripe, at once he goes in with his sickle, because the harvest has come.

(Mark 4:26–29).

Stripped of their multiple interpretations and traditions, Jesus' words seem simple and obvious. Is it possible, then, that Jesus was talking about gardening all along, and his words were given meaning by 'those with ears to hear'? (Mark 4:23). Was the Jesus of the Christian tradition merely a construct of active interpretation?

Like the traditions of Jesus, the film has a significant undercurrent of social critique. Chance passes graffiti on the wall: 'American aint shit cuz the white mans got a god complex.' Indeed, Chance is a white man who is readily accepted into positions of power because intelligence agencies can find no scandal in his past. Louise the maid makes this observation as she watches Chance on a talk show:

It's for sure a white man's world in America. Look here: I raised that boy since he was the size of a piss-ant. And I'll say right now, he never learned to read and write. No, sir. Had no brains at all. Was stuffed with rice pudding between th' ears. Shortchanged by the Lord, and dumb as a jackass. Look at him now! Yes, sir, all you've gotta be is white in America, to get whatever you want. Gobbledy-gook!

Standing before the White House, Chance tells a security guard that a tree is 'very sick and needs care', evoking (but reversing) Jesus' curse of the fig tree on his way into Jerusalem (Mark 13:12–14, 20–26). The streets of the nation's capital are dangerous: Chance is 'rescued' and taken into a white man's palace. Although Chance never voices his critique overtly (unlike Jesus), he watches like the omnipresent divine eye, saying 'I see'.

And if we were to push the association of Chance with Jesus, we might note the flat response of Chance to everything that happens in the film. Apparently, Peter Sellers practiced in front of a mirror for hours to get just the right passive, non-judging, kindly, compassionate look on his face. This also resembles the 'face' of Jesus in the contemporary public eye, and indeed, in many artistic renderings of the god-man. It may be why Sellers so adamantly opposed the inclusion of the out-takes in the DVD which show him trying to repeat a message from the street thugs with a gangster twang; when he keeps messing up his lines, he laughs and jokes, breaking Chance's flat affect and the illusion of (divine) sympathy created throughout the film.

Finally, there are a few rather vague references to the 'resurrection motif' found in many Christ-figure films. Ben can face death 'much easier'; he finds new life in 'drinking blood' (transfusions). Eve finds a new life with Chance. But other than walking on the water and some 'chance' good fortune, there are no miracles or healings. In fact, the remote control does *not* work!

Hal Ashby's flip at the close of this odd little film accomplishes much more than the novella by Jerzy Kosinski was able to do. By turning Chance the Gardener into Jesus the Christ, Ashby puts the viewer into the position of the 'one being watched from above', and challenges the viewer's assertions of truth and reality. In particular, he challenges the understanding of the historical Jesus: Was Jesus such a simple innocent? Was he only talking about gardening? Have Christians projected their own (mis)understanding onto Jesus so that he is no longer even recognizable at first glance? Surprisingly, only the South African Publications Control Board ordered that the final scene showing Chance walking on the water be cut from the South African release, as it might offend many Christians.

Jane S. Webster

Further reading

Warren Carter and John Paul Heil (1998) *Matthew's Parables: Audience-Oriented Perspectives*. Washington, DC: Catholic Biblical Association of America.
Arland J. Hultgren (2000) *The Parables of Jesus: A Commentary*. Grand Rapids, MI: Eerdmans.
Jerzy Kosinski (1970) *Being There*. New York, NY: Harcourt Brace Jovanovich.
Joshua Meyrowitz (2009) 'We Liked to Watch: Television as Progenitor of the Surveillance Society', *The Annals of the American Academy*. 625: 32–48.
Ben Witherington, III (1994) *Jesus the Sage: The Pilgrimage of Wisdom*. Minneapolis, MN: Fortress.

BEN-HUR (1959)

[Production Company: Sam Zimbalist. Director: William Wyler. Screenplay: Lew Wallace, (novel); Karl Tunberg, (screenplay). Cinematography: Robert L. Surtees. Music: Miklós Rózsa. Cast: Charlton Heston (Judah Ben-Hur), Jack Hawkins (Quintus Arrius), Haya Harareet (Esther), Stephen Boyd (Messala), Hugh Griffith (Sheik Ilderim), Martha Scott (Miriam), Cathy O'Donnell (Tirzah),

Sam Jaffe (Simonides), Finlay Currie (Balthasar / Narrator), Frank Thring (Pontius Pilate), Claude Heater (Jesus).]

William Wyler's *Ben-Hur* (1959) is the quintessential 'sword and sandal' epic. It is arguably one of the most identifiable Biblical-era epic films to come out of Hollywood during the 1950s and 1960s when such films were riding a wave of popularity. The film helped establish Charlton Heston, still basking in critical acclaim for his portrayal of Moses in Cecil B. DeMille's *The Ten Commandments* (1956), as a cinematic icon. Indeed, Heston won a Best Actor Oscar for his portrayal of Judah Ben-Hur, and the film went on to win another ten Oscars, including Best Picture, Best Director, Best Supporting Actor, Best Cinematography, and Best Musical Score (for Miklós Rózsa's magnificent composition). *Ben-Hur* was also a huge commercial success, earning $90 million for an initial investment of $15 million; it earned $40 million in its first year alone, and helped rescue the ailing MGM studios from bankruptcy.

The novel *Ben-Hur: A Tale of the Christ* was published in 1880 by Lew Wallace (1827–1905), a Union General of the American Civil War whose own life was filled with adventure and accomplishments in a number of fields. Wallace was not only an acclaimed military leader (he fought at the battle of Shiloh in 1864, and assisted in the defence of Washington, D.C.), but also a successful lawyer in Indiana, and an eminent politician (serving as a Senator for Indiana from 1856–60, as Governor of New Mexico from 1878–81, and as the American minister to Turkey from 1881–85). Nevertheless, Wallace is best remembered for the novel *Ben-Hur* which became an international bestseller; it sold 300,000 copies in ten years, and made its author a much-sought-after celebrity. Once the novel became successful and began to capture the imagination of the public, there were a number of attempts to produce stage versions of it, the most successful of which premiered in 1899 and ran for 20 years. Wallace kept a tight control on the production of these plays. Wanting to remain true to his own deeply held religious convictions which had given birth to the novel in the first place, Wallace forbade the stage appearance of Jesus Christ, for in his mind the portrayal of the Son of God by a human actor was blasphemous. In consequence, a bright blue light was used to indicate Christ's presence on stage.

Wyler's 1959 film was not the first time that Lew Wallace's novel had been made into a movie. Earlier cinematic versions of *Ben-Hur* were produced, including a silent version by Sidney Olcott, Frank Oakes Rose and H. Temple, lasting only 15 minutes, which appeared in 1907. Another silent version by Fred Niblo appeared in 1925, which starred Roman Navarro as Ben-Hur, and, at a cost of nearly $4 million, was the most expensive silent movie ever made.

Much of Wyler's film was shot on location at Cinecittà Studios in Rome and various surrounding towns in Italy; filming took nine months to complete. Everything about *Ben-Hur* was done on a grand scale; the film lasts over three and a half hours, had a huge budget and an all-star cast, and required 300 sets to be built to accommodate the breadth of the vision being contemplated. Indeed, the outdoor sets for the famous chariot race at the time were the largest ever produced for a film. Special 65mm cameras, costing $100,000 each, were used in the filming; these provided larger print negatives and a wide-screen format with much greater clarity and detail. While there are many memorable scenes within the film, including wide-screen shots of the Roman army on march through Judea and Jerusalem, and an action-packed naval battle between the Roman fleet and some Macedonian pirate ships, it is the chariot race in the Jerusalem circus, in which Ben-Hur takes on his arch-rival Messala and exacts a bloody revenge, which remains the defining feature of the film. Eighteen chariots were constructed for the race and 15,000 extras were used in the filming of the racing sequences which took five weeks to complete. It is not surprising that Andrew Marton and Yakima Canutt, the second unit team who were responsible for the filming of the chariot race scenes, received a special award from the National Board of Review of Motion Pictures. Largely on the basis of the spectacle of this chariot race the publicity posters for the *Ben-Hur* film proclaimed it 'The Entertainment Experience of a LifeTime!'

The sub-title of Wallace's novel ('A Tale of the Christ') is an important indicator of the author's religious beliefs and intentions in writing the novel. Wallace deliberately set out to create a richly textured fictional story which is set against the backdrop of the life of Jesus of Nazareth. This feature is perfectly preserved within Wyler's film, which opens with a pre-title depiction of the Christmas story and the visit of the Three Magi and concludes with the crucifixion of Jesus Christ. The story of Judah Ben-Hur's life is thus set within the narrative framework of a biography of Jesus Christ.

Indeed, Judah Ben-Hur encounters Jesus Christ twice within the film; both instances are carefully crafted scenes which complement one another and recall the words of Jesus recorded in Mark 9:41 and Matthew 10:42 ('whoever gives a cup of cold water'). The first encounter takes place as a gang of condemned prisoners – Ben-Hur among them – is being marched by Roman guards northwards from Jerusalem through Galilee toward Tyre on the Mediterranean coast in order to serve as slave-rowers on a Roman galley. The prisoners stop in the town of Nazareth where the local villagers are forced by the soldiers to provide water from their well for everyone to drink. However, the Roman decurion singles out Ben-Hur for special punishment and specifically prohibits anyone from quenching his thirst. Ben-Hur collapses on the ground in desperation, and cries for God to help him. At this point Jesus, in defiance of the decurion's orders, comes forward and gives him some water to drink, reviving his spirits and enabling him to go on.

The second encounter takes place four years later, in Jerusalem, at the time of Jesus' trial and condemnation. Ben-Hur is standing among the crowd on the Via Dolorosa watching Christ carry his cross toward Golgotha when he suddenly recognizes Jesus as the man who had given him water in Nazareth. When Christ collapses under the weight of the cross, and is being whipped by the Roman soldiers escorting him, Ben-Hur breaks through the crowd and brings him a cup of water. This act of reciprocal compassion is a crucial scene within the film, even though it represents a departure from Wallace's original novel.

Interestingly, both scenes are shot in such a way that the viewer never sees a close-up of the face of Jesus himself. Nor, for that matter, do we ever hear Jesus say anything within the film although his words are recounted by others. Instead we see the impact of Jesus reflected in the faces of those looking on, including Ben-Hur and the Roman Decurion in Nazareth. This is a marvellous technique of drawing the film viewer into the scenes, and recalls Wallace's stipulation for the stage productions of *Ben-Hur* that Jesus Christ could not be portrayed by an actor, but had to be represented by a bright light.

Another indication of the importance of Jesus' act of kindness occurs during the slave galley sequence. Just before the battle begins the Roman counsel Quintus Arrius gives orders that Ben-Hur ('Number 41') be unchained from his oar. One of the fellow slaves asks Ben-Hur why he had been freed. 'I don't know', replies Ben-Hur, 'Once before a man helped me. I didn't know why then.' This scene is also linked to the first 'cup of water' scene musically (the same musical theme, which the film's composer Miklós Rózsa entitled 'The Prince of Peace', is heard in both sequences). The 'cup of cold water' motif recurs at the end of the scene. The ship commanded by Quintus Arrius is wrecked, and Quintus Arrius and Ben-Hur cling to a raft in the water until they are rescued by another Roman galley. Once safe on board, Quintus Arrius offers Judah Ben-Hur a cup of water.

Ben-Hur also recalls the cup of cold water offered him by Jesus at yet another point in the film: after Ben-Hur discovers that his mother and sister are still alive, but ill and living in the Valley of the Lepers.

He strides away from the site purposefully and encounters the faithful Balthasar who is overjoyed that he has found Jesus, the promised Son of God, after so many years of searching. Balthasar invites Ben-Hur to accompany him to a hillside where Jesus is delivering a speech (the Sermon on the Mount!). Ben-Hur stops to scoop a drink from a nearby stream and says to Balthasar, 'When the Romans were marching me to the galleys, thirst had nearly killed me. A man gave me water to drink. I went on living. I should have done better if I'd poured it into the sand.' His anger and distress over what has happened to his family have broken him. We next see Balthasar at the crucifixion where he is joined by Ben-Hur and together they look up at Christ on the cross. Judah says, 'This is where your search has brought you, Balthasar. He gave me water, and a heart to live. What has he done to merit this?' The execution of the peace-loving Jewish rabbbi at the hands of the Roman imperial power is incomprehensible to Judah Ben-Hur, and even to the ever-faithful Balthasar.

There is an explicit ideological struggle between Judaism and Rome running throughout the film, with the Jewish people portrayed as a believing nation who are denied freedom by the pagan Roman empire which oppresses them. This struggle is, of course, personified in the clash between Judah Ben-Hur and Messala, and the outcome can only be the victory of the Jew over the Roman, the moral over the immoral. Yet Judah Ben-Hur's final triumph over his Roman nemesis Messala is not the end of the story, for the impact of the atoning death of Jesus Christ upon Judah Ben-Hur and his family has still to be dramatized. Interestingly, the Jewishness of the early followers of Jesus Christ is asserted without apology within Wyler's film; the only indication that Christianity may eventually attract non-Jewish adherents comes in the form of the Alexandrian Balthasar, who makes four appearances in the film, beginning with his visit to the Bethlehem stable as one of the three Magi. In effect, nascent Christianity is presented as the culmination of Jewish hopes and expectations, with love and forgiveness being the characteristic features of a new way of life which transcends the political preoccupations of the world.

The final words of Judah Ben-Hur within the film indicate the redemptive power of Christ's death upon him. Judah returns to his home where he finds the faithful servant Esther, who has returned with his sister Tirzah and his mother Miriam, cleansed from their leprosy during the violent storm which accompanied Christ's death. Judah, too, has been transformed by the death of Christ. Recalling Jesus's words from the cross recorded in Luke 23:34, he explains to Esther, 'Almost the moment he died, I heard him say, "Father, forgive them, for they know not what they do" … And I felt his voice take the sword out of my hand.'

Following on from Wyler's classic film version of *Ben-Hur*, Lew Wallace's story has continued to attract the interest of filmmakers and audiences alike. A children's cartoon version directed by Al Guest and Jean Mathieson appeared in 1988, and another 80-minute children's cartoon version directed by William Kowalchuk Jr. appeared in 2003, featuring the voice of Charlton Heston as Ben-Hur in his final cinematic role. A full-bodied two-part TV miniseries directed by Steve Shill was first aired on the Canadian Broadcasting Corporation (CBC TV) on 4 and 11 April 2010. Ridley Scott, whose Oscar-winning film *Gladiator* (2000) marked a cinematic revival of the 'sword and sandal' epics, views Wyler's *Ben-Hur* as a major influence on his film (Scott 1994). Clearly Lew Wallace's story continues to capture the imagination of film makers, although most productions since 1959 clearly trade on the popularity of William Wyler's classic which set the standard and defined the parameters of the story cinematically.

Larry J. Kreitzer

Further reading

Derek Elley (1984) *The Epic Film: Myth and History*. London: Routledge and Kegan Paul.

Larry J. Kreitzer (1993) *The New Testament in Fiction and Film*. Sheffield: JSOT Press.

Jeff Rovin (1977) *The Films of Charleton Heston*. Secaucus, New Jersey: The Citadel Press.

Ridley Scott (1994) Documentary: *Ben-Hur: The Making of an Epic*, in the 50th anniversary DVD release (4 DVD set).

James H. Smylie (1972) 'The Hidden Agenda in *Ben-Hur*', *Theology Today* 29(3): 294–304.

Jon Solomon (2001) *The Ancient World in the Cinema*. New Haven, CN: Yale University Press.

Gordon Thomas (2006) 'Getting It Right the Second Time: Adapting *Ben-Hur* for the Screen', *Bright Lights Film Journal* 52. Available online at www. brightlightsfilm.com/52/benhur.htm.

BLADE RUNNER (1982)

[Production Company: Michael Deeley. Director: Ridley Scott. Screenwriters: Hampton Fancher and David Peoples. Original Novel: Philip K. Dick, *Do*

Androids Dream of Electric Sheep? (1968). Cinematography: Jordan Cronenweth. Music: Vangelis. Art Director: David Snyder. Cast: Harrison Ford (Rick Deckard), Rutger Hauer (Roy Batty), Sean Young (Rachael), Edward James Olmos (Gaff), Daryl Hannah (Pris), William Sanderson (J. F. Sebastian), Joe Turkel (Dr. Eldon Tyrell).]

In the summer of 1982, Ridley Scott's *Blade Runner* failed miserably at the box office and suffered critical derision. Pauline Kael joked in the *New Yorker* (12 July 1982) that if scientists ever invented a test to detect humanness then 'Ridley Scott and his associates should hide'. Writing for the *Chicago Tribune* (25 June 1982), Gene Siskel judged that, despite its visual appeal, the film was 'empty at its core'. Specific criticism most frequently targeted Harrison Ford's flat voiceover narration and the film's forced happy ending, both last-minute studio additions after test audiences had found the film depressing and hard to follow. Scott lost artistic control of *Blade Runner* shortly after shooting ended because of budgetary overruns resulting from continuous rewrites and problems on the set. Thus, the film released in 1982 did not fully render its director's artistic intentions.

Blade Runner was rescued from cinematic obscurity by burgeoning cable television and video markets, where it gained a cult following. Its success in home markets and the rediscovery of a work print closer to Scott's original conception led to the 1992 release of the so-called 'director's cut'. This darker version of the film eliminated the voiceover, restored Scott's preferred more ambiguous ending, and reinserted a key scene known as the 'unicorn reverie'. Yet, while a commercial success, it still represented a compromise between the director's vision and studio interests. It was not until the film's twenty-fifth anniversary that Ridley Scott was permitted full artistic control over what became known as the 'final cut' (2007).

The existence of at least seven different versions of *Blade Runner*, including television and international releases, adds considerably to its mystique. Moreover, the absence of a single definitive edition appropriately reflects the crisis of identity that is at the heart of this film. This identity crisis is symbolically expressed through the difficulty of distinguishing between 'real' humans and genetically engineered 'replicants', created by the powerful Tyrell Corporation to serve as slaves on off-world colonies. Replicants, whose physical and mental abilities surpass those of humans, are kept in line through the fail-safe of a pre-programmed four-year lifespan, that supposedly prevents them from developing emotions and thereby attaining full personhood. Like the biblical deity, the replicants' creator, Dr Eldon Tyrell, has limited their lifespan to discourage the rebellion of his wayward creation (Gen. 6:1–2). By the year 2019, replicants have been outlawed on earth after an attempted revolt and are to be 'retired' (i.e. executed) upon detection by members of a special police unit called 'blade runners'. All of this background information is established by crawl text at the beginning of the film.

The film's main storyline follows the efforts of Rick Deckard, a reluctantly reinstated ex-blade runner, to retire a group of advanced NEXUS 6 replicants, led by combat model Roy Batty, that have illegally returned to earth and are attempting to infiltrate the Tyrell Corporation. We later learn that they wish to confront their 'maker' and force him to extend their pre-programmed lifespan. Much of the film's overt biblical resonance lies in this anticipated confrontation between Creator and Creation. Playing upon the Bible's second creation story (Gen. 2–3), especially as interpreted in John Milton's *Paradise Lost* and Mary Shelley's *Frankenstein* (and its cinematic adaptations), the film as a whole becomes an extended reflection on personhood and what it might mean to be human.

In Genesis 2–3, Adam and Eve are expelled from Eden after choosing to disobey God by eating from the forbidden tree of knowledge. Milton's epic poem follows an Augustinian interpretive tradition by reading this biblical story as an account of humanity's fall and the introduction of original sin into the world. Situating the story within a larger cosmic drama, Milton makes Satan the instigator of humanity's first sin. The poem ends with Adam's vision of the coming Christ, which provides evidence of God's continued providential care for fallen humanity. Shelley intentionally reworks motifs found in Genesis 2–3 and *Paradise Lost* in her gothic novel *Frankenstein*. Here the Creator is depicted as an arrogant scientist who is reluctant to assume responsibility for having created an abomination. Conflicted and rejected by its maker, the monster ultimately demands a reckoning from Dr Frankenstein and kills him. Shelley's work challenges traditional readings of Genesis that blame humanity for the existence of evil and misery and look for a theological remedy expressed in dogmatic belief structures.

Blade Runner taps into this intertextual conversation through intentional references to these earlier works (Desser 1991: 53–8). Like much of *Paradise Lost*, its story takes place in hell as established by the fiery industrial landscape revealed in the film's opening shot. We never see the much-touted off-world colonies although they are advertised in Edenic terms. If Deckard represents Adamic humanity, he never inhabited Paradise but resides instead in an already fallen world. Like

Satan and his angels in *Paradise Lost*, the replicants have rebelled against God/Tyrell and been cast into hell (Luke 10:18). They are jealous and resentful of humanity to whom they are superior in so many ways.

The film's climactic confrontation between Batty and Tyrell borrows heavily from *Frankenstein*. Like Dr Frankenstein, Dr Tyrell is a human scientist who has arrogantly encroached upon the divine sphere by playing Creator. Moreover, both scientists have abdicated responsibility for their hapless creations. Indeed Tyrell has allowed the replicants to be enslaved and exploited for financial gain. Both creatures have been marginalized and abused because of their difference and, as a result have developed resentment toward humanity. Although he greets Batty as his 'prodigal son' (Luke 15:11–32; in later versions of the film, Batty reciprocates by calling him 'father'), Tyrell is noticeably apprehensive during their interaction. Ultimately, the replicant (like Frankenstein's monster) kills his abusive maker. The death of the god-figure in both works makes it clear that neither Shelley's novel nor *Blade Runner* allows for the possibility of theological redemption.

Blade Runner also includes a second confrontation between Batty and Deckard. Their harrowing rooftop chase ends with Deckard clinging helplessly to a jutting beam. Having visually transformed himself into a Christ figure by driving a nail through his numbing hands, Batty chooses to save his enemy shortly before his own life expires. Whereas Milton's Satan acts as an adversary to Adam, Batty becomes Deckard's saviour. Bearing witness to Batty's final moments, which include an eloquent lamentation on the inevitability of death, affects Deckard. He finally resolves to leave the city with Rachael (a replicant and the film's Eve figure). In the happy ending of the film's original theatrical release, the couple is last seen traveling across a green Edenic landscape. Later releases end more ambiguously with the couple leaving Deckard's apartment. In the absence of theological redemption, the film advocates seeking transcendence through relationships.

Blade Runner uses the mythic structure of Genesis 1–3, as filtered through the works of Milton and Shelley, to complicate any simple dichotomy between 'real' and 'constructed' human identity. Dr Tyrell advertises his creations as 'more human than human', a claim that becomes increasingly evident as the film unfolds. Blade runners identify replicants using the Voigt-Kamf (V.K.) Empathy Test, which measures involuntary dilations of the pupil produced by emotional responses. We see this test administered twice in the film. On the first occasion, the replicant Leon demonstrates much more emotion (specifically anxiety and fear) than does the dispassionate blade runner examining him.

In the voiceover narration of the original release, Deckard admits that blade runners have become as emotionless as the replicants they hunt. On the second occasion, it takes an extraordinarily long time for Deckard to determine that Rachael is a replicant, possibly because she herself is initially unaware of this fact. Her creator had implanted childhood memories and provided photographic evidence of her fictional past. But in this film, memory and photographic evidence do not provide a reliable foundation for identity. Ironically, Rachael behaves more humanly after discovering that she is not human. Her mannerisms soften; she displays emotion; she saves Deckard's life; and, under duress, she confesses her desire for him (Gen. 3:16b). Similarly, Leon and Batty grieve and seek to avenge the deaths of their companions. Batty ultimately demonstrates empathy by saving Deckard after teaching him to empathize with the fear felt by hunted replicants.

As the film progresses, the boundary between human and nonhuman begins to dissolve as Deckard falls in love with Rachael, and (at least in later versions of the film) begins to wonder whether he might be a replicant himself. This interpretation is supported by the reinstatement of Deckard's unicorn reverie, which adds significance to the origami unicorn Gaff leaves for him to find at the end of the film. Presumably, Gaff could only be aware of this dream if Deckard's private thoughts and dreams result from documented programming.

As a science-fiction film, *Blade Runner* reveals many of the real issues and concerns of its era by positing a fictional future dystopia in which audiences can examine their desires and fears at a safe distance. The 1980s witnessed a surge in corporate takeovers, conglomerates, and media empires. Anxiety over a hole in the ozone layer and genetic engineering entered public consciousness. Many Americans were beginning to perceive Asians as an economic threat to western hegemony. *Blade Runner* gives expression to these concerns as well as additional apprehensions over the possible consequences of globalization, over-population, and capitalistic exploitation (Redmond 2008: 21–5).

The film depicts an ecologically ravaged, media-saturated world tightly controlled by an elite corporate minority. Following the classic science-fiction film *Metropolis* (Fritz Lang 1927), *Blade Runner* literalizes the distinction between the upper- and lower-class. The wealthy and the police force that supports them inhabit lofty tower-apartments, such as Dr Tyrell's penthouse suite on the 700th floor of a ziggurat-like pyramid (Gen. 11:1–9). Workers populate street-level inner-city ghettos, where freedoms are eroded and life devalued. Only the genetically qualified are allowed to emigrate off-world.

In this setting, the fact that *Blade Runner* defines humanness as the capacity to feel empathy is deeply ironic. If the film's human characters demonstrate little empathy for one another, they demonstrate even less for replicants, the 'skin jobs' they define as nonhuman. According to ads for the off-world colonies, replicant slaves can be used as their human masters see fit. The replicants seen in the film are runaway slaves attempting to 'pass' as humans. The doubly marginalized female replicants are sexually exploited. Pris is described as a 'pleasure model' and Zhora is an exotic dancer with the stage name Miss Salome (the name traditionally given to the daughter of Herodias, Mark 6:17–29; Matt. 14:3–11). Both die violently amidst mannequins that represent their objectification. *Blade Runner* illustrates the systematic dehumanization of those defined as 'other' by virtue of their origin, race, gender, or genetic status.

To establish an appropriately dark mood for this future dystopia, *Blade Runner* liberally borrows key elements of *film noir* and the closely related 1940s and 50s detective genre. This influence is evident in the film's visual style including rain-lashed urban streets, the play of shadows, a *femme fatale* sporting 1940s fashions and hairstyles, and marked class distinctions as scenes shift from penthouse apartments to seedy dives. Deception, narrative gaps, and a deliberately confusing plotline impede our alienated protagonist in his search for answers and meaning. Like *film noir*, *Blade Runner* envisions a sinister world characterized by moral ambiguity and an endemic sense of hopelessness punctuated by occasional blues saxophone solos.

Intentionally or not, these *noir* elements bring the film into conversation with the book of Ecclesiastes. Like Deckard's jaded voiceover and Batty's repeated references to all his eyes have seen, the first-person narrator of Ecclesiastes expresses a sense of hopelessness and alienation rooted in lived experience in and observation of a crooked world (Ecc. 1:1–2). Counter to the sensibilities of more traditional biblical books, this one posits a world in which good will not necessarily triumph over evil (7:15–17; 8:14), human activity has no ultimate significance (1:3–4), and absolutely everything is overshadowed by the inevitability of death (6:1–6). Nor is there is a discernible providential order in the universe to ease humanity's existential plight (5:1–2).

Blade Runner's connection to Ecclesiastes is perhaps most evident in Batty's determined efforts to extend his life. 'It's not an easy thing to meet your maker,' he says with double significance when confronting Tyrell. The maker in question can only offer empty words of comfort encouraging Batty to reconcile himself to his impending end, 'The light that burns twice as bright burns half as long, and you have burned so very, very brightly ... Revel in your time.' Later the dying Batty laments that all the wonders he has witnessed will be 'lost like tears in rain' (1:11–12; 2:16). Humanity's existential dilemma also finds expression in Gaff's final words to Deckard, 'It's too bad she won't live [referring to Rachael]; but, then again, who does?' The original release attempts to soften these words by assuring audiences in voiceover that Rachael lived happily ever after beyond her programmed expiration date. Later versions, however, allow Gaff's statement to stand without comment. We only see the couple leave together presumably to seek what enjoyment they can from their short and futile lives (9:7–10).

Rhonda Burnette-Bletsch

Further reading

Scott Bukatman (1997) *BFI Modern Classics: Blade Runner*. London: BFI Publishing.
David Desser (1991) 'The New Eve: The Influence of *Paradise Lost* and *Frankenstein* on *Blade Runner*', in Judith B. Kerman (ed.) *Retrofitting Blade Runner*. Bowling Green, Ohio: Bowling Green State University Popular Press. pp. 53–65.
Sean Redmond (2008) *Studying Blade Runner*. Leighton Buzzard: Auteur.
Paul M. Sammon (1996) *Future Noir: The Making of Blade Runner*. New York, NY: itbooks.
Richard A. Schwartz (2001) *The Films of Ridley Scott*. Westport, CT; London: Praeger.

BLUE (1993)

[Production Company: Marin Karmitz. Director: Krzysztof Kieślowski. Screenplay: Krzysztof Piesiewicz, Agnieszka Holland, Edward Zebrowski, Slawomir Idziak. Cinematography: Slawomir Idziak. Music: Zbigniew Preisner. Cast: Juliette Binoche (Julie Vignon – de Courcy), Benoît Régent (Olivier), Florence Pernel (Sandrine), Charlotte Véry (Lucille), Hugues Quester (Patrice), Yann Trégouët (Antoine), Alain Ollivier (the lawyer).]

Blue is an award-winning film by the Polish film director Krzysztof Kieślowski (1941–96), the first part of his acclaimed trilogy *Three Colors*, the titles of which are derived from the three colours of the French flag. Although the official titles of the films in the trilogy are in French, and dialogue of the films is mainly in French, they are

widely known by their English titles and we shall use the English title
and subtitles of the dialogue throughout this discussion. The three films
are given over to exploring the three philosophical ideals of the French
Revolution and what they might mean for the modern world: *Blue*
concentrates on the meaning of Liberty, *White* the meaning of Equality,
and *Red* the meaning of Fraternity. *Blue* won the award for Best Film
at the Venice Film Festival in 1993, an early measure of its critical
success, and an indication of its importance as a cinematic venture
into post-modernism. Juliette Binoche also won the award for Best
Actress at the festival, in what many regard as the best performance of
her career.

As a film-maker Kieślowski is well-known for his engagement with
Biblical themes and moral issues, perhaps best exemplified by his *Dekalog*
(1988), a series of ten films based on the Ten Commandments which is
set in a modern Warsaw housing estate and deals with the complexities
of life there. In his films Kieślowski often concentrates on the inner
struggle that human beings experience when they are confronted
with difficult moral choices or faced with capricious fate, blind chance,
or tragic circumstance. The basic plot of *Blue* fits comfortably within
this description, as it is concerned with how a woman deals with the
death of her husband and daughter in a car accident and begins to
rebuild her life following their loss.

The central character in *Blue* is Julie de Courcy, whose husband
Patrice is a respected classical composer. Patrice has just begun work
on a musical concerto commissioned to celebrate the Unification of
Europe and intended to premiere in twelve European cities, but the
piece is left unfinished because of the accident. Patrice's untimely
death strikes Julie so deeply that she struggles to find her way forward. Recovering in the hospital from the car accident which killed
her husband and daughter, Julie attempts suicide by taking some pills
from the nursing station's drug cabinet. But her will to survive is too
strong and she cannot swallow the pills.

Once she is released from the hospital she sets about systematically
stripping herself of anything to do with her past as a way of asserting
her Liberty. She severs contact with people, arranges to have the
family home sold, gets rid of all of her family possessions, and destroys
her husband's musical manuscripts. She has a brief passionless affair
with Olivier, her husband's assistant, who has long been in love with
her, only as an attempt to kill his love for her by proving to him that
she is as imperfect as other women. She moves to a secluded neighbourhood in Paris, renting a bare apartment in a building with no
children, and establishes herself in liberated isolation. She studiously

avoids contact with people, particularly anyone who reminds her of the past and what she has lost. A young man named Antoine, who had witnessed the fateful car crash, seeks her out in order to return a necklace with a cross on it that he found near the car. He offers to tell her what he knows about the incident, but she dismisses him, saying she does not want to know anything about it. Olivier too tracks her down in Paris, but again she asserts her independence and Liberty and sends him away. She visits her mother in a care-home, but finds that her mother is not very lucid and confuses her with another daughter. Julie summarizes her own fragile state of mind when she explains to her mother that her husband and daughter are dead, and says, 'Now I have only one thing left to do: Nothing. I don't want any belongings, any memories. No friends, no love. Those are all traps.'

Nevertheless, Julie's innate goodness and genuine compassion inevitably mean that relationships with other people do begin to form, notably a friendship with a young woman named Lucille who lives downstairs in the apartment block. Lucille is a free spirit, and works as a stripper in the Pigalle neighbourhood, but is regarded as a prostitute by the rest of the people in the apartment building who want to have her evicted. Julie will have nothing to do with any eviction petition, and this earns her Lucille's friendship and admiration.

Lucille becomes the unwitting agent of Julie's journey to wholeness when she rings her up in agitation one night and begs her to come down to the strip-club where she is working. When Julie arrives Lucille explains that in the middle of a dance routine she noticed that her father was one of the men in the audience. Julie listens, non-judgementally, and while they are talking Lucille points to a news report being shown on television about Patrice's unfinished concerto, which was now going to be finished by Olivier. The news report shows some pictures of Julie and Patrice, as well as some photographs of Patrice with another woman that Julie does not recognize. This picture sets Julie on a trail of discovery, and she learns from Olivier that the woman was Patrice's long-standing mistress, a lawyer named Sandrine.

Julie eventually tracks Sandrine down and discovers that she is pregnant with Patrice's son. Sandrine is afraid that Julie will hate her now. But Julie is unable to do so. Recognizing that the necklace Sandrine is wearing is identical to the one Patrice had given her, she realizes that Patrice must have loved Sandrine. Julie eventually makes arrangements for Sandrine and her unborn son to have the house in the country that she and Patrice had lived in. This confirms Sandrine's opinion of Julie's essential goodness, based on what Patrice had told her about his wife: 'That you are good. That you are good and generous. That's what you want to be. People can always count on you. Even me.'

Julie returns to Olivier, and together they complete Patrice's concerto on *The Unification of Europe*. This is fitting: earlier in the film there was a suggestion, put forward in the form of a question by an inquisitive journalist, that Julie was herself responsible for her husband's music. That she must have at least collaborated with him in writing his music is evident in her familiarity with it: the written score triggers the music to play in her head.

The film reaches its climax as the seven-minute chorus of this finished concerto is heard while a montage of images is presented. A sequence of scenes involving each of the characters whose lives have been touched by Julie is shown. We see images of Julie and Olivier making love, of Antoine fingering the cross-necklace given him by Julie, Julie's mother resting in her nursing home, Lucille in her strip-club, and Sandrine undergoing an ultra-sound scan of her unborn son. The chorus we hear is a sublime and other-worldly setting for words taken from Paul's First Letter to the Corinthians (1 Cor. 13:1, 2 [minus the phrases 'and all knowledge and have all faith'], 4, 7–8, 13). It is sung in Greek, although English subtitles are provided in some versions of the film's release, although curiously not in all American editions. Somewhat confusingly, the English subtitles do not correspond exactly with what is sung in the film, but are as follows:

> Though I speak with the tongue of angels,
> If I have not love, I am become as hollow brass.
> Though I have the gift of prophecy,
> And understand all mysteries and all knowledge,
> And though I have enough faith,
> To move the mightiest mountains,
> If I have not love,
> I am nothing.
> Love is patient,
> Love is kind,
> It bears all things,
> It hopes all things,
> Love never fails.
> For prophecies shall fail,
> Tongues shall cease,
> Knowledge shall wither away.
> And now shall abide faith, hope and love,
> But the greatest of these three is love.

Two of the phrases ('I am nothing' and 'the greatest of these is love') are stressed within the sung composition by being repeated three times, indicating the transformative power of love and where human beings stand without it. In effect, Julie's attempts to find her Liberty by means of rigorous independence and enforced isolation, by a rejection of the past and a suppression of what is painful, are all shown to be futile. The unification of her being, as suggested by the chorus of the concerto on *The Unification of Europe*, can only be achieved through love. And love invariably involves other people, just as a chorus is never a solo but is always sung with others.

The final frames of the film, following this montage of the people in Julie's life, are a close-up of her, looking slightly off-camera out of a window onto the world, with tears beginning to stream down her face. This is the only time that we see her crying in the film, and it demonstrates that her journey to wholeness and recovery is under way.

Kieślowski has a reputation as an innovative film-maker whose films are marked by a unique cinematographic style conveying intimacy through the use of colour, the creative juxtaposition of motifs, and the interlocking of themes, all placed within a realistic human setting. *Blue* stands as a fine example of Kieślowski's craft, and several features are worth noting briefly. In terms of how the camera is used within this film, there is a great deal of close-up work, focusing on Julie herself, and fixing her centrally within the frame. Often the camera focuses in on what Julie herself sees, in effect drawing the viewer into her world and helping to communicate a sense of her interiority. Not surprisingly given the title, the colour blue is used frequently within the film, usually as a way to symbolize or call attention to Julie's melancholic state, grieving over her loss and seemingly detached and separated from the world. For example, several scenes show Julie swimming, alone and isolated, in a blue-lit pool; and she takes a blue crystal chandelier from the blue room in their family home with her to her rented apartment in Paris as one of the very few mementos of her former life.

Music is an essential component of *Blue*, and the film is blessed with a haunting score written by the composer Zbigniew Preisner, a long-time collaborator of Kieślowski who also wrote the music for *Dekalog*. At four different points in the film Kieślowski creatively uses music together with a fade-out and fade-in technique as a means of symbolizing the suspension of time. The storyline picks up exactly where it was before the pause, but during the interval it is music that fills the space. Then there are a number of important scenes which show Julie receiving a musical gifting, where music from the proposed symphony for *The Unification of Europe* comes crashing upon her consciousness and she hears a fragment of the work in her head. Visually, this is sometimes accompanied by deliberate concentration on blue colours within the shot, again to emphasize the private interiority of the experience. Finally, when Julie works on finishing the score of Patrice's concerto for *The Unification of Europe* she does so in a blue pen, a fitting touch to this cinematic masterpiece.

Larry J. Kreitzer

Further reading

Geoff Andrew (1998) *The 'Three Colours' Trilogy*. London: BFI Publishing.
Janina Falkowska (1999) 'The Double Life of Veronique and *Three Colours*: An Escape from Politics?', in Paul Coates (ed.) *Lucid Dreams: The Films of Krzysztof Kieślowski*. Wiltshire: Flicks Books. pp. 136–59.
Annette Insdorf (1999) *Double Lives, Second Chances: The Cinema of Krzysztof Kieślowski*. New York: Miramax Books.
Krzysztof Kieślowski and Krzysztof Piesiewicz (1998) *Three Colours Trilogy: Blue, White, Red*. London: Faber and Faber.
Emma Wilson (1998) '*Three Colours: Blue*: Kieślowski, Colour and the Postmodern Subject', *Screen* 39: 349–62.

BREAKING THE WAVES (1996)

[Production Company: Zentropa. Director: Lars von Trier. Screen writer: Lars von Trier. Co-written by Peter Asmussen. Cinematography: Robby Müller. Music: Joachim Holbek. Art director: Karl Juliusson. Cast: Emily Watson (Bess) and Stellan Skarsgård (Jan).]

The main character in Lars von Trier's film, *Breaking the Waves*, is Bess, a young, innocent girl who is known for being somewhat simple. She is raised in a strict Calvinist community in a small coastal village in the north of Scotland. The elders in the church rule over what looks like a perfect patriarchal society. They set the agenda. They interpret God's Word and decide about people's fate, even beyond death. In this society, women are to occupy themselves with womanly work; they are to be obedient, control their feelings and hide their grief and sorrows.

Bess finds it difficult to meet the expectations of her community. Against their will she marries a stranger, an outsider to the community.

His name is Jan, an oil-rig worker in the North Sea. Bess is a virgin when she marries Jan, as she has waited for her one and only love. Her love is sincere and she devotes herself fully to Jan. After enjoying a short but blissful honeymoon, Jan must return to his job on the oil-rig. Bess is devastated at being left behind, and the women closest to her, her mother and sister-in-law, try to console her.

Seeking comfort in prayer, Bess asks God to send Jan back home. Jan comes back much sooner than planned, seriously injured after an accident at the oil-rig. She is convinced that God has answered her prayer. She is grateful to God that Jan has survived the accident, but she believes that Jan's condition is her fault. Jan is paralysed from neck down, and severely depressed. There is no doubt in her mind that the accident is God's work, intended as a test of her love for Jan. Bess decides that she will do whatever she can to prove her love for Jan, in order for him to be able to walk and be well again. Thus, when Jan asks her to have sex with other men and then tell him about her experience, Bess agrees.

Despite warnings from her community, Bess gradually becomes more immersed in prostitution. She is denounced by her church and her family, due to her behaviour. But Bess believes it is her responsibility to please Jan and do what he wants, and thereby consummate his healing. Ultimately it proves deadly for her. She is fatally injured when she boards a fishing ship despite its crew's reputation for violently mistreating prostitutes. After her death, the elders in her community decide that she does not deserve a funeral-service as she will in any case go to hell. In the film's final scene, Jan is back on his feet, supporting himself with a stick. Together with his friends, Jan steals her body and throws it into the sea. Her body fails to show up on the ship's sonar. Bells from heaven ring out, invoking God as the agent of her disappearance.

The innovative camerawork in von Trier's *Breaking the Waves*, the close-ups and the hand-held camera, which was to become standard in the *Dogma 95* film-making movement, is a trademark of von Trier's films. Von Trier was strongly influenced by the work of another Danish director, Carl Theodor Dreyer, especially his 1928 film *Joan of Arc*. This is particularly obvious in his cinematographic style, particularly his frequent and lengthy close-ups. In many ways Bess resembles Dreyer's Joan of Arc, and the striking performance by Emily Watson (for which she earned an Oscar nomination for Best Actress in a Leading Role) echoes Renée Jeanne Falconetti's performance as Joan of Arc, which is considered among the finest in cinema history (Schepelern 2010).

The movie raises a number of theological questions and concerns, disclosed most clearly in the conversations between Bess and God. In these conversations Bess talks to God and God talks back, through Bess herself, who thereby takes on the role of a biblical prophet (see Jer. 1:7). Even if the voice is the same, the tone is different, being both deeper and harsher when God talks. The tone is fitting to the message. The God who speaks through Bess is harsh and merciless. He wants Bess to be a good girl, but because Bess is in fact 'a stupid, little girl', God decides to test her love for Jan. If she is able to stand the test, Jan will live. Bess therefore equates obedience to Jan with obedience to God. When God disapproves of her, God withdraws. Thus Bess loses contact with God when she escapes the abuse in her first visit to the fishing ship. But she is reconnected on her second visit to the ship. God tells her *he* is with her on this trip, but the trip proves to be a fatal one for Bess.

The God who speaks with Bess corresponds fully to the God as apprehended by the Calvinist church in which Bess was raised. This is a God who is full of anger and revenge; *he* is in charge and he exerts his control through *his men*. Only those who obey God (or his representatives) and act accordingly have a hope for the future; they alone are welcome to the church and eventually into heaven. When Bess gets into trouble the church is not able to assist her. She is excommunicated from her community, doomed to live as an outsider and eventually consigned to hell, at least in the eyes of her community. Even her mother does not dare to let her in when Bess seeks her help. Only her sister-in-law and her physician, the other outsiders to this community, try to help her, but in vain.

Regardless of the director's intention, Bess is often considered a plausible image of Christ for a contemporary version of a 'passion play'. Bess's sacrifice proves to be effective; her degradation and death are not in vain. The allusion to the resurrection at the end of the film, symbolized by Jan's resurrection from his bed and Bess' resurrection from death with the 'empty tomb' and heavenly church bells, reinforce the interpretation of Bess as Christ-figure.

While there is no consensus regarding a definition of a Christ-figure (Kozlovic 2004; Deacy 2006), I would propose two basic criteria: that there be some direct and specific resemblance to Christ (though a full replication in every detail is not essential); and that the fundamental message associated with the possible Christ-figure has to be consistent with the life and work of Christ, and not contrary to his message about liberation and love. Movies in which the Christ-figure is female raise significant issues both about Christ's identity and about women's

ability to represent Christ, whether it is on the movie-screen or at
the altar in church. Hence, female Christ-figures can help us focus on
the classical christological question of the human and the divine, as well
as the theological significance of Jesus' historical context, particularly
his sex.

Bess fulfills these criteria. Indeed, contrary to the judgement she faces
from her community, she is an incarnation of the traditional understanding of love as *agape*. Her love is the unselfish love that does not
seek its own. Her love knows no limits, but sacrifices itself for others,
even unto death. However, the harmful effects of sacrificial love
quickly become evident in her life. She is easily convinced by Jan that
she should prove her love for him by consenting to his will. In doing
this, Bess appears to be obeying the will of God, as Jan's will is in fact
God's will. Because Bess is utterly controlled by Jan, she refuses to
listen to the warnings of those who fear for her life. Her sole desire is
to do whatever she can to save Jan; according to Jan's words, his life
is in her hands. He will only be healed if she is willing to sacrifice
herself. Because she also believes this to be true, Bess is unable to
protect herself from being harmed, even killed, by Jan's perverse
inclinations.

Since the 1960s, feminist theologians have raised compelling questions
about the Christian model of love as self-sacrifice and its impact on
women's lives. Anders Nygren's book on *Agape och Eros*, originally
published in the 1930s, has been a touchstone for the Christian theological discourse about love. Nygren pits *agape*, unselfish love against *eros*,
which he considers a form of selfish love. He views *agape* as a divine
love that never seeks its own interests. *Agape* is the Christian ideal, but
human sinfulness prevents us from attaining it fully. *Agapic* love
sacrifices itself for others, just as Christ did on the cross. *Eros* signifies
the opposite – a love controlled by selfish desires and essentially *not*
Christian. Hence *eros* always becomes the negative form of human
love, something to be resisted and overcome. Feminist theologians
have criticized such traditional understandings of divine and human
love. They are particularly critical of the tendency to idealize *agape* as
sacrificial love, as women have been raised to think too much about
others and too little about themselves. From the perspective of women's
experience, it becomes highly questionable to label what women so
often lack, namely self-confidence and a strong self-image, as bad or
even sinful.

Such feminist-critical analysis of self-sacrificial love provides a
helpful lens through which to view von Trier's *Breaking the Waves*.
In the best possible light, von Trier's film can be viewed as a critique

of the traditional interpretation of Christ's sacrificial death, in which the father demands the death of his son. In recent decades many theologians have criticized this traditional interpretation, emphasizing instead the importance of understanding Jesus' death on the cross as a consequence of his liberating life of protest that he lived. Jesus chose to overturn the norms and values of the society he lived in, as well as to live and work on the margins, and thus challenged both worldly and spiritual authorities. Like Jesus, Bess counters the values and norms of the society, thereby becoming an outsider in her own religious and familial context.

In my view, however, Bess is not in fact a Christ-figure. As a naive girl, she is destined from the outset to be on the margins, as she is unable truly to comprehend what is happening around her. She herself is not imbued with agency, in contrast, for example, to Sister Helen in Tim Robbins' *Dead Man Walking*, who may also be perceived as a Christ-figure (Pennington 2012: 190). Bess is a powerless woman in a society controlled by men. In her patriarchal society man's salvation is secured by the perfect sacrifice of the woman. She is utterly a victim of the powerful, of those who take control of her life. Hence, instead of being an agent of love, Bess ends up as a victim of violence, betrayed by her community, her husband, and, ultimately, also God. In *Breaking the Waves* God sides with the powerful against the powerless, in a stark contradiction to the God who is revealed in the person and the liberating work of Jesus Christ, according to the Gospels and the Christian tradition.

Arnfríður Guðmundsdóttir

Further reading

Christopher Deacy (2006) 'Reflections on the Uncritical Appropriation of Cinematic Christ-Figures: Holy Other or Wholly Inadequate?', *Journal of Religion and Popular Culture*. 13.

Ken Derry (2012) 'Believing Is Seeing: Teaching Religion and Violence in Film', in Brian K. Pennington (ed.) *Teaching Religion and Violence*. New York: Oxford University Press. pp. 185–217.

Arnfríður Guðmundsdóttir (2002) 'Female Christ-figures in Films: A Feminist Critical Analysis of Breaking the Waves and Dead Man Walking', *Studia Theologica* (*Scandinavian Journal of Theology*). 56(1): 27–43.

Anton K. Kozlovic (2004) 'The Structural Characteristics of the Cinematic Christ-figure' *Journal of Religion and Popular Culture* Vol. 8. Available online: www.usask.ca/relst/jrpc/art8-cinematicchrist.html (accessed 24 August 2011).

Brian K. Pennington (ed.) (2012) *Teaching Religion and Violence*. New York: Oxford University Press. pp. 185–217.

Peter Schepelern (2010) 'From Dreyer to von Trier', available online at www.
english.carlthdreyer.dk/AboutDreyer/Themes/From-Dreyer-to-Trier.aspx
Lars von Trier and Christian Braad Thomsen (2007) 'Trier on von Trier', in
Jolyon Mitchell and Brent Plate (eds.) *The Religion and Film Reader*. New
York and London: Routledge. pp. 230–32.

Further viewing

The Passion of Joan of Arc (Theodor Dreyer, 1928)
Dead Man Walking (Tim Robbins, 1995)

CAPE FEAR (1991)

[Production Company: Amblin Entertainment, Cappa Films, Tribeca Productions.
Director: Martin Scorsese. Screenplay: Wesley Strick. Cinematography: Freddie
Francis. Cast: Robert De Niro (Max Cady), Nick Nolte (Sam Bowden), Jessica
Lange (Leigh Bowden), Juliette Lewis (Danielle Bowden).]

Martin Scorsese made *Cape Fear* for Universal Studios in return for
their having financed (to great controversy, as outlined elsewhere
in this volume) *The Last Temptation of Christ* in 1988, and it proved to
be the director's biggest budget film to date (costing $34 million), as
well as his biggest box office success, generating over $79m at the US
box office alone. For an unapologetically commercial picture, and a
remake at that of a 1962 thriller of the same name directed by J. Lee
Thompson, it is all the more surprising that the Bible should play
such a paramount role in this film. Judging solely from the sheer
number of biblical references, *Cape Fear* would appear to be Scorsese's
most religiously fecund film. Yet this is not a conventional or reverential retread of any Biblical narrative or motifs. Despite overt reference
to a number of Pauline, Gospel and Old Testament passages or stories
(such as Psalms and, especially, the Book of Job), the Bible is harnessed,
even perverted and bastardized, by the lead character, Max Cady, for
his own destructive purposes. Cady is a newly released prison inmate
who wreaks vengeance on the defence lawyer, Sam Bowden, who he
believes betrayed him for burying a report testifying to his 16-year-
old victim's alleged promiscuity, when he was on trial 14 years earlier
for assault and rape.

In marked contrast to Clint Eastwood's *Gran Torino* (2008), which
resonates with a number of core biblical passages without referring to
them explicitly, *Cape Fear* uses the Bible both as a recurring prop and
as the engine that propels forward the movie's plot. The very first

scene introduces us to Cady in his prison cell, in which he has collected a library that includes Dante's *Inferno*, Nietzsche's *Thus Spake Zarathustra*, and the Holy Bible itself. Cady himself is covered in tattoos, the majority of which take the form of biblical quotations and references. On his left forearm is imprinted 'Vengeance is mine NT: Romans, XII, 19' while engraved on his right arm is 'My Time IS AT HAND. NT: Matthew, XXVI, 18'. Tattooed on his left bicep are the verses 'I have put my trust in the LORD GOD in him will I trust Ps 91, 2' as well as 'THE LORD IS THE AVENGER NT: I Thessalonians 4,6'. Perversely, then, Cady is 'the Word made Flesh' (cf. John 1:14); virtually every sentence he utters contains a biblical quotation or theme. When he advises Bowden's daughter, Danielle, against judging her parents for their misdemeanours he cites Jesus' final words in Luke: ' ... forgive them; for they know not what they do' (Luke 23:34). Cady tends to compare his suffering in prison to Paul's suffering for the sake of his gospel (Gal. 5:11; 1 Thess. 3:4; Reinhartz 2003: 73). In Cady's words to Bowden: 'You don't know what suffering is, Councillor. Like it says in Galatians 3, have you suffered so many things in vain ... ' (Gal. 3:4). Finally, Cady, like Paul, can speak in tongues, as he demonstrates in the overblown, apocalyptic showdown at the end of the picture on the houseboat in the perilous waters of Cape Fear, before he exclaims that he is 'bound for the Promised Land'.

Cady, then, presents himself as a divine vessel, acting out God's wishes. But, thoroughly immersed though he is in biblical language – and notwithstanding his glossolalia – his campaign for retribution against the lawyer and his family is not the work of a beneficent celestial instrument of salvation, but more closely resembles that of an avenging demon or Devil-figure. Despite his antagonism towards Bowden for the lawyer's lies and transgressions, Cady himself is deceitful. Cady denies, for example, any culpability for killing the family dog at the same time that he castigates Sam Bowden for his mendacity. Although he has read the Bible, Cady appropriates it for his own base purposes, to the point that he violates it as sacred text (cf. Reinhartz 2003: 74). Moral inversionism indeed lies at the very kernel of Cady's raison d'être. He may ask Bowden's wife, Leigh, towards the end whether she is 'ready to be born again', but he also intends to rape and sexually assault her. There is nothing salvific or edifying about his language or intentions – 'A few minutes alone with me, darling, and you'll be speaking in tongues.'

Yet God seems entirely absent from, and irrelevant to, Cady's scheme. Cady may see himself as acting on a higher authority, and as carrying out God's work, but God is a rather superfluous agent in

Cady's universe. Cady is a completely autonomous figure. He may derive from a Pentecostal background in the Deep South, but he is not part of any Christian church or indeed any type of community (see Reinhartz 2003: 79). He acts alone and independently. He also appears to be superhuman – he appears and disappears at will, he is always one step ahead of the law, and he is able to withstand all kinds of suffering, including a severe beating at the hands of three hired thugs with bicycle chains and baseball bats (he turns the tables and out-manoeuvres his assailants). He is impervious to tortures such as boiling water and candle wax: 'Granddaddy used to handle snake knives in church, Granny drank strychnine. I guess you could say I had a leg up, genetically speaking.' As he explains to Sam: 'I spent fourteen years in an eight by nine cell surrounded by people who were less than human. My mission in that time was to become more than human.' Cady even claims to having usurped God, Nietzschean style. In addition to Nietzsche, he cites from the seventeenth century theologian Angelus Silesius: 'I am like God and God like me. I am as large as God, he is as small as I. He cannot be above me nor I beneath him be.'

In what sense, therefore, can we 'read' *Cape Fear* as a biblically literate or consonant film? The dilemma is even more sharply posed by the film's equating the suffering of the Bowden family as an updated treatise on the trials of Job, which, as Reinhartz puts it, amounts to a structuring device for this film (2003: 68). Cady counsels Bowden to 'Check out the Bible, councillor – the book between Esther and Psalms', namely the Book of Job, which we subsequently see Bowden reading in bed. Job was a righteous man and a servant of God, whose faith was put to the test in a wager between God and Satan. Job is deprived of his sons and daughters, his livestock, his servants and his reputation, and is afflicted with a severe bodily affliction (extending 'from the sole of his foot to the crown of his head'; Job 2:7) – all to test the durability of his faith. Despite his suffering, Job refuses to break off relations with God: 'The Lord gave, and the Lord has taken away; blessed be the name of the Lord' (Job 1:21). Subsequently, however, Job accuses God of being indifferent to the human condition and even of murder: 'From out of the city the dying groan, and the soul of the wounded cries for help; yet God pays no attention to their prayer' (Job 24:12).

There are obvious parallels between the suffering of Job and the plight of the Bowden family. Cady forewarns Bowden that 'I'm going to make you learn about loss'. If so, however, Cady here identifies himself not with God or with Christ, as the biblical tattoos on his body would imply, but with Satan, who was responsible for the heavenly wager (Job 1:9–10; cf. Reinhartz 2003: 76). Moreover, whereas in the Book of Job Satan is merely one of the attendants in the heavenly court – a quasi-legal figure – the Satan that Cady really approximates is the superhuman entity or beast of the apocalypse on display in the Book of Revelation, where he is identified as 'the deceiver of the whole world' (Rev. 12:9; cf. John 12:31, 14:30).

The nature of the devastation that attends the Bowden family also differs from that of Job and his family. In Job 2:9, Job's wife scorns her husband for maintaining his belief in God after all of the misfortune that has befallen him; she urges him to 'Curse God, and die'. In marked contrast, Sam Bowden's wife, Leigh, sees the *survival* of the family unit, not its demise, as being the critical issue at hand (see also Reinhartz 2003: 75–6): 'I'd like to know just how strong we are, or how weak. But I guess the only way we're going to find that out is just by going through this.'

The fact that the Bowdens do survive also differentiates them from their biblical counterparts. And whereas Job is 'blameless and upright' (Job 1:1), the Bowdens are not, nor is their punishment a test of piety but rather of endurance. As Reinhartz puts it, 'religious faith is not an issue in this film' (2003: 76). The only character with any overt faith commitment is Cady, and it is a perverted one at that.

Differences are also evident in the film's conclusion. On the surface, it would seem that the survival of the Bowdens is parallel to the restoration of Job and his family. God bestows upon Job 'twice as much as he had before' (Job 42:10), including a new family comprised of seven sons and three daughters (Job 42:13). But, even here, the differences are palpable. Physically, they do – barely – manage to evade the clutches of Cady, who has drowned, but they have degenerated into savages (Reinhartz 2003: 76). It is almost impossible to distinguish Sam from Max by the end – they are both fighting like animals for sheer survival. Sam has descended to Max's level when he attempts to crush Max Cady's head with a large rock while babbling 'I'm going to kill you'. In the final scene, we see the whole family literally rising from the mud to which they have descended.

While they have survived physically, it is not clear that they have survived emotionally or psychologically. According to Danielle's final voiceover: 'We never spoke about what happened – at least not to each other'. She also concludes that 'if you hang on to the past, you die a little every day'. Danielle would seem to be saying that, rather than learn from their former sins, in accordance with Cady's previous declaration to Sam that 'You might say I'm here to save you', the family is in collective denial about, and has even built a protective wall around, all the circumstances which led to Cady's incursion into their dysfunctional lives (Deacy 2001: 127). This is not to say the family is incapable of being redeemed from their sins; following Origen, one could argue that the process of redemption has merely begun, and is in no way complete (Deacy 2001: 135).

This type of reading, however, would endow the film with a theological scaffolding that is in fact absent from the film itself. In speculating about what has happened to the family, and what the implications of not confronting the past might be, I am reminded of a film which happened to be on release in the same month as *Cape Fear* – Barbra Streisand's *The Prince of Tides* (1991). This film is also about a family that falls apart precisely because they are unable to talk about a traumatic episode from the past. The Wingo family, from South Carolina, were victims of a brutal assault and rape, which many decades later has resulted in the attempted suicide of one of the family members. Significantly, that film also stars Nick Nolte, whose character, Tom Wingo, confesses to his psychiatrist: 'God help me, the silence was worse than the rape'. Robert Jewett has written at some length about how the biblical motifs relating to what Paul says in 1 Corinthians 14:25 concerning the need to disclose through prophecy 'the secrets of the heart' resonate with this film (1999: 23–37). Reading Jewett's analysis, I wonder whether Streisand's film might not, in spite of its more allusive and tangential engagement with scriptural subject matter, comprise a no less durable starting point for exploring the intersection between the Bible and film, than Scorsese's more brazen and, at face value, more persuasive rendering would suggest. That said, *Cape Fear* is a complex and provocative movie whose ironic use, if not misuse, of key biblical themes and characters, Old and New Testament alike, plays upon our assumptions that the mere citation of scripture is sufficient to provide divine sanction for one's actions. *Cape Fear* takes Bible-film analysis to a new level, whereupon the greater, and more explicit, the use of scripture, the more divergent and theologically problematic, such a reading becomes.

Christopher Deacy

Further reading

Christopher Deacy (2001) *Screen Christologies: Redemption and the Medium of Film*. Cardiff: University of Wales Press.

Lawrence S. Friedman (1997) *The Cinema of Martin Scorsese*. Oxford: Roundhouse Publishing.

Robert Jewett (1999) *Saint Paul Returns to the Movies: Triumph over Shame*. Grand Rapids and Cambridge: Eerdmans.
Adele Reinhartz (2003) *Scripture on the Silver Screen*. Louisville and London: Westminster John Knox Press.

CHILDREN OF MEN (2006)

[Production Company: Universal Pictures. Director: Alfonso Cuarón. Screenplay: Alfonso Cuarón, Timothy J. Sexton, David Arata, Mark Fergus, and Hawk Ostby, based on the novel *The Children of Men* by P. D. James. Cinematography: Emmanuel Lubezki. Cast: Clive Owen (Theo Faron), Julianne Moore (Julian), Michael Caine (Jasper), Clare-Hope Ashitey (Kee), Pam Ferris (Miriam).]

The intersection of the Bible with *Children of Men* is subtle yet all the more profound for that subtlety. Christian and biblical images are woven throughout the film to provide glimmers of hope in an otherwise hauntingly bleak landscape. Set in England in 2027, the film opens up a world in which mass and unexplained infertility has stemmed reproduction worldwide for the past 18 years. Responses have varied in the face of the impending demise of humankind. The dominant theme is the breakdown of social mores, as groups of penitents and flagellants appear briefly bearing signs claiming, 'Infertility is God's punishment' and urging onlookers to 'Repent'. A fascist police state in England uses an iron fist to provide some semblance of social order, tightly controlling citizen movements and systematically rounding up illegal immigrants (called 'fugees', an abbreviation of 'refugees') for deportation. Citizens are freely offered 'Quietus', a medication that triggers a serene death for those who choose to depart this world.

The cinematography underlines the bleak context, as the camera lingers over images of poverty, graffiti, caged immigrants awaiting deportation, and people living on the margins of 'civilized' society. The gritty, dreary mood is enhanced through the predominance of grey-blue colouring and dim lighting. Overall, the film is 'apocalyptic' in the popular cultural sense of imaging a dystopian world with no future and no prospects for human flourishing. As Theo states in the film, 'I can't really remember when I last had any hope, and I certainly can't remember when anyone else did either. Because really, since women stopped being able to have babies, what's left to hope for?' Yet the film is also 'apocalyptic' in the root sense of being revelatory. The narrative instills a vision of hope and perseverance in the face of a corrupt and bankrupt world.

The source of hope for this otherwise hopeless world is a child. The immediate biblical connection is, of course, the child of God, sent in human form as Jesus. The film opens with the introduction of the main character whose name, Theo (shortened from Theodore) evokes the Greek word for 'God'. A mid-level bureaucrat who once had a wife and child and radical aspirations for a just and open society, Theo now finds some small comfort in alcohol, which helps him through each day. His personal world reflects the bleakness of life around him. In contrast, his ex-partner, Julian, continues her fight for justice, and is now aligned with a group of radicals attempting to provoke a popular uprising to destabilize the repressive government. Julian's optimism for a just world stands in stark contrast to the despair of Theo ('God'), who is presented as having given up on the world, washing his hands of its darkness and sin.

Eventually, however, Theo is provoked to action by Julian, who is the archetype of the Holy Spirit. She first appears in the film bathed in bright sunlight, a stark contrast to the otherwise dim lighting of the film. Her role is iconographically indicated by the tattoo on the right side of her neck depicting a dove in flight, a well-recognized symbol of Christian hope – and Holy Spirit. She sends Theo on a mission to help change the world. At this point in the film it is as yet unclear whether Theo's character symbolizes the Father or the Son, but as events unfold the viewer recognizes that Theo is the catalyst for world renewal rather than its provider. As the Christ paradigm requires, Theo gives up his life in order that others shall live. Yet in the final scene, as Theo reveals that he is bleeding from his side from a bullet wound, Kee cries out 'God!' leaving the ambiguity of his metaphoric identity unresolved.

Biblical language and imagery are invoked in a few other key scenes that revolve around Kee, the young African woman whom Theo must shepherd to safety. She carries in her womb a child, potentially the first child to be born on Earth in 18 years. The paternity of the child is ambiguous, not unlike that of Jesus. After the birth of the child, there is an explicit connection of the baby with Jesus when Sid, the helper turned betrayer, sees the newborn swaddled in dirty, tattered clothes and exclaims 'Jesus Christ ... Jesus Christ!' The salvific role of the child is anticipated even before his birth. When Kee first reveals to Theo her distended abdomen, Theo likewise expresses his amazement through the words 'Jesus Christ!' Theo articulates words not heard for 18 years, 'She's pregnant!', to which the newly elected leader of the radicals responds, 'Yeah, it's a miracle, innit?'

When Theo asks Kee who fathered the child, she responds, 'I'm a virgin', thus evoking images of Mary the mother of Jesus. Quickly, she reveals her joke, telling Theo there were in fact many men who potentially could have impregnated her. In this way, Kee is a stark contrast to Mary, whose virgin state is glossed in the biblical narratives and developed in Christian tradition. But like Mary, Kee is young and afraid: she carries a child whose paternity is shrouded in ambiguity, and flees from those who would take her baby. Like Joseph, Theo cares for both the mother and the child that he has not fathered. Theo stays by his companion's side, helps her to safety and oversees the delivery of the baby. Such allegorical links to the Christian nativity story are further strengthened by the day chosen for the opening of the film in 2006: December 25 (Vineberg 2007).

Biblical figures likewise populate the landscape of the film. When the bus is stopped and searched as it passes through the security checkpoints of the Bexhill Refugee detainment camp, Miriam diverts attention from Kee by furiously crossing herself and invoking the name of the archangel Gabriel. Homeland security officers remove her from the bus to a fate that will include torture and probable death, but her act of selflessness allows Kee to pass through unnoticed.

In an earlier scene, Theo pays a visit to his wealthy and well-connected cousin, who has turned the Battersea Power Station into a government funded 'Ark of the Arts' meant to preserve past culture. In clever homage to rock artists Pink Floyd, director Alfonso Cuarón has a large inflatable pig visibly bobbing over smokestacks in the background. This image is a reference to the album cover for *Animals* (1977), an allegorical critique of capitalism, in which the Battersea Power Station serves as a symbol of the decay of the modern age. In the film, the Power Plant houses artistic opulence, yet the very presence of famous art pieces creates cognitive dissonance in the viewer. As Theo awaits his cousin he looks upon Michelangelo's Statue of David, standing alone in a bare hall. The usual cacophony of colours against which the stark simplicity of the marble statue stands has now been lost; there is no contrast, no beauty. David, the virile king of Israel, depicted naked with power and grace, is rendered impotent in this new context.

When Theo's cousin arrives, he notes that he was unable to save another famous Michelangelo statue: 'La Pieta was smashed before we got there.' Yet this image of Mary cradling her now dead adult son is not lost in the film. Cuarón notes that he deliberately constructed a later scene to invoke this image by placing in the background a woman holding the body of her son when Theo and Kee exit the Russian apartments in the internment camp.

This was a reference to a real photograph of a woman holding the body of her son in the Balkans, crying with the corpse of her son. It's very obvious that when the photographer captured that photograph, he was referencing *La Pieta*, the Michelangelo sculpture of Mary holding the corpse of Jesus. So: We have a reference to something that really happened, in the Balkans, which is itself a reference to the Michelangelo sculpture. At the same time, we use the sculpture of David early on, which is also by Michelangelo, and we have of course the whole reference to the Nativity. And so everything was referencing and cross-referencing, as much as we could.

(Cuarón in Voynar 2006, para. 37)

The biblical and spiritual themes of the film are underscored by the original composition of Sir John Tavener, who describes his soundtrack as 'musical and spiritual reaction to Alfonso's film' (Tavener in Broxton 2006), and includes pieces with titles such as 'Song of the Angel', 'The Lamb', 'Mother of God, Here I Stand', and the lengthy 'Fragments of a Prayer' (which occurs regularly throughout the film). When Kee and Theo carry the newborn baby out of a building under siege, as the police and radicals engage in a vicious gun battle, the soundtrack is completely silent. As they walk down the stairs and out of the building passing residents and combatants, many cross themselves or fall to their knees in viewing the miracle baby. This adoration is not carried out by shepherds and magi, but it is adoration nonetheless.

Children of Men is adapted from a book of the same name by renowned mystery novelist P. D. James (and is a marked departure from her usual genre). The film focuses primarily on the second half of the book, and shifts characters and major plot threads to the point where the film is connected to the book only by its basic premise of a bleak, dystopian world in which mass infertility has stifled hope. Although Schwartzman (2009) sees in the title a broadening of the messianic identity 'Son of Man' to 'Children of Men', this is not James' intention in the novel, nor is it at all obvious in the movie itself. The book is very explicit in linking the title, and thus the narrative, to the Bible through the Anglican Book of Common Prayer. At an ad hoc burial for one of their traveling companions, Theo recites from memory Psalm 90:1–4, taken from the prayer book's burial service:

Lord, thou has been our refuge: from one generation to another. Before the mountains were brought forth, or even the earth and the world were made: thou art God from everlasting, and world without end. Thou turnest man to destruction: again thou sayest, Come again, ye children of men. For a thousand years in thy sight are but as yesterday: seeing that is past as a watch in the night.

(James 1992: 281)

These verses encapsulate the plot premise: God created the world, God can turn the world over to destruction, and God can renew the world, the latter conviction expressed in the words 'come again, ye children of men'.

In the film, an unseen hand plays a large role in the unfolding events. No explanation, medical or otherwise, is given for the mass infertility that created the dystopia in the first place, nor is the backstory for Kee's pregnancy provided. Yet with this new baby there will be a future, or at very least, the hope of a future. There are no guarantees that more pregnancies will follow, but the film closes with the imposing image of a large freighter bearing down on the small rowboat in order to carry Kee and her baby to safety under the protection of the 'Human Project'. The name of the freighter: *Tomorrow*.

Richard S. Ascough

Further reading

Jonathan Broxton (2006) '*Children of Men*: John Tavener', *Movie Music UK*, available online at http://web.archive.org/web/20070228105041/ http://www.moviemusicuk.us/childrenofmencd.htm (accessed 15 September 2011).

P. D. James (1992) *The Children of Men*. London: Penguin.

Sarah Schwartzman (2009) '*Children of Men* and a Plural Messianism', *Journal of Religion and Film* 13(1) available online at www.unomaha.edu/jrf/vol13.no1/ChildrenMen.htm. (accessed 11 September 2011).

Steve Vineberg (2007) 'Rumors of a Birth', *Christian Century* 124(3): 44.

Kim Voynar (2006) 'Interview: *Children of Men* Director Alfonso Cuaron', *Cinematical* (December 25), available online at http://blog.moviefone.com/2006/12/25/interview-children-ofmen-director-alfonso-cuaron (accessed 16 September 2011).

CLOSE ENCOUNTERS OF THE THIRD KIND (1977)

[Production Companies: Columbia Pictures Corporation, EMI Films, Julia Phillips and Michael Phillips. Director: Steven Spielberg. Screenwriters: Steven Spielberg, Hal Barwood, Jerry Belson, David Giler, John Hill, Matthew Robbins, and Paul Schrader. Cinematography: Vilmos Zsigmond. Cast:

Richard Dreyfuss (Roy Neary), Teri Garr (Ronnie Neary), François Truffaut (Claude Lacombe), Melinda Dillon (Jillian Guiler), Bob Balaban (David Laughlin).]

The movie's title (sometimes abbreviated as 'CE3K') derives from the writings of astronomer and 'ufologist', J. Allen Hynek. According to Hynek (who consulted on the film, and plays a bit part), the third and closest kind of encounter with an unidentified flying object (UFO) or extraterrestrial alien is direct contact between alien beings and human beings (see also the work of the French ufologist, Jacques Vallée). The movie's conclusion features such an encounter, and earlier encounters of the first and second kinds are depicted as preparing the way for it. The movie was immensely popular with both viewers and critics upon its release, and it has remained so ever since. It received numerous awards and is often listed among the greatest films ever made. The following comments refer to the 'director's cut', except as noted.

The story is set in present-day, late twentieth-century USA, with brief scenes set in Mexico, Mongolia ('special edition' only), and India. The primary plot begins in Indiana and ends in Wyoming. The film bears a general resemblance to biblical stories of prophets who are 'called' by God but resist that call, such as Jeremiah, Ezekiel, or especially Jonah. Roy Neary, Jillian Guiler, and other earthlings have been 'invited' to meet the aliens, in the words of Claude Lacombe (who was modelled on Vallée). Lacombe correctly interprets the earlier encounters and orchestrates the final one. For Roy at least (and probably also the others), this invitation is more like an offer that cannot be refused, for it takes the form of a compulsion that torments his mind and body, ripping him away from his ordinary life, and destroying his family. As he says, 'I don't think I know what's happening to me – I'm really scared.' For Roy at least this trauma eventually results in vindication and perhaps even satisfaction; however, the experience does not result in any prophetic message or activity, for him or anyone else.

The movie's only explicit reference to a biblical text is mediated through both film and television. In an early scene in the Nearys' family room, the television is turned on. On its screen is Cecil B. DeMille's 1956 movie, *The Ten Commandments*. A second, even more indirect reference, which is not explicit but more important to the story, is the movie's use of the song, 'When You Wish Upon A Star', from the Disney movie *Pinocchio* (1940). The CE3K score draws upon the music (but not the words) of this song at various crucial moments of the story. The Pinocchio stories (Collodi 1883) feature a wooden puppet who wants to become a real boy. In one of his adventures, Pinocchio is swallowed by a whale (in the Disney version; a large fish in Collodi's book), but then finds his 'father,' the craftsman Geppetto. This 'big fish' story in turn brings to mind the book of Jonah. Like Pinocchio, Roy 'finds' himself by passing through 'the belly of Sheol' (Jonah 2:2).

Other possible intertextual relations between the film and the Bible take the form of visual, verbal, or symbolic resemblances. These connections require interpretation from the viewer. Ominous, tumultuous storm clouds with frequent flashes of light within them gather over Jillian's house just before her son is abducted by the aliens, and similar clouds appear again over the Devil's Tower monolith just prior to the arrival of the alien ships. These boiling clouds recall the story of Moses at Mount Sinai (Exod. 19–20) as well as other images of God as a thunderstorm in the Jewish scriptures. (Similar scenes have appeared in *The Ten Commandments* and various movies since, ranging from *Ben-Hur* [1959] to *Pleasantville* [1998]). During Roy's initial encounter with an alien ship, half of his face is 'sunburned' (presumably from the ship's radiation), and this may correspond to the shining face of Moses after he returns from Sinai (Exod. 34:29–30) or of Jesus at the transfiguration (Matt. 17:2, see also 2 Cor. 3:7, 13).

Devil's Tower National Monument, the great stone monolith in Wyoming where the movie's final and closest encounter is set, could easily be seen as a sort of holy mountain. Of many human 'invitees' to the alien encounter (as Lacombe supposes), only twelve make it as far as the government's 'decontamination camp' at the foot of the Tower, recalling the tribes of Israel, the scouts sent by Moses to the promised land, and the disciples of Jesus. Of these twelve only three continue up onto the mountain itself, eluding government capture, and only two of them (Roy and Jillian) make it as far as the 'arena' on the Tower's top where the climactic 'third kind' encounter between the aliens and a large group of scientists occurs. As they climb the huge rock, Roy tells Jillian not to look back at the pursuing military helicopters, not unlike the angels' advice given to Lot and his wife (Gen. 19:17–26), but then it is Jillian who grabs Roy and saves him from falling as they approach the summit.

In the movie's final scenes, the alien spaceships themselves resemble huge, brightly lit holiday ornaments, but also the wheels within wheels and moving lights of Ezekiel's visions (1:4–21, 10:6–19). Roy is eventually taken into the enormous alien mother ship and perhaps even 'transfigured' or metamorphosed into an alien body, and then like Ezekiel he is 'taken away' (RSV 3:14) – or better, like Elijah, he is taken by a 'chariot of fire' and a 'whirlwind into heaven' (2 Kings 2:11) – as the movie ends. Yet Roy never preaches 'the day of the

Lord' (as in Joel 1:15, Zeph. 1:14, or Zech. 30:3) or announces doom or judgement like some ancient prophet; instead, like Job, he just wants answers to his own pressing questions. Furthermore, like Jesus's disciples, he has abandoned everything in his quest (Mark 10:29, Matt. 19:29, Luke 18:29).

Roy knows somehow that the encounters 'mean something' as Lacombe also says (this and similar phrases are repeated several times during the movie), and he wants to know what they mean. During the final encounter, Roy tells Lacombe, 'I just want to know that it's all really happening.' He seems content as he enters the alien ship, but whether his questions have been answered is less clear. In contrast, Jillian says 'I'm just not ready [to go] yet' and she is satisfied by the return of her young son. It may be presumptuous to read the contrast between Roy and Jillian as gender disparity – after all, the twelve 'invitees' seem evenly divided between men and women – but it may also be Hollywood stereotyping.

Despite (or because of) the Sinai-like quality of the final encounter on the top of a mountain, 'what it means' remains unclear to the viewers. Undoubtedly something has 'really happened', and there have been revelations – aliens, apparently benevolent ones, are indeed 'out there', perhaps closer than you think – but many questions remain unanswered. The film resolves one mystery by narrating an even greater one (compare Mark 4:11, Matt. 13:11, Luke 8:10). There is no indication that the aliens have any message or other gifts (let alone salvation) to offer humankind. The return of the abductees and the aliens' acceptance of Roy onto their ship may indicate a covenant between humanity (as represented by the scientists) and the alien visitors. As in the Bible, however, the details of the agreement are fuzzy at best, and whether either party has truly agreed to anything remains to be seen.

Other religious or theological elements in the movie include a large group of apparently Buddhist monks in India. Lacombe discovers these monks chanting the simple tune of five tones that the aliens apparently implant in the mind of each human they encounter. When Lacombe asks where the music came from, the monks all point toward the sky. Like God, the spaceships 'speak' this simple tune. Jillian's boy plays the same tonal sequence on his toy xylophone before he is abducted, and the scientists play variations on the theme during the final encounter to initiate greetings with the alien ships, initially using human musicians but then a computer. One of the scientists says that they are establishing 'a basic tonal vocabulary'.

Music may not be the divine language in CE3K, but it is evidently a universal language. Perhaps it is even a primal language that exists prior to and separate from any need to communicate a message, and thus requires no translation. Nevertheless, the problem of translation is prominent throughout this movie. Lacombe's English is not good, and he hires David Laughlin to be his translator and associate. Laughlin is also a cartographer, and both his translation and map-making skills prove to be crucial in the unfolding of the story. The emphasis on the importance of decoding and interpretation that this character (as well as the five-note melody) brings to the story is an unusual and valuable feature in the context of the alien encounter movie genre more generally. Alien encounter movies often downplay what would probably be immense difficulties in understanding if such an encounter ever occurred (compare *Star Trek*'s 'universal translator').

Shortly before the end of the movie, a Christian priest leads a diverse group of what look like astronauts in an antiphonal blessing which apparently comes from the Catholic prayer book, the 'Blessing of Pilgrims' (see also Ps. 91:11). These astronauts, who are apparently prepared to depart on the alien ship, play no prior part in the story, and the overtly religious qualities of this scene seem especially strange in a movie that is otherwise almost entirely devoid of such features. At the last minute, Lacombe insists that Roy should be added to this group of potential pilgrims. Of the group, only Roy is chosen by the aliens to board the ship and accompany them when they leave.

The aliens themselves take on three distinct humanoid forms. The first alien to emerge from the ship is very tall with long, spider-like arms and legs. This being is followed by a large group of short, chubby, child-sized aliens who mingle with the humans and select Roy from the group of potential pilgrims. Finally, after Roy has disappeared into the mother ship, a third alien form emerges to bid the humans farewell, using human (Curwen-Kodály) sign language to convey the familiar tonal sequence. This alien has a long neck and expressive face. Whether this is Roy with a transformed body is uncertain. In an interview that appears among the movie's 'collector edition extra features', Spielberg says that he wanted to show that the aliens themselves were a collection of diverse peoples.

In a segment that Spielberg added to the 'special edition' of the movie at the studio's insistence (according to the interview noted above), the child-aliens take Roy by the hand and escort him into the ship. The starship's interior appears to be an enormous open space containing an alien city. Roy weeps and is then showered with sparkling lights, shortly after which the third alien form emerges from the ship. Spielberg later deleted the scene in the ship's interior from the 'director's cut' because he wanted to leave what happens inside the alien ships to the viewer's imagination. It becomes another of the unknowns of this movie.

George Aichele

Further reading

C. Collodi (Carlo Lorenzo) (1883) *The Adventures of Pinocchio*. Public domain.
J. Allen Hynek (1988) *The UFO Experience: A Scientific Enquiry*. New York: Ballantine (originally published 1972).
Jacques Vallée (1987) *UFO's in Space: Anatomy of a Phenomenon*. New York: Ballantine (originally published 1965).

Further viewing

2001: A Space Odyssey (Stanley Kubrick, 1968)
Starman (John Carpenter, 1984)
Contact (Robert Zemeckis, 1997)

COOL HAND LUKE (1967)

[Production Company: Warner Brothers. Director: Stuart Rosenberg. Screenplay: Donn Pearce and Frank R. Pierson. Cinematography: Conrad Hall. Cast: Paul Newman (Lukas Jackson), George Kennedy (Dragline), J. D. Canon (Society Red), Robert Drivas (Loudmouth Steve), Lou Antonio (Koko), Strother Martin (the Captain), Jo Van Fleet (Arletta), Morgan Woodward (Boss Godfrey), Clifton James (Carr), Luke Askew (Boss Paul), Marc Cavell (Rabbit).]

Cool Hand Luke is a remarkably complex film. Taking cues from its most famous line, it is fundamentally a movie about communication and, more ominously, the 'failure to communicate'. Another theme is the struggle for individuality despite the pressures of alterity and community. It is also a movie about God and redemption. Finally, it explores friendship and intercession with all their blessings and burdens.

As *Cool Hand Luke* opens, Lukas 'Luke' Jackson, a former war hero, is arrested in a rural Florida town for mindlessly cutting the heads off of parking meters. Luke is sentenced to three years on a prison road crew. The prisoners are guarded by hardened men, all under the leadership of a no-nonsense warden, the Captain. Luke is first opposed then befriended by a fellow prisoner, a Cajun named Dragline. Luke's strong sense of independence begins to emerge. The prison administration, however, is firm to the point of brutality and has little patience for independent prisoners. Luke's mother dies while he is in prison. Afraid that Luke will attempt escape, the Captain orders Luke to solitary confinement. Luke emerges with a new sense of rebellion and promptly escapes. Recaptured, Luke is given harsher punishment. He escapes yet again, and is subjected on recapture to even more brutal retribution which seems to break his spirit. Luke's repeated escapes inspire the other inmates; on Luke's third attempt, Dragline also runs away. Seeing that Luke's rebellion has become too alluring, Luke is killed. As the film ends, the recaptured Dragline is heard telling the story of Luke, a 'natural born world shaker'.

Cool Hand Luke, released in 1967, was one of the earliest films scrutinized by biblical scholars. Ironically (or, perhaps, elegantly), for a film that takes communication as one of its themes, references to the Bible are subtle. Luke Jackson is a Christ figure. Luke is a prisoner who cannot quite fit in society. His father is unknown to him; his relationship with his mother is complex. His name invokes the biblical gospel. The barter among prisoners is the provision of a 'cold drink', on one hand, a typical southern expression for a carbonated soda, but, on the other hand, a possible allusion to Matthew 10:42 ('whoever gives even a cup of cold water to one of these little ones in the name of a disciple – truly I tell you, none of these will lose their reward').

Many allusions are visual. Cross shapes pepper the mis-en-scène at key moments (window panes, fences, etc.), and the final shot is an aerial view of the road crew working on a crossroad with images of a smiling Luke superimposed. In one scene, after he has been severely beaten for rebelling, Luke is surrounded by other inmates who lay him on a dinner table and hover around with questions and stories. Exasperated, Luke shouts 'stop feeding off me', a perverse reference to Luke 22:19 ('This is my body, which is given for you. Do this in remembrance of me'). Stuck indoors by a rainstorm, bored and looking for 'something to do', Luke enters into a bet, managed by Dragline, that Luke can eat 50 boiled eggs in an hour. He trains under Dragline's tutelage for days. The contest is arduous (as one might imagine) but he eventually triumphs. In the final shot of the episode, a half-naked Luke, left by his companions to lie among the scattered remains of egg-shells, lies cruciform on a wooden table. The camera, shot downward onto the figure of Luke, pans back leaving a vista of Jesus on the Cross, styled in posture and lighting after a medieval or renaissance altar piece, the broken shells making him nimbate.

Even more Jesus and biblical allusions cluster around the relationship between Luke and his mother. Luke is visited by his dying mother,

Arletta, who is borne to him by Luke's brother, John, and Luke's nephew in the bed of an old pick-up truck. Their conversation is halting. They speak of Luke's inability to conform, his persistent desire to 'go his own way', and refer light-heartedly to Luke's problematic childhood, his absent father, and Luke and Arletta's own strained relationship. Luke calls her 'Arletta', never 'mother'. She has come to say goodbye and to tell Luke she has willed all her property (including the childhood farm) to John. He concedes she should. She insists it was because she had always loved Luke more, slighting his brother; now, in her death, she hopes to address the inequity. As Luke turns from her to return to prison, he gives a hortatory address about fearing the law to his young nephew. John gives him a banjo and the admonition of his own: 'Now there ain't nothin' to come back for.' The conversation among the triad of mother and brothers is laden with broken sentences, unclear references, and unspoken feelings and sentiments. They fail to communicate.

Though the characters cannot speak clearly, the film itself does. The scene is bracketed by the popular country hymn 'Just a Closer Walk with Thee' in the background. This hymn is an earnest, repeated and mournful request for a 'closer walk' with Jesus. The lyrics express feelings of sinfulness and desire for Jesus' companionship and encouragement. The plaintive wailing of the song's melody mimics the lyrical alternations between despair and prayer. This song establishes the inner turmoil and conflicted desire, rage, love, nostalgia, and more churning beneath the (affectedly) casual conversation between mother and (wayward) son.

Arletta dies, and word is sent to Luke via a telegram. Upon learning the grave news contained in the yellow paper casually handed to Luke, the other inmates pull back from him to give him some privacy. Taking his banjo, Luke slowly and mournfully sings a rather bawdy song, 'Plastic Jesus'. The song, clearly intended to be irreverent, bouncy and bright, is about a plastic Jesus that is stuck to the dashboard of a car – a kitchy, tacky token of religious sentiment. Later verses celebrate a plastic Virgin Mary who is likewise attached to the dash: 'Going 90, I ain't scary / 'cause I got the Virgin Mary / to care for me / and save my soul from Hell.' Luke, metaphorically in Hell (in prison on a brutally hot night), has definitely not been saved, nor was his mother a Virgin. The viewer is left to wonder about the meaning of the song for Luke. Was this a favorite 'hymn' of his road-running mother? Does it awaken memories of happier days? Is it the only 'religious' song Luke knows? Whatever the reason, it is the only dirge offered by the 'plastic Jesus' of Cool Hand Luke for his 'Sweet Madonna' mother.

Arletta's visit to Luke recalls Jesus' parable of the prodigal son (Luke 15:11–24). Here we see the triad of parent, responsible older sibling, and prodigal young man pushed forward in years. The indulgent parent has, again and again, welcomed the prodigal home with feasting and fatted calves, displaying 'more joy' in him than in the faithful brother. True to human nature, this family dynamic does not breed deeper love but, instead, encourages recidivism in the prodigal, fosters resentment in the elder brother, and concludes with the despair and a final turning away of the parent. In this case, too much grace produces lawlessness.

But too much law is equally troublesome. Luke's road crew is guarded by 'Boss Godfrey', a mysterious man in mirrored sun-glasses, called 'No-Eyes' by Dragline. He is hardly blind. This 'eyeless' sentry (his gaze always dumbly reflects back on the viewer) never speaks, but he is a deadly rifle shot. The Captain he serves only wants 'peace and quiet'. His reign is arbitrary and brutal; 'peace' is aggressive punishment of any potential uprising.

The Captain's decision to put Luke in solitary confinement after Arletta's death creates the film's dramatic crisis. 'The box' is a wooden shed exposed to the sun and heat. Prisoners are forced to strip naked and put on a white linen night-shirt. Luke is given three days in this 'grave'. He emerges obsessed with escape. With each attempt, Luke is brought back, chained, and beaten more brutally. Displayed and humiliated before his peers, Luke is the subject of the Captain's sermon (from atop a mount) which opens with the film's iconic line: 'What we've got here is failure to communicate.' Eventually Luke is forced to spend days digging, filling in and redigging a trench (his own grave), interspersed with brutal beatings. Broken at last, Luke clasps at the legs of the Captain, crying, 'O God, make this stop.' The (now divinized) Captain answers the prayer; he gently takes up the broken prisoner, calls him 'son', and orders him to be cleaned and fed and given a bed. For a time, the broken Luke is grovelling. Yet, given a chance, he again escapes. Realizing that he cannot be broken, the guards finally shoot Luke. He is last seen in the back seat of the Captain's car, being taken to prison (a journey surely too far to save him). Luke turns and smiles. The Captain's somewhat arbitrary decision to put Luke in solitary confinement has baptized Luke into an unquenchable spirit for freedom. Too much authority, like too much indulgence, produced lawlessness.

The film as a whole is preoccupied with prayer, God, and (divine) authority. In an early scene, the prison road crew is caught by a sudden and violent thunderstorm. As the other inmates run to shelter,

Luke stands alone, shouting at the God who rides upon thunderstorms, challenging him to strike Luke down. Luke is enraged by a God who neither helps nor destroys. Luke's favourite term for God is 'the old Man', also a colloquial American expression for one's father ('my old man'). Like Luke's actual father, God is absent and silent. For Luke God is harsh and violently strict, a 'hard case'. Within the film's narrative, the Captain is a cipher for God. He too is strict authority even as he is arbitrary; he is author of order and commander of violence; he is a distant viewer who watches without comment but speaks most directly about the importance of communication.

During his final escape, Luke takes refuge in a church from a fierce rainstorm. Alone, he enters into a prayer of complaint: God has been too long absent, too long silent. Luke calls for 'some sign, any sign' of God's presence, even as he rages against God's (lack of) justice and order. The police arrive, bringing Luke's prayer to an abrupt halt and supplying the only answer given to his prayerful pleas. Dragline enters with the Judas-like task of talking Luke into surrender. Luke goes to the window and shouts, 'What we've got here is failure to communicate' – his last words. He is shot in the chest by Godfrey, the blind sentry now become the unspoken Word of God. Dragline attacks Godfrey, knocking off his sunglasses. Godfrey now, finally, sees and is seen. The scene evokes Mark 15:39: 'Now when the centurion, who stood facing him, saw that in this way he breathed his last, he said, "Truly this man was God's Son!"'

God, the Bible and images of Jesus pervade the movie, but what sort of 'Jesus' is Cool Hand Luke? He is in no way sinless. Though certainly over-punished, the movie never suggests Luke is innocent. His beatings do not bring healing to others, though his rebellions and escapes do awaken hope and morale among his fellow inmates. Luke's own 'Gethsemane' in the abandoned Church may be the best clue. As a Christ figure, Cool Hand Luke decidedly emphasizes the humanity of Jesus, even as he is critical of a silent God. The cup does not pass from Luke, nor is the will of God made clear, let alone accomplished. Through it all, God remains silent, a cosmic failure to communicate that nevertheless speaks clearly.

Robert Paul Seesengood

Further reading

Matthew McEver (1998) 'The Messianic Figure in Film: Christology Beyond the Biblical Epic', *Journal of Religion and Film* 2(2), available online at www.unomaha.edu/jrf/McEverMessiah.htm.

Adele Reinhartz (2009) 'Jesus and Christ-Figures', in John Lyden (ed.) *The Routledge Companion to Religion and Film*. New York, NY: Routledge. pp. 420–39.

Jeffery A. Smith (2001) 'Hollywood Theology: The Commodification of Religion in Twentieth-Century Films', *Religion and American Culture: A Journal of Interpretation* 11(2): 191–231.

Warren Sloat (1968) 'Cool Hand Luke', *Christian Century* 85(15): 457–8.

CRIMES AND MISDEMEANORS (1989)

[Production Company: Orion Pictures. Director: Woody Allen. Screenplay: Woody Allen. Cinematography: Sven Nykvist. Cast: Martin Landau (Judah Rosenthal), Anjelica Huston (Dolores Paley), Woody Allen (Cliff Stern), Sam Waterston (Ben), Alan Alda (Lester), Mia Farrow (Halley Reed).]

Although famous for comedy, many of Woody Allen's films convey the pessimism more often associated with his idol Ingmar Bergman (e.g. *Interiors* [1978]; *Another Woman* [1988]; *Shadows and Fog* [1991]). In deploying both a comic and tragic storyline, *Crimes and Misdemeanors* crafts a middle path between entertainment and artistic pessimism. Yet it is pessimism that Allen values more highly, in the same way that Judah in *Crimes and Misdemeanors* esteems dark Schubert over flowery Schumann.

The comedy is the familiar Allen tale of a neurotic loser, in this case, a film-maker named Cliff Stern. Cliff disdains popular film/TV and portrays himself as a documentary artist, but he lacks funds for his current documentary on philosopher Louis Levy (Primo Levi?), who urges love and responsibility in a world without God. Cliff's wife Wendy convinces Lester, her successful-TV-producer brother, to hire Cliff to film his biography for the PBS Creative Minds series. Cliff falls in love with his assistant on the project, Halley Reed. Everything soon goes wrong (another typical Allen pattern). Despite his life-affirming message, Levy commits suicide before Cliff can complete his documentary. Cliff sabotages his PBS opportunity with a film that compares Lester to Mussolini and a talking ass. Realizing Cliff's worst fears, Halley agrees to marry Lester.

The film's second, and dark, story line depicts the trials of the wealthy Judah Rosenthal, noted ophthalmologist. Judah's handling of his problems gives the film its title, which echoes Dostoevsky's famous *Crime and Punishment* while indicating a different story. While the film explores the psychological consequences of murder, Judah is no Raskolnikov.

In the opening scene, Judah speaks apologetically about God's watchful eyes at a dinner celebrating his philanthropic leadership in opening a new ophthalmology wing. Sparks of his father's piety have stayed with this self-confessed skeptic, and he wonders amusingly if his father's lessons about God's eyes account for his chosen profession. Childhood pieties, however, have not prevented Judah's crimes: two years of adultery, lies, embezzlement and other dirty deeds (at which his criminal brother Jack hints).

Now, his mistress Dolores' demands for marriage threaten his privileged life(style). In crisis, Judah confesses to a rabbi named Ben, who is his patient and the sibling of Lester and Wendy. Ironically, this rabbi is going blind. Ben urges Judah to confess to his wife and to hope for her forgiveness. Soon the two engage in a debate they have had repeatedly: Judah claiming the world is amoral and pitiless, Ben averring that a higher power and moral structure exists. In a later scene, Judah seems to argue these points with Ben again, but in fact is engaging in an interior dialogue. In a diatribe, rebutting his internalization of Ben's position, Judah chooses Jack's notions of reality over Ben's kingdom of heaven and his privileged life over the luxury of Ben's idea of God.

Despite fears about guilt's destructiveness and about the darkness without the law, Judah orders a hit on Dolores (Schubert music accompanies her murder). Dolores' lifeless, soulless eyes remind Judah of God's all-seeing eyes and send him into a delirium of guilt and fears of capture. A detective, who pales in comparison to Dostoevsky's Porfiry, asks questions, but Jack's threats counter Judah's Raskolnikov-like desires to confess. In another crucial interior view, Judah remembers a Seder at which his father chose God over truth in an argument with Judah's cynical aunt. Not comforted by his aunt's claim that uncaught murderers can go (psychologically) free, Judah, like his father and Ben, fears that the world is a cesspool without God. Judah's Raskolnikov-like return to his childhood faith, however, is not the end of his story.

The two stories and sets of characters merge at the wedding of Ben's daughter. Judah finally meets Cliff as he plots the perfect murder (in response to Halley's engagement). Knowing Cliff to be a film-maker, Judah assumes they are speaking of movie scripts and offers a murder story with a twist: the murderer transcends guilt to return to his privileged life. When Cliff calls the story incredible, Judah claims that people live with such crimes daily. When Cliff finds this horrible, Judah admits it is a chilling story. When Cliff suggests instead a tragedy in which the culprit assumes responsibility for his own sins in God's absence (compare Levy's final voiceover), Judah laughingly suggests that Cliff watch a Hollywood film for such a happy ending. Ironically,

Judah is presenting his story as a movie script, and the film repeatedly pairs Judah's story with Hollywood films. In a further irony, the next scene mimics a happy ending: Judah walks away with his wife, and blind Ben dances with his newly married daughter.

As they dance, a montage replays previous scenes with a voiceover by Levy about the creation of character, choice by choice (thus the flashbacks) in the pursuit of love and meaning in a meaningless world. Harsh realities – murder, suicide, lost love – exist alongside (the pursuit of) temporary happiness. This montage undercuts the murderer's 'happy ending', mixing small decisions (Cliff's misdemeanors) with large ones (Judah's crimes). The montage thus reminds one that the film is not Judah's story alone and that the film does not simply endorse Judah. It offers an ensemble of characters/worldviews.

Biblical allusions abound. Judah's name suggests the Jewish tradition that he leaves behind. It also recalls biblical characters willing to sell (or to dispense with) their 'brother' (see Gen. 37:26–28; Matt. 26:14–16) and those saving their life, instead of losing it for the kingdom (e.g. Mark 8:34–9:1). Despite these dire biblical warnings, Judah keeps his life and thereby translates scripture into a death-of-God world. Similarly, the film's Seder, instead of celebrating a people's liberation, features the cynic's claim, with reference to the Holocaust, that God does not act to redress injustice.

This cynical claim permeates the film as a whole, which questions the credibility of the biblical view of character (ethos). The film disputes the scriptural theodicy that the good/wise prosper and the evil/foolish perish (*Match Point* [2005] and *Cassandra's Dream* [2007] reprise Allen's concern with this theodicy). Pairing this theodicy with an ontological notion of the good, scripture asserts this divine justice to be visibly, materially verifiable. While it admits anomalies and has dissenting voices in Job and Ecclesiastes, scripture typically handles problems, as Judah's father does, by postponing visible justice to the next world (e.g. Revelation). The deployment of guilt in modern Protestantism and in psychology transfers visible justice instead to the psyche's invisible realm (compare Foucault [1978] on the development of the self-monitoring, modern individual). Allen's neurotics, who are always in analysis, struggle with guilt as much as failure. Like Raskolnikov, they could not 'get away' with murder even if they could avoid detection. In a sense, Judah represents the ultimate fantasy – a life beyond guilt – for Allen's neurotics.

In biblical terms, Judah means that God's moral order is passé. Judah belongs to a Bergman film or to a film noir Job. When Judah depicts himself as a victim and takes justice into his own hands, he creates a character/world that even he recognizes as chilling and as a cesspool. Despite its comic storyline, the film has no righteous characters. At least, the final montage joins scenes with the philosopher's words to reinforce the notion that Cliff is guilty of misdemeanour – lesser – forms of Judah's crimes. He attempts adultery and plots murder.

In this world, as in other Allen films, such as *Hannah and Her Sisters* (1986) and *Stardust Memories* (1980), God is inactive. The blind rabbi, the film's only possible saint, symbolizes religious faith's blindness to this harsh reality, as does Judah's father who chooses God over truth. No divine revelations occur. The final conversation between Judah and Cliff is no whirlwind. Neither the religious wisdom of Judah's father nor Ben is ever on target. In his last significant speech, Ben speaks of luck, not providence, as the best plan. He is no Tiresias. In striking contrast to the worlds of classic tragedy and scripture, the blind do not see. Although an ophthalmologist, Judah helps no one see. He cannot prevent Ben's encroaching blindness. He renders Dolores' eyes vacant. He deliberately blinds everyone to his crimes, even himself. Finally, he hides his life in plain view as a movie script. (Incidentally, critics have accused Allen of doing this throughout his career). Cliff knows himself no better. Contrary to all evidence, he also fashions himself as victim. Claiming he is too good a film-maker to succeed, he sabotages himself while mocking the pretensions of others.

The final montage, however, pairs scenes of Cliff and his niece with the philosopher's words about those who find the ability to go on in a meaningless world. Appropriately, Cliff's favorite movie is *Singin' in the Rain* (1952). Further, as Levy speaks of hope in future generations, the film's final shot is blind Ben dancing with his newly married daughter to the accompaniment of 'I'll Be Seeing You'. Any wisdom lies in such juxtapositions.

Allen claims the film was a rejoinder to the too positive ending of *Hannah and Her Sisters*, in which each sister is happily married. Everything is relative then, and everything in the ensemble film comes with its own refutation, or, better, its own 'banana peel', as comedy undermines every position enunciated in the film. Comedy may indeed be 'tragedy plus time', but the film deflates this cliché by placing it in the mouth of a talking ass. Perhaps, Judah 'gets away' with murder, but he admits it is a chilling story. Perhaps, Levy's affirmation of life and self-fashioning is the film's message (Allen characters often tout such philosophies). But Levy is a suicide, and he claims that humans have been unable to imagine a completely loving God, or an 'ideal', as this philosopher believes gods to be human constructions. Further, neither main character finds love, which Levy claims one needs 'to stay' in this world.

Can anyone live in a meaningless world in which life and character are only what one makes of them? In contrast to Albert Camus' more successful struggle with the philosophical question of suicide in *The Myth of Sisyphus* (1955), Levy cannot. Neither can the religious who retreat blindly to their faithful certainties. Cliff sings bumbling on in the rain. Judah self-fashions chillingly. Can those watching sing along in that rain?

The film's ensemble nature and its juxtapositions leave it to the audience. Only they see, and what they see are the movies. They see Judah's movie script. They see the life-affirming philosopher who, quite significantly, appears in the film only in Cliff's documentary clips. Further, as the film cuts back and forth between the stories of Judah and Cliff, it often connects them with movie clips. Cliff watches old movies whose scenes parallel the scene just seen in Judah's story. This intertextuality forcefully reminds one of the camera and of the watchful audience. These eyes have replaced God's. The movies, not the law, interpret life.

Richard Walsh

Further reading

Pau Gilabert Barberà (2009) 'Woody Allen and the Spirit of Greek Tragedy: from *Crimes and Misdemeanors* to *Match Point*', *BELLS* (*Barcelona English Language and Literature Studies*) 11: 1–18.

Stig Bjorkman (1994) *Woody Allen on Woody Allen: In Conversation with Stig Bjorkman*. London: Faber and Faber.

Albert Camus (1955) *The Myth of Sisyphus*. Trans. Justin O'Brien. New York, NY: Alfred A. Knopf.

Michel Foucault (1978) *The History of Sexuality: Volume 1: An Introduction*. Trans. Robert Hurley. New York, NY: Random House.

Sam B. Girgus (1993) *The Films of Woody Allen*. Cambridge: Cambridge University Press.

Sander H. Lee (1997) *Woody Allen's Angst: Philosophical Commentaries on His Serious Films*. Jefferson, NC: McFarland.

Mary P. Nichols (1998) *Reconstructing Woody: Art, Love, and Life in the Films of Woody Allen*. Lanham, MD: Rowman & Littlefield.

Mark W. Roche (1995) 'Justice and the Withdrawal of God in Woody Allen's Crimes and Misdemeanors', *The Journal of Value Inquiry* 29(4): 547–63.

DAVID AND BATHSHEBA (1951)

[Production Company: Twentieth Century Fox. Producer: Darryl F. Zanuck. Director: Henry King. Screenplay: Philip Dunne. Music: Alfred Newman.

Cast: Gregory Peck (David), Susan Hayward (Bathsheba), Jayne Meadows
(Michal), Kieron Moore (Uriah), Raymond Massay (Nathan).]

My students hate this film. It is boring, the acting is wooden, and it
has a distinctly dated feel. But like any biblical film, it is of particular
interest for the way it handles the biblical text – in this case, with
considerable freedom. *David and Bathsheba* turns the biblical account
into something it is not: a love story. With its focus on the psychological development of its hero, David, and on the course of his
relationship with the poised but vulnerable Bathsheba, *David and
Bathsheba* is not a typical sword-and-sandals action-filled big-budget
biblical spectacle (even the contemporary classic biblical love story,
Cecil B. DeMille's *Samson and Delilah* [1949] has spectacle galore). It
is not a typical 1950s Hollywood love story either, for it does not
neatly conform to the cinematic moral code of the 50s according to
which adultery must end tragically for the participants. Although
David and Bathsheba are punished (by their own guilt for breaking
the law, and when their child dies), the film ends with an affirmation
of the strength of their love and, equally important, with God's
blessing. Not only does it seek to explain (and, to some extent,
excuse) David's adultery with Bathsheba for a 50s audience, it also
makes their relationship David's route to a restored relationship to God.

David and Bathsheba has much in common with the Woman's Film
of the 40s and 50s (Gunn 1996: 92–9, Babington and Evans 1993:
74–6). It reflects tensions and questions about gender identity in
America in the aftermath of World War II, when women had entered
the work force in large numbers and experienced a greater degree of
independence and economic self-sufficiency. Faced with the problem
of balancing sexuality, marriage, family, and independence, women
were seeking improved opportunities for fulfillment. Men, too, were
struggling with their roles. On more than one occasion, David holds
forth about the real meaning of 'manhood', and in word and deed
demonstrates the importance of sensitivity to a woman's perspective.
King David can be viewed as an example of masculinity in mid-life
crisis and Bathsheba as a 1950s version of the New Woman (on their
portrayals as reflecting contemporary issues, see Babington and Evans
1993: 79–89, Gunn 1996: 91–9). David is successful but prey to
feelings of inadequacy as he tries to come to terms with the burden
of kingship (Kelso 2002: 172–87). He is estranged from his family,
bored, cynical about religion and about his accomplishments ('royalty
is a fraud') discontented and resigned to his lot ('we have to go on
living', he tells Michal).

Like David, Bathsheba is not content with her lot. She is not satisfied in the role of neglected wife and decides for herself what to do about it, in full awareness of the consequences. Perhaps she is not totally aware of all the consequences, but she never makes excuses for herself and she has principles. Upon discovering that she is pregnant, she rejects the idea that David give up the kingdom for her and they flee to Egypt, as well as the proposal that something be done about Uriah. But she accepts responsibility ('I wished him dead'), and she is not afraid to die. As they embark on their liaison, she insists, 'If the law of Moses is to be broken, David, let us break it in full understanding of what we want from each other.' David's objection that she cannot be his wife because 'you're not free' is dismissed by her with 'If I *were* free', which is hardly a naive remark.

After an opening scene that shows David fighting alongside members of a scouting party that includes Uriah (Henry King's David is a very different king from the David of 2 Samuel 11, who remains at home when the army goes to war), we quickly come to recognize that the king is disillusioned and unhappy. He has two immature sons, the petulant Absalom and the sniveling Amnon, a wife who despises him, no friends (Jonathan is dead, and those around him either serve or want something from him), and he has lost the innocent faith of his youth. Life has lost its meaning. What he needs is the right woman, a woman who will accept him for himself: 'I need the kind of understanding that only one human being can give to another. I need someone to share my heart.' Enter Bathsheba.

The bathing scene is the turning point in David's fortunes in both text (negatively) and film (more positively). It gave Henry King an opportunity to showcase his star's sex appeal, and much was made of the scene in the film's publicity. Susan Hayward bathes behind a screen in what even at the time was not considered particularly revealing (compare Alice Krige's full frontal nudity in *King David* [1985]). In a slow-paced scene, the camera moves back and forth between David, whose face displays rapt attention, and Bathsheba. Increasingly closer zoom shots into Bathsheba's bath chamber make the audience privy to more than David can see from the rooftop, but create the illusion that what we see is what incites David.

In the Bible their encounter takes only three verses (2 Sam. 11:2–4), leaving the reader with many questions. Did David take Bathsheba by force? Was she free to say no? Did she know she was being watched? Did she want to be seen? *David and Bathsheba* fills these gaps by having David respond to Bathsheba's professed submission to his will ('You are the king ... You have sent for me and made known to me your will, what

else is there for me to say?') with a long speech in which he prides himself
for refusing ever to take anything by force. Bathsheba then admits that she
planned to be seen and knew David was watching. Having Bathsheba
not only willing but also culpable makes David look less blameworthy
than the biblical David at Bathsheba's expense, but it also has the important effect of presenting Bathsheba as self-assured and determined, and
thus appealing to a female audience. She is the victim of an unhappy
marriage, and she wants more. She sets out to get it using the means
available to her, her sexuality. She wants 'to please' the king. But she has
her conditions: this can be no casual relationship; she wants to be his wife.

Here we find a conflict at the heart of the film: the tension between a
woman's desire for self-determination and fulfillment, which leads
Bathsheba to take matters into her own hands, and patriarchal constraints
on her options, which lead her to seek that fulfillment through a man
(who just happens to be king). Nowhere is this more clearly expressed
than in a dialogue between David and Uriah, in which David expounds,
'Is it possible that you believe that [Bathsheba] does not think or feel?
A woman is flesh and blood, Uriah, like us. Perhaps even more so
because we give her so little to think of but matters of the flesh.'

In order to show both David and Bathsheba in a better light, the film
makes their marital partners look bad. Not only does Uriah prefer the
battleground to the bedroom, he is also a heartless follower of the
letter of the law who would invoke the law to have his wife stoned if
he had reason to suspect her of adultery. Uriah must be an unsym-
pathetic figure so that David's betrayal is not totally undeserved. *David
and Bathsheba* even has Uriah himself ask to be put in the forefront of
the fiercest fighting (cf. 2 Sam. 11:14–15).

David's unhappy relationship with Michal helps explain his emotional
vulnerability to Bathsheba. Though there are some hints of the theological and political tensions of the biblical account, with its interest in
the legitimacy of David's claim to Saul's kingdom (Exum 1996: 60–1),
in *David and Bathsheba* the rift between David and Michal is reduced
to a quarrel between husband and wife about who is to blame for the
breakdown of the marriage. The fault is entirely that of Michal, portrayed as a nagging, spiteful shrew, and not – as is possible to conclude
from the biblical story – a woman whose love has justifiably turned to
hate (2 Sam. 6:16). Later, Michal along with David's son Absalom
will be the witnesses who accuse Bathsheba of adultery.

Whereas biblical law demands the death of both parties in adultery,
in *David and Bathsheba* only Bathsheba's death is called for, because,
declares Nathan, she was a 'faithless wife'. Although it emphasizes that
in Israel the king is subject to the law, *David and Bathsheba* is

inconsistent in not applying the law to David in this case. In focusing on Bathsheba's guilt, the film is typical of classical cinema of the 40s and 50s in its need to show the 'bad' woman punished, and then either killed off or redeemed. Bathsheba is punished by the death of her son, her own guilt, and the people's fury, and redeemed by David, who prays to God to spare her life. But the film is also critical of the double standard that punishes the woman more severely than the man, as well as of the idea of justice not tempered by mercy. In a scene that calls to mind the New Testament account of the woman caught in the act of adultery (John 8:1–11), a woman pleads in vain for mercy as she is being stoned by an angry mob. Where is the guilty man? As a guilty man himself, David tries to take all the blame for his adultery with Bathsheba, but Nathan will not hear of it. David nonetheless insists, 'But even if she sinned, she has done no evil'.

David's opposition to the legalistic, intolerant version of religion represented by Nathan makes him a sympathetic character. The God David knew in his youth was a god of goodness and mercy, not Nathan's 'god without mercy, a god who thinks only of his justice'. But somewhere along the line, says David, he 'lost' God. In their first scene together, David, who wears on all his clothes the star of David, a reminder of the new nation of Israel, clearly finds Nathan tedious and is happy to leave religious affairs to him. He is sceptical about divine involvement in human affairs. When Uzzah dies after touching the ark of the covenant, David attributes his death to natural causes (cf. Sam. 6:6–7). Nathan says the drought is the result of sin, but David objects, 'We've had droughts before'. Although there was already a shortage of water when David began his affair with Bathsheba, Bathsheba is blamed for bringing the drought, as well as famine, and the wrath of God against Israel. When Nathan, and the people, demand that Bathsheba die for her sin, David says that he has heard the word of Nathan but he must hear the verdict directly from God.

In the film's climactic scene, David goes to the Tabernacle, where he offers a heartfelt prayer, cast in the 'thees' and 'thous' that biblical movies use for proper religious effect. After praying for his people, for Bathsheba's life, and for God to remember the boy who loved him, David dramatically touches the ark with both hands. Earlier, when Uzzah touched the ark to prevent it from falling, he was struck dead. When David touches the ark and does not die, it is a sign of God's forgiveness and God's favor upon the contrite king, as is the rain that immediately begins to fall. In the Bible, in contrast, touching the ark brings death simply by virtue of the numinous, overwhelming holiness of the ark, regardless of one's intentions, worthiness or unworthiness (in addition to 2 Sam. 6:6–7, see Lev. 16:1–2; Num. 4:15; Josh. 3:3–4). Although David never touches the ark in the Bible, there is a point in the story where the ark does symbolize David's relationship to God. When Absalom's rebellion causes David to flee Jerusalem, and his faithful followers want to bring the ark with them, David tells them to take the ark back, saying, 'If I find favor in the eyes of the Lord, he will bring me back and let me see both it and its abode' (2 Sam. 15:25).

In *David and Bathsheba*, David saves Bathsheba's life, but Bathsheba also saves David. She loves him for who he is, and helps him rediscover the God of his youth, with whom he had a close relationship. When the angry mob is outside, calling for Bathsheba to be brought out to die, she asks David to play the harp and sing one of his boyhood songs for her. He chooses the twenty-third psalm, and, as he reflects on his early closeness to God, he realizes that only God can save Bathsheba.

David and Bathsheba ends with David and Bathsheba walking out into the sunlit rain, leaving the punishments that will befall David's house for another day: the rape of David's daughter (2 Sam. 13); the death of three of his sons (2 Sam. 13:28; 18:15; 1 Kings 2:23–25); Absalom's attempt to usurp the throne (2 Sam. 15–18, alluded to in the film); a revolt by northern tribes, formerly loyal to Saul (2 Sam. 20); and a vindictive David perhaps duped on his deathbed into making Solomon king (1 Kings 1).

J. Cheryl Exum

Further reading

Bruce Babington and Peter William Evans (1993) *Biblical Epics: Sacred Narrative in the Hollywood Cinema*. Manchester: Manchester University Press.

J. Cheryl Exum (1996) 'Bathsheba Plotted, Shot, and Painted' and 'Michal at the Window, Michal in the Movies', in *Plotted, Shot, and Painted: Cultural Representations of Biblical Women*. Sheffield: Sheffield Academic Press. pp. 19–53 and 54–79.

David M. Gunn (1996) 'Bathsheba Goes Bathing in Hollywood: Words, Images, and Social Locations', in Alice Bach (ed.) *Biblical Glamour and Hollywood Glitz. Semeia* 74; Atlanta, GA: Scholars Press. pp. 75–101.

Julie Kelso (2002) 'Gazing at Impotence in Henry King's *David and Bathsheba*', in George Aichele and Richard Walsh (eds) *Screening Scripture: Intertextual Connections between Scripture and Film*. Harrisburg, PA: Trinity Press International. pp. 155–87.

Further viewing

King David (Bruce Beresford, 1985)

DEAD MAN WALKING (1995)

[Production Companies: Havoc, Polygram Filmed Entertainment, and Working Title Films. Screenplay and Director: Tim Robbins. Cinematography: Roger Deakins. Original music: David Robbins. Art direction: Tom Warren. Cast: Susan Sarandon (Helen Prejean), Sean Penn (Matthew Poncelet), Robert Prosky (Hilton Barber), Raymond J. Barry (Earl Delacroix), R. Lee Ermey (Clyde Percy), Scott Wilson (Chaplain Farley).]

Based on Helen Prejean's book of the same name, *Dead Man Walking* portrays a developing relationship between Sister Prejean and Matthew Poncelet, a death row inmate sentenced for rape and murder. The Bible plays an important role in the relationship between Prejean and Poncelet, and in the film's dialogical argument about capital punishment.

Helen employs biblical texts as sources of comfort and challenge with Matthew, telling him that 'there are some passages in there about when Jesus was facing death and lonely you might want to check out'. During his final walk to the execution, she cites Isaiah 43:1–2:

> Do not be afraid. For I have ordained thee. I have called thee by thy name. Thou art mine. Should thou pass through the sea I shall be with thee. Should thee walk through the fire thou shall not be scorched.

> (film transcription)

This same text is the basis of the hymn 'Be Not Afraid' that she sings to Matthew shortly before his execution. Helen uses the Bible to challenge Matthew to take responsibility for his crimes, suggesting that he 'look at the gospel of John, chapter 8, where Jesus said, "You shall know the truth, and the truth shall make you free"' (John 8:32).

Outside the interactions between Helen and Matthew, this film uses biblical texts primarily in the depictions of conflicting views on capital punishment. Supporters of the death penalty twice refer to *lex talionis* in the Hebrew Bible. During an execution protestors hold signs reading 'An eye for an eye' and 'A life for a life'. Other signs convey support for retributive violence ('Kill a Killer', 'Revenge is Sweet'), as does a preacher carrying a large Bible, who proclaims, 'Jesus also said, "He who lives by the sword shall die by the sword"' (Matt. 26:52). Those protesting the execution hold many signs, but only one is partially visible: 'Jesus said, "Let he who is without sin cast the first stone"' (John 8:7). These conflicting signs reflect the film's dialogical portrayal of diverse and conflicting perspectives within biblical texts regarding violence, and the appropriation of these disparate views to support antithetical positions on the death penalty (Rindge 2010). *Lex talionis* is also cited in a conversation between Prejean and a prison guard:

> Guard: You know how the Bible says, 'An eye for an eye'?
> Helen: You know what else the Bible asks for? Death as a punishment for adultery, prostitution, homosexuality, trespass upon sacred grounds, profanin' the sabbath, and contempt to parents.

Helen points to the hypocrisy of applying *lex talionis* while neglecting other Torah laws demanding capital punishment. By (re)contextualizing *lex talionis* within its broader literary context, Prejean undermines the officer's selection of only one of many prescriptions for the death penalty.

The film never specifies which *lex talionis* statement in the Torah (Exod. 21:22–25; Lev. 24:17–22; Deut. 19:16–21) is the intended referent, perhaps reflecting an American cultural familiarity with the principle of *lex talionis* but an ignorance regarding its original literary function(s). In the Bible, *lex talionis* is twice applied in specific cases: any harm committed against a pregnant woman is to be visited upon the injurious party ('life for life, eye for eye ... '; Exod. 21:22–25); a person who gives false testimony shall receive the same punishment that would have been applied to the defendant ('life for life, eye for eye ... '; Deut. 19:16–21). The function of *lex talionis* here as a *protection* for defendants contrasts sharply with its use by characters in the film as a warrant to *harm* defendants.

The one use of *lex talionis* in the Torah as a general principle concludes with an emphasis on its equitable application: 'There shall be one law for you, for the alien and for the native there shall be: for I am YHWH your God' (Lev. 24:22). Such a consistent enforcement of capital punishment diverges from the film's depiction of the death penalty's discriminatory application. Attorney Hilton Barber declares: 'You're not going to find many rich people on death row; Matthew Poncelet's here today *because he's poor*.' Barber suggests that Poncelet's accomplice – convicted of the same crimes – avoided a death sentence only because he had a better lawyer. Prejean's book details the tendency for the death penalty in America to target poor (and especially black) people.

In the Ancient Near East, violence could beget escalating types of violence; *lex talionis* could minimize such violent spirals by limiting punishment to match the crime. One was forbidden, for example, to respond to bodily injury with murder. Characters in the film who cite *lex talionis* do so, however, not to reduce violence but to perpetuate it. The film illustrates conflicting voices (biblical and contemporary) regarding capital punishment. Chaplain Farley rebukes Helen for protesting against an execution asking: 'Are you familiar with the Old Testament? "Thou shalt not kill?" "If anyone sheds the blood of man, by man shall his blood be shed."' Helen retorts: 'Yes, Father. Are you familiar with the New Testament, where Jesus talks about grace and reconciliation?'

Contextualizing Genesis 9:6 within a broader canonical perspective problematizes Farley's citation of one biblical text as decisively authoritative on capital punishment. So too, however, does Farley's citation demonstrate Helen's perspective as reflective, not of 'the Bible', but of one biblical voice out of a diverse chorus. Her reference to the New Testament and Jesus suggests her own 'canon within the canon', one that is Christocentric. The stereotypical contrast regarding the disparate attitudes toward violence in the Hebrew Bible and New Testament is unfortunate, given the schizophrenic perspectives on violence in both testaments (Rindge 2011).

Helen's generalized *imitatio Christi* resurfaces in her explanation for befriending Poncelet ('I'm just trying to follow the example of Jesus, who said that every person is worth more than their worst act') and in Robbins's comment:

> There are many religious people who justify execution by quoting the Bible. ... People like Sister Helen are more into the spirit of Jesus Christ, and what he represents, and ultimately ask the question: could you see Jesus Christ pulling the switch, becoming actively involved in an execution?
>
> (DVD audio commentary)

Farley's citation (see above) omits the conclusion of Genesis 9:6 and – therefore – the stated reason for applying the death penalty to murderers: 'for in God's image [God] made humanity'. Omitting this *imago dei* reference is significant given the film's tension regarding the (divine) humanity of Poncelet. Disregard for Poncelet's humanity surfaces in accusations that he and his ilk are 'mad dogs, maniacs'. A radio host mocks those who suppose Poncelet is 'a child of God'. Earl Delacroix, Walter's father, calls Poncelet 'an evil man' and 'scum'. Hope's father, Clyde Percy, insists: 'This is not a person! This is an animal! No, I take that back; animals don't rape and murder their own kind. Matthew Poncelet is *God's mistake*.'

Prejean's affirmation of Matthew's humanity and divine imprint is symbolized by the gradual reduction in the physical barrier between the two, and her initiation of physical contact by placing a hand on and kissing his shoulder. Her affirmation culminates in declaring – in explicit contrast to the radio host – 'You are a son of God, Matthew Poncelet.' Farley's omission of *imago dei* is noteworthy given the correlation between perceptions of Matthew's humanity and attitudes toward his execution. The assistant District Attorney, persuading the pardon board not to grant clemency, remarks: 'Matthew Poncelet is not a good boy; he is a heartless killer.' Barber tells Matthew: 'What we have to do is present you as a person, as a human being, … *it's easy to kill a monster, but it's hard to kill a human being*' (emphasis added). Helen tells Matthew that his rants 'are making it so easy for them to kill you, coming across as some kind of crazed animal, Nazi, racist mad dog *who deserves to die*' (emphasis added). Whereas *imago dei* is a warrant in Genesis 9:6 for capital punishment, it functions in the film as an argument for mercy and clemency.

The film's balance of conflicting views is evident in applying *imago dei* to Walter and Hope, Poncelet's two victims. Empathy with them is enhanced by interspersing flashbacks to their brutal rape and murder. Walter and Hope are humanized as Helen listens to the stories and grief of their respective parents. Robbins calls such scenes crucial since they take Helen's 'experience into a different realm'. For Robbins, opposition to the death penalty requires empathy with victims and their families. 'If you ignore them', he notes, 'if you create an enemy out of them, I don't feel you are really doing justice to the real … moral issue involved in the taking of a human life' (DVD audio commentary).

The film examines the possibility of simultaneous solidarity with criminals and victims' families. Reflecting a certain dualism, Hope's parents tell Helen she must choose one side or the other. Clyde Percy maintains: 'Now you can't have it both ways. You can't befriend that murderer and expect to be our friend too!' The film concludes with the possibility of reconciling these opposing sides. Appearing at Poncelet's funeral, Earl Delacroix tells Helen: 'I don't know why I'm here; I got a lot of hate.' Helen suggests, 'Maybe we could help each other find a way out of the hate?' But Earl's response – 'I don't know; I don't think so' – seems to reject the possibility of such mutual healing. Yet in the final scene Helen and Earl kneel side by side and pray, signaling a sliver of hope that viewers might recognize – in an opponent's view – a modicum of valid experience.

The film uses the Bible to express conflicting socio-political perspectives. After rebuking Helen for protesting against the death penalty, Farley opines: 'Look at Romans: 'Let every person be sub-ordinate to the higher authorities; for there is no authority except from God', and those who oppose it will bring judgement upon themselves' (Rom. 13:1a). This text legitimizes Farley's participation in a system that kills people, and critiques Prejean for protesting the same system. Helen's opposition to systemic execution is partially rooted in her perception of Jesus as someone who rejected socio-political norms:

> Helen: You say you like rebels; what do you think Jesus was?
> Matthew: Ah, well, he wasn't no rebel.
> Helen: Sure he was, he was a dangerous man.
> Matthew: What's so dangerous about 'love your brother'?
> Helen: Because his love changed things. … All those people who nobody cared about, the prostitutes and beggars and poor, finally had somebody who respected and loved them, made 'em realize their own worth; they had dignity, and they were becoming so powerful that the guys at the top got real nervous so they had to kill Jesus.

The social disruption Jesus models for Helen diverges sharply from the submission to authority Farley endorses.

The film both invites and rejects comparisons between Poncelet and Jesus. Helen rejects Matthew's suggestion that he and Jesus were killed for similar reasons: 'No, Matt, no, not at all like you. Jesus changed the world with his love; you watched while two kids were murdered.' Several details do, however, portray Poncelet as a Jesus figure. He is called 'son of God' shortly before his execution, and he petitions Helen to care for his mother (cf. Mark 15:39; John 19:26–27). Matthew is executed in a vertical cruciform position, his arms extended perpendicularly from his body. While possibly due to cinematic reasons, this altered pose (lethal injection victims lie horizontally) invokes the crucified Jesus.

Such parallels invite consideration of the primary similarity between Jesus and Poncelet: state execution as a convicted criminal. Matthew's poverty is a reminder of Jesus' status as a poor, marginalized figure, and how his socio-economic status contributed to his crucifixion. Jesus' execution is a reminder of America's status as an Empire that does to poor, mostly black, men what the Roman Empire did to marginalized people deemed to be dangerous and disposable.

Reminders of Jesus as a crucified criminal pervade the film in the form of the crucifix. Helen wears a crucifix in at least 26 different scenes. In the first of these, a metal detector goes off during her initial visit to Matthew, and the camera zooms in to reveal Helen's crucifix as the cause. This audible alarm anticipates the subsequent conflict Helen will embody in her solidarity with Matthew and resistance to execution. Her familiarity with this image of an executed criminal leads her not to legitimate violence but to oppose it.

Matthew S. Rindge

Further reading

Helen Prejean, C.S.J. (1993) *Dead Man Walking*. New York: Vintage Books.
Adele Reinhartz (2003) *Scripture on the Silver Screen*. Louisville, KY: Westminster John Knox Press.
Matthew S. Rindge (2010) 'Teaching the Bible *and* Film: Pedagogical Promises, Pitfalls, and Proposals', in *Teaching Theology and Religion* 13(2): 140–55.
——(2011) 'Troy Davis and the Biblical Case(s) for Violence', *Huffington Post*, available online at www.huffingtonpost.com/matthew-s-rindge-phd/tory-davis-biblical-violence_b_974662.html

Further viewing

Angels with Dirty Faces (Michael Curtiz, 1938)
Dead Man Walking (DVD audio commentary by Tim Robbins)
The Green Mile (Frank Darabont, 1999)

DOGMA (1999)

[Production Company: View Askew Productions. Director: Kevin Smith. Screenplay: Kevin Smith. Cinematography: Robert Yeoman. Cast: Ben Affleck (Bartleby), George Carlin (Roman Catholic Cardinal), Matt Damon (Loki), Linda Fiorentino (Bethany Sloane), Salma Hayak (Serendipity), Jason Lee (Azrael), Jason Mewes (Jay), Alanis Morissette (God), Kevin Smith (Silent Bob), Alan Rickman (Metatron), Chris Rock (Rufus).]

Dogma is a road movie in which two fallen angels seeking to return to heaven are opposed by a cast of human and non-human characters who realize that, should the angels succeed, all of creation would be destroyed. The film is intelligent, humourous, and (unconventionally) religious, but it depicts Roman Catholic theology and personnel in an unflattering way and is crude and profane by almost anyone's standards. When it was first released, the movie provoked a flood of hate mail as well as three death threats against Kevin Smith, the author and producer of the film.

The complicated plot of *Dogma* hinges on a supposed loophole in Catholic teaching about *plenary indulgences*, which are offers of the remission of all temporal punishment in purgatory. In the film, it is assumed that plenary indulgences unconditionally guarantee entry into heaven at death. An angel named Loki has quit his position as Angel of Death with the encouragement of his angel-friend, Bartleby. As a result, both angels have been cast out of heaven. Eager to return, they set out to travel to Redbank, New Jersey, where a Catholic Church is planning to offer plenary indulgences to all who pass through the church doors on a certain day. Loki and Bartleby reason that they can wreak mayhem upon the crowd, become human (by cutting off their wings), pass through the church doors, and then reemerge from the church, at which point they will be killed by the police who will have gathered. God will then be obligated to re-admit them to heaven. What Loki and Bartleby fail to factor into their plan is that such a sequence of events would prove God fallible, thereby undoing all of creation.

A woman named Bethany Sloane is commissioned by the angel Metatron to stop Loki and Bartleby from carrying out their plan. Bethany is Catholic – not a lapsed Catholic, but one who is none-theless highly ambivalent about her faith. Reluctantly she accepts the dubious mission. Her assistants in the venture are the 'prophets' (potheads) Jay and Silent Bob, as well as the supposed thirteenth apostle, named Rufus, and a muse named Serendipity. Meanwhile, the demon Azrael attacks Bethany and her posse in order to assist Loki and Bartleby. Azrael wants the angels to succeed in their quest because he would prefer non-existence to eternity in hell. Indeed, it turns out that Azrael has orchestrated the entire plan, even incapacit-ating God on one of God's occasional trips to earth in human form. The story reaches a climax when all the characters converge on the church in New Jersey. God is rescued from a comatose state in a nearby hospital and returns to power, preventing Loki and Bartleby from succeeding in their mission. Creation is thereby preserved, although the ultimate destiny of the two angels is left ambiguous.

The plot of *Dogma* takes off from Genesis 6:1–4, in which angels ('sons of God') descend to the earth. This brief story was retold and expanded in ancient extrabiblical literature, including several books ascribed to Enoch, and it provides the framework for other films such as the 1987 film *Wings of Desire* and its 1998 remake *City of Angels*. But whereas the other films showed angels who *wanted* to live on earth (as in the Genesis passage), the angels in *Dogma* dislike earth and want to return to heaven.

The Bible itself never actually portrays a primordial expulsion of angels. The sons of God mentioned in Genesis 6:1–4 depart willingly, the figure cast out in Isaiah 14 was not an angel but the King of Babylon portrayed in mythic terms, and the expulsion of angels in Revelation 12 happens not at the beginning but at the end of time. But whatever the original meaning of Isaiah 14:12–20, by as early as the New Testament era readers were interpreting this lament for the 'bright morning star' as a description of Satan's expulsion from heaven as a consequence of his arrogance (compare Luke 10:18; Rev. 12:7,12). A related ancient motif concerned the jealousy of Satan and the angels on account of attention that God had showered on Adam and his kind. In *Life of Adam and Eve*, parts of which date back to very early in the Common Era, Satan is instructed by the archangel Michael to worship Adam. He staunchly refuses, declaring that he was created *before* Adam – hence Adam should be worshiping Satan, not vice versa! Such envious pride is featured also in *Dogma*: at first the angelic duo just want to 'go home', but midway through the quest, Bartleby snaps, and begins to rant about God's preferential treatment of human beings.

The angel Loki is described as a former angel of death. Both biblical testaments depict a destroying angel – an agent of God – who slays the unrighteous. In Exodus 12:23 the destroyer kills the firstborn in each Egyptian household (see also 2 Sam. 24:11–16; 1 Cor. 10:10). Ancient nonbiblical texts, such as *The Testament of Abraham*, elaborate on the figure of the destroying angel or angel of death and give him a distinct identity and profile. In the film, Loki temporarily resumes the role he held before his expulsion from heaven, slaying the board members of a corporation whose iconic logo is a golden calf. Loki's fellow angel, Bartleby, is said to be a Watcher. Watchers, mentioned in Daniel 4:13, 17 and 23, figure prominently in the Enoch-literature as a category of angel. *1 Enoch* 6–36 is known as 'The Book of the Watchers'. Watcher-angels also figure prominently in *Wings of Desire* and *City of Angels*, where, as in *Dogma,* the Watchers observe the comings and goings of human beings and monitor their thoughts.

Some of the most interesting improvisations on biblical themes in *Dogma* pertain to the figure of God. At the film's opening, God is enjoying a holiday in human form, playing Skee ball at the New Jersey shore disguised as an old man. The notion of God incarnate in human form is a central element of New Testament proclamation concerning Jesus (see John 1:14). In the film, the incarnate God is attacked by the Stygian Triplets, beaten into a coma, and taken as a 'John Doe' to a nearby hospital, neither dead nor able to return to heaven; New Testament authors had likewise presumed that Jesus was assaulted by human adversaries in the devil's employ (see Luke 22:3, 53; John 13:27; 1 Cor. 2:8).

At the end of the film God appears in the guise of a woman who smells the flowers and does handstands against a tree. When she speaks, however, her voice is enough to destroy all within earshot. This alleged destructive effect is the reason given by Metatron for his functioning as God's voice through biblical history and into the present: direct perception of God's own voice would have annihilated all who heard it. A voice from heaven is mentioned in several places in the Bible and frequently in Rabbinic literature as the *bat kol* (literally, 'daughter of a voice'; in the Bible see, for example, Ezek. 1:28; Jer. 25:30; Matt. 3:17; Luke 9:35; and Rev. 11:12). In none of these or other biblical passages is the voice said to have destructive effect.

The flower-child figure of God at the end of *Dogma* belies her presumed identity with the biblical deity who instituted mass killings through a destroying angel, but this same tension is found in the Bible itself, where the God of love also executes the unfaithful. *Dogma* deals with the tension by implying that God has now given up God's former ways. This solution incorporates the popular but false notion that the 'God of the Old Testament' is wrathful and the 'God of the New Testament' is a God of love; in reality, both the Hebrew scriptures and the Christian scriptures portray God as complex, sometimes expressing love but also demanding righteousness and executing vengeance (see, e.g. Gen. 19:24–25 and Ps. 118:1–4; 1 John 4:16 and Rev. 14:20).

The names, mythical figures, and plot elements come from various sources: the Bible, extrabiblical lore, world mythologies, and Kevin Smith's fertile imagination. 'Loki' is the name of a Norse God. The character Rufus ('the thirteenth apostle') tells of his days with Jesus, alluding to various parts of the Gospel accounts and claiming that the biblical authors deliberately omitted him from the roll of the Twelve because he was black. The character Bethany Sloane is supposedly the last scion of Jesus – a distant descendant of one of Jesus' siblings. The character Metatron serves in the film as chief angel and voice of God; an angel by this name is never mentioned in the canonical biblical texts, but appears in *3 Enoch,* the Talmud, and ancient and medieval Jewish mystical writings. The character Serendipity is a muse – a type of goddess known from Greek mythology. The characters of the two prophets, Jay and Silent Bob, may allude to the two prophets or 'witnesses' of Revelation 11. The character Azrael is a demon, specifically a fallen muse; his name was associated with the angel of death in some later nonbiblical traditions. The Stygian Triplets (three demonic, hockey-stick-wielding youths working for Azrael) are not known from any ancient literature, although the modifier *Stygian* is an adjective referring to the river Styx in Greek mythology about Hades.

In plotting the angels' quest, Bartleby quotes Matthew 16:19, where Jesus declares to Peter, 'I will give you the keys of the kingdom of heaven, and whatever you bind on earth will be bound in heaven, and whatever you loose on earth will be loosed in heaven'. This verse is the scriptural authority for the Catholic doctrine of papal infallibility. Bartleby reasons that since the church's celebration and offer of plenary indulgences has a papal sanction, God will be forced to abide by it. Roman Catholics' selling of indulgences (said to release persons from time in purgatory) was a factor that contributed to the Protestant Reformation, and the portrayal in the film of the vain and self-absorbed Cardinal Glick may vaguely recall some of the more corrupted aspects of theology and practice in that era. Nonetheless, the notion that a church leader could truly guarantee entry into heaven at the time of death and that under certain circumstances God would be powerless to prevent abuse of such a system, caricatures Catholic theology.

Persons easily offended by crude references to sex or by profanity (particularly the f-word), or by deliberately comic and unnuanced references to Christian teaching will find plenty to take offence at in *Dogma*. Viewers not bothered by such elements may find the plot of the film fresh, Smith's use of biblical and extrabiblical motifs ingenious, and the film's dialogue at times devastatingly funny. *Dogma* is not as irreligious as it might seem: while the film pokes fun at beliefs ('dogma'), it affirms that God is real and celebrates humans' faith in her.

Susan R. Garrett

Further reading

Susan R. Garrett (2008) *No Ordinary Angel: Celestial Spirits and Christian Claims about Jesus*. New Haven: Yale University Press.
Kimberley Jones (10 August 2001) 'Mr. Smith Goes to Austin'. *Austin Chronicle*, available online at www.austinchronicle.com/gyrobase/Issue/story?oid=oid%3A82630 (accessed 11 November 2011).
Andy Seiler (24 October 2001) 'Kevin Smith is seldom "Silent"'. *USA Today*, available online at www.usatoday.com/life/movies/2001-08-24-kevin-smith.htm (accessed 11 November 2011).

Further viewing

Wings of Desire (Wim Wenders, 1987)
City of Angels (Brad Silberling, 1998)

FRANKENSTEIN (1931)

[Production Company: Universal Studios. Producers: Carl Laemmle Jr. and E. M. Asher. Director: James Whale. Cinematographers: Arthur Edeson and Paul Ivano. Screenplay: Garrett Fort and Francis Edward Faragoh; based on the novel by Mary Shelley. Cast: Colin Clive (Henry Frankenstein), Boris Karloff (The Monster), Mae Clarke (Elizabeth), John Boles (Victor Moritz), Edward Van Sloan (Dr Waldman), Frederick Kerr (Baron Frankenstein), Dwight Frye (Fritz).]

James Whale's 1931 *Frankenstein* cinematically adapts Mary Shelley's novel to establish a powerful myth of social order. The film begins with a post-production preface: a formally dressed Edward van Sloan steps from behind a curtain to warn us about 'the story of Frankenstein, a man of science who sought to create a man after his own image without reckoning upon God'.

The movie, which may 'thrill' or 'horrify', deals with 'the two great mysteries of creation – life and death'. Thrusting us immediately into this dichotomy, the movie opens with a graveyard collection of skewed crosses, a life-size crucifix, peasants' grieving faces, a priest's faint prayers, and multiple shots of a skeletal Grim Reaper who taunts that religion may console, but it does not spare. When the grave-digger departs, two lurking men exhume the deceased and cart his body to their next prospective site – a hanging corpse that they reject because of its broken neck. Looking for body parts to reanimate, this pair heralds the possibility of new life. Next, we visit a lecture hall where fermented brains reside in impersonally labeled jars reduced to the 'life' of educational props. We hear Dr Waldman describe the criminal's brain as 'degenerate'. The wording suggests an original 'goodness' not unlike that in the Genesis creation story. In Genesis, however, mortality follows quickly as a divine curse. The film's remaining scenes establish a new curse: resurrecting the dead disrupts human social order.

After Dr Waldman, Henry Frankenstein, and Elizabeth (no last name given) arrive, the film slows while everyone awaits the lightning storm – heaven's force of nature – the only missing ingredient in the creation experiment because it is beyond the scientist's control. As with Shelley's novel, and the Prometheus myth of her title, fire generates life. Without lightning, no scientific knowledge and apparatus can enliven the scientist's spatchcocked corpses' pieces. Like us, Henry becomes merely one of the spectators to the orderly staged scientific experiment. We see no *creation ex nihilo* and no omnipotent creator.

Although Dr Waldman labels Henry as 'erratic', 'strange', and 'crazy', much like Shelley's egomaniac who confesses his overreaching to Captain Walton, we see Henry's passion for new life tempered with patience – painstakingly constructing his experiment and awaiting the storm. Of course, Henry is not entirely powerless. This pristinely dressed male usurps female productivity, just as the film credits 'Mrs Percy B. Shelley'. Revising the Genesis mortality punishment and recalling the stories of Lazarus and Jesus, Henry resurrects the dead, exclaiming, 'In the name of God. Now I know what it feels like to be God.' Reminiscent of Shelley's Frankenstein who yells, 'Great God!' as the creature comes to life, Henry's exclamation amends the film's opening preface. If interpreted as a dedication to the divine, 'In the name of God' might mollify religious objectors. Of course, some may wish to interpret his preface as blasphemy; however, the movie does not go so far. Even Dr Waldman, who criticizes Henry's experiments as a 'mad dream' and an 'insane ambition', does not accuse him of breaking any religious or moral taboos. Further, after Henry corrects his teacher regarding 'the great ray which first brought life into the world', we may legitimately wonder if Waldman is merely jealous of Henry's progress.

Surpassing his professor's knowledge, Henry identifies the primal source as lightning, which recalls the first creation of Genesis – light. Henry's work depicts a scientific discovery rather than blasphemy. Henry Frankenstein's 'In the name of God' suggests a human–divine partnership of human prudence awaiting divine power. Such a partnership leaves behind ancient taboos and medieval Christianity, sanctioning modern science.

In order to establish its mythic worldview, the film must privilege a social order over any individual. Evoking the Genesis story but not Shelley's, Whale's creator addresses his new being without condescension or fear. Initially, Henry plans to educate his creation: 'He is only two days old. Wait till I teach him things, till I rouse the human in him.' Henry's temporary endorsement of his creation's learning departs from the Genesis creator who punishes knowledge acquisition in the fall story and Shelley's creator, who treats his creation callously. Fritz, Henry's deformed and inarticulate assistant whom he has dehumanized, endangered, and demeaned (calling him a 'fool' and an 'idiot'), becomes jealous when he witnesses Henry's preferential treatment of the newborn creation. As in the biblical stories of Cain and Abel (Gen. 4:1–15) and the Prodigal Son (Luke 15:11–32), as well as Shelley's novel, the jealous one turns violent. Although aware that Fritz tortures the Monster with a blazing torch, Henry does nothing. He simply abandons his terrified creation to danger. Like the God of the fall, flood, Babel, and Job, as well as Victor Moritz, Henry fails to protect his creation from harm, leaving the Monster alone to face danger. Like a confused Job, the Monster does not understand Fritz's aggression. But unlike Job, faith and trust in the creator will not save him. Although Henry succeeds as a scientist, he fails as a father because he does not explain or protect against the lurking danger.

Defending himself against torture, the Monster murders Fritz. Although Henry realizes that Fritz probably deserves the creature's retaliation, Henry abandons his creation once again, this time to the Monster-bashing Dr Waldman. Breaking his promise to painlessly destroy the Monster, Waldman begins dissecting the living creature until the Monster strangles him to death in self-defense. Had Henry not abandoned his creation, neither murder would have occurred.

The third murder also ensues from parental neglect. A father abandons his young daughter at a lake's shore, where her flower floating game with the Monster leads to her unintended drowning. Both the girl and the Monster are too ignorant to grasp the consequences of their actions.

As the film progresses, its focus transfers from the father-son relationship between Henry and the Monster to the relationship between Henry and his own father. In order to ensure the perpetuation of the House of Frankenstein, the Baron insists that Henry resume his family responsibilities and abandon his experiments and creation. Unlike Shelley, who is much more concerned with the creature's socialization and personality, Whale portrays the Monster only as a plot device – a threat to society. Boris Karloff's make-up, grunting, and laboured gait fit the Monster's lack of characterization and generic name, casting the creature outside human order. Like many bible stories, such as Exodus, the film emphasizes the continuation of the chosen, not those outside. But because Frankenstein's experiments threaten family and social orders, he must trade them for the good life of blue-blood lineage. Resuming his role among the gentry, Henry confesses to Elizabeth, 'It's like Heaven ... to be with you again.'

The film ultimately pits Frankenstein against the Monster, who appears to be defending itself against his own creator. This conflict, however, is peripheral to the main theme of the film and the Monster's guilt or innocence, like its needs and desires, is not really in view any longer. Like many horror films of his time, Whale's film focuses on class and social order. The ethos is simple: abide by your place in the class structure. The privileged House of Frankenstein must continue to thrive – enjoying exquisite wine; preserved orange blossom adornments; and, above all, male heirs. With Henry's wedding date secured, the film must dismiss the Monster, not because its brain is abnormal, but because its creation violates a social order. Even if its creator had attempted to socialize it, there is no place for the Monster in the House of Frankenstein. Operating as a *Bildungsroman*, Whale's film insists that Henry reject his low-class, decaying laboratory; restore his father/Baron-son relationship; renew his friendship with an upper-class male; marry a refined woman; and father an heir. One could read much of biblical narrative as a similar call to know one's place in an ordered world. James Whale's *Frankenstein* acts as a myth that establishes a social charter defining human worth for a designated group.

Modern viewers may wonder why this social charter appealed to Depression audiences. For all its assertion that the House of Frankenstein must prevail, the film's penultimate scene credits the mob – not the Baron or his son – with eradicating the threat of the Monster to society. Without proof of anyone's murder, the mob unleashes its drunken anger, which the Baron has predicted, upon the Monster, while the impotent Henry has been transported to the safety, orderliness, and affection of the Frankenstein household. As in Matthew 27:23–27, the people succeed in securing the scapegoat's sacrifice while the elite wash their hands and remain safe. Although initially thrilling to view, the mob's primitive frenzy quickly frightens and repulses. At the end of the day, most viewers would probably prefer a peaceful order. The film restores concord through the status and authority of the House of Frankenstein. Audiences are ultimately assured that a mob mentality will not prevail and that those in charge can be counted on. The film's final scene – added to the original screenplay which originally ended with the mob's victory – depicts a harmonious triumph as the Baron toasts to the House of Frankenstein. The film has progressed from the neglectful creators of Genesis and Shelley to the divine sovereign of Exodus who protects his chosen people. Such a future would appeal to Depression audiences longing for the assurance of class security and social order.

While Shelley concludes with overreaching proscriptions, Whale concludes with socially responsible prescriptions. As the film leaves behind the gloomy laboratory tower for the opulent Frankenstein manor, we realize that Henry's errors lie less in abusing his assistant and failing to protect his creation and more in failing to protect his future bride and jeopardizing the Frankenstein legacy. To rectify his errors, he must privilege family and social order over personal ambition. No doubt, from the graveyard to the burning windmill, Whale concedes a debt to the lower class into which he was born. Thereafter, however, Whale's additional scene finalizes his mythic vision, which resolves our fears by reinstating the class distinctions of social order. Much like a reading from Genesis through Exodus, *Frankenstein* transports us from the 'thrill' of creation to the stability of social ethic.

P. Jennifer Rohrer-Walsh

Further reading

Timothy Beal (2002) *Religion and its Monsters.* New York: Routledge.

Paul Cantor (1984) *Creature and Creator: Myth-making and English Romanticism.* Cambridge: Cambridge University Press.

Donald F. Glut (1984) *The Frankenstein Catalog.* Jefferson, North Carolina: McFarland & Company.

——(1973) *The Frankenstein Legend: A Tribute to Mary Shelley and Boris Karloff.* Metuchen, NJ: The Scarecrow Press.

Mary Shelley (1977, orig. 1818) *The Essential Frankenstein.* New York: Byron Preiss.

FROM THE MANGER TO THE CROSS (1912)

[Production Company: Kalem. Director: Sidney Olcott. Screenwriter: Gene Gauntier. Cinematographer: George K. Hollister. Cast: Robert Henderson-Bland (Jesus), Percy Dyer (the boy Jesus), Gene Gauntier (Virgin Mary), Alice Hollister (Mary Magdalene), Sidney Olcott (blind man), Samuel Morgan (Pilate), James D. Ainsley (John the Baptist), Robert G. Vignola (Judas), George Kellog (King Herod), Montague Sidney (Joseph), Jack J. Clark (John the Disciple).]

Sidney Olcott's five-reel travelogue genre Jesus movie follows a harmonizing, episodic plot structure of Jesus' life that is divided into three roughly equal parts: Infancy and Period of Youth; Calling, Miracles, and Scenes in the Ministry; and Last Days. Olcott uses two types of intertitles in his film: scripture references for individual scenes; and seven chapter-like intertitles. The chapter-like intertitles are superimposed on simple art work, making the film a pastiche of scripture, art, and moving pictures.

The film's harmonizing tendencies are most obvious in the scripture intertitles which occasionally are incorrectly referenced, and at other times do not match their scenes. For example, one set of intertitles pairs the healing of one blind man at Jericho (Mark 10:46) with the Gospel of Matthew, even though that gospel has two men healed; and another time it pairs Judas's complaint regarding the anointing woman with Matthew's gospel, although it is only John's gospel that identifies Judas as the complainer (John 12:4–6).

In 1911, the Kalem Company sent Olcott to the Mediterranean to film one-reel spectacles, and his Jesus film was apparently an afterthought, the brainchild of Gene Gauntier, who was already well known for her work with Olcott. The film's travelogue genre is made clear in its third intertitle which states: 'The scene of this history is the Holy Land.' A map of Palestine follows, identifying all the towns where the film was shot. The fourth intertitle concludes the film's preface with the words, 'With scenes filmed at Jerusalem, Bethlehem and other authentic locations in Palestine.'

By the late nineteenth century, travel to exotic lands was more easily accessible to upper middle-class Europeans and Americans. But, since most Americans were still unable to travel abroad for pleasure, they depended on touring lecturers to describe far off places. As a result, traveling exhibitions of 'uncivilized heathens' presented by church mission societies and city museums became quite popular. Thus, the appeal of Sidney Olcott's film (it was Kalem Company's most popular film, eventually bringing nearly one million dollars in profits), was due in part to its ability to combine audience curiosity about exotic peoples and places (Egypt and Palestine) with the familiar – their knowledge of the Jesus story; especially as seen in the popular James Tissot illustrations of *The Life of Christ*. In fact, the head of Kalem Company gave Olcott's entourage a copy of Tissot's illustrations when they left for the Mediterranean. And the opening scene of Olcott's film where Mary carries a water pot is such an obvious replication of Tissot's 'The Holy Virgin in Her Youth', that audiences who had seen Tissot's travelling exhibition would have been primed to view Olcott's film almost as a moving picture version of Tissot's *The Life of Christ*.

Tissot travelled to the Holy Land twice in the 1880s where he sketched and photographed scenes and people that would become the basis for his meticulously detailed paintings. His series of 350 illustrations of the life of Christ were shown to critical acclaim and enthusiastic audiences in Paris, London, and New York before being bought by the Brooklyn Museum in 1900. As one clergyman, the Rev. Lyman Abbott, noted at the time, 'to look upon these pictures ... is to come as near to living the Christ's life as is permitted to anyone living in this modern world' (Gardner 2009).

Olcott's renderings of the Tissot paintings are particularly evident in the following scenes: 'The Holy Virgin in Her Youth', 'The Annunciation', 'The Anxiety of Saint Joseph', 'The Magi in the House of Herod', 'Jesus Found in the Temple', 'The Youth Jesus', 'Saint John the Baptist Sees Jesus from afar', 'The Marriage at Cana', 'Mary Magdalene at the Feet of Jesus', 'Jesus, Mary Magdalene, and Martha at Bethany', 'Jesus Wept', 'Judas Goes to the Chief Priests', 'Communion of the Apostles', and 'The First Nail'. But whereas Tissot's paintings occasionally reveal his fascination with Spiritism, Olcott rejected Tissot's portrayals of angels, the devil, and his dramatic Easter scenes. This is most obvious in Olcott's rendering of Tissot's 'The Annunciation' which copies Tissot's painting down to the checkered wall design in Mary's home, but without the accompanying angel Gabriel. Instead, Olcott substitutes a hazy light for the angelic image. Although Satan would become an important character in future Jesus films, only Pasolini (*The Gospel According to St. Matthew*, 1964) and Dornford May (*Son of Man*, 2006) would portray angels onscreen.

Olcott's film adds elements of the travelogue genre to the nineteenth century realism of Tissot's illustrations. And like Tissot's paintings which never show a close-up of Jesus' face, Olcott prefers to film his Jesus character in long shots. In fact, Robert Henderson-Bland, who plays the role of the adult Jesus, is so similar in facial features and stature to Tissot's Jesus that from a distance, he appears as if he might have been Tissot's model for Christ.

Charles Foster writes that when Olcott and his crew first met Robert Henderson-Bland, 'Bland walked into Olcott's hotel room wearing a long golden wig, dressed in a white flowing robe. "I am Jesus Christ," said Bland. "I will portray myself in your film." Bland told them he had received a vision during the night, and that God had told him he was His chosen son. "Frankly, we thought he was mad," said Olcott. "But we didn't argue. He was obviously what we wanted"' (2000: 229).

Olcott's film represents an important period in the history of religious film – and of film in general – with its presentation of Jesus as one who reflects the domestic (late Victorian) piety of early twentieth-century American religion. Throughout the film, the portrayal of women at the feet of Jesus marks Jesus as a domestic, feminized figure. He belongs to women, he uplifts them, and they and their religion belong to the home. Women are among the few characters that Jesus looks at directly. Mary Magdalene is an important figure in the film, and although she is not explicitly identified as the sinful woman of Luke 7 (Olcott does not include the story of the woman caught in adultery [John 8:1–11], a woman traditionally identified as Mary

Magdalene), Gene Gauntier believed that 'Mary, Martha's sister, and Mary Magdalene were one and the same person' (Dench 1915: 77). Significantly, in Olcott's rendering, it is the dark-veiled Mary who comes to tell Jesus about her brother's death by kneeling, sobbing, and kissing Jesus' legs and feet (cf. John 11:20–21). As a result, Olcott explains the plot to kill Jesus in terms of Judas' reaction to Mary Magdalene's emotion-filled anointing and in terms of Jesus' blasphemous 'I Am' statement in the Jerusalem Temple (John 8:58), rather than as a response to Jesus' political threat to Roman (or British or American) imperialism.

Following the composite, harmonistic structure of most Christmas pageants, Olcott draws from both Matthew and Luke to construct his birth narrative. Contra Matthew, both Mary and Joseph receive the announcement of Jesus' birth in Nazareth, and contra Luke, Joseph is pictured as a carpenter. Combining Matthew and Luke, both shepherds and wise men follow the star to the manger in Bethlehem to worship the newborn. But Olcott is most creative when constructing the scenes of Jesus' childhood in Nazareth. In one scene, evocative of Victorian family parlor life, Mary reads from a scroll to Jesus (who wears a yarmulke) while Joseph watches from the background, working a piece of wood. Later, the dutiful son is seen under the watchful care of Mary as he carries a jar of water. And when he is twelve, Mary and Joseph peer through a Temple window as Jesus teaches the priests and scribes; his right hand's two raised fingers denote his dual nature as human and divine.

In the film's most stunning scene, Olcott copies Tissot's 'The Youth Jesus', where the carpenter boy carries a board across his shoulders as his parents watch. But in a brilliant stroke, Olcott positions Jesus in such a way that as he enters the sunlight the shadow of the plank across his shoulders makes a cruciform on the ground. His mother sees the shadow and covers her mouth in fright, thus bringing to an end the opening third of the film. This naturalistic scene, to which Jesus is oblivious, functions 'literally' as a foreshadowing of Jesus' destiny, and is a harbinger of film's future storytelling possibilities. Cecil B. DeMille (*The King of Kings*, [1927]), George Stevens (*The Greatest Story Ever Told*, [1965]), and Martin Scorsese (*The Last Temptation of Christ*, [1988]) will, in their own unique ways, also use crosses proleptically as revelatory images of Jesus' destiny.

The middle section of Olcott's film, however, lacks the creativity of the opening scenes, since Olcott resists inventing scenarios for Jesus' adulthood which might otherwise give a sense of cohesion to the plot. As the story turns to Jesus' public ministry, Olcott omits John's baptism of Jesus. Instead, Jesus is just barely observable off in the distance, walking on the horizon (John 1:36). The location then moves to the

Sea of Galilee, where Jesus calls some fishermen to follow him. Not coincidentally, this is the point at which the viewing audience sees the adult Jesus in medium long shots for the first time. Despite teaching scenes on the lake and in homes, there are no scriptural intertitles to help viewers identify Jesus' words. Instead, his ministry is a series of wavy-hand miracles and domestic tableaus with women, including two anointing scenes.

Olcott includes many more scenes of Jesus teaching than do other silent Jesus films, centering the teaching on two revelatory 'I am' statements from the Gospel of John (8:58; 18:6). The plot's turning point comes with the first of these, made in the Jerusalem temple. Jesus walks away from the stone-wielding priests who huddle together, plotting against him.

Judas's dissatisfaction with the anointing at Bethany provides the first clear, dramatic counterpoint to the film's aloof, magisterial Christ. Judas emerges from the group of disciples and the undefined crowds to take on the adversarial role that moves the plot toward its climax. After the triumphal entry, more healings, and the cleansing of the Temple, Judas, now in dark clothing, haggles with the priests over the betrayal price. In the extensive upper room material – including footwashing, meal, and communion – Judas's identification and departure (notably before communion) are prominent.

In Gethsemane, Judas brings the soldiers by lamplight. After the kiss, Judas and the soldiers fall back in revelatory awe, as in John 18:6. Olcott completes Judas's story – the repentance and the hanging – before turning to Jesus' Roman trial and his mockery by Herod. There is no trial before the Sanhedrin (anticipating *King of Kings*, [1961]; *Godspell*, [1973]; *The Last Temptation of Christ*, [1988]; and *Jesus of Montreal*, [1989]), but the Jewish priests point accusingly at Jesus from the background as Pilate questions Jesus. Likewise, the murderous crowd repeatedly demands Jesus' execution despite the scourging (which Pilate watches), the ecce homo scene (John 19:5), and Pilate's hand-washing (Matt. 27:24). After mocking Jesus as he sits on a stone pillar, Pilate's soldiers take Jesus to Golgotha. Simon is whipped in order to force him to carry Jesus' T-shaped cross (Tissot's Jesus also carries a T-shaped cross).

The audience sees Golgotha from afar, sharing the distant perspective with the watching women. As the camera moves closer, it looks down upon the head and torso of a fully clothed Jesus. He writhes in pain as soldiers nail him to the cross and raise it into the air. A fade to black leads to a final Scripture card: For God so loved the world, that he gave his only begotten Son, that whosoever believeth in him should not perish, but have everlasting life (John 3:16). Notably, there is no Easter morning scene at an empty tomb. In this sense, the film is a precursor of later Jesus films such as *Godspell* (1973), *Jesus Christ Superstar* (1973), *The Last Temptation of Christ* (1988), *Jesus of Montreal* (1989), *Son of Man* (2006), which also reject the traditional Easter story.

Jeffrey L. Staley

Further reading

Judith Buchanan (2007) 'Gospel Narratives on Silent Film', in *The Cambridge Companion to Literature on Screen*, Cartmell, Deborah and Imelda Whelehan (eds). Cambridge: Cambridge University Press, pp. 47–60.

Ernest A. Dench (1915) *Making the Movies*. New York: Macmillan.

Charles Foster (2000) 'Sidney Olcott and the *Making of From the Manger to the Cross*', in *In Stardust and Shadows: Canadians in Early Hollywood*. Toronto: Dundurn. pp. 215–42.

James Gardner (2009) 'So What Was the Fuss All About?' Arts and Entertainment, *The Wall Street Journal* 17 December, available online at http://online.wsj.com/article/SB10001424052748704779704574553760776109266.html (accessed 22 July 2011).

Gene Gauntier (2003) 'Filming *From the Manger to the Cross*. The First Moving Picture of the Life of Christ Made in the Land Where He Lived and Died'. Condensed from a 1927 reminiscence by a major player and scenarist of the film. Four-page DVD insert. Image Entertainment.

Ken Johnson (2009) 'Jesus, Illustrated: Tissot's New Testament'. Art Review. *New York Times* 17 December.

Alison McMahan (2002) *Alice Guy Blaché: Lost Visionary of the Cinema*. New York: Continuum.

Herbert Reynolds (1992) 'From Palette to Screen: The Tissot Bible as a Sourcebook for *From the Manger to the Cross*', in Roland Cosandey, André Gaudreault and Tom Gunning (eds) *Une Invention du diable? Cinéma des premiers temps et religion*. Sainte-Foy: Éditions Payot Lausanne. pp. 275–310. *Sidney Olcott en Egypte et en Palestine*. Available online at www.youtube.com/watch?v=TNo3kzJGGdw (accessed 22 July 2011).

Jeffrey L. Staley, and Richard Walsh (2007) *Jesus, the Gospels, and Cinematic Imagination: A Handbook to Jesus on DVD*. Louisville, KY: Westminster John Knox Press. pp. 11–16.

W. Barnes Tatum (2004) 'Sidney Olcott, From the Manger to the Cross'. In *Jesus at the Movies: A Guide to the First Hundred Years*. Rev. and Expanded. ed. Santa Rosa: Polebridge. pp. 23–33.

GODSPELL (1973)

[Production Company: Columbia Pictures Corporation. Director: David Greene. Screenplay: David Greene and John-Michael Tebelak. Cinematography:

Richard G. Heimann. Music: Stephen Schwartz. Cast: Victor Garber (Jesus), David Haskell (John/Judas), Katie Hanley (Katie), Lynne Thigpen (Lynne).]

Like *Jesus Christ Superstar*, another Jesus film from 1973, *Godspell* was first a play (both in 1971). Stephen Prothero observes that while *Superstar* represents the brooding angrier side of the sixties, '*Godspell*, by contrast, is a product of the sixties' bright side. … [Jesus] prays for a day when 'Earth shall be fair/And all her people one' (2003: 135). He further notes that these plays and films allowed the playwright John-Michael Tebelak, 'to rescue Jesus from the church' and reclaim a Jesus from and in the world (2003: 135). *Godspell* did so with upbeat humour and spirit, asking its audiences to rise to the occasion – with Jesus.

At the beginning of the film the camera pans over graffiti to a bustling New York City, as a voiceover narrator – God the Creator – intones: 'I will make him [man] gardener for his own re-creation'. This creation monologue implies that Jesus will infiltrate the city in invisible ways. John the Baptist comes with a cart, wearing a mock-military jacket with shoulder tassels and a fish symbol on the back. The film briefly shows each disciple in the midst of the city, focusing on the uniqueness of each person. John, with his shofar and winking appearances, calls the disciples to leave their hectic lives; they leave their old lives and identities abruptly behind, dropping books and shoes and purses. The city suddenly becomes empty as the troupe heads to the Bethesda Fountain in Central Park for the playful baptism by John.

The group exchanges their urban weariness for playful joy, expressed in story, song and dance. During the day the sun is always shining, brightening up the junkyard compound where Jesus and the disciples make their home. The junkyard represents the detritus of society, reclaimed and made beautiful and useful by the new community. In making this space the base for their 'urban school' with Jesus, they have chosen to live in the ugliest part of the city. They venture out daily from their junkyard home into the heart of the city – occupying parks, the Cherry Lane Theatre (where the play was first performed), streets, the harbour, and the tops of skyscrapers. In these moments Jesus and the believers, not the wealthy status quo, 'own' the city. They turn the chaos, loneliness and filth of the city into something worth celebrating.

Godspell picks up on the Bible's ambivalence about the city. Richard Walsh argues that the film perpetuates the biblical notion of the negative rejection of the city in favor of a garden paradise (2003: 74). But *Godspell* is more ambivalent about the city: John intentionally crosses into Manhattan on the Brooklyn Bridge; even the garden and sea scenes confine Jesus and the disciples within the boundaries of the great city. Their pilgrimages are bounded by bridges, the Statue of Liberty, skyscrapers, and Central Park. As they dance and sing and teach through the city, they are celebrating it. In the end, however, the empty city refills with people, embedding the echoes and traces of joy in the capitalist society that New York represents. Walsh relates, 'Despite its surface alienation, then, *Godspell* actually renders Jesus' teaching consumable for post-1970s America by situating it in American Romanticism and in capitalist consumerism' (2003: 74). This romanticism is deconstructed; the garden paradise is to be found only in the heart of the city. Likewise, Jesus is found, not in the outlying boroughs or small towns, but only in the urban chaos, which swallows and reincorporates the troupe in the end.

As Jesus and the disciples roam the city, they inventively play out a selection of gospel stories. Jesus' teachings are actually expounded collectively with the disciples in *Godspell*. Sometimes he starts off the story but he is also an audience member. Often the disciples start the teachings and parables and Jesus follows up, explains, or helps them act out the teachings. For example, the disciples start each line of the Beatitudes but Jesus finishes the lines in a kind of call and response. Walsh notes that *Godspell* draws on the Gospel of Matthew, Luke (for the parables), John (for the passion), Q, and Thomas, even as the film 'rejects canonical language games' (2003: 74). He also argues persuasively that *Godspell* veers toward the hypothetical Q sayings (as Luke presents them) with Q's 'apocalyptic voyeurism' (2003: 80–81) in a sort of soft-shoe apocalypse. Jesus always compassionately frames and guides the teachings. When John the Baptist protests over 'love your enemies', however, Jesus slaps his left cheek. John begins to hit Jesus back, then thinks better of it, pretending his raised hand is a phone receiver, and they embrace, thereby illustrating the 'commandment'.

Throughout the brief (100 minute) film Jesus teaches and exemplifies love and compassion. In his enactment of Matthew 25:32–46, Jesus divides the disciples into sheep and goats. The goats (because of their selfish acts) receive Jesus' pronouncement, 'A curse is upon you'. The blessed sheep (because of their charitable acts) bound happily away with Jesus; they round a corner and are gone. But immediately Jesus and the sheep peek their heads around the corner and Jesus says, 'Come on', waving his arm and embracing the goats. Jesus turns the dialectic of eternal punishment versus eternal life inside out, and the result is a universalist, all-inclusive teaching of love and salvation.

In the christology or 'jesusology' of this film, Jesus is a wise innocent with a simple, hopeful message. For example, when Jesus, in briefs, approaches John at the fountain, he says, 'I want to get washed up.' Jesus emerges from the water in a Superman shirt with suspenders and stripped clown pants and red clown shoes. He is clean-shaven with an Afro hairstyle. Jesus as clown draws the viewer in with serious play (see Walsh 2003: 77; Staley and Walsh 2007: 71 and Cox 1969: 139–40 on Jesus as clown in the film *Parable*). John and the disciples believe immediately that he is the one. They refer to him as 'Master', 'good Master', 'Lord', 'Rabbi' (by Judas), 'Messiah', 'son of God', and of course, 'Jesus'. John begins to call him 'Jesus Chr ... !' during the teaching of 'turn the other cheek', but he catches his use of the term as cursing when he looks at Jesus. The disciples also consider him God from first sight until the end; in the resurrection scene, the disciples sing 'Long Live God' and this song joins with 'Prepare Ye the Way of the Lord', providing a full circle in the film.

Jesus is also deeply human, relying on touch, eye contact and gentle emotion to teach the disciples. At one point he claims, 'I read feet', to deflect an uncomfortable proleptic saying about his impending death. 'It says "Rejoice"', says Jesus. The disciple looks at the bottom of his shoe and responds, 'No, it says, "Keds".' This Jesus has no power to heal or read feet or work miracles or save himself. Yet he is still God – albeit one that is incarnate and human – throughout the film.

While the viewer may realize that this Jesus does not do miracles, one of the disciples believes he magically made a tree grow. The disciples are under his 'spell': 'The dimension of liminality in the film suggests a further significance of the film's title: *Godspell* as the spell of God, the fascination, the ecstasy of God, the mystical experience of God' (Baugh 1997: 47). Jesus' 'clowning' is serious play; Jesus means business, even as love and compassion are central. Gerald Forshey suggests that, in contrast to Zeffirelli's *Jesus of Nazareth* (1977), *Godspell*, like *Superstar* (1973), has 'banned the supernatural' (Forshey 1992: 169). But Pamela Grace disagrees:

> In keeping with the film's many contradictions, the ending does not indicate that the film chooses to avoid the miraculous or traditional notions of the afterlife, since there are numerous references to Jesus' father in heaven, who will reward the good with eternal happiness.
>
> (2009: 91)

Yet there is no bodily or physical resurrection; Jesus is absorbed into the heart of the busy city once the disciples turn a corner. Jesus' followers walk back into the city, into their lives, but as transformed peacemakers. The real miracles occur in the human heart, in those who make a difference in the crowd. The abbreviated Passion begins on the wharf after the tugboat trip. The authorities, represented by a monster puppet operated by the disciples, are vaguely named 'Pharisees' by Jesus. The change in camera angle from straight on to low angle increases the tension. This is the one scene where Jesus expresses anger, as he asserts his authority and dismantles the monster. The other authorities are symbolized at his 'crucifixion' on the fence by the police cars with their lights that Judas summoned. When the cars arrive outside the compound, Jesus kisses Judas on the 'other' cheek.

According to Prothero, the script and songs 'affirm, among other things, the divinity of Jesus and the truth of the resurrection' (2003: 134). There is also traditional theology at the last supper. Jesus uses a symbolically red door as the table and proclaims, 'This is my body. ... This is my blood. ... The blood of the covenant shared for the forgiveness of sins.' This Jesus sees an atoning purpose to the supper – and his foreshadowed death. Jesus begins the erasure of the disciples' clown makeup in a 'face washing' instead of foot washing scene but refuses to have the heart on his forehead and the lines under his eyes removed.

The Manhattan of this Jesus story is a parallel universe to the real city. It also serves as a stand in for Jerusalem. During the time of Jesus the city stops; it empties out to provide the stage for the Jesus story in order to highlight it against the backdrop of soaring skyscrapers and Central Park. The empty spaces provide room for theatre improv through which the actors, and the viewers, can imagine a different type of urban community. One of the songs, 'You Are the Light of the World', refers to the city as 'the city of God', sung as the group drinks wine and cheerfully sails around the Statue of Liberty on a boat decorated with an American flag, with the Twin Towers of the not-yet-completed World Trade Center eerily in the background. The soft shoe dance on one of the Towers (and on the digital sign in Times Square) in the number, 'It's All for the Best', evoke, for present-day viewers, the universe since 9/11. The disciples sing, 'We can build, a beautiful city, yes we can. ... and call it the city of love', around Bethesda Fountain and hope reigns again.

Jesus and his disciples form an early version of 'Occupy Wall Street' (2011), with a counter-cultural message of love, forgiveness, and anti-capitalism. 'When will God save the people? Not thrones and crowns, but men?' sing the disciples after the baptism. The lilies of the field, not the golden calf/the Wall Street bull, symbolize Jesus' followers. 'No man can serve God ... and money', declares Jesus. The film critiques wealth – and the wealthy – for example in the song 'Turn Back, O Man' and the parable of the rich man and Lazarus. Still, Jesus answers the Pharisaic monster by advising the payment of taxes to Caesar, as he does in the Gospels (Mark 12:13–17). Margaret Miles states that 'Despite popular films' largely dismissive treatment of *religion*, films are profoundly interested in *values*'. (1996: 21, note 7). *Godspell* is a low-budget Hollywood film about religion and values, and this description fits with Miles' definition of religion as 'a sense of relatedness' (1996: 14). *Godspell* engages the viewer in re-examining relationships – to money and possessions, to work, to the city, to each other, and to God. The call is open-ended; viewers leave the theatre, rounding the corner back into their lives, having heard another version of the gospels.

Tina Pippin

Further reading

Lloyd Baugh (1997) *Imaging the Divine: Jesus and Christ-Figures in Film*. Kansas City, MO: Sheed & Ward.
Harvey Cox (1969) 'Christ the Harlequin', in *Feast of Fools: A Theological Essay on Festivity and Fantasy*. New York, NY: Harper & Row. pp. 139–57.
Gerald E. Forshey (1992) *American Religious and Biblical Spectaculars*. Westport, CT: Praeger.
Pamela Grace (2009) *The Religious Film: Christianity and the Hagiopic*. New Approaches to Film Genre. Chichester; Malden, Mass.: Wiley-Blackwell.
Peter Hasenberg (1992) 'Clown und Superstar: Die Jesus-Musicals der 70er Jahre'. *Film-Dienst Extra, 40*.
Margaret R. Miles (1996) *Seeing and Believing: Religion and Values in the Movies*. Boston, MA: Beacon Press.
Stephen Prothero (2003) *American Jesus: How the Son of God Became an Icon*. New York, NY: Farrar, Straus and Giroux.
Jeffrey L. Staley and Richard Walsh (2007) *Jesus, the Gospels, and Cinematic Imagination: A Handbook to Jesus on DVD*. Louisville, KY: Westminster John Knox Press.
Richard Walsh (2003) *Reading the Gospels in the Dark: Portrayals of Jesus in Film*. Harrisburg, PA: Trinity Press International.

Further viewing

Parable (Rolf Forsberg, 1964)
Cotton Patch Gospel (Michael Meece, 1988)

THE GOSPEL ACCORDING TO ST. MATTHEW (1964)

[Production Company: Arco/Lux. Director: Pier Paolo Pasolini. Screenplay: Pier Paolo Pasolini. Cinematography: Tonino Delli Colli. Cast: Enrique Irazoqui (Jesus Christ), Margherita Caruso (Mary, younger), Susanna Pasolini (Mary, older), Marcello Morante (Joseph), Mario Socrate (John the Baptist).]

In autumn 1962, while in Assisi for a seminar on spirituality and the movies, Pier Paolo Pasolini (1922–75) started reading the gospels, decades after his last encounter with them. Overwhelmed by the beauty and power of Matthew's Gospel, which he experienced – as he later described it – as a 'tremendous energy' and 'intensification of vitality' (quoted in Gambetti 1964: 14), he spontaneously decided to film it. Perceiving the narrative style of Matthew as already cinematic and screenplay-like, he had the immediate inspiration to follow the gospel 'point for point [...], without making any script and without any reduction. I will faithfully translate, in images, without omission to or deletion from the story. Even the dialogue must be strictly that of Saint Matthew, without even a line of explanation or feeder lines: because no images or words inserted can ever be of the poetic height of the text' (quoted in Schwartz 1992: 424).

Pasolini remained true to his intention concerning the dialogue – this same principle was later intended to govern his never-realized project on Saint Paul – but he could not avoid omissions. To be sure, his printed screenplay (cf. Gambetti 1964) included the whole Gospel, and he shot about 70,000 metres (229,658 feet) of footage, enough for a four hour epic. The film itself was cut to 3,749 metres (12,300 feet), and had a running time of 137 minutes. Despite the widespread opinion that Pasolini remained almost 'scrupulously faithful' to the Gospel (Green 1990: 73), a closer look reveals many changes with significant interpretative impact (cf. Zwick 1997: 162–84). The film even includes scenes found not in Matthew but in one of the other three canonical gospels, particularly in the passion sequence, which borrowed heavily from John's gospel. Of the over 150 sections (pericopes) in Matthew's gospel Pasolini adapted only 86 to his film, and many of these are fragmentary. For example, he incorporated only three of the parables and deleted all of Jesus' sayings on the last days (Matt. 24–25). By contrast, he included almost every scene that shows Jesus in conflict with the religious authorities. Moreover, Pasolini reordered the sequence of many of the episodes. For example, by including some of the sayings on discipleship and divisiveness (Matt. 9:35–10:39) immediately after the call of the disciples (Matt. 4:18–22), he reinforced the tone of conflict to the point that it became a key theme in his cinematic text. In light of these changes, as well as of the creative mise-en-scène, it is apparent that, despite the reputation of this film as 'faithful' to Matthew's Gospel, Pasolini had in fact created a new gospel of his own.

A significant element in this new creation was the decision regarding the filming location. Pasolini initially intended to film in Israel, and to this end he travelled to Israel to search for suitable locations. This journey is documented in the movie *Sopralluoghi in Palestina* (1965); (cf. Steimatsky 1998; Zwick 2008: 211–15). But disappointed by Israel's pervasive modernity he finally selected Apulia and the Basilicata in the poor, underdeveloped South of Italy as his Judea and Galilee, making the rundown town of Matera his Jerusalem, as Mel Gibson also did some four decades later. In this ambiance he selected only amateur actors. Most of these actors were people from the region, but a number were friends from Rome, including his later biographer Enzo Siciliano as Simon of Bethania, the writer Natalia Ginzburg as Mary of Bethania and the now famous philosopher Giorgio Agamben as the disciple Philip. That he cast his mother Susanna as the aged Mother of Jesus is a rather blatant indication of Pasolini's lifelong self-identification with Christ as the persecuted and suffering Righteous One.

At the movie's premier at the Venice festival in September 1964, some young fascists caused an uproar before the screening, because they expected that any film about Jesus made by a director who was a homosexual, atheist and Marxist would inevitably be blasphemous. Their suspicions were not entirely unfounded, for shortly before this premier, Pasolini had been accused of blasphemy for his short feature film *La Ricotta* in which he had explored different burlesque and dramatic approaches to filming Jesus' crucifixion. But to the surprise of all – not only the fascists – the movie was not blasphemous but reverential. Indeed, for many of Pasolini's left wing friends, his gospel was much too pious, whereas for his right wing opponents it was too political and sociocritical. Nevertheless, the film received critical acclaim. In addition to the special prize of the main jury in Venice the movie also won the prize of the Catholic jury and later received extended standing ovations in a private screening in Rome for approximately one hundred bishops of the Vatican council. Soon the film was being appreciated even by intellectuals who were far removed from the Church and from Christian faith. After a screening in Notre Dame Cathedral in Paris, Jean-Paul Sartre admitted that Christ was a blind spot in the thinking of the leftists.

Despite his self-identification as an atheist and a Marxist, Pasolini was a deeply spiritual man, a great admirer of Saint Francis of Assisi, to whom his 1966 film *Uccellacci e Uccellini* (*The Hawks and the Sparrows* [1966]) pays homage. Pasolini was a man who studied mystics and the history of religions, a man who in many of his other films portrayed Christ figures, for example, in *Teorema* (1968), and a man who considered religion to be an indispensable resource for a society about to drown in consumerism. His public disavowal of Christianity was related not to religion per se but to homosexuality; this distancing was one way to cope with the complexities of sin and guilt imposed by a rigid 'Christian' morality. Nevertheless, Pasolini remained deeply affected by his Catholic upbringing and was aware that his Marxism was very close to Christian socialism.

Pasolini's complex personality and ideas resulted in a highly original movie that crossed traditional borders of genre and style and breathtakingly combined a political, contemporary reading of the gospel with strong elements of popular religion, Christian iconography and art. The latter is present primarily in the influence of early Italian renaissance painters such as Masaccio and, even more important, Piero della Francesco, whom Pasolini quoted not only in the robes and hats of the priests and Pharisees but also in the opening shot of the pregnant Mary, which refers to Piero's famous *Madonna del Parto* in the Chapel of Monterchi near Arezzo, Italy.

Despite the influence of religious paintings, Pasolini came to see that the 'sacred style' that he had developed in his earlier films *Accattone* (1961) and *Mamma Roma* (1962) did not suit the adaptation of a gospel to the screen. The characteristics of sacred style, such as frontality, symmetry, centering or blank backgrounds, which were derived from Christian iconography, worked well as a means of investing secular stories with deeper, anthropological and even religious layers of meaning. But when used to tell a religious story the sacred style resulted in overload. Pasolini therefore moved to a cinema of 'contamination', which he sometimes also called a 'cinema of poetry'. This cinema combines very different aesthetic concepts which are held together by a governing artistic craftsmanship. In the case of *The Gospel According to St. Matthew* such concepts include cinematic expressionism (as in Carl Theodor Dreyer's *The Passion of Jeanne d'Arc* (1928), one of Pasolini's favourite films), the radical documentary style of 'cinéma vérité', Italian neorealism, poetic and sometimes also magical realism (in the portrayal of Jesus' miracles), and finally, Robert Bresson's ascetic Phenomenological

Realism. This amalgam of inspiring sources and styles resulted in a vibrant portrait of Christ that remains unique in the history of cinema. This Christ is powerful and energetic, tender and soft, enraged and patient, demanding and forgiving, rigorous and merciful, hieratic and human. Accustomed to the softened, sweet Christ figures in devotional art, many critics judged Pasolini's Christ to be too austere: he did not smile enough. This judgement overlooked his rare but striking and highly moving gestures of joy and trust in his Father.

This type of Christ required a special actor. Max von Sydow, whom George Stevens chose for *The Greatest Story Ever Told* (1965) would have suited Pasolini well. Pasolini initially imagined poets such as Yevgeny Yevtushenko or Allen Ginsberg as Christ, but then he himself fell victim to the deeply rooted and highly popular Nazerene style. On this basis he cast the beautiful young Spanish student Enrique Irazoqui as Jesus. Despite his rather traditional 'look', however, Pasolini's Christ is different from all the others, not only in his readiness for conflict and criticism but also in his authority and sublimity. Pasolini's personal attitude to Christ was ambivalent, but the movie itself supports the complex Christology that he himself articulated:

> I do not believe that Christ was the Son of God, because I am not a believer – at least not consciously. But I believe Christ to be divine and I believe there was in him a humanity so great, rigorous and ideal as to go beyond the common terms of humanity.
>
> (quoted in Schwartz 1992: 425)

Pasolini explicitly wanted to present the gospel from the perspective of a believer and to tell the story of Christ as the story of the Son of God (cf. Faldini/Fofi 1986: 82). To succeed in this aim, he aligned himself with the 'soul of a believer' (ibid.):

> I have done everything, to conserve the true essence of Matthew's story, also with a hidden agenda: to attack a certain fanatic Marxism and Laicism. I wanted to understand thoroughly, until I am able to see the religious reality with the eyes of a believer.
>
> (quoted ibid.: 79; translation mine)

But Pasolini himself was not very far away from this imagined believer. In a letter from June 1963 to Alfredo Bini, his producer, he wrote:

> Christ's humanity is propelled by such a strong inner force, by such an unquenchable thirst for knowledge and for verifying

knowledge, without any fear of scandal and contradiction, that with relation to it [i.e. Christ's humanity] the "divine" metaphor crosses the bounds of the metaphorical, to the point that it almost becomes a reality.

(quoted in Gambetti 1964: 20; translation mine)

In following this almost dogmatically correct appraisal of Christ Pasolini did not end with the cross and the burial, but also depicted the final epiphany and commission on the mount (Matt. 28:16–20). And he did not hesitate to include many miracles, even spectacular ones such as the Feeding of the Multitudes or the Walking on Water, which are clearly written from a post-Easter perspective. Pasolini later felt uncomfortable with his miracles; he thought them to be too 'baroque', too explicit. But in his artistic intuition he had found an appropriate way to portray them: in a very simple, direct and nonillusionistic mode, in a gesture of what Heinrich von Kleist termed 'second naivité' in his famous treatise *On the Marionette Theatre* (1810). Pasolini's seemingly simple approach, that uses the 'basic features of movie magic' that had been invented by cinema pioneer Georges Méliès (1861–1938) and his avoidance of special effects, prevent the viewer from misunderstanding the miracles as historical accounts.

Also impressive is his rendering of Jesus' lengthy discourses. In accordance with the scholarly view of the composite nature of the Sermon on the Mount (Matt. 5–7), Pasolini conveys this text in an extended sequence of small preaching units that take place at different times and places, during which Jesus appears only in close-up. In this way, Pasolini establishes the direct relevance of Jesus' words to his viewing audience.

Pasolini's powerful and poetic movie revitalises the universal quality of the gospel's message. To give expression and emphasis to this universal quality, he used music both old and modern, both sacred and political, of both western and 'third world' origins. With its only slight historicization in costumes and decoration, Pasolini avoided the trap of a forced 'historical correctness' and instead succeeded in conveying the sense that his story is both timeless and eternal.

In its insistent advocacy for the poor, for justice and equality and its emphatic criticism of violence and suppression, Pasolini's 'gospel' in retrospect seems not only to be deeply rooted in the dialogue between Christianity and Socialism, but also to anticipate liberation theology, which later found its starting point in Gustavo Gutierrez's book

A Theology of Liberation (1971). At the same time as his film draws attention to the gap between the rich and the poor, the powerful and the powerless, Pasolini's dedication of the movie to the memory of Pope John XXIII also sends a message of hope that Christianity may be a force for good in the present time.

Reinhold Zwick

Further reading

Franca Faldini and Goffredo Fofi (eds) (1986) *Pier Paolo Pasolini – Lichter der Vorstädte*. Hofheim: Wolke Verlag.

Giacomo Gambetti (ed.) (1964) *Il Vangelo secondo Matteo. Un film di Pier Paolo Pasolini*. Mailand: Garzanti.

Naomi Green (1990) *Pier Paolo Pasolini. Cinema as Heresy*. Princeton, NJ: Princeton University Press.

Barth David Schwartz (1992) *Pasolini Requiem*. New York, NY: Pantheon Books.

Nao Steimatsky (1998) 'Pasolini on Terra Sancta: Towards a Theology of Film'. *The Yale Journal of Criticism* 11: 239–58.

Reinhold Zwick (1997) *Evangelienrezeption im Jesusfilm*. Würzburg: Echter.

——(2008) 'Imaginationen des Heiligen Landes im Bibelfilm'. *Jahrbuch für Biblische Theologie* 23: 203–22.

Further viewing

La Ricotta (Pier Paolo Pasolini, 1963)
Teorema (Pier Paolo Pasolini, 1968)

GRAN TORINO (2008)

[Production Company: Matten Productions, Double Nickel Entertainment, Gerber Pictures, Malpaso Productions, Media Magik Entertainment, Village Roadshow Pictures, WV Films IV, Warner Bros. Pictures. Director: Clint Eastwood. Screenplay: Nick Schenk. Cinematography: Tom Stern. Cast: Clint Eastwood (Walt Kowalski), Christopher Carley (Father Janovich), Bee Vang (Thao), Ahney Her (Sue).]

At first glance, *Gran Torino*, Clint Eastwood's dissection of racial enmity and the changing economic contours of a once booming blue-collar Michigan suburb would not seem to be a prime candidate for a treatise on the interrelation between the Bible and film. The protagonist, a retired Ford worker who bemoans the influx of largely Hmong immigrants into his formerly all-white neighbourhood, has no use for the Bible. The Bible is not explicitly cited in the film – no one is seen reading it, citing from it, or even using it as a prop. That the Bible is nevertheless present, however, is intimated by the allusion to Psalm 18 in the opening scene, in which Benedetto Marcello's early eighteenth century composition 'Psalm XVIII' is heard in the film soundtrack. This allusion occurs at just the moment that we are first introduced to Walt Kowalski. Walt is standing at the front of a Roman Catholic church at the funeral of his wife, and, characteristically, snarling at the irreverence shown by his grandchildren, one of whom has her navel pierced and exposed and texts on her mobile phone during the service, and the triteness of the baby-faced priest, Father Janovich, who begins the service by defining death as 'a bittersweet occasion'. The words of King David's ode to God for having delivered him from his enemies and enabling him to accede to the royal throne have at best a tangential connection to the film. Walt has a contempt for the church – he attended only out of devotion to his wife – and refuses to go to confession. In this light, King David's attestation that 'The Lord is my rock, and my fortress, and my deliverer … in whom I take refuge' (Ps. 18:2) is out of character for a man suspicious of outside intervention of any kind. He is estranged from his mercenary family – his sons want to move him to a retirement home so that they can sell his house, and his granddaughter is set on inheriting Walt's prized 1972 Gran Torino – and hostile to his Hmong neighbours, whom he calls 'damn barbarians', 'jabbering gooks', 'zipperheads' and 'slopes'.

Aside from legitimate scholarly and ecclesiastical debates about the moral purity of David – his eight marriages and an adulterous relationship with Bathsheba (and subsequent murder of her husband, Uriah the Hittite), opportunism, savagery in battle and bad parenting hardly make him a positive role model – he was nevertheless a God-fearing man who made Jerusalem the capital of Israel, transferred the ark of the covenant there, embarked on a military expansion policy which transformed Israel into the greatest power in the region of Palestine and Syria, evoked loyalty and unity among the twelve tribes, and was favoured by God. His importance extended beyond his place in Israelite history, as it is from David's lineage that the Messiah was to come (Ps. 89:4). With some justification, David celebrated the fact that 'The Lord rewarded me according to my righteousness; according to the cleanness of my hands he recompensed me. For I have kept the ways of the Lord, and have not wickedly departed from my God' (Ps. 18:20–21). One would be hard pressed to equate David's achievements with those of Walt Kowalski who hardly has clean hands after his experiences in Korea, which continue to afflict him. As he explains to his teenage Hmong neighbour, Thao, Walt has 'got blood on [his] hands' and is 'soiled'. Unlike David, Walt cannot declare: 'I was blameless before [God], and I kept myself from guilt' (Ps. 18:23).

That said, the David of Psalm 18 is hardly a pacifist. Albeit with God's sanction, David pursued his 'enemies and overtook them; and did not turn back till they were consumed' (Ps. 18:37). To a point, this applies also to the plot of *Gran Torino* which, like Eastwood's *Unforgiven* (1992), is a meditative, but nonetheless highly graphic, testimony to the cost, personally, societally and even theologically, of violence. In *Gran Torino*, the violence is primarily gang-related. At the beginning of the picture, Thao is in danger of falling in with the local Hmong gang that count some of Thao's relatives among its members. In order to be initiated into this gang, Thao has to steal Walt's Gran Torino. Throughout, the gang torment Thao and his family; finally they rape his sister, Sue.

Without exactly disobeying his priest, who counsels him against retaliation, Walt finds a way (through self-sacrifice) of vanquishing the gang, thereby exercising the vengeance. By this point in the film, Walt has made his confession to Father Janovich and has become a father-figure to Thao and Sue. Technically, then, like King David, Walt has triumphed over Thao and Sue's adversaries, who have become his own. As in the words of the psalm, 'I thrust them through, so that they were not able to rise; they fell under my feet' (Ps. 18:38).

The film, however, does not play this triumph out completely, for it is Walt who, literally, falls to his (own) death. At the final confrontation with the gang, he is shot when he reaches into his jacket pocket. The gang members believe he is about to pull a gun, and no doubt Walt intends them to think so. But all he is armed with is a cigarette lighter. Metaphorically, for both Walt and King David, it is the 'assailants' who 'sink' (Ps. 18:39), and both could say, with some justification, that 'those who hated me I destroyed' (Ps. 18:40). Walt has found a way of eliminating the gang without any further bloodshed and without involving Thao. As a policeman points out to Thao at the end of the picture, the gang will be locked up for a very long time. Ironically, in his earlier films such as the *Dirty Harry* (1971–88) franchise, the Eastwood protagonist had no qualms about using his .44 magnum to dispatch those who assail or threaten him.

We see a similar, but far more nuanced, delineation at work in *Unforgiven*, where Eastwood's William Munny certainly administers violence, to the point of killing a number of unarmed men in the saloon shootout at the end of that picture. In *Torino*, however, Eastwood's character does not dispense violence. He receives it. The violence in *Unforgiven* is driven by a quest for purity and justice, and it comes at a heavy personal price, leading to Munny's isolation and exile. In *Gran Torino*, by contrast, the violence – Walt's sacrifice – has no intrinsic value but is merely a means to an end: the salvation of the neighbourhood. Violence may be part and parcel of Eastwood's oeuvre over the decades, but there is something more theologically profound at work in *Gran Torino* than either in *Unforgiven* (Vaux 1999: 109–20; Jewett 1999: 147–61) or in the barbarism that legitimates David's attack. King David may ostensibly be doing God's work, but the effect is the same as when Dirty Harry cleanses the San Francisco streets of those who terrorize the helpless. David's cause may be higher than Harry's, more virtuous and transcendental in scope, but both figures operate on the principle that it is good to eradicate the enemy by violent, and retributive, means (cf. Ps. 18:47–48). In *Gran Torino*, however, there is a surprisingly nuanced dimension at work, whereby it is the guilt and other negative effects of violence that come to the fore.

Ironically, therefore, despite being a film that appears to pay merely lip service to the institutions and structures of religion, *Gran Torino* turns out to be a theologically efficacious work. As in *Mystic River* (2003) and *Million Dollar Baby* (2004), Eastwood situates contemporary moral questions (retributive justice and euthanasia, respectively) within an explicitly Catholic framework. *Gran Torino*'s explicit themes may pertain to race, immigration, multiculturalism, masculinity, violence, gang culture, vigilantism, tradition and ageing, but the allusion to Psalm 18 in the organ music that is heard during the film's opening scene opens up a surprisingly rich, if inconsonant and critical, engagement with core Old Testament notions of justice and war. The film also engenders questions of healing, redemption and sacrifice which tie in well with other biblical passages and characters.

On one level, *Gran Torino* could be interpreted as a familiar Hollywood staple in the Ebenezer Scrooge mould whereby a lonely, caustic, misanthropic older man is transformed into someone with compassion and virtue (as in *As Good as it Gets* [1997]). Sara Vaux, however, has also recently likened Walt Kowalski to Nicodemus. Vaux argues that 'Walt shifts from a stagnant person into Nicodemus, someone ready to be reborn into the lives of Sue and her family in a forward-moving journey toward confession and release' (Vaux 2011: 181; cf. John 7:50–51; 19:39). Once Walt lets his defences down he is able to see the healing benefit of confession, admitting to the priest he had earlier derided, that he has never been close to his two sons and that he has committed other misdemeanours that have stricken him with guilt.

A superficial reading may also suggest that the theme of atonement is present in this film. Thao's mother makes him work for Walt by way of making amends for the attempt to steal his car. Thao has to repay his debt by working for the man he wronged, in a manner that seems congruent to Leviticus 25:25 where redemption specifically takes the form of money payments for the recovery of property. This approach has its limitations, however. The Hmong family are not practising Christians but have a very different culture and way of life. The film suggests that their family is much stronger and richer than Walt's own. Whereas Walt's sons and grandchildren begrudge having to turn up to their mother and grandmother's funeral and wake, the children of the family next door value and participate gladly in the Hmong ritual – the child blessing ceremony – that is taking place at the same time as the funeral for Walt's wife. Later, when the Hmong shaman correctly discerns that Walt has unresolved unhappiness from his past, Walt mutters to himself that he has 'more in common with these gooks' than with his own 'rotten, spoiled family'. To attempt to read the film through a limited, Western, Christo-centric lens would be to miss the point. For the Hmong, mountain people of South East Asia, and later for Walt, it is not one tradition nor the holy book of one particular faith that supplies all of the answers.

There is a legitimate debate to be had over whether the film's symbolism remains within the realm of Christianity. This most readily applies in the 'vengeance' scene in which the gang shoots Walt as he reaches into his pocket for his lighter. Not only is his death a sacrifice of self so that others may live, but as he falls, his arms are outstretched in cruciform pose, and a trickle of blood flows from a wound in his hand. This imagery might be taken to suggest that Walt Kowalski has joined the ranks of those other cinematic Christ-figures who die in order that others might live (e.g. Lucas Jackson [Paul Newman] in *Cool Hand Luke* [1967], Randle P. McMurphy [Jack Nicholson] in *One Flew Over the Cuckoo's Nest* [1975]; Kozlovic 2004; Deacy 2008).

But the Christ-comparison is not the film's overarching focus. Rather than reduce Walt to the structural patterns or correlations of the central figure of one tradition, a more effective New Testament parallel is the Good Samaritan of Luke 10:25–37. The parable insists on the importance of helping one's neighbour, even if, and especially when, that neighbour hails from a different cultural, ethnic, class, social or religious background. Both Walt and the Samaritan of Luke's Gospel demonstrate compassion, perhaps unexpectedly so. Samaritans were outcasts in the ancient world. For a Samaritan to come to the aid of a man on the road from Jerusalem to Jericho 'who fell among robbers, who stripped him and beat him, and departed, leaving him half dead' (Luke 10:30), is about as unpredictable as Walt Kowalski, now the lone white face, and a bigoted one at that, in an ethnically diverse, racially dysfunctional neighbourhood, putting his life on the line in order to protect Thao and Sue. The film explicitly asserts that it is not words that will secure freedom from sin and guilt – it is actions that matter, up to and including the ultimate act of putting one's life on the line.

Significant though these parallels might be, a final word of caution is warranted. If the Bible is truly significant in this film, one may ask why few reviewers or interpreters of the film, outside of explicitly religious texts or websites, have uncovered them. Perhaps *Gran Torino* is really about the relationship between a man and his car, which is not an insignificant theme, according to two documentaries that appear on the DVD on American car culture. One of them, *Manning the Wheel*, is quite literally about men and their penchant for cars; the second documentary also comments on the 'special bond' between men and their vehicles. It is worth thinking about the possibility that films which aim to reach a popular audience and to wrestle with issues that are at the kernel of biblical and other religious texts may have to downplay or perhaps even camouflage the religious, theological and/ or biblical elements in these films. This possibility may serve as a salutary warning, to those biblical or theological commentators intent on finding Christ-figures and other biblical resonances in film, that such approaches, for good or ill, have yet to find currency outside of more specialized theological and biblical circles.

Christopher Deacy

Further reading

Christopher Deacy (2008) 'The Pedagogical Challenges of Finding Christ Figures in Film', in G. Watkins (ed.) *Teaching Religion and Film*, Oxford: Oxford University Press. pp. 129–40.
Robert Jewett (1999) *Saint Paul Returns to the Movies: Triumph over Shame*. Grand Rapids; Cambridge: Eerdmans.

Anton K. Kozlovic (2004) 'The Structural Characteristics of the Cinematic Christ-Figure', *Journal of Religion and Popular Culture* 8(1), available online at www.usask.ca/relst/jrpc/art8-cinematicchrist.html (accessed 24 August 2011).

S. A. Vaux (1999) *Finding Meaning at the Movies*. Nashville: Abingdon Press.

——(2011) *The Ethical Vision of Clint Eastwood*. Grand Rapids: Eerdmans.

THE GREATEST STORY EVER TOLD (1965)

[Production Company: United Artists. Director: George Stevens. Screenplay: George Stevens and James Lee Barrett, from the book by Fulton Oursler, and the writings of Henry Denker. Cinematography: William C. Mellor and Loyal Griggs. Music: Alfred Newman. Cast: Max von Sydow (Jesus Christ), Charlton Heston (John the Baptist), Dorothy McGuire (Virgin Mary), José Ferrer (Herod Antipas), Richard Conte (Barabbas), Martin Landau (Caiaphas), David McCallum (Judas Iscariot), Claude Rains (Herod), Ed Wynn (Old Aram), Shelley Winters (Woman of No Name), Telly Savalas (Pontius Pilate), Donald Pleasence (The Dark Hermit/Satan), John Wayne (Roman Centurion), Joanna Dunham (Mary Magdalene), Joseph Schildkraut (Nicodemus).]

Accused of being overlong, overslow, overdramatic, and overstuffed with Hollywood stars, a commercial failure blamed for setting back the Hollywood Jesus film (Channel Four *Jesus Christ Movie-Star* 1992), George Stevens' *The Greatest Story Ever Told* was, nevertheless, a thoughtful, atmospheric, and quietly compelling meditation on the life of Christ, with an evocative film score, impressive locations, some powerful and distinctive acting, and some very fine scenes.

The film begins in a low-key way with credits slowly displayed to the sound of a reflective and untriumphalist music score. A voice-over intones the words of John 1:1 ('In the beginning was the Word, and the Word was with God, and the Word was God'), the first of many references to the Fourth Gospel. The face of Max von Sydow, the actor playing Jesus, appears in a Sistine Chapel ceiling painting. Aesthetically arresting images of the traditional birth story (dismissed by critics as 'picture-postcard') are presented, before political reality in Roman Judea imposes itself and the camera pans over scenes of violence, rape, and ritual slaughter.

The voice of John the Baptist is heard while the camera soars over grand canyons before it focuses in on John as he baptizes (in the frigid Colorado River). Jesus appears for baptism, and we are treated to penetrating close-ups of the two men. The Arizona Rockies are then shown to good effect as Jesus faces temptation at the hands of the genial, civilized and quietly reasonable dark hermit, Satan. Further vistas are opened up as the preaching of John echoes again over the terrain, literally illustrating the chorus from Handel's Messiah: 'Every valley shall be exalted, and every mountain and hill shall be brought low' (Isa. 40:4). A choral climax with Jesus on top of a promontory ends the scene, and the greatest story ever told has truly begun.

With another three and three quarter hours to run, the film has time to develop familiar elements of that story drawn from all four Gospels: Jesus' Teaching of his Disciples, The Woman Taken in Adultery, Salome's Dance, The Sermon on the Mount, The Investiture of Peter, Jesus' Rejection at Nazareth, The Raising of Lazarus, Jesus' Teaching in the Temple, The Last Supper, Judas' Kiss, The Trial before Caiaphas, The Trial before Pilate, Peter's Denial, The Crucifixion and the Resurrection.

Camera man-turned-director and academy-award winner, George Stevens was responsible for such classic films as *A Place in the Sun* (1951), *Shane* (1953), *Giant* (1956) and *The Diary of Anne Frank* (1959). Stevens had established a formidable reputation for himself before he turned to *The Greatest Story Ever Told*, a film 'he surely intended … as the signature work of his brilliant career', according to Charlton Heston, whose autobiography recounts that chilly baptismal experience in Glen Canyon (Heston 1995: 297). A perfectionist, with a deep Christian conviction, Stevens had been preparing for the project for some years and was given a free hand by United Artists to develop it.

The American poet and historian Carl Sandburg (1878–1967) was involved in the writing of the script and, while the dialogue is occasionally banal (in the Last Supper scene, for example, Jesus addresses his disciples as those 'who have walked with me down all those dusty roads'), it is also, on occasion, beautiful, poetic and subtly nuanced, or sharp and arresting: 'Baptist, I have orders to bring you to Herod' to which the Baptist responds: 'I have orders to bring you to God!'; 'Which God is he supposed to be the son of?', asks Pilate before Jesus is arraigned before him; 'The whole thing will be forgotten in a week', says Caiaphas, when news of the disappearance of Jesus' body is reported to him. 'I wonder', says Nicodemus.

In contrast to other characters, Jesus' language, as also that of Heston's John the Baptist, is largely inspired by the King James Version of the Gospels. In one scene, however, at the Raising of Lazarus, von Sydow was allowed to improvise a particularly striking prayer, which is compiled from passages such as Exodus 15:11, Deuteronomy 32:39 and Ezekiel 37:9:

Who is like thee, O Father in heaven, majestic in holiness, mighty in wonders, terrible in glorious deeds? Who can deliver out of thy hand? For you wound, and you heal. You kill, and you make alive. Come, ye four winds, and breathe upon this man, that he may live.

As with most Christ films based on the Bible, *Greatest Story* often conflates materials from all four Gospels. Lazarus, for example, is presented as the scribe of Mark 12:34 ('You are not far from the Kingdom of God, Lazarus') as well as the rich young ruler (Mark 10:17–22). As previously mentioned, the script draws particularly on John's Gospel. Jesus uses the imagery of light in his speech in the Temple, for example, and at the Last Supper, the words of this Gospel are used to amplify the Synoptic account considerably. Uniquely, too, Stevens' Jesus appropriates Paul, by reciting 1 Corinthians 13.

Like other directors before him, but to the point of obsession, Stevens drew on centuries of Christian art, poring over classical paintings of Christ, and drawing inspiration from the most celebrated traditional models. In the Last Supper scene, for example, Jesus and the disciples are seated at a long table, in a line, as in Leonardo da Vinci's famous painting. The music accompaniment to the film was provided by the American composer, Alfred Newman (1900–1970), who composed the scores for many Hollywood musicals. Frequently subtle, subdued or unobtrusive, his music is extremely effective in creating the film's atmosphere.

Filmed in Arizona, California, Nevada and Utah, the settings give the film a monumental feel. Canyonlands National Park (Moab, Utah), for example, was the location for The Sermon on the Mount, and such dramatic settings recall the great big-sky Westerns of the Hollywood cinema, especially of course Stevens's own *Shane* (Babington and Evans 1993: 141).

The pace throughout the film is slow, even stately, with frequent close-ups of Jesus' and the disciples' faces. The film's slightly other-worldly atmosphere is particularly apparent in the Raising of Lazarus, where the juxtaposition of light and darkness, sound and silence, create a memorable effect. The crucifixion takes place almost in slow motion, lending a meditative as well as a reverent quality to the event, although John Wayne's centurion and his American-accented 'Truly, this man was the Son of God!' introduces a risible element into an otherwise moving scene.

Some memorable performances also characterize the film. Jesus' nobility of character, firmness of purpose, certainty of mind, and sadness of spirit are conveyed well by von Sydow. Few have represented John the Baptist with such power and vigour as Charlton Heston.

Acting as Jesus' alternative inner voice, Donald Pleasence's bald, portly, middle-aged Satan (the Dark Hermit), with his mixture of humour and menace, and his specious advocacy of the good life, has never been so colourfully portrayed. Telly Savalas as Pilate, Martin Landau as Caiaphas and Claude Rains as Herod the Great also give creditable performances.

It is in the Temptation scene perhaps that clues are most conspicuously offered with respect to the film's historical, social, cultural and religious context. 'Long hard climb, wasn't it?', Pleasence's Satan says to Jesus, with commiseration, as he reaches the summit, and the hermit's cave. And then with geniality, naturalness and a quiet reasonableness,

> Come on in, if you like. Some think the whole of life should be hard like that. An easy life is a sinful life. That's what they think. Not so. Life should be as easy as a man can make it.

Von Sydow's Jesus responds to him in a more formal, scripted way, however, citing the Hebrew Bible throughout in reply to his blandishments, and stiffly rejecting the force of his rationalism and secularism with a spirituality that characterizes the mystical, Byzantine Christ portrayed so powerfully by the actor.

Set against a gigantic orange moon that enhances their effect (a feature that will reappear in Mel Gibson's *The Passion of the Christ* Gethsemane sequence), the traditional temptations of the Synoptic narratives are each presented to the viewer, though in a different order from that of Matthew and Luke. The hermit first offers Jesus food, which is the first temptation in both Synoptic accounts; then the world, which is the third Matthean/second Lukan temptation (cf. Matt. 4:8–10; Luke 4:5–8); then the temptation to throw himself down from the height (the second Matthean/third Lukan temptation, set in the temple (cf. Matt. 4:5–7; Luke 4:9–12); and finally, the temptation to turn stones into bread, which is again the first Matthean and Lukan temptation (cf. Matt. 4:3–4; Luke 4:3–4).

Some have seen in the natural phenomena presented here – gigantic moon, desolate wilderness, striking vistas, high mountain, hermit's cave, etc. – the trial of Jesus as the 'natural man' pursuing 'the Emersonian ideal of self-reliance, so important not only to American literature and ideology but to the Western movie genre as well' (Stern *et al.* 1999: 158–9). The inclusion in the temptation sequence formed by the motif of 'food' and 'bread' highlights, however, the emphasis on the nature of evil as submission to the seductive power of materialism.

Where ideology and social context are concerned, therefore, Babington and Evans are right to comment:

> At a time of growing counter-culture revulsion against materialist and consumerist excess, it seems logical, where conventionally devout audiences might equate the diabolical with pride and rebellion against the creator, that for more socially critical Christians and others the Devil should rather be identified with materialism and its consequences.
>
> (1993: 143)

'The film is very much one with 1960s ideals of meditation and inner change as the responsibility of the individual', they declare, and 'evil is portrayed through images of comfortable, middle-class conformism' (144).

Despite its obvious merits, Stevens' film failed to do well at the box office, giving it an undeserved place among all-time box-office flops. Made for an estimated $20 million, by December 1969, it had grossed only $12 million worldwide, according to The Internet Movie Database. Such a return was virtually a death warrant for the genre, at least until the 1980s when the biblical epic (e.g. *King David*, [1985]) or the Christ film (e.g. *The Last Temptation of Christ*, [1988]) began to make a limited reappearance.

Audience response was apathetic and impatient with its length and pace. In consequence, the film's running time was reduced. Originally 260 minutes, it was cut eventually to 197 minutes for British audiences and 190 minutes for American ones (Butler 1969: 155–56). Critics, too, were scathing. Though appreciative of its many strengths, 'an opulent, empty film which lacked the thing it needed most to succeed – inspiration', was Butler's overall estimation (Butler 1969: 156), while others were much less generous (see Hochman 1974: 408–10). One critic, Philip T. Hartung, thought that the film lay midway between 'a masterpiece' and 'a disaster' (Tatum 1997: 99).

Time, however, has mellowed these reactions and the film is given higher estimation now than it was by its first spectators and critics. On 29 September 2011, for example, 3,623 Internet Movie Database users had given it a weighted average vote of 6.3/10. Frequent television screenings, and the availability of the film on DVD and other electronic media, have brought it anew to contemporary audiences who have come to appreciate its fine cinematography, its dramatic settings, its splendid scenes, the fine acting by its principals, its reflective and meditative treatment of the Christ story, and its delicate treatment of religious sensitivities, especially its treatment of Jews and Judaism.

William R. Telford

Further reading

Bruce Babington and P. W. Evans (1993) *Biblical Epics: Sacred Narrative in the Hollywood Cinema*. Manchester: Manchester University Press.
Ivan Butler (1969) *Religion in the Cinema*. New York, NY: Barnes.
Charlton Heston (1995) *In the Arena. The Autobiography*. London: HarperCollins.
Stanley Hochman (ed.) (1974) *A Library of Film Criticism. American Film Directors. With Filmographies and Index of Critics and Films*. New York, NY: Ungar.
Adele Reinhartz (2007) *Jesus of Hollywood*. New York, NY: Oxford University Press.
Richard C. Stern, Clayton N. Jefford, and Guerric DeBona (1999) *Savior on the Silver Screen*. New York, NJ: Paulist.
W. Barnes Tatum (1997) *Jesus at the Movies: A Guide to the First Hundred Years*. Santa Rosa, CA: Polebridge.
William R. Telford (1997) 'Jesus Christ Movie-Star: The Depiction of Jesus in the Cinema', in C. Marsh and G. Ortiz (eds) *Explorations in Theology and Film. Movies and Meaning*. Oxford: Blackwell. pp. 115–39.

Further viewing

Channel Four (10 April 1992) *Jesus Christ Movie-Star*

THE GREEN PASTURES (1936)

[Production Company: Warner Bros. Pictures. Directors: Marc Connelly, William Keighley. Screenplay: Marc Connelly (based on the novel 'Ol' Man Adam an' His Chillun' by Roark Bradford). Cinematography: Hal Mohr. Cast: Rex Ingram (Adam / De Lawd), Oscar Polk (Gabriel), Eddie 'Rochester' Anderson (Noah), Frank H. Wilson (Moses), Myrtle Anderson (Eve), Ida Forsyne (Ms. Noah).]

The Green Pastures tells several stories from the Hebrew Bible/Old Testament and one from the New Testament. The biblical stories include the creation of the earth (Gen. 1), Eve and Adam (Gen. 2–3), Cain and Abel (Gen. 4), Noah (Gen. 6–9), Moses' call, his negotiation with Pharaoh, his death, and the arrival of the Israelites at the Jordan river (Exod. 3–12; Deut. 34), the treatment of a prophet in Babylon, and the crucifixion. The film is based on the successful Broadway play, *The Green Pastures*, which Marc Connelly, a white American man, wrote and adapted from Roark Bradford's novel 'Ol' Man Adam and His Chillun' (1928). The play ran for five years with 1,779 performances from 1930–35, and won the Pulitzer Prize in the first year. The all-black cast played in racially segregated theaters throughout the United States. When the cast travelled in racially segregated southern cities, the actors stayed with African American families and in segregated hotels, ate at black-only restaurants, and sometimes played before white-only audiences, which provoked protest from local Black organizations such as the National Association for the Advancement of Colored People (NAACP).

The film was one of the most successful films of 1936. It was a top ten film in the New York Times and listed among the Best American Films in the National Board of Review. Nevertheless, critics often agreed that the film paled in comparison to the play, in which Richard B. Harrison, a highly regarded and mesmerizing actor, played the main character, De Lawd. His acting presence made *The Green Pastures* a 'classic' (Daniel 1986: 1). In 1931, Harrison had received the NAACP's prestigious Spingarn Medal recognizing him as the most influential African American during that year. When he died in March 1935, the play also died. While the play appeared in the United States only, the film was also shown abroad, but several countries, such as Italy, Latvia, China, and Australia, banned the film, not for its racist portrayal of African Americans but for what they believed was a blasphemous characterization of God.

The reliance on an exclusively African American cast for the representation of biblical characters is relatively unique in the history of film, but it is also controversial. After all, as Connelly explained, his play attempts 'to present certain aspects of a living religion in the terms of its believers ... thousands of Negroes in the deep South' (Connelly 1958). To many contemporary critics, this statement hints at the manifold stereotypes about African American religiosity, life, and culture perpetuated in the film, and slots its characters into familiar stereotypical roles of Uncle 'Toms, Coons, Mulattoes, Mammies, and Bucks' (Bogle 2007). Today, the film is barely known and rarely seen. Interestingly, the DVD version begins with a disclaimer by the production company, reminding viewers that films 'are a product of their time' and that the apparent racial and ethnic prejudices displayed in the movie have to be understood accordingly; they 'reflect a part of our history that cannot and should not be ignored' even though they 'are wrong today'.

Since the first appearance of the play in 1930 and the film in 1936, opinion about *The Green Pastures* has changed significantly. While white critics and commentators praised the play as a major contribution to American theater into the 1960s (Cordell *et al.* 1935; Barnes 1969), reviewers of the post-Civil Rights era exposed the film's racial stereotypes and racist assumptions as a reflection of American society and culture (Evans 2008), especially the century-long tradition of blackface minstrelsy (Bogle 2007). Commentators also observed that the play helped white Americans to escape economic despair and disillusionment during the time of the Great Depression and to immerse themselves into the 'faith and hope and simple beauty' projected onto Southern black life and religion (Daniel 1986: 2). They noted that the play ignored the brutal lynchings and blatant segregation in the South (Evans 2008) and that play and film alike portray African Americans as simple-minded, pious, and submissive Uncle Toms, living obediently and quietly the lessons of their faith. Consequently, the film must be understood as an 'allegory of accommodation' produced during an era in which 'the plantation genre peaked in appeal and popularity' (Winokur 1995: 7; see, e.g. *Jezebel* [1938] or *Gone with the Wind* [1939]). As such, both play and film signify 'ghettoization and segregation' in the United States (Winokur 1995: 8).

The first scene shows a grandpa and his grandson ringing the church bells; slowly, the Sunday school teacher and his pupils gather for their weekly Bible study. The Sunday school class frames the film, linking the interspersed biblical stories into a coherent narrative. The teacher, Mr. Deshee, introduces the biblical stories with references and images from the lives of the children in his class. He tells his students that God looks like their preacher, Heaven is the place of a big and happy fish fry, and, except for white flowing clothes and wings, the angels look like the members of their congregation. The next scene leaves the Sunday school behind and shows God joining the fish fry festivities of his angels. Meanwhile 'The Hall Johnson Choir', which debuted as the 'Hall Johnson Negro Choir' in 1928, sings spirituals in the background. Then, on a whim, God creates the sun and earth out of firmament. Soon God realizes that he made good farmland and, leaving Heaven through a big white plantation gate, he goes down to earth to welcome Adam. God is pleased about his creation and decides that Adam needs a 'family'. Adam agrees ('Yes, Sir') and as God calls her name, Eve instantly appears right next to Adam. God tells them to behave themselves 'cause you both a new kind of experiment with me and I ain't sure you can make it'. When God visits earth again, Cain already slaughtered Abel. Increasingly,

God despairs about his creation, even as his confidante, the Archangel Gabriel, tries to cheer him up. God is not consoled: 'Even being God ain't no bed of roses.'

Throughout the film, God is the central character, gradually realizing that the idea of mercy through suffering applies even to him: 'Did he mean even God must suffer?'. This God is not omniscient but learns in the interaction with his creation, an idea reminiscent of Carl Jung's *Answer to Job* (Collins 1991). Overall, then, the film promotes the idea of suffering as being redemptive (a classic plantation doctrine) and portrays African Americans as joyful, carefree, and simple people who are endowed with a deep yet harmless religiosity (Evans 2008). Read within the historical-cultural context of American slavery and racial discrimination, the film reinforces resignation rather than resistance to structures of domination. It advances 'plantation christianity' and not 'slave christianity' (Winokur 1995: 8).

Yet the storyline does not merely center on the anthropomorphic God. It also stresses the increasing depravity of humanity. The issue is dramatically highlighted in a scene that depicts the Babylonian king. He is surrounded by beautiful women and well-clothed and leisurely smoking men, and a few women dance provocatively in short silky dresses before him. He orders his entourage to 'shoot down' an Israelite prophet after the prophet condemned the excesses of Babylonian life and empire. In this scene, staging and costumes resemble a 1920s Harlem nightclub, thus visually equating the 'depraved' lifestyle in Babylon with African American urban life in the North (Winokur 1995: 11).

The film's climax is Jesus' crucifixion. When God sits pensively in the large garden surrounded by the crowd of angels, the concerned Archangel Gabriel inquires if God is alright. God explains that he reflects on the notion that mercy comes from suffering. Then one of the angels looks down to earth from behind the closed gates and exclaims: 'They are going to make him carry it up that high hill. They are going to nail him to it. That's a terrible burden for one man to carry.' God's eyes suddenly brighten, he smiles and exclaims: 'Yes!' Yet Christ himself remains invisible, physically absent, and merely imagined. He represents the ultimate authority figure because '[t]he audience is aware of Him only through the realization of de Lawd, who sees/feels the drama of the crucifixion as a kind of new transcendental awareness of charity'. Invisibility signifies power and its impact is felt by the empathetic God and his angels, African-Americans all. Absent yet present, Christ is like the white film-maker and white America, the 'masters' whose orders have to be obeyed though they are never seen in the film. Hence, 'this offscreen, intangible Christ' must also be understood as 'a representative of plantation Christianity' (Winokur 1995: 14–15). The last scene returns us to the Sunday school. The little boy who helped pull the bell in the first scene is now sleeping in the arms of his grandpa in the pose of a pieta in which the boy is Christ and the grandfather the Madonna. Film critic Morris (2008) suggests that 'Connelly actually confuses' viewers with this last scene because it seems as if 'the little black boy [is] now Christ'. Or does Connelly's last scene suggest that Christ's suffering and death is like 'a comfortable nap in Uncle Tom's arms after a boring but harmless Bible lesson' (Morris 2008)?

In the end, *The Green Pastures* is not a vehicle for racial reconciliation in America; neither does the film offer a non-sexist future. Male characters predominate and the few women rarely if ever speak or act in meaningful and non-stereotypical ways. The film also promotes a heterosexist agenda by stressing family life, for instance, in the retelling of the Eve and Adam and Noah stories. Certainly, the film presents an infantilizing and demeaning African American religiosity; it blends out the real-life challenges of racial oppression, lynching, segregation, and poverty that African American communities faced on a daily basis prior to, during and after the 1930s. Connelly's retelling of the Bible made it safe for white American audiences to watch African Americans without feelings of guilt or fear. Requests for reparation or repentance from white society are absent and African Americans are depicted as forgiving and kind. After all, the film's message is that they learned mercy through their suffering. As such, *The Green Pastures* is a must-see film for understanding the historical, cultural, and religious pervasiveness of racism in the United States, as promoted in American film and biblical interpretation.

Susanne Scholz

Further reading

Clive Barnes (1969) *50 Best Plays of the American Theatre*. New York: Crown Publishers.

Donald Bogle (2007) *Toms, Coons, Mulattoes, Mammies, and Bucks: An Interpretive History of Blacks in American Films*. 4th ed. New York: Continuum.

Brendan Collins (1991) 'Wisdom in Jung's Answer to Job', *Biblical Theology Bulletin* 21(3) (Fall): 97–101.

Marc Connelly (1958) *The Green Pastures: A Fable Suggested by Roark Bradford's Southern Sketches, 'Ol' Man Adam an' his chillum'*. New York: Holt, Rinehart and Winston.

Kathryn Coe Cordell, William H. Cordell and William Lyon Phelps (1935) *The Pulitzer Prize Plays, 1918–1934*. New York: Random House.

Thomas Cripps (1977) *Slow Fade To Black: The Negro in American Film, 1900–1942*. New York: Oxford University Press.

Walter C. Daniel (1986) '*De Lawd': Richard B. Harrison and The Green Pastures*. New York: Greenwood Press.

Curtis J. Evans (2008) 'The Religion and Racial Meanings of *The Green Pastures*', *Religion and American Culture* 18(1) (Winter): 59–93.

Alan Gevinson (ed.) (1997) *Within Our Gates: Ethnicity in American Feature Films, 1911–1960*. Berkeley: University of California Press.

G. S. Morris (2008) 'Thank God for Uncle Tom: Race and Religion Collide in *The Green Pastures*', *Bright Lights Film Journal* 59, available online at www.brightlightsfilm.com/59/59greenpastures.php

Mark Winokur (1995) '*The Green Pastures* as an Allegory of Accommodation: Christ, Race, and the All-Black Musical', *Film & History* 25(1–2): 6–16.

Further viewing

Halleluja (King Vidor, 1929)
Jezebel (William Wyler, 1938)
Gone with the Wind (Victor Fleming, 1939)

INDEPENDENCE DAY (1996)

[Production Company: 20th Century Fox. Director: Roland Emmerich. Screenplay: Roland Emmerich, Dean Devlin. Cinematography: Karl Walter Lindenlaub. Cast: Will Smith (Captain Steven Hiller), Bill Pullman (President Thomas J. Whitmore), Jeff Goldblum (David Levinson), Mary McDonnell (First Lady Marilyn Whitmore), Judd Hirsch (Julius Levinson), Robert Loggia (General William Grey), Randy Quaid (Russell Casse).]

The highest grossing film of 1996, and a veritable cultural phenomenon at the time of its release, *Independence Day* combines a number of cinematic genres, narratives, and themes which can be traced, directly or indirectly, to the Bible. The focus of this discussion will be on *Independence Day* as a disaster film, and on one of its main narrative themes: retribution.

Independence Day deals with an alien invasion taking place between 2 July and 4 July. On 2 July, a gigantic alien mother ship enters the Earth's atmosphere, releasing smaller spaceships that hover over the Earth's major cities. Computer expert David Levinson discovers the transmission signal which the aliens are using to plan their attack.

He and his father Julius are able to warn the American President, Thomas J. Whitmore, and together they make a narrow escape after the aliens destroy Washington DC, Los Angeles and other major cities around the world. On 3 July, a counterattack led by Captain Steven Hiller is launched. The attack fails and Hiller is the only pilot who survives, after crash landing his plane in the desert. He manages to capture one of the aliens. In the desert, he is picked up by a group of survivors led by the supposedly alien-abductee and crop-duster pilot Russell Casse. Hiller, with the captured alien and its spacecraft, and Casse rejoin the President and his entourage at Area 51, where they learn about the plans of the aliens. A nuclear attack on an alien spacecraft over Houston fails and the President and his daughter visit the fatally injured First Lady in hospital, where she dies from her injuries. On 4 July, Levinson comes up with the idea of attacking the mother ship with a computer virus. Together with Captain Hiller, he embarks on the mission to plant the virus in the mother ship's main computer. The mission succeeds and the activated virus causes a malfunction in the alien's defense system. Combined forces around the world launch the decisive and successful attack against the alien invaders.

Given *Independence Day*'s alien invasion storyline combined with scenes of destruction on a massive scale, the film fits within two important genres: science fiction and the disaster film. The late 1990s saw a rash of disaster/apocalyptically themed films released by Hollywood. In his book *Disaster Movies: The Cinema of Catastrophe*, Stephen Keane formulates a definition of the genre of disaster films, and in particular the films that were released in the 1990s. Keane's observations are certainly pertinent to *Independence Day*. The disaster films of the 1990s, Keane argues, cannot be read and understood without 'reference to previous disaster cycles or, conversely, the altogether hyperbolic pro-spect of imminent doom' (2001: 73). Since most films, including *Deep Impact* (1998), *Armageddon* (1998), *End of Days* (1999), and another Emmerich film, *Godzilla* (1998), were released by the end of the decade, this cycle of disaster films was labeled 'millennial movies'. The success of the disaster films of the late 1990s can be explained by several factors. The most important factor, argues Keane, was that they 'tapped into the "pop millenarianism" of the time; the tabloid stories, television documentaries and best-selling books which effectively worked in turning "anxiety" into "interest"' (2001: 74).

In the opening scene of the film, the apocalyptic tone is immediately set by the use of REM's song 'It's the end of the world as we know it (and I feel fine)' (1987). The foreboding nature of the song is maintained for the first quarter of the film, in which the aliens hover close to Earth while waiting to strike. Interestingly enough, once the news of the aliens coming is broken, the story focuses not so much on possible impending doom, but on the jubilant responses to the visitors. Especially in Los Angeles, huge crowds are ready to welcome the supposedly friendly aliens.

The film's most obvious use of apocalyptic imagery emerges once the evil nature of the aliens has been established. Much has been made of the film's impressive use of computer generated imagery (CGI), particularly in the scenes depicting the destruction of the White House, New York and Los Angeles. *Independence Day*'s imagery of destruction is indeed impressive, though straightforward. More importantly, the destruction has strong biblical connotations. The alien invaders announce themselves shrouded in a cloud of smoke and fire. The first appearance takes place over the desert of Iraq, and soon the alien invaders are spotted around the world. *Independence Day*'s smoke and fire imagery is strongly reminiscent of Exodus 13:21 as well as of the book of Revelation, where fire is the dominant motif for destruction (compare Rev. 16:8, 'the angel poured his bowl on the sun, and it was allowed to scorch them with fire'). The film's most impressive scenes involve gigantic waves of fire, rolling in slow motion towards unfortunate people as well as the film's spectator.

If *Independence Day*'s representation of destruction has biblical connotations, the selection of those who survive and those who perish is equally biblical. Destruction is selective and moralistic, echoing the book of Revelation, which emphasizes the pure and the elected (compare Rev. 14:4) versus those who are beyond salvation. John Shelton Lawrence and Robert Jewett have called this idea of moral selection the 'retribution principle'. In a large number of disaster films, and *Independence Day* is no exception, there is a relationship between the violation of sexual mores and punishment by the forces of nature: 'The contemporary images of disaster parallel those biblical stories in which the pattern of retribution for sexual infidelity and frivolity is deeply embedded' (2002: 314). The retribution principle follows archaic biblical conventions, as Lawrence and Jewett argue: 'sin brings disaster, while virtue brings success and escape from disaster' (2002: 315).

Three characters are most explicitly connected to sin in *Independence Day*. All are women. One of them is able to redeem herself, while the other two are not. This gendered aspect of retribution has not gone unnoticed by other theorists of the genre, who identify the misogynistic tendencies of many disaster films. In *Independence Day*, female sin is unambiguously coupled to the institution of marriage.

The most obviously sinful character is Tiffany (Kiersten Warren), who is a good friend and colleague of Jasmine (Vivica A. Fox). Both women work as exotic dancers, but while Jasmine is saved by a last minute marriage to Hiller, shortly before he and David go on the mission to plant the virus in the alien mothership, Tiffany is the first to die when the aliens attack Los Angeles. Marriage thus functions as a way to re-subordinate the woman, and those who defy marriage are eventually punished. This same dynamic is evident in Hosea 2:19, in which God tells Israel: 'And I will take you for my wife forever; I will take you for my wife in righteousness and in justice, in steadfast love, and in mercy', and in Ezekiel 16, where marriage is used as a metaphor for the relationship between God and his people. In the film, this pattern is illustrated by the character of First Lady Whitmore (Mary McDonnell). Her marriage to the President has gone cold; they are not together when the President flees Washington, DC. The First Lady survives the attack, but later succumbs to her injuries, after she has confessed her sin as an independent or wayward wife.

Furthermore, one of the more prominent male characters unceremoniously killed in the first half of the film, is also the most feminine male character. David's gay boss, Marty (Harvey Fierstein), is killed in the attack on New York; he is caught in a wave of fire while neurotically shouting at his therapist on the phone in his car. The scene is played for laughs, thereby fueling the criticism that gay characters in mainstream twentieth-century Hollywood cinema are often the objects of ridicule (Russo 1987). Within the parameters of the retribution principle, Marty's death is consistent, since, as a gay man, he cannot be saved by marriage.

The one male character capable of redeeming himself, after being ridiculed by everyone in the film, is the alcoholic Vietnam veteran Russell Casse (Randy Quaid). His redemption is achieved through the act of self-sacrifice: he flies his plane into the heart of the alien mothership, thereby delivering the final blow. The act of self-sacrifice can be read within the framework of Revelation. Russell's voluntary death echoes Revelation's martyrs who chose to die for a righteous cause, although the comparison between Russell and the martyrs of Revelation (compare Rev. 6:9–11, where the martyrs appear for the first time in some detail) is implicit rather than explicit.

Russell's character can be read, however, within the discourse of Hollywood's appropriation of the Apocalypse and the act of self-sacrifice. The Hollywood appropriation of martyrdom situates it in the larger context of the redemption of humankind, which can be achieved by preventing the Apocalypse. The Hollywood martyr sacrifices his or her life in order to save the whole of humanity (Copier 2011). However, if one looks more carefully, saving mankind often serves as a pretext for the redemption of the martyr's nearest family. Contrary to classical conceptions of martyrdom, which confine the act within the limited definition of a willingness to die for one's belief, Hollywood's reworking of martyrdom is connected to the reconciliation and continuation of the family. Russell, the improbable hero, defeats the aliens, saves mankind, but most of all, through death, earns the respect of his three children.

The reconciliation of the family is also represented in less extreme terms through the character of Julius (Judd Hirsch), David's father. If *Independence Day* eschews direct references to Judeo-Christian morals, values and traditions, this character stands out as the film's only truly religiously motivated character. Julius, who lost his faith after his wife died, continues to be a caring father to David, unwittingly helping David to come up with the virus strategy against the aliens. In turn, David consolidates his father's religious re-awakening by handing him the Torah and a yarmulke shortly before he goes on his mission with Steven. *Independence Day*'s message of unity in the face of evil is repeatedly exemplified in the film's blatant glorification of the United States as the world's leading superpower. On a smaller scale, however, religious unity is propagated by Julius leading prayers while being under attack. One of the bystanders is pulled into the circle of prayer by Julius. When he stammers he 'is not even Jewish', Julius deadpans him by replying, 'Nobody's perfect'. In a film fixated on presenting dichotomies (aliens versus humans, believers versus non-believers, sinners versus the redeemed, the chosen ones versus the doomed ones), this short scene offers a much-needed, albeit small, glimpse of religious inclusion in the face of extraterrestrial adversity.

Laura T. Copier

Further reading

Laura T. Copier (2011) *Preposterous Revelations: Visions of Apocalypse and Martyrdom in Hollywood Cinema 1980–2000*. Sheffield: Sheffield Phoenix Press.

Stephen Keane (2001) *Disaster Movies: The Cinema of Catastrophe*. London: Wallflower.

Geoff King (2000) *Spectacular Narratives: Hollywood in the Age of the Blockbuster*. London: I.B. Tauris.

John Shelton Lawrence and Robert Jewett (2002) *The Myth of the American Superhero*. Grand Rapids: Eerdmans.

Michael Rogin (1998) *Independence Day*. London: BFI.
Vito Russo (1987) *The Celluloid Closet: Homosexuality in the Movies*. Rev. ed.
New York: Harper and Row.

Further viewing

Mars Attacks! (Tim Burton, 1996)
War of the Worlds (Steven Spielberg, 2005)

INTOLERANCE: LOVE'S STRUGGLE THROUGH THE AGES (1916)

[Production Companies: Triangle Film Corporation, Wark Producing. Producer:
D. W. Griffith. Director: D. W. Griffith. Screenplay: D. W. Griffith. Cinematography:
G. W. Bitzer. Music: Joseph Carl Breil. Art Director: Walter L. Hall. Cast:
Lillian Gish (Woman Rocking the Cradle), Mae Marsh (the Dear One),
Robert Harron (the Boy), Vera Lewis (Ms. Jenkins), Howard Gaye (Christ
in the Judean story), Alfred Paget (Prince Belshazzar), George Siegmann
(Cyrus), Tully Marshall (The High Priest of Bel).]

As the title suggests, Griffith's 1916 film is about intolerance through
the ages, and love's capacity to overcome it. *Intolerance* tells four parallel
stories: the conquest of Babylon by Cyrus, Jesus's persecution by the
Pharisees in Judea, the Huguenots' persecution by the Medicis, and a
modern love story in the face of corporate control. All four stories
work together to argue against the control of populations, against war
and against the violent suppression of populations. The film ends with
a scene of millennial peace, in which war and killing are ended and
love triumphs. In all but the modern romance, however, love does
not actually overcome intolerance, but is thwarted by it. The modern
story, prioritizing love in the nuclear family, is therefore designed
to give the last word. It also carries the bulk of Griffith's political
message – a critique of censorship.

Intolerance offers Griffith's defensive reaction to the demands for
censorship of his earlier very successful but deeply racist film, *Birth of a
Nation* (1915) (Rogin 1989: 518–20; Hansen 1991: 164). In 1916,
Griffith published a pamphlet in response to the criticism of *Birth*, and
to the attempts to censor it. Entitled *The Rise and Fall of Free Speech
in America*, the pamphlet defends *Birth* and connects intolerance to
censorship throughout. The heading 'Intolerance: The Root of All
Censorship' appears on almost every other page. He writes,

'Curtailment of individual liberty is the curse of the nation.' Censorship is a far worse national ill in Griffith's mind than slavery and racism. Even though the film weighs in against the violent suppression of populations, its most vigorous argument, against censorship, is clearly meant to further the racializing work of Griffith's earlier film. In this light, the use of biblical themes in the film is somewhat troubling, as they are meant to exonerate his earlier work. They also help to set out his ambitions for American film as a universal language able to end intolerance. The association of tolerance with racism discloses the limits of that discourse. Although Griffith's notion of intolerance seems completely different than our own, his film was an important voice in the development of tolerance discourse, which continues to create insiders and outsiders – those who tolerate and those who are tolerated (Jakobsen and Pellegrini 2003: 50–66).

The Judean story is the shortest of the four parallel tales. The purpose of the Judean story seems primarily to align Griffith's project with Jesus, and thereby to give it biblical authority. The Judean story is the second to be introduced, following the modern story. Beginning only seven minutes into the film, it helps to frame the entire film. An intertitle sets the stage: 'Ancient Jerusalem, the golden city whose people have given us many of our highest ideals, and from the carpenter shop of Bethlehem, sent us the Man of Men, the greatest enemy of intolerance.' Griffith reminds the viewer that the work of the film is like the work of Jesus. Its images of hypocritical Pharisees who seek attention when they pray are akin to the film's other intolerant censoring characters, such as the modern story's social reformers. Adele Reinhartz points out that Griffith made some effort to diminish the anti-Semitic depiction of the Pharisees, in response to protests by B'nai Brith, which resulted in cutting scenes of the Pharisees crucifying Jesus, leaving only twelve minutes remaining (1998: 10).

The Babylonian story is the most elaborate in terms of cinematic spectacle, perhaps because it relays Griffith's aspirations for film as a universal language. Lillian Gish, Griffith's favored actress, reports that he called film 'a great power that had been predicted in the Bible as the universal language … [which] was going to end wars and bring about the millennium' (cited in May 1980: 73). In her autobiography, Gish recalls that when Griffith began filming *Intolerance*, he said, 'I've always said I would rebuild Babylon for you. Now I'm going to do it' (1969: 165). The Babylon story celebrates the medium of film, with its hugely elaborate set, costume design and choreography. As film scholar Miriam Hansen has pointed out, one of the intertitles at the beginning of Act II states (inaccurately) that with the destruction of Babylon, 'a universal written language (the cuneiform) was made to become an unknown cypher upon the face of the earth'. This intertitle makes the connection between the lost universal language of Babylon and Griffith's hopes for the medium of film (1991: 183–4). Babylon is depicted as a wondrous place of religious tolerance, aesthetic luxury, and sexual openness, indicating what Griffith had in mind when he advocated for tolerance.

In the Babylonian story, the empire tragically falls because of religious intolerance. Belshazzar, the religiously inclusive ruler of Babylon, is betrayed to Cyrus of Persia by insiders. Upset over Belshazzar's worship of Ishtar, the goddess of love and war, the High Priest of Bel opens the city gates in the wee hours of the morning, after the city has spent itself celebrating the success in repelling Cyrus's first siege. Griffith's portrayal of Babylon runs contrary to the biblical text, where Belshazzar is depicted as an arrogant and blasphemous enemy of Yahweh (Dan. 5) and Cyrus as the great liberator of the Israelites from Babylon (Ezra 1, Isa. 45). In *Intolerance*, however, Belshazzar is the hero, and Cyrus the villain. Belshazzar is tolerant, an 'apostle of religious freedom', trying to establish a universal religion. Cyrus, by contrast, was loyal to Shamash, the sun God. Griffith idealized Babylon as a lost space of religious universalism and tolerance because he felt that with demands for censorship, film was under attack – not unlike Babylonian language and the Babylonian vision for universal religion.

As William Drew points out, Griffith was making liberal use of scholarship on Babylonian religion. Scholarship of his time suggested that Belshazzar's father, Nabodinus, had tried to create a more universal and centralized religion of Marduk (1986: 43). It was thought that Babylon was betrayed from the inside by those who opposed this innovation, and, like Cyrus, preferred a system of local deities. Griffith embellished this historical hypothesis, substituting Belshazzar for Nabodinus, Ishtar for Marduk, and regarding Cyrus as a villain. He also borrowed religious iconography from scholarship, but on ancient Assyria, rather than Babylon. The reliefs used by Griffith to ornament the great Babylonian hall are similar to those found at the ancient Assyrian palace of Ashurnasirpal II at Nimrud in northern Iraq. These included a stylized tree of life, winged human-headed deities, and eagle-headed winged figures.

Freedom to pursue a more tolerant universal religion' is associated in Griffith's Babylon with the pursuit of pleasure and sexual freedom. The worship of Ishtar is visualized in extended orientalizing scenes of scantily clad women dancing and languishing in the 'Temple of

Love'. In Griffith's idyllic world of Babylon, people are not controlled by laws. They are allowed to pursue their own pleasures and interests, sexually and religiously. Access to pleasure was central to Griffith's imagination of cinema, and he paired it with religious and sexual openness as a way of arguing against the censorship of film. Griffith appears to be advocating for a world in which pleasure and access to sex are easily available and not curtailed by law.

Nonetheless, there is ambivalence toward Babylon in *Intolerance* that serves to orient the viewer to appreciate the modern story's outcome. As film critic Russell Merritt points out, even though ancient Babylon is portrayed positively, its pleasures are the cause of the city's downfall, since its night of revelry and feasting means that there is no one available or sober to protect the city when it is betrayed. Merritt writes, 'The spectacle of this city has a divided purpose: to reveal the pleasures of glittering sumptuousness and to repeat one all-powerful commandment: "Don't"'. (1979: 20). The pursuit of pleasure is both desired and judged. Babylon does not censor pleasure but comes to harm because of it. The world of Babylon is, ultimately, not to be emulated.

In contrast, the happy ending of the modern story suggests that contemporary society may have at its disposal the resources to right Babylon's error. It appears that those resources are film and the family. Both allow the viewing public safe pleasures, decadence without the consequences. The modern story prioritizes access to pleasure, but it also offers the family as the most fulfilling way to pursue pleasure. It treats social reformers as parallel to Babylon's anti-Ishtar (anti-pleasure) Babylonian High Priest of Bel. Against a backdrop of social unrest caused by capitalist exploitation of workers, social reformers try to legislate away pleasure, including dancing, prostitution, and alcohol. Ms. Jenkins works with a team of Vestal Virgins to advocate laws for social reforms. Their reforms interfere with the lives of the other characters, including the two central characters, the Boy (Robert Harron) and the Dear One (Mae Marsh), who meet, fall in love, marry, and have a child. The Boy and the Dear One are continually separated by various plot twists – many caused by the reformers' meddling – until the very end. Critics have noticed the way in which the modern story prioritizes the nuclear family form, idealized in the successful heterosexual pairing of the Boy and the Dear One (Hansen 1991, Rogin 1989).

Intolerance was not a box office success. Reviewers found it too experimental, and jarring in its innovative parallel cutting. The most famous critique of *Intolerance* came from Sergei Eisenstein. Eisenstein acknowledges his debt to Griffith's cutting style in developing his own distinctive Soviet technique of montage, but felt that *Intolerance* failed to achieve its unifying metaphor. In his view, montage should create a dialectical 'unity, which in the inner stress of contradictions [between juxtaposed disparate shots] is halved in order to be re-assembled in a new unity on a new plane, qualitatively higher, its imagery newly perceived' (1977: 235–36). Montage produces a set of contradictions that are sublated into metaphor, rather than remaining in the realm of representation (1977: 241). In other words, ideally, the contradictions would indicate to the viewer that a larger metaphor or commentary was being offered, one that went beyond the representation of people and places in the storyline. In Eisenstein's judgement, Griffith was not able to make the historical parallels work together metaphorically; he 'made no attempt at a genuinely thoughtful abstraction of phenomena – at an extraction of generalize conclusions on historical phenomena' (1977: 244). For Eisenstein, Griffith's work does not depart from the bourgeois structure of the Dickens' narratives that he emulated. Rather, 'the montage concept of Griffith, as a primarily parallel montage, appears to be a copy of [Dickens'] dualistic picture of the world, running in two parallel lines of poor and rich toward some hypothetical [and never realized] "reconciliation"' (1977: 235). Eisenstein wanted film to comment on and radically provoke change to these kinds of social divisions, not simply to reinforce them by representing them.

Despite these faults, or perhaps because of them, *Intolerance* deeply influenced the development of classic Hollywood film style. The film also forged the continued association of Hollywood with Babylon and the film industry with luxury and pleasure. As a testament to this fact, the Hollywood Highland Center Mall in Los Angeles – built in 2001 and now a major tourist destination – reproduces parts of Griffith's set in its 'Babylon Court'. The mall is also home of the Kodak Theater, where the Academy Awards take place. In Babylon Court, a replica of just one of Griffith's huge double arches in the great hall of Babylon frames the Hollywood sign. The walls and floors are adorned with the faux-Babylonian reliefs used by Griffith. Babylon Court celebrates Hollywood glamour and spectacle, as well as the consumerism that Hollywood generates. It is unlikely that many people shopping in Hollywood's Babylon Court pause to consider the ideological origins of Griffith's project to advance film as a universal language and to limit censorship. It is worth noting, however, that the film history chosen to help sell merchandise is bound up with a defense of racism in the name of tolerance and the use of scripture to authorize this point of view.

Erin Runions

Further reading

William M. Drew (1986) *D.W. Griffith's Intolerance: Its Genesis and Its Vision*. Jefferson, NC: McFarland and Co.

Sergei Eisenstein (1977 [1944]) 'Dickens, Griffith, and the Film Today', in *Film Form: Essays in Film Theory*. San Diego, CA: Harcourt.

Lillian Gish (1969) *The Movies, Mr. Griffith, and Me*. Englewood Cliffs, NJ: Prentice-Hall.

Miriam Hansen (1991) *Babel and Babylon: Spectatorship in American Silent Film*. Cambridge, MA: Harvard University Press.

Janet Jakobsen and Ann Pellegrini (2003) *Love the Sin: Sexual Regulation and the Limits of Religious Tolerance*. New York, NY: New York University Press.

Lary May (1980) *Screening Out the Past: The Birth of Mass Culture and the Motion Picture Industry*. Oxford: Oxford University Press.

Russell Merritt (1979) 'On First Looking into Griffith's Babylon', *Wide Angle* 1: 12–21.

Adele Reinhartz (1998) 'Jesus in Film: Hollywood Perspectives on the Jewishness of Jesus', *Journal of Religion and Popular Culture* 2(2), available online at www.unomaha.edu/jrf/JesusinFilmRein.htm.

Michael Rogin (1989) 'The Great Mother Domesticated: Sexual Difference and Sexual Indifference in D.W. Griffith's *Intolerance*', *Critical Inquiry* 15(3): 510–55.

JESUS CHRIST SUPERSTAR (1973)

[Production Company: Universal. Director: Norman Jewison; Screenwriters: Melvyn Bragg, Norman Jewison; Tim Rice (book); Cinematography: Douglas Slocombe; Music: Andrew Lloyd Webber, Tim Rice (lyrics); Art director: John Clark. Cast inc.: Ted Neeley (Jesus); Carl Anderson (Judas); Yvonne Elliman (Mary Magdalene).]

Jesus Christ Superstar is the story of a reluctant Messiah, a misunderstood martyr. The movie depicts the religious authorities and the government in collusion, sordid gain and greed serving as the covenant between them. Jesus contests this state of affairs in the Gospels and in the movie, as evidenced by the 'Cleansing of the Temple' scene in the movie which depicts all manner of modern paraphernalia for sale: postcards, drugs, female bodies, weapons, guns, and grenades. Cash registers ring up the merchandise; mirrors abound, in true 1970s fashion. But notice also the 'ancient stuff' – camels, sheep, and birds. Jesus knocks it all over. And the point is made concerning then and now: when a person contests the sites of religious, political, social, and economic power, he or she will be crucified. In the midst of his rampage in the temple, the religious establishment looks on, preferring expediency and longevity over truth (see Dostoevsky's 'The Legend of the Grand Inquisitor' in *The Brothers Karamazov*).

The movie opens silently in the desert of Israel. Immediately we are exposed to one of the movie's primary techniques: the blurring of the lines between the ancient context and the contemporary, as we see the ruins of an ancient compound flanked by modern scaffolding. In the distance we see a bus advancing; it has words in both Hebrew and Arabic on the side, perhaps alluding to the Six Day War of 1967. The cast, with their 70s hair and clothing, pours out of the bus abuzz with upbeat energy and smiles, even as they unload a giant cross from the roof of the bus. This opening recalls the beginning of Mark's Gospel, which likewise opens in a desert and foreshadows Jesus' crucifixion (1:4, 8).

The first three minutes also present and provide impressions about the characters. Mary Magdalene, an exotic-looking woman who has an Asian or Native American look about her, is already putting on make-up. Herod, who will appear as an effeminate, dangerously silly and hedonistic character, is brushing his hair. Pilate is donning impressive imperial robes. Judas, a black man, is already in his red costume and has separated himself from the group, looking upon them with a disdainful, superior eye. The priests have donned black robes and black hats and stand outside the circle. An 'inner circle', literally, forms, surrounding Jesus who stands in the center. Those in the inner circle dance in a way that signifies worship and homage. The Roman soldiers, dressed in purple muscle shirts, silver helmets, and brandishing spears, also stand outside the circle but opposite the religious authorities. The positioning of the characters places the Romans, the Jewish religious authorities, and Judas in the same negative category, anticipating their collusion against Jesus later in the movie.

Just before the five-minute mark, Jesus dons the white robe that is the usual uniform of the cinematic Christ; we view him from the back, his blonde, long-haired self raising his arms to the sun as the music of the *Jesus Christ Superstar* theme song plays in the background. Then we see his face – it is a transcendent, powerful, awe-inspiring scene. The cast takes its place on the set of the ruins and then the title of the movie appears on screen.

The movie is heavy on characterization and conflict. The characters drawn most strongly are Jesus, Judas, and Mary Magdalene; Pilate, Herod and Caiaphas and their minions are also vividly portrayed. The intensity of the characters and their relationship to one another is conveyed especially through eye contact. The conflict centers most forcefully on the relationship between Jesus and Judas. Indeed, Judas takes on the oppositional role played by Satan in the Gospels. He tries at every turn to tempt Jesus to abandon his destiny. Where Jesus is associated with white clothing, white skin, and light, Judas is black-skinned and wears red, a colour often associated with Satan.

The movie conflates the Gospel accounts of Judas and thereby creates a composite character (see John 6:71; 12:4; 13:2, 27, 29, 31; 14:22; 18:2, 3, 5 and Matt. 27:3–10). The Judas of *Jesus Christ Superstar* is a much more sympathetic character, especially in the social context of the 70s in the US. Judas is the stereotypical, pragmatic revolutionary. He signed on to a movement that would transform society through grass-roots organizing against 'the man'. He then sees the movement getting carried away, pushing the boundaries too hard, too fast. He calls for a stripping away of 'the myth from the man'. He asks Jesus (ironically?): 'Listen, Jesus, don't you care for your race?'

Race plays a crucial, if ambiguous, role in the film. What does race mean, in the time of Jesus, the Gospels, or the 1970s hippie era? What is Jesus' race? And what does race mean when a black man confronts a white man, when both have American accents and are acting out the roles of first-century Jews? The issues of race and war, specifically, the Vietnam war, intermingle, as Judas stands in the scorching heat in front of five army tanks.

Despite his self-righteousness, Judas is confused. The priests play on his concern for the poor. As in the Synoptic Gospels, Judas betrays Jesus with a kiss (Mark 14:45; Matt. 26:49; Luke 22:47). Filled with remorse, Judas goes to the authorities and returns the money, understanding that his name will be forever associated with betrayal. In a heartbreaking moment, he sings the song of his foil, Mary Magdalene, 'I Don't Know How to Love Him' and wonders if Jesus loves him. At that moment, he hears the sounds of Jesus being nailed to the cross; he runs to the desert as the darkness covers the land and laments that he has been used by God, anticipating Jesus' own song later in the Garden. The camera work becomes wildly choppy, the music is stressful, and he runs to a tree and hangs himself with the rope from his waist while screaming at God, 'You have murdered me!' The image of a black man hanging from a tree sickeningly recalls the lynchings so strongly associated with the fight for civil rights in the US.

Judas reappears later in white robes, apparently resurrected before the Crucifixion takes place. He is flanked by many white-outfitted, scantily clad women as they all sing the *Jesus Christ Superstar* theme song. The scene flashes back and forth psychedelically between the dancers and Golgotha.

Not only does Jesus have a conflicted relationship with Judas throughout the movie, he also appears in tension with the rest of the disciples as well. They are presented as self-absorbed, navel-gazing groupies who lack a sense of understanding, drive, or purpose. They want to be part of a 'copacetic' movement that positions them well, allows them to drink wine, peace-out, and be famous someday by association with a person who really does sacrifice dearly, unto death, even if they themselves eschew the notion of deep sacrifice. They are wannabes. Jesus says of them: 'Men like you can be so thick and slow.'

As his remark about the slowness of the disciples shows, the Jesus presented in *Jesus Christ Superstar* is exceedingly human. He is often, though not always, impatient, tortured, and irritated with those around him. In the Sermon on Mount he smiles and has children on his lap. He then experiences the devotion of the crowd. The dancers are, once again, in contemporary clothing and are shown dancing in slow motion. Jesus smiles appreciatively but sees the Roman soldiers advancing in the background, their silver helmets and spears gleaming in the sun. The camera flashes to Judas who appraises it all with a distressed look. Jesus glances from Judas to the Romans, knowingly, and sings 'Neither you Simon, nor the 50,000; nor the Romans nor the Jews; nor Judas nor the Twelve, nor Judas, nor the priests nor the scribes, nor doomed Jerusalem itself, understand what power is, understand what glory is, understand at all, understand at all.'

After the Cleansing of the Temple scene, a tortured, tired Jesus walks alone to a dry, rocky area. In the midst of his anguished plaint/Passion prediction, people in need of healing pour forth from the rocks demanding healing. He is overwhelmed by their need and demand. He does touch and heal them (one of the few times that miracles enter the plot) but there are just too many.

The Garden of Gethsemane scene constitutes the turning point for Jesus. He has it out with God:

> Then I was inspired; now I'm sad and tired … Surely I've exceeded expectations … Let them hate me, hit me, hurt me, nail me to their tree … Show me there's a reason for your wanting me to die … Watch me die. See how I die.

In the midst of his angst, the film flashes forward to various depictions of the crucifixion. Jesus then meets his fate by Judas' kiss; he is tried by Pilate, interviewed by Herod, and crucified. At the end of the film, all the actors, except the one who played Jesus, quietly, pensively, load the bus and leave. Jesus glides across the screen faintly before the sun. The music falls silent. The credits roll.

Mary is perhaps the most ambiguous character in the film. She is appealing because she is so real, so conflicted, so vulnerable, such a round character, unlike, say, Peter, who is rather flat. Her signature piece, 'I Don't Know How to Love Him', is a powerful song of the heart's knowing, of real transformation. She is the one character throughout the movie who remains truly devoted to Jesus, even when she does not fully understand what that means or what it might cost. She is mistreated by Judas, who castigates her, or at least her 'profession', at every turn. Jesus defends her, with a reference to John 7:53–8:11 (the so-called story of 'the adulteress woman'), by challenging Judas or anyone else to throw stones at her. Jesus seems to appreciate her attention to his physical needs, to 'what I need right here and now', but belittles her by mentioning how she 'prattles through her supper'. It is important to note, however, that this depiction of Mary Magdalene, like much of the film's characterization of Judas, has no basis in scripture (Clark-Soles 2010a: 35–42; Clark-Soles 2010b). Contrary to the Gospels themselves, Mary Magdalene has become a mulatto whore who is a site of contest between two alpha males, here a black one and a white one.

The film raises some important social and theological questions. Particularly troubling to some viewers has been the negative portrayal of Caiaphas and the Pharisees, which may reinforce the stereotypes of Christian anti-Semitism (Humphries-Brooks 2006; Reinhartz 2007: 197–22). Questions of race are also a concern, given that Jesus is white with an American accent while Mary, the sexualized Other, is not white and Judas, the betrayer, is black. Those familiar with the Bible will take issue with the way the movie conflates the materials of the canonical Gospels, especially during the Passion scenes. On the other hand, the movie is appealing for the way it brings the ancient story to life and helps us to imagine these people as real people, with mixed motives, bodies that sweat, yearn for sex, get sleepy after too much wine, and die. Mary is loving and devoted and willing to embrace a mystery that exceeds her present knowing. Judas reminds us that we all have mixed motives and are prone to fooling ourselves; most of us become scared when the stakes get too high. Also compelling is the intermingling of past and present, suggesting that the struggles of this ancient, reluctant messiah, continue to be relevant to the present.

The movie depicts Jesus as a man struggling, as we all must someday, with his perceived destiny. This Jesus is no 'God-striding-across-the-earth' as depicted in the Fourth Gospel. The scene in the Garden is poignant. His closest companions fall asleep repeatedly in his darkest hour while he has it out with God. He is exhausted and unsure, his brow furrowed and his face sweaty and weathered. He succumbs to God's will but without a sense of triumph; rather it is a Jobian moment of 'and though he slay me, I will trust in him' (Job 13:15). This fact disturbs some, though for others it is the very element that provides a 'way in' to the Jesus story.

Some find in *Jesus Christ Superstar* a mere cultural artifact; others a political statement that still enjoys some relevance. Still others experience the movie as an existential journey of sorts. Without a doubt, *Jesus Christ Superstar* continues to captivate and provoke viewers.

Jaime Clark-Soles

Further reading

Jaime Clark-Soles (2010a) *Engaging the Word: The New Testament and the Christian Believer.* Louisville, KY: Westminster John Knox Press.

——(2010b). 'Introducing the Real Mary Magdalene', in *Teaching the Bible*, the Society of Biblical Literature, available online at http://sbl-site.org/ educational/TBnewsletter.aspx (accessed November 2010).

Stephenson Humphries-Brooks (2006). *Cinematic Savior: Hollywood's Making of the American Christ.* Westport, CT: Praeger. pp. 55–67.

Adele Reinhartz (2007) *Jesus of Hollywood.* New York, NY: Oxford University Press.

Jeffrey L. Staley and Richard Walsh (2007) *Jesus, the Gospels, and Cinematic Imagination: A Handbook to Jesus on DVD.* Louisville, KY: Westminster John Knox Press.

JESUS OF MONTREAL (1989)

[Production Company: France: Centre National de la Cinématographie, Gérard Mital Productions; Canada: Max Films Productions Inc. National Film Board, Super Ecran, Téléfilm Canada. Director: Denys Arcand. Screenwriter: Denys Arcand. Cinematographer: Guy Dufaux. Major Cast Members: Lothaire Bluteau (Daniel Coulombe), Catherine Wilkening (Mireille), Johanne-Marie Tremblay (Constance), Rémy Girard (Martin), Robert Lepage (René), Gilles Pelletier (Father Leclerc).]

Jesus of Montreal combines the genres of Jesus film and Christ-figure film. Jesus films retell the story of Jesus in 'historical' terms, based on the canonical Gospels (e.g. *King of Kings* [1961], *Jesus of Nazareth* [1977]).

Christ-figure films portray a hero resembling Jesus and/or theological conceptions of Christ, for example, as redeemer, saviour, suffering servant. The Christ-figure is a rich source of imagery, since both the bible and Christian tradition contain myriad images and symbols that can be expressed in movie characters and plots.

In the film, a band of five underemployed Montreal actors, led by the charismatic Daniel Coulombe, are engaged by a Catholic priest to update a passion play, a series of Gospel scenes traditionally staged during Lent. Although the production is a hit, church officials are outraged at its portrayal of Jesus, and try to shut it down, leading to tragedy for Daniel and his troupe. Daniel becomes a Christ-figure, whose story becomes increasingly identified with that of Jesus.

The Passion play scenes, which are enacted at different points in the movie, claim to depict a Jesus who is closer to the historical figure than are the Gospels, because they are (ostensibly) based on 'recent new discoveries' and 'computer-assisted analysis'. The theologian who advises Daniel claims that his church-funded university will not allow him to publish his findings, so the play will be a way of spreading the truth about Jesus. Ironically, the play is also put on by the church, which is why it is quickly cancelled.

The play makes several surprising, and tendentious, claims about Jesus. He is identified as Jeshua ben Panthera, the illegitimate son of a Roman soldier and Mary of Nazareth. The evidence offered is that Jesus was known as 'son of Mary', not 'son of Joseph'. Since Jewish men of Jesus' time were normally identified by their fathers' names, being called 'Mary's son' might indicate that Jesus had no legal father. Another piece of 'evidence' is a reference to a soldier named Panthera, who was discharged from his post in Galilee in 6 CE. There actually is an inscription on a German tombstone, dated to the first century CE, referring to a Tiberius Julius Abdes Panthera, a Phoenician archer. This, however, hardly constitutes evidence that Panthera was the father of Jesus. Jesus *is* referred to as son of Mary in Mark 6:3 (cf. Luke 4:22), but the accusation that Jesus was 'the bastard of an adulteress' is a slur that arose a century after his death. Possibly, the term 'Jesus son of Panthera' is a corruption of the phrase *Iēsous huios parthenou* ('Jesus son of a virgin'). The usual explanation of the title 'son of Mary' is that Joseph had died by the time Jesus reached adulthood.

Another portrayal of Jesus supposedly based on scholarship is that he was a magician, whose attraction for people was primarily his ability to cure illnesses and work wonders – even to raise the dead. This claim may be based on Morton Smith's *Jesus the Magician* (1978), which

compared the Gospel stories of Jesus as a miracle-worker to contemporary accounts of magicians and sorcerers, considered unsavoury
characters in antiquity. In Judaism, magic was seen as a kind of witchcraft
that relied on demonic spirits; in Mark, the accusation that Jesus performs miracles through the power of Beelzebub reflects this view
(3:22–27). Jesus refutes the accusation by pointing out that Satan
cannot cast out Satan. Although scholars admit that Jesus was a faith
healer and exorcist, they do not see this as his main appeal; rather,
many emphasize his social and theological teachings, such as concern
for the poor, and the kingdom of God.

The most surprising assertion made in the play is that the Gospels
were not written down until 'a hundred years' after Jesus' death.
Although the dating is uncertain, most scholars date Mark at around
70 CE, some 35 to 40 years after Jesus' death, and John, before 100 CE
(60 to 70 years post-crucifixion).

Some aspects of the portrayal of Jesus in the play do reflect scholarly consensus – the idea that the primary content of his teaching was
the kingdom of God, not his own divinity or messianic identity; his
self-identification as the son of man ('human being'). It is true that
crucifixion, portrayed very graphically in the film, was regarded as so
horrific and shameful that the cross was not portrayed in Christian art
for several centuries after Jesus' death (late fifth century CE). The
intense, dark-eyed Daniel shatters the Jesus-film stereotype of Jesus as
'the blue-eyed boy of Bethlehem', and defies the portrayal of Jesus
as a calm, stoical figure with calm foreknowledge of his destiny.

Why does the passion play present such a deceptive view of the
'real' Jesus? The accusation made in the play that the evangelists 'lied'
and 'embellished' could just as well be levelled at the film. The point
of the extreme depiction of Jesus is that 'we think we all know' what
he was all about (as the character Constance says), but most of us have
little basis upon which to judge claims to the contrary. The obvious
fact that the play is *not* the life of Jesus but a performance is made clear
by the elaborate and inventive way it is staged: it takes place at night;
it ingeniously uses different settings, props and lighting; the same
actors play different characters; the lights of Montreal form a backdrop; a
security guard ushers the audience from station to station. As part of a
movie, the play achieves effects that could never be reproduced on
stage. The claim that the Catholic church is hostile to Daniel's passion
play is belied by the fact that St. Joseph's Oratory – a famous Catholic
shrine in Montreal – is one of the main settings of the movie.

While the Jesus of the Passion play is 'demythologized' – ostensibly
purged of legendary and theological elements – the central character

in the film, Daniel, mirrors many traditional Gospel stories, and even apocryphal legends. Like Mark's Jesus, he is a 'mystery man' with an obscure past. Like the young Jesus in Luke and the infancy gospels, he is reputed to have been a child prodigy who graduated first in his class at the Conservatory. Despite great public interest in Daniel, the media never interview him; everything the public knows about him is 'hearsay'. There are rumours that he is a spiritual seeker who visited India and Tibet; similar extra-biblical legends exist about Jesus' early life. When he first meets Constance, Daniel is homeless (Matt. 8:20; Luke 9:58). Like Jesus in traditional art from renaissance paintings to Warner Sallman's famous *The Head of Christ*, he wears white.

Daniel gathers about him a band of disciples who form an alternative family (cf. Mark 3:31–34), and become increasingly devoted to him. The choice of four rather than twelve reflects the number of canonical Gospels, symbolized in the film by the four satiric versions of the Passion play improvised by the actors: *Comédie Française*, Method Acting, Street Slang, Kabuki. The actresses have symbolic names. Constance ('faithfulness') is the mother of the group: she has a daughter, she nurtures Fr Leclerc, and she wears blue, like the Virgin Mary in Catholic art. Most of the meals in the film are associated with her: the soup kitchen, communal breakfasts in her apartment. She also serves as a Martha figure, who serves the others and looks after their bodily needs (Luke 10:38–42). Mireille's name echoes Mary, and her portrayal as sexually exploited identifies her with the tradition of Mary Magdalene as repentant prostitute (a part she acts in the play). Like the Magdalene, she functions as 'apostle to the apostles', encouraging the troupe to remain true to their artistic vision: 'What we have is precious; we have to keep on going'. Her last name, Fontaine ('fountain' – she first appears 'walking on water' while filming a commercial), evokes the image of 'living water' in the story of the woman at the well (John 4).

Other Gospel characters and incidents mirrored in the film include Father Leclerc (a name that literally means 'the scribe'), who is initially supportive of the actors, but like the 'chief priests and scribes', ultimately opts to protect his own position in the service of Rome. The actor in the opening scenes of the film who proclaims Daniel as the 'really good actor' is a John the Baptist figure. The agent who 'wants his head' for her advertising campaign is reminiscent of Herodias, who literally has the prophet beheaded (Mark 6:14–29). The lawyer, Richard Cardinal (whose surname evokes a high official in the Catholic church), plays the Devil (Matt. 4:1–11), who offers Jesus the holy city (Montreal, founded by missionaries) if he will compromise his ideals.

Mireille's beer commercial audition reconfigures the incident of the 'cleansing of the temple' (John 2:13–16), where Jesus overturns the tables of the moneychangers. Daniel, infuriated by the degrading treatment of the women actors, upends the refreshment table, shatters TV equipment, and drives out the leering agents and advertising executives from the studio with a 'whip of cords' made of electrical cables. Daniel/Jesus is arrested and tried by civil authorities ('Pontius Pilate', represented by the judge, played by writer-director Arcand). As in the Gospels, the secular authorities (the judge, the psychiatrist) are easier on Jesus/Daniel than the religious authorities (the priest, the church).

Finally, Daniel/Jesus 'dies' on the cross, after a brief 'resurrection', he 'descends into hell' (the subway); Mireille bends over his body in a classic Pieta tableau. After his death, Daniel offers salvation by literally sharing his body and blood – his organs – with others; he now lives on in them. A doctor proclaims his body a 'Godsend'. The three hospitals where the women take the wounded Daniel are significant: the Montreal General Hospital (secular society) has no room for him; St. Mark's (Christianity) has no time for a human, suffering Jesus; the *Jewish* General Hospital is the one that treats him with human compassion. Daniel is buried in a simple casket; at the bottom, in the whorls on the wood, is the ancient symbol of Christ, the *ichthys*. The disciples decide to build a theatre – their church – to keep the message of Daniel alive. Martin, the movie's Peter figure, will be its first artistic director.

The final scene in the subway, the site of Daniel's death, has two women singing Pergolesi's *Stabat Mater*, a hymn about the grieving Virgin that ends with a resurrection prayer. The upward sweep of the camera culminates in the empty cross on Mount Royal, symbolizing the resurrection hope. In the end, the portrayal of Jesus in the passion play is edgy and challenging, but the Christ-figure Daniel figure is familiar and comforting. The divine figure (Jesus Christ) is demythologized, the human character (Daniel) is mythologized.

This film is Arcand's critique of contemporary Quebec society, a sequel to his *The Decline of the American Empire* (1985). Pre-1960, Quebec was dominated by the Catholic church, founded on traditional values of religion and family, hard work, honesty, respect and hospitality. However, Quebec was also regarded as a cultural and economic backwater. The Quiet Revolution of the 1960s imparted new pride in French language and culture, the growth of entrepreneurship, democratization, social programs, and openness to American culture. Arcand's savage attack on the 1980s decadence in *Decline* lies behind

Jesus of Montreal. Montreal society is portrayed as shallow and corrupt; Daniel preaches a return to the holiness of human existence: salvation must be found within; don't give up hope in the meaningfulness of life; walk in solidarity; forget yourself and love one another; live simply. Daniel's apocalyptic ramblings in the subway, which paraphrase the so-called 'little apocalypse' of Mark 13, prophesy the inevitable downfall of the Quebec outpost of the 'American empire', Montreal. In the end, the film offers salvation in the form of authentic human existence based on values of caring, trust and hope.

Mary Ann Beavis

Further reading

Adele Reinhartz (2007) *Jesus of Hollywood*. New York: Oxford University Press. pp. 31–39.

Richard C. Stern, Clayton N. Jefford, and Geric Debona (1999) *Savior on the Silver Screen*. New York: Paulist Press.

W. Barnes Tatum (2004) *Jesus at the Movies: A Guide to the First Hundred Years*. Rev. and Expanded ed. Santa Rosa: Polebridge Press.

JESUS OF NAZARETH (1977)

[Production Companies: Lew Grade (ATV, Great Britain) / Vincenzo Labella (RAI, Italy). Director: Franco Zeffirelli. Screenwriters: Anthony Burgess, Suso Cecchi d'Amico, and Franco Zeffirelli. Cinematography: Armando Nannuzzi and David Watkin. Cast: Robert Powell (Jesus), Olivia Hussey (Virgin Mary), Peter Ustinov (Herod the Great), Michael York (John the Baptist), Christopher Plummer (Herod Antipas), Simon Peter (James Farentino), John Duttine (John), Keith Washington (Matthew), Ian McShane (Judas), Anne Bancroft (Mary Magdalene), Laurence Olivier (Nicodemus), James Mason (Joseph of Arimathea), Ian Holm (Zerah), Anthony Quinn (Caiaphas), Stacy Keach (Barabbas), Rod Steiger (Pontius Pilate).]

On Palm Sunday, 3 April 1977, Pope Paul VI, in his address to the crowds in St. Peter's Square, expressed unprecedented praise for a specific film by commending it for viewing that night. The film was Franco Zeffirelli's *Jesus of Nazareth* (1977). Unlike the big-screen biblical epics of the 1950s and 1960s, this cinematic story of Jesus was for the small screen – television. The first telecasts of *Jesus of Nazareth* occurred during that Easter season in Italy, Great Britain, and the

United States. The initial telecasts of this mini-series in the United States took place over the NBC network in primetime on Palm Sunday and Easter Sunday, 3 and 10 April, in two three-hour presentations. (On both evenings, I watched in my home with a colleague at Greensboro College, Henry Black Ingram. He and I had recently taught together a course we called, 'A Cinematic Quest for Jesus'.)

Jesus of Nazareth represented an Anglo-Italian collaboration between ATV, a British television and production company, and RAI, the Italian state television network. It was Lew Grade of ATV who approached Franco Zeffirelli about directing the film. Zeffirelli recalled how he, as an Italian Roman Catholic, had been deeply affected by the Vatican II document, *Nostra Aetate*, that in 1965 had underscored the Jewishness of Jesus, emphasized the kinship between Judaism and Christianity, and condemned anti-Semitism. With the prospect of having more screen time for telling the Jesus story for television and a commitment to tell the Jesus story as a Jewish story, Zeffirelli accepted the invitation by Lew Grade – himself a Jew – before Christmas 1973. The film, of course, also tells the story of Christianity's beginnings within Judaism. Zeffirelli used his varied experiences in theater, opera, television and movies, to assemble a company of proven actors to surround Robert Powell, whom he cast as Jesus of Nazareth.

Like others before him, Zeffirelli examined sites for filming his Jesus movie in the Middle East before finding his 'Israel' in North Africa, in Morocco and Tunisia. On location in these two Muslim countries, the shoot lasted from September 1975, until May 1976. Synagogue scenes in the movie included members of the ancient Jewish community on the Isle of Djerba, off the coast of Tunisia. Notable representatives of Judaism, Christianity, and Islam were consulted during the production process, and they commented favorably about the film when completed. Even prior to its American television debut, however, Zeffirelli's film survived public controversy. Comments by the film-maker referred to the forthcoming movie's portrayal of Jesus as an 'ordinary man'. The misperceived affront to Jesus' divinity occasioned protest by Protestant fundamentalists. A fierce letter-writing campaign against General Motors led GMAC to drop its contracted television sponsorship, which was taken over by Procter and Gamble. Nevertheless, since its debut, *Jesus of Nazareth* has become a regular visitor in homes during the Christmas and Easter seasons. In the role of Jesus, Robert Powell has the appearance of traditional visual images and he often speaks with the solemnity of his cinematic predecessors.

Zeffirelli's *Jesus of Nazareth* extended the trajectory of those Jesus movies that had harmonized the four canonical gospels into a continuous narrative, including the Hollywood Jesus epics of the previous decade, Nicholas Ray's *King of Kings* (1961) and George Stevens' *The Greatest Story Ever Told* (1965). The Zeffirelli film, in later VHS and DVD formats, has the longest running time of them all: 382 minutes, nearly six and a half hours.

Cinematically, *Jesus of Nazareth* has its own distinctive beginning. Zeffirelli places his Jesus story within the context of first century Jewish messianic expectation. In the opening scene, the camera takes viewers into the interior of the synagogue at Nazareth. The rabbi holds an open scroll and comments with words that begin, 'In the hour when the King-Messiah comes … '. The sequences that follow bring together familiar stories related to Jesus' birth, infancy and early years, drawn primarily from the Gospels of Matthew and Luke. Included are: the annunciation to Mary and her visit to her already pregnant kinswoman Elizabeth, who later has her newborn son John circumcised (Luke 1:26–66), and the reluctance of Joseph to wed Mary his pregnant betrothed (Matt. 1:18–25); the Roman census, the journey to Bethlehem, the birth of Mary's son Jesus, and his visitation by shepherds (Luke 2:1–20), and the meeting with three kings from afar (Matt. 2:1–13); the circumcision of Jesus (Luke 2:21), and the flight of Mary, Joseph, and the babe to Egypt to escape King Herod (Matt. 2:14–15). Mary's mother Anna, known from the apocryphal Infancy Gospel of James, plays a prominent role early in the film.

These episodes, and others created out of the imagination of the film-makers, are used to dramatize the Jewish heritage of the child born to Mary and adopted by Joseph. These scenes contain numerous affirmations that Jesus is indeed the promised Messiah and are punctuated by the recitation of the traditional credo, the *Shema*, 'Hear O Israel … ' (Deut. 6:4–5). Such moments as Jesus' *bar mitzvah* (created scene) and his pilgrimage to Jerusalem with his parents (Luke 2:41–52) prepare the viewers for Jesus' own mission.

Zeffirelli's sweeping story, beautifully filmed, effects the transition from Jesus' early years to his own public ministry by invoking John the Baptist as Jesus' forerunner (Matt. 3:1–6; Mark 1:1–6; Luke 3:1–6; John 1:29–34). John appears clad in the garb of a prophet inveighing against Herod Antipas and his wife Herodias (Matt. 14:3–12; Mark 6:17–29). Subsequently, at riverside, John baptizes those who respond to his call for repentance. The viewer sees Jesus for the first time as an adult through the eyes of John when Jesus presents himself for baptism (Matt. 3:13–17; Mark 1:9–11; Luke 3:21–22). Jesus already knows whose and who he is. With no follow-up testing in the wilderness, he immediately returns to the synagogue at Nazareth

(Luke 4:16–30). He reads the passage from the scroll of Isaiah that begins, 'The Spirit of the Lord is upon me … '. (Isa. 61:1). He then claims that this text has been fulfilled in the hearing of those present. Already Jesus encounters the charge of 'blasphemer' that will eventually contribute to his execution.

Zeffirelli shapes the geographical outline of Jesus' public activity in accordance with the Synoptic Gospels of Matthew, Mark, and Luke. This means: an early ministry of teaching and healing in Galilee, a single journey to Judea, and the events of the final week in Jerusalem. A partial listing of stories related to Jesus' ministry in Galilee displays the inclusive, harmonizing character of the screenplay: his exorcism of a boy with an unclean spirit (Luke 4:31–37; Mark 1:21–28); a miraculous catch of fish in the presence of Simon, not yet known as Peter (Luke 5:1–11); Jesus' dining in the house of the tax collector Matthew (Matt. 9:9–13; Mark 2:13–17; Luke 5:27–32), as the setting for his parable of the prodigal son (Luke 15:11–32), which prompts reconciliation between Matthew and Simon Peter; Jesus' healing Jairus' daughter (Matt. 9:18–26, Mark 5:21–43, Luke 8:40–56); the dance of Herodias' daughter and the execution of John the Baptist (Matt. 14:3–12; Mark 6:17–29); Jesus' feeding crowds with five loaves and two fish (Matt. 14:13–21; Mark 6:32–44; Luke 9:10–17; John 6:1–15); his dining in the house of a Pharisee and being anointed by a sinful woman, identified in the film as Mary Magdalene (Luke 7:36–50); his sending forth his twelve disciples (Matt. 10:1–16; Mark 6:6–13, Luke 9:1–6); and then the confession by Simon that Jesus is the Messiah (Matt. 16:16; Mark 8:29; Luke 9:20), and the blessing by Jesus upon Simon Peter, the rock on which his church will be built (Matt. 16:17–19).

Although the film does not locate the confession of Simon Peter as occurring in the vicinity of Caesarea Philippi (Matt. 16:13; Mark 8:27), this episode does constitute the turning point in Jesus' ministry in Galilee, because only now does Jesus begin to talk with his disciples about his impending death in Jerusalem, 'The Son of Man … will be rejected … ' (Matt. 16:21; Mark 8:31; Luke 9:22). In the film, two of the best known, and often-filmed, gospel occasions serve as the brief transition between Galilee and Jerusalem. They are presented without the dramatic flair often associated with them in the cinematic tradition: the Sermon on the Mount, consisting here only of the Beatitudes and the Lord's Prayer (Matt. 5:3–11, 6:9–13); and the raising of Lazarus from the dead at Bethany (John 11:1–44).

In addition to depicting well-known events from Jesus' last week in Jerusalem, the film has relocated to these days several events that occur in other settings in the Gospel of John. The following list of stories in the film from the last week also notes these relocated events: Jesus' entry into Jerusalem (Matt. 21:1–9; Mark 11:1–10; Luke 19:28–40; John 12:12–18); his disturbance in the temple (Matt. 21:10–17; Mark 11:15–17; Luke 19:45–46; note John 2:13–22); the adulterous woman (note John 7:53–8:11); the healing of a blind man (note John 9:1–41); the visit of Nicodemus (note John 3:1–15); the Last Supper, with words over bread and wine (Matt. 26:26–29; Mark 14:22–25; Luke 22:17–20); Jesus' arrest in Gethsemane (Matt. 26:26–56; Mark 14:32–52; Luke 22:40–53; John 18:2–12); Judas' suicide by hanging (Matt. 27:3–10); Jesus' appearance before Caiaphas (Matt. 27:57–67; Mark 14:55–65); Jesus' trial before Pilate and the release of Barabbas (Matt. 27:1–26; Mark 15:1–15; Luke 23:1–25; John 18:28–19:16); his way to the cross (Matt. 27:27–32; Mark 15:16–22; Luke 23:26–32; John 19:17); crucifixion, with six of Jesus' seven last words from the cross (Matt. 27:33–66; Mark 15:23–47; Luke 23:33–56; John 19:18–42); and – beyond his death – the empty tomb and resurrection appearances (Matt. 28; Mark 16; Luke 24; John 19–20). The film concludes with a version of the words of promise uttered by the resurrected Jesus to his disciples: 'I am with you every day until the end of time' (Matt. 28:20).

Such listings of episodes, however, misrepresent the texture of the narrative. Stories from the gospels are not strung together disconnected side by side but woven together into a flowing narrative. This is accomplished by imaginative story-telling, the creation of scenes, and conversational dialogue. One-dimensional characters in the gospels become weightier figures in the film. Nicodemus and Joseph of Arimathea appear as active members of the Sanhedrin, sympathetic to Jesus. Then there is Zerah – a leader within the Sanhedrin, without any textual basis in the gospels. He becomes Jesus' principal adversary in Jerusalem. Zerah's manipulations detract from the malevolent roles often assigned to Judas, Caiaphas, and the Jewish crowds. But in this film, unlike the gospels themselves, Pontius Pilate – as Rome's man – at last accepts responsibility for Jesus' fate, or destiny, by verbally declaring, 'Jesus of Nazareth is guilty of treason by proclaiming himself king and is sentenced to be crucified.' Thus Zeffirelli uses several strategies for undercutting an anti-Semitic reading of his Jesus story.

That Jesus is a child of first century Judaism is unmistakable. That he is the anticipated King-Messiah is also unmistakable – although his kingdom is not of this world, as he tells Pilate (John 18:36). But the definitive nature of Jesus' messiahship, already confessed by Peter, appears on the lips of Nicodemus in Jerusalem. As Jesus hangs on the distinctive lattice-like cross, Nicodemus stands nearby, gazing upon him and reciting the Suffering-Servant passage from Isaiah 53 that includes these words: '[H]e was oppressed and afflicted ... He was brought as a lamb to slaughter ... '. This identification of Jesus as the Suffering-Servant had been anticipated visually through recurring images of lambs and sheep and by John the Baptist's reference to Jesus after his baptism as 'the lamb of God' (John 1:29, 36). This use of the Suffering-Servant text with reference to the crucified Jesus anticipates its citation in Martin Scorsese's *The Last Temptation of Christ* (1988) and Mel Gibson's *The Passion of the Christ* (2004).

Viewers of Zeffirelli's expansive cinematic chronicle of Jesus' life should be aware not only of how he used the Synoptic Gospels to shape the geographical outline of Jesus' public activity, but also how he uses the Gospel of John to create a dramatically coherent portrayal of Jesus as the Christ. In Galilee and on his southward journey, Jesus speaks about God and God's kingdom, sometimes through his familiar parables (from the Synoptics). Only after Peter's confession of Jesus' messiahship does Jesus in Judea and Jerusalem speak openly about himself through his God-like 'I am' sayings (from John 11:25; 9:5; 14:6; film sequence). Cinematically, Franco Zeffirelli's *Jesus of Nazareth* represents the finest retelling of the Jesus story among those films that harmonize the four canonical gospels.

W. Barnes Tatum

Further reading

W. Barnes Tatum and Henry Black Ingram (1975) 'Whence and Whither the Cinematic Jesus?', *Religion in Life*. 44(4): 470–78.
Franco Zeffirelli (1986) *The Autobiography of Franco Zeffirelli*. New York: Weidenfeld & Nicolson.
——(1984) *Franco Zeffirelli's Jesus: A Spiritual Diary*. Trans. Willis J. Egan, S. J. San Francisco: Harper & Row. [Italian original, 1977.]

JOAN THE MAID: THE BATTLES/THE PRISONS (1994)

[Production Company: Pierre Grise Productions. Director: Jacques Rivette. Screenplay: Christine Laurent, Pascal Bonitzer. Cinematography: William

Lubtchansky. Music: Jordi Savall. Cast: Sandrine Bonnaire (Joan), Stéphane Boucher (La Hire), André Marcon (the Dauphin).]

Through its reticent depictions, elliptical editing, and mysterious silences, Jacques Rivette's *Jeanne la Pucelle* (*Joan the Maid,* 1994) creates a world that is simultaneously down-to-earth and sacred, a world reminiscent of the narrative realm of the Bible. Far more than many biblical films, in which characters in long robes express twentieth or twenty-first century attitudes, *Jeanne la Pucelle* conveys reverence for the human world and for what may lie beyond – an attitude in keeping with the humility of the Hebrew and early Christian authors of the Bible. Through its cinematic style, Rivette's film also implies that we humans are neither masters of history nor clear-seeing observers of the present.

Because of Rivette's stylistic restraint and meticulous adherence to historical records, *Jeanne la Pucelle* is widely seen as the most historically accurate cinematic depiction of the life of Joan of Arc. The picture was highly praised by leading critics; Joan Acocella, in the 15 November 1999 issue of *The New Yorker,* described the film as 'the best Joan movie ever made'. The primary source for the film was *Jeanne d'Arc par elle-même et par ses témoins* (*Joan of Arc by Herself and Her Witnesses*), an austere account written in 1962 by the renowned medieval historian Régine Pernoud. The book consists of quotations from the trial transcripts – judges' questions, Joan's answers, and statements by numerous witnesses – linked by brief introductions and commentaries. The voluminous details collected by the court scribes over the course of Joan's Trial of Condemnation (1431) and her post-mortem Trial of Rehabilitation (1455) provide a lively sense of the heroine's life and personality. As one historian points out in regard to the Maid, 'thanks to the transcripts of her trials we know more details of her short life than we do of any other human being before her time (including Plato, or Alexander of Macedonia, or Julius Caesar, or Jesus Christ) and for several centuries thereafter' (Pernoud and Clin/ Adams 1999: xv–xvi).

Rather than inventing chatty dialogue, in the manner of popular historical film-makers who seek to give us a sense of 'being there', Rivette restricts himself primarily to the words in the court documents. One liberty the director allowed himself was to use questions and answers recorded during the Trial of Condemnation in his brief depiction of the Inquest at Poitiers, when most of the same issues arose. The transcripts of the earlier Inquest were lost or destroyed within a few years of the hearing, but the findings were still extant at the time of the Trial of Rehabilitation and were cited in its records (Pernoud 1994: 67).

Rivette, a film scholar, critic, and influential member of the French New Wave, is considered a director's director little interested in attracting large audiences. His films often use pauses and extended takes to achieve their effects, and some of his works are several hours long. *Jeanne la Pucelle* was released as two films: *Jeanne la Pucelle 1: Les batailles* (*Joan the Maid 1: The Battles,* 1994, 160 minutes) and *Jeanne la Pucelle II: Les prisons* (*Joan the Maid II: The Prisons,* 1994, 176 minutes). A few years later, the two films were made available on videotape and then DVD, in shortened form (112 and 116 minutes respectively) in French with English subtitles by Facets Video Company. In 2009, the British distributor Artificial Eye released a full-length English-subtitled DVD.

The first few minutes set the tone for the film: music suggestive of the medieval church and court fills the air as the opening credits roll against a pitch black background. Then the first image appears, announcing the film's indebtedness to its sources: three women, wearing the long black robes and white headdresses associated with medieval European matrons and present-day nuns, slowly walk toward the camera, stopping partway through an interior courtyard. The woman in the center, elderly and supported by the others, speaks:

> I had a daughter, born in wedlock, who had the sacraments of baptism and confirmation. I raised her in fear of God, respect for the tradition of the Church, in so far as her age and her simple condition permitted. Having grown in fields and pastures, she went to church often …

An intertitle, white against pure black like the opening credits, interrupts: 'Le 7 novembre, 1455, en Notre-Dame de Paris'. Viewers familiar with Joan's history will identify the Maid's mother, Isabelle Romée, even before her name is provided, and many will recognize the year of the Trial of Reconciliation. More significantly, those who have read even brief excerpts from the court transcripts will note the emphasis on obedience to the Church. In the trial that led to her burning, Joan was convicted of being a relapsed heretic, an apostate, and an idolater. In her post-mortem 1455 trial, the charges were nullified; and in 1920 the Maid was canonized a saint by the Church that had executed her four centuries earlier.

The opening scene ends with an abrupt cut to black, a silent pause, and then a cut to a young woman and a middle-aged man sitting on a crude horse-drawn cart in a working courtyard outside a large stone house. Joan (the extraordinarily impressive Sandrine Bonnaire) and her uncle have been waiting in Vaucouleurs for six months to see Robert de Baudricourt; the year is 1429. Across the courtyard, we watch as a blacksmith shoes a horse. The uncle is about to return to his family in Domrémy, but Joan insists on staying behind. The young girl's conviction, persistence, and quiet dignity eventually win over a squire, Jean de Metz, who takes Joan to Baudricourt, who finally gives her a few men to escort her to the Dauphin in Chinon.

Before Joan leaves Vaucouleurs, she prays, presumably to the three celestial figures she believes have been inspiring and guiding her: Saints Michael, Margaret, and Catherine. Joan's conversations with her 'voices', as she often called them, have been a favorite subject of painters and film-makers, who usually portray the saint looking upward, and sometimes depict the apparitions that Joan sees. Rivette's scene supports the idea that, in film, the unseen and unheard are sometimes more powerful than anything that appears on the screen or heard on the soundtrack. As Joan prays, we do not see her at all. The blacksmith's wife, gazing respectfully through an open door, quietly reports to her husband what she sees: 'She sits on the chest. Her eyes shine. Her lips move. I don't hear anything.' Later in the film, Rivette does show Joan praying, but the emphasis is on the period in Joan's life when the saints' voices are failing her, shaking the confidence she possessed when she felt that her every move was part of a divine plan. Throughout the film, Rivette respects his subject and his audience by maintaining a neutral stance toward Joan's voices; he neither confirms their reality nor negates it through ridicule or psychological explanation.

Joan's uneventful journey from Vaucouleurs to Chinon is the sort of detail that most films omit. However, its very simplicity recalls the numerous journeys of figures in the Hebrew Bible as well as the itinerant life of Jesus. Rivette uses the journey to ground the sacred in the everyday, much as Pasolini did in his 1964 film *The Gospel According to St. Matthew,* when he showed Mary somewhat awkwardly climbing onto a donkey at the beginning of the flight into Egypt (Matt. 2:13–15). Rivette also uses the journey to demonstrate the transformation in the attitude of young swordsmen toward the teenaged girl who wants to lead soldiers into battle. Joan rides off with six male escorts, five of whom she has just met. The party is shown traveling in silence through fields and forests in the dead of winter. At one point, two of the men stop along a trail to urinate, talking about their sexual interest in Joan as they relieve themselves. That night, protectively sleeping in the straw on either side of the Maid, they express shame about their earlier intentions. They have already begun to see Joan as someone far different from an ordinary woman.

Joan begins her transformation by cutting off her long hair and putting on male clothing. As the transcripts of the Trial of Condemnation amply demonstrate, the Maid's male attire was a prime concern of the Inquisition judges. Joan's cross-dressing, they claimed, not only violated a biblical prohibition (Deut. 22:5); it was also a visible form of idolatry, a demonstration of heresy. The jurists' endless questions and expressions of outrage betray a deep conviction that, in modern argot, 'clothes make the man'. The transcripts show the clerics using threats of divine punishment in their repeated attempts to strip Joan of the clothing that protected her and allowed her to lead men into battle. If the Church could unmake a soldier by stripping her of male garments, it could also make a king by dressing a weak, unimpressive man in royal attire. Rivette's coronation scene demonstrates the Church's ability to exert power over worldly events by bestowing or removing the materials that cover the body. With rich irony, the director makes the starkly simple ceremony one of the most deeply moving scenes in the film. Charles, the Dauphin, walks forward humbly, wearing only a white cotton robe and white socks, garments that would seem more suitable for a newborn baby or, perhaps, for a grown man in the privacy of his bedchamber. The Dauphin prostrates himself fully on the bare marble floor before three bishops. He then rises to his feet and stands in silence as the clerics dress him in layers of royal robes, adding white shoes and gloves, and finally bestowing on him a sword and crown. Joan, who made the event possible, stands on the sidelines, wearing her usual suit of armor, looking as if she had just left the battlefield.

Concern with the symbolism of clothing has a long history in Christianity. But a deliberate rejection of attachment to such material concerns goes back to the story of Jesus, who is reported to have said, 'Do not worry ... what you will wear. Is not ... the body more than clothing?' (Matt. 6:25–26) and 'From anyone who takes away your coat do not withhold even your shirt' (Luke 6:29). Jesus was later crucified in full humiliating nakedness. Through the centuries, Christianity has smoothed over Jesus' anti-materialism just as it has covered his private parts with loincloths in depictions of the crucifixion. Rivette's film evokes a sense of a pre-ecclesiastical rawness, which departs from a long history of euphemism, sentimentality, and institutional justification.

The Bible hovers over the story of Joan of Arc, and Rivette's film, as the Judeo-Christian urtext that explained the world to the Maid and her contemporaries and, through its New Testament narratives about Jesus, provided the basic structure for the life of a Christian saint. The parallels between Joan's life and the life of Christ are striking: a gifted young person of humble birth, who has a strong sense of being divinely guided on an important mission, leaves home, gives up any possibility of domestic life, acquires a following, and performs deeds that appear to be miraculous; the authorities order a trial; the hero, abandoned by those who should be supporters, is brutally executed; later, the hero's great virtue and significance are officially recognized and he or she is declared a saviour. This overall narrative structure lends itself to popular literature and film, even in instances where the central figure is not nearly as important as Jesus or Joan. The general pattern has become so standardized in films about Christian heroes that I have identified it a genre – the hagiopic – a picture about a holy or saintly hero (Grace 2009). Rivette does not emphasize the parallels between Joan's story and that of Jesus as much as some film-makers do, but he does include a few phrases of Joan's that refer directly to the Gospels. The Maid tells the Dauphin that her voices call her 'Daughter of God' (an echo of the New Testament phrase, 'Son of God'; e.g. John 1:1–18); as she is led to the stake, she asks for 'forgiveness to all', recalling Jesus' prayer that his killers be forgiven, 'for they know not what they do' (Luke 23:24) and before her death, Joan calls out to Jesus, just as Christ called out to his heavenly father (Matt. 27:46). Rivette's film distances itself from the stylistic clichés of the popular hagiopic as it harks back to its ultimate source: the biblical stories of heroic men and women who acted upon their religious beliefs.

Pamela Grace

Further reading

Pamela Grace (2009) *The Religious Film: Christianity and the Hagiopic*. New Approaches to Film Genre. Chichester; Malden, MA.: Wiley-Blackwell.

Douglas Morrey and Alison Smith (2009) *Jacques Rivette*. Manchester: Manchester University Press.

Régine Pernoud (1994) *Joan of Arc by Herself and Her Witnesses*. Lanham, MD: Scarborough House.

Régine Pernoud and Marie-Veronique Clin (1999) *Joan of Arc: Her Story*, trans. and rev. by Jeremy duQuesnay Adams. New York, NY: St. Martin's Griffin.

Marina Warner (2000) *Joan of Arc: The Image of Female Heroism*. Berkeley, CA and Los Angeles, CA: University of California Press.

Bonnie Wheeler and Charles T. Wood, (eds) (1996) *Fresh Verdicts on Joan of Arc*. New York, NY and London: Garland Publishing, Inc.

KAGEMUSHA (1980)

[Production Companies: Toho Studios and Twentieth Century Fox. Director: Akira Kurosawa. Screenplay: Akira Kurosawa and Masato Ide. Cinematography: Takao Saitó. Music: Shin-ichiro Ikebe. Cast: Tatsuya Nakadai (Shingen Takeda and the Kagemusha), Tsutomu Yamazaki (Nobukado Takeda), Ken'ichi Hagiwara (Katsuyori Takeda). Language: Japanese. Running time: 179 minutes.]

Even those who have never heard of Akira Kurosawa may well have seen his films or, more likely, remakes of his films. *A Fistful of Dollars* (1964), the 'spaghetti Western' that launched the careers of Clint Eastwood and Sergio Leone, is a remake of Kurosawa's *Yojimbo* (1961), and the unforgettable *Magnificent Seven* (1960) is an Americanization of his 1954 *Seven Samurai*. This cross-reference between Japanese samurai and American cowboy is no accident. Both trade on the myth of individual honour code, integrity, and steely personality, and both are tropes that work out post-war identities of the two nations. But the differences between them are telling as well. In the movies of someone like John Ford, to whom Kurosawa readily acknowledges his inspirational debts, the American cowboy goes it alone by flouting the conventions that he thinks are holding him back from personal (that is, national) greatness. Kurosawa leverages that insistent American individualism into a samurai virtue. The result is an ambivalence between traditional expectations of unquestioned loyalty to and absolute sacrifice for his lord on one hand and a more universal sense of personal fulfillment and a more public application of justice on the other.

The historical context that allows Kurosawa to explore this tension is the 1867 abolition of the samurai system, when almost two million samurai were abandoned by their lords and became *ronin*, 'wandering samurai'. *Seven Samurai, Yojimbo,* and *Sanjuro* (1962) all center around the ronin, whose traditional values clash with their personal sense of justice and integrity. This exploration comes into focus for the first time, ironically, not in a samurai film but in Kurosawa's 1952 film *Ikiru* on post-war Japan. The film depicts the last days of a lifelong Tokyo bureaucrat, nicknamed 'Mummy' because he looks like a walking dead man. The 'Mummy' has been diagnosed with terminal stomach cancer and given six months to live. Only then does he realize that his life has been an utter waste. He spent his life in unrequited loyalty to his family and to a meaningless bureaucracy, but he now realizes he has never truly lived. He is born again – to the tune of

'Happy Birthday' – only when he dedicates his life to building a playground for a local community.

In the 1980 film *Kagemusha*, Kurosawa traces the samurai code to sixteenth-century Japan, just before the start of the Tokugawa Shogunate that would not end until the 1867 edict. *Kagemusha* might be a prequel to his earlier samurai films, but it brings Kurosawa's decades-long meditation on the samurai spirit to a conclusion.

And what a conclusion it is! With the brilliant cinematography and relentless narrative that are hallmarks of Kurosawa films, *Kagemusha* follows the brief stint of a thief forced to play the powerful warlord Shingen Takeda's double, a *kagemusha* ('shadow warrior'), because of his uncanny resemblance to him. Shingen is vying for control with other warlords, most prominent among them Nobunaga Oda and Ieyasu Tokugawa. In 25 years, Ieyasu would indeed unify Japan and found the Tokugawa Shogunate. For now, in 1573, Shingen is the most fearsome of the warlords, and he is marching towards Kyoto, the crown jewel that would earn him the coveted title *shogun*, effectively making him the supreme ruler of Japan. The march is cut short by an assassin's bullet that mortally wounds him. Before his death, he instructs his retainers to keep his death a secret from his enemies, his subjects, even his family for three years so the Takeda clan could consolidate itself. Enter the kagemusha.

It is the film's conceit that the kagemusha remains nameless. He is a thief snatched from the crucifixion ground to be the lord's double. Reluctant, and ignorant of Shingen's death, he schemes to steal away in the middle of the night with stolen loot. When he discovers the lord's dead body and realizes the immense burden, not to mention the inherent danger, of being the lord's double, he resolutely refuses the role. Then, during Shingen's burial, veiled as an offering of a large urn of sake to the lake god, a transformation takes place. In the narrative flow of the film, the kagemusha has a change of mind when he overhears rival spies who witness the spectacle predicting the demise of the Takeda clan if they can confirm Shingen's death. They guess that might be the case but are still not entirely sure. That prompts the kagemusha to volunteer his service in a last-ditch effort to save the clan. But Kurosawa places the kagemusha's transformation just after the burial. He pleads with the generals: 'I want to be of use *to him*' (emphasis added). He does not aspire to be of use to the clan or to the people but *to Lord Shingen* himself. This act signals a resurrection or identification theme in which the dead lord's spirit inhabits the kagemusha and unites with his spirit, much as Paul describes in Romans 6:5: 'For if we have been united with [Christ] in a death like his, we will certainly be united with him in a resurrection like his'. The thief is rescued from the cross but lives to take the lord's throne and name. From this point onward, the kagemusha is so identified with the lord that he is simply called Shingen.

In a blood-crimson psychedelic dreamscape the kagemusha meets the deceased Shingen who chases him but soon disappears altogether. The kagemusha wanders about his dream looking for the lord but in the end finds only himself. He wakes up screaming in fright, not of the encounter but of being surrounded by enemies. Shingen is raised and is now living in him. The kagemusha is now Shingen. When the kagemusha witnesses his attendants giving up their lives to protect him from enemy fire, his identification with Shingen is complete. So complete that in the climactic battle in which the Takeda army is annihilated, he picks up a lance and charges the enemy line, alone, even though he has already been exposed as an imposter and expelled from the clan. Rejected by his own people, he nonetheless dies for them in a messianic self-sacrifice. The film ends with his lifeless body flowing past the clan's submerged standard in a river of time. He dies as Shingen. Though it comes from a very different cultural and historical context, this narrative is a variation of adoptionist Christology: '[the Son] was appointed Son of God in power according to the spirit of holiness by resurrection from the dead' (Rom. 1:3).

That Kurosawa would use biblical themes in a Japanese period piece seems to make little sense. Maybe that is why few if any film critics in the West have picked up on the biblical thread. I suspect the reason is that the cross-resurrection-adoption complex intrigued Kurosawa, and he used the resurrection theme in particular as a way of resolving his samurai problem. Crucifixion as punishment for crime was adopted by the Japanese from Christian missionaries; the Japanese condemnation of twenty-six missionaries to the cross in 1597 was therefore a deliberate allusion to, and perversion of, Christ's crucifixion.

In *Kagemusha*, however, crucifixion is highlighted not as punishment but as a fate from which the kagemusha is delivered and the means by which he is adopted as the supreme master of the clan. There is life beyond the cross. This resurrection theme is especially prominent in a scene I consider to be the best visual commentary on the valley of the dry bones (Ezek. 37). A messenger with fluttering standards on his back runs like a wind through a deathly still castle and over steps strewn with blood-splattered, motionless soldiers. As he passes, soldiers rise up one by one; despite the commotion the soldiers never rise up out of order. It is the runner, the divine spirit, who sweeps over the dry bones and calls up the mighty army of Ezekiel. The concept of *kamikaze*, literally 'divine wind', is of course indigenous to Japan, but it is also a spirit of vengeance. The kamikaze protects the Japanese people by destroying their enemies, whereas the spirit of Ezekiel gives life and promises restoration. Likewise, possession by ghost is standard fare in Japanese literature, but only an improper burial would normally give rise to a wandering ghost looking for a host to possess. Kurosawa reverses that process in *Kagemusha*. It is Shingen's burial, not his death, that occasions the kagemusha's identification with the lord's identity and his ambition. The reason? In the Christian story the resurrection follows not death but burial.

What then is Kurosawa saying about the samurai spirit? Since the earliest time the samurai-warrior spirit was one of honour, integrity, and loyalty that revolves around duty to the master, even unto death. One Western interpreter observes that the 'way of the samurai', *bushido*, '[eulogizes] such virtues as reckless bravery, fierce family pride, and selfless, at times senseless, devotion of master and man' (Steenstrup 1979: 74). While he used the samurai to exemplify these virtues in his previous films, Kurosawa was clearly also troubled by the samurai's narrow, blind loyalty to their masters. That is perhaps why Kurosawa sought to transform the samurai code of conduct into public virtues. The heroes in *Seven Samurai* transform their loyalty to masters into a commitment to protecting poor villagers, whose social class places them beneath the samurai and whom it would have been unthinkable for the aristocratic samurai to deign to rescue in traditional Japan. The protagonist in *Yojimbo*, a ronin determined to transgress the samurai code by playing the rival lords against each other, succumbs at the end to his innate samurai sense of justice and, with enormous personal sacrifice, helps a family of a lower caste. The absence of this samurai tension in the Western remakes makes those films inherently less satisfying.

Appealing to the Christian theme of resurrection permits Kurosawa to anticipate a future revival of the samurai sense of honour, loyalty, and integrity. Yes, the samurai code has been badly damaged and, worse, co-opted by unscrupulous warlords to further their selfish ambitions. The death of Shingen, both as the lord himself and vicariously through his kagemusha, and the drowning of his clan standard, signal the passing of one phase. But just as the kagemusha begins to care deeply for the clan and the people, enough for him to sacrifice himself on their behalf, so can the samurai sense of loyalty be broadened to include the larger public. In the same way, the protagonist in *Ikiru*, a modern samurai dying of cancer, is able to transform his loyalty to a bureaucracy into a sacrificial giving that benefits disadvantaged girls. In spite of his death, his spirit of generosity lives on, hence the title of the film, which literally means 'to live'. The flip side contains a warning. The kagemusha's death is efficacious only if the new samurai spirit can inhabit souls diligent at transforming it. In the last act of *Ikiru*, even though the bureaucrat's sacrifice inspires his inebriated co-workers to emulate his virtues, the film ends with the bureaucrats' retreating back into a listless and meaningless existence of office bureaucracy in sober daylight.

In spite of the upbeat note, there is a dark, perhaps even nihilistic, side to Kurosawa's samurai. In his masterpiece *Ran* (1985), a film inspired by *King Lear,* the samurai code of absolute loyalty exemplified by the third son is rewarded with an untimely death. The transformed samurai virtue of responsibility beyond the clan's boundary might go beyond narrow patronage, but ultimately it fails to break the national boundaries of Japan. This subtle nationalism is already adumbrated in *Ikiru*. The dying bureaucrat is inspired by a young underling who left her government office position to make toys. 'Why toys?' he asks. 'I feel like I am playing with every baby *in Japan'* (emphasis added). In his 1990 film *Dreams,* a critical and box office failure, Kurosawa has a World War II Japanese commander apologize to the ghosts of soldiers for having sent them to their deaths. Not a word of remorse, however, to the countless victims in East and Southeast Asia who lost their lives to aggression engineered by the same soldiers. A year later, his *Rhapsody in August* opened to public outcry when a modern Japanese American played by Richard Gere apologizes to his elderly aunt who lived through the war and still lives in Japan for the atomic bombing of Nagasaki. The film remains silent on the context of the Pacific conflicts and victims of Japanese militarism.

Sze-kar Wan

Further reading

Peter Cowie (2010) *Akira Kurosawa: Master of Cinema.* New York: Rizzoli.

David Desser (1983) *The Samurai Films of Akira Kurosawa.* Ann Arbor: UMI Research Press.

Akira Kurosawa (1982) *Something like an Autobiography.* English trans. New York: Knopf.

Stephen Prince (1991) *The Warrior's Camera: The Cinema of Akira Kurosawa.* Princeton: Princeton University Press.

Donald Richie (1998) *The Films of Akira Kurosawa.* 3rd ed Berkeley: University of California Press.

Carl Steenstrup (1979) *Hōjō Shigetoki (1198–1261) and his Role in the History of Political and Ethical Ideas in Japan.* London: Curzon Press.

Mitsuhiro Yoshimoto (2000) *Kurosawa: Film Studies and Japanese Cinema.* Durham: Duke University Press.

Further viewing

Ikiru (Kurosawa, 1952)
Seven Samurai (Kurosawa, 1954)
Yojimbo (Kurosawa, 1961)
Sanjuro (Kurosawa, 1962)
Ran (Kurosawa, 1985)
Dreams (Kurosawa, 1990)

KING OF KINGS (1961)

[Production Company: Samuel Bronston Productions, Metro-Goldwin Mayer; Director: Nicholas Ray. Screenwriter: Philip Yordan (with uncredited narration by Ray Bradbury). Music: Miklós Rósza; Cinematographer: Manuel Berenguer, Milton R. Krasner, Franz F. Planer. Major Cast Members: Jeffrey Hunter (Jesus), Siobhán McKenna (Mary), Hurd Hatfield (Pontius Pilate), Viveca Lindfors (Claudia), Rip Torn (Judas), Orson Welles (narrator) (uncredited).]

Nicholas Ray's 1961 *King of Kings* was a deeply American film, an epic life of Jesus that engaged a panoply of interwoven issues in American civic discourse at the end of the 1950s: World War II and the Holocaust, still fresh in the memories of many Americans, the creation of the State of Israel in 1948 shortly after the war's end, Christian anti-Semitism, and the subsequent Cold War between Communism and the West, including anti-Communist McCarthyism. The year before it was released, *Exodus*, Leon Uris' 1958 blockbuster novel depicting Jewish struggles to settle in Palestine before and after the Holocaust, had been made into a major film starring Paul Newman as a blue-eyed Jewish freedom fighter. *King of Kings* featured a profoundly human and very Jewish Jesus (the blue-eyed Jeffrey Hunter), who preached only peace, love and brotherhood, executed not by his fellow Jews over any theological differences, but by the Roman occupiers of Judea, who, faced with the very real threats of Judean rebel movements, feared Jesus' ability to provoke an actual revolt against Rome.

King of Kings sets the story of Jesus firmly within the context of Roman occupation of Judea/Palestine and the oppression of the Jews. Its arresting opening scenes allude unmistakeably to the all-too-recent

Holocaust. Helmeted Roman soldiers pile up the bodies of dead Jews into pits, as the sonorous voice of Orson Welles announces that this slaughter took place almost a century before the death of Jesus, when the Roman general Pompey entered Jerusalem and desecrated the Temple there.

Despite its length and its many small vignettes, the film's basic plot is simple. Roman oppression generates Jewish resistance. When Pontius Pilate, governor of Judea in the third decade of the first century repeats Pompey's earlier desecration by placing images in the Temple, the rebel leader Barabbas advocates armed revolt. At the same time, though, a new miracle-working prophet has appeared in Judea. Hearing of this new prophet, Barabbas seeks to meet him, hoping that he might provide the prophetic authorization for his armed revolt. But this new prophet, Jesus, is Barabbas' diametric opposite, who preaches only 'love, peace, and the brotherhood of man'. The voiceover narrator calls them 'the messiah of war', and 'the messiah of peace'.

Caught between these opposing stances is Jesus' disciple, Judas. When Jesus comes from the Galilee to Jerusalem to preach his gospel of peace at the Temple, Barabbas enlists Judas' support. If Jesus can free the Jews from Roman oppression without bloodshed, he deserves to be proclaimed King, and Barabbas will bring his men in support. At the same time, Pilate, who has been gathering intelligence about both messiahs, fears that their supporters will join forces in an effective uprising. While Jesus preaches peace in Jerusalem, Barabbas incites a riot outside the temple. The Romans repulse and massacre the rebels. As the rebels despair, Judas resolves to force Jesus' hand, convinced that when Jesus himself is threatened by Roman force, he will work miracles against them. To this end, Judas goes to the high priest Caiaphas and denounces Barabbas and Jesus. Although both are guilty of sedition against Rome, at the order of Pilate, only Jesus dies, while Barabbas goes free. From here on the plot harmonizes the canonical gospels. Jesus is crucified, taken down and buried. Three days later, his tomb is found empty; the resurrected Jesus meets his followers in encounters that are either shown or narrated by Welles. The film closes with shots of the male disciples gathered on the shore, and then only Peter, and, finally, the shadow of Jesus.

To construct a fundamentally Jewish pacifist Jesus tragically caught in the historical contingencies of first-century, Roman-occupied Judea, the film utilized diverse techniques. Unusual among life of Jesus films, Philip Yordan's script drew extensively from accounts of the history of Judea under Roman rule by Flavius Josephus, the first-century Jewish historiographer and participant in some of the events he relates. The plot and the dialogue drew selectively from all four canonical gospels. Catholic traditions absent from the biblical texts regularly supplement the story. Yet a great deal is supplied by the creative imaginations of the screenwriter, whose invention of events and dialogue closely resembles ancient techniques often called midrash, which freely invent and develop characters, actions and speech to fill the gaps in the biblical accounts.

The representation of Jesus as explicitly Jewish is accomplished in various ways. The gospels differ substantially on whether Jesus was called rabbi (often in John, never in Luke, twice in Mark, and only by Judas in Matthew, whose Jesus tells his disciples to eschew the title altogether). The film's Jesus is repeatedly called rabbi by many, including John the Baptist. In a scene with no basis in the gospels, let alone Josephus, John sees Jesus returned from his sojourn in the desert and says, 'There's your new rabbi.' In another expansion of the extant stories, at the last supper, Jesus prays the traditional Hebrew blessing over the bread, and over the wine, before giving them to his disciples.

King of Kings plays up those sayings of Jesus that construe him as a pacifist, while conveniently ignoring those sayings such as Matthew 10:34, in which Jesus says, 'I come not to bring peace, but a sword'. The film omits Jesus' admonition in Luke 14:26 that only those who hate father and mother [etc.] can be his disciple, and lacks not only the vignettes of an angry Jesus cursing a fig tree that failed to yield figs out of season (Matt. 21:19–21; Mark 11:13–14; Luke 21:29–30), but the more significant attack on the commerce in the temple courtyard that, according to Matthew, Mark and Luke, is the event that triggers Jesus' arrest (Matt. 21:12–13; Mark 11:15–18; Luke 19:45–47). *King of Kings'* 'Messiah of Peace' is no apocalyptic prophet preaching the imminent end (Mark 1:15; Matt. 4:17): these pronouncements and others are absent, including those detailed descriptions of war, famine and desolation predicted in Mark 13, Matthew 24 and Luke 21.

Numerous strategies emphasize that responsibility for the death of Jesus lay primarily with the Romans. The lengthy introduction establishes the historical context of Roman oppression, combining selective use of ancient materials with authorial invention. Josephus does indeed recount Pompey's defiling entrance into the temple (*Antiquities* 14.58–72). Entirely fictional, however, is an early scene evoking Nazi book-burning, when a terrified Jew silently implores Pompey for a small scroll the general had found inside the temple, as the altar flames flicker in between them, suggesting that Pompey might burn it, or have this man killed as he has just killed a line of priests standing between him and the holy of holies. Alluding perhaps to Josephus' claim that Pompey actually took nothing from the temple (*Antiquities* 14.72), he does none of these.

Selectivity and imagination together cast the ordinary people of Judea and the Galilee in opposition to the Romans, and to the Judean puppet government and high priests, including the major figures of Herod Antipas and the high priest Caiaphas. Whereas the canonical gospels, to varying degrees, cast Pharisees and Sadducees as opponents of Jesus, the film downplays their roles. Once, briefly, the narrator tells us that Jesus angered the scribes and Pharisees, who plan to kill him, but they clearly lack the ultimate authority to execute him, and their charge of blasphemy is of no interest to Pilate. Those who actually debate and determine Jesus' fate are instead a group of seven: the pro-curator Pilate and his wife, the puppet ruler Antipas, his wife, Herodias, her daughter, Salome, the high priest Caiaphas, and a fictitious but central character, a Roman centurion called Lucius.

While the film presents the gospel accounts of trials before Jewish authorities only in a brief prefatory remark by Pilate, it elaborates extensively on Pilate's trial of Jesus, harmonizing elements from all four gospels. Particularly important is an entirely imaginary scene between Pilate and Lucius, now appointed as Jesus' lawyer. When Lucius argues that Jesus' divine claims do not threaten Rome, Pilate agrees that religious disputes are irrelevant: only the accusations of anti-Roman activity matter.

Conspicuous by its absence is the particularly egregious language unique to the Gospel of Matthew, where Jews accept full responsibility for the death of Jesus with a saying that gave license to Christian persecution of Jews for millennia: 'His blood be on us and on our children' (Matt. 27:25). On the contrary, the film presents ordinary Jews as Jesus' supporters; even the occasional Jew who dismisses Jesus' teaching as 'words' is treated generously in the film, when the disciple John simply says, with kindness: 'Your friend didn't understand'. Particularly clever is the film's explanation for Pilate's release of Barabbas. Where the gospels, and traditional Christian interpretation, envision undifferentiated hostile Jews, clamoring for Barabbas and against Jesus, *King of Kings* offers an historically specific, and theologically neutral explanation. Barabbas' followers were at least better organized (if not more numerous) and shouted louder. As throughout the film, historical particularity replaces theological meaning.

The creation of a fictitious centurion named Lucius, whose name hints at a possible identification with the evangelist Luke, serves many purposes. Appointed early in the film to observe Jesus and his followers, Lucius takes verbatim notes when Jesus preaches at length on a mountain (uttering words combined from the differing accounts in Matt. 5–7 and Luke 6:17–49, where Jesus speaks on a level plain). He reads back Jesus' words to Pilate from a scroll in a scene that tacitly suggests how, if not actually where, the gospel writers might have received their information. He repeatedly verifies that Jesus preaches only peace, perhaps most tellingly in a wholly invented scene in which Jesus seeks to see John the Baptist in prison, and tells the conveniently present Lucius that he has come to free John. When Lucius is skeptical about Jesus' ability to spring John from his cell, Jesus replies, 'I come to free John *in* his cell', and indeed, that is what we see: extending his hand to John, Jesus assures John that he was indeed the one whom John awaited and thereby gives John inner peace before he dies.

In the trial before Pilate, Lucius does double duty. First, he facilitates a transparent retrojection of American legal proceedings into the first century, when Pilate now appoints him as Jesus' lawyer. Second, advocating for Jesus, he both argues, and secures Pilate's assent to one of the film's central tenets, that the Jewish charges of blasphemy against Jesus are of little import; the only significant legal question is whether Jesus is guilty of sedition against Rome. Lucius bookends the biography of Jesus in the film. Even before his delegation by Pilate, a much younger Lucius protects the child Jesus when Roman soldiers come to his family village, and at the crucifixion, Lucius proclaims, 'Surely, this man was the Christ', a line that comes close to the words all three synoptic authors attribute to a Roman centurion (Matt. 27:54; Mark 15:39; Luke 23:47).

Gender and women's rights were not yet pressing issues when *King of Kings* was made. Yet here, too, an analysis of its omissions, inclusions and inventions is instructive. Many ordinary women who interact with Jesus in the canonical gospels – Peter's mother-in-law (Matt. 8:14; Mark 1:30), the gentile mother of a possessed daughter whom Jesus heals (Matt. 15:21–28; Mark 7:24–30), the Samaritan woman in John 4, Mary and Martha (Luke 10:38–42, also John 11:1–6; 17–44; 12:2) – are absent from the film. Not only does the film omit the many ordinary women in the gospel accounts, but also it focuses almost entirely on female characters who exemplify feminine virtue and vice. Often drawing extensively on later Christian traditions, extensive invented scenes cast Mary the mother of Jesus as the wise, mature exemplar of maternal virtue, and Mary Magdalene as a repentant prostitute, although, as numerous feminist scholars (see

Schaberg 1992) have pointed out, there are no biblical warrants for such a depiction. Pilate's wife, who appears only in the Gospel of Matthew as a somewhat sympathetic character (Matt. 27:19), here serves as a model for the appeal of Christian truth to an aristocratic Roman woman.

Other fictional scenes depict Herod Antipas' wife, Herodias and her daughter, Salome, as craven sexual predators who seek John's death because he rebukes them for their sexual immorality. Salome's name does not occur in the Gospel accounts of the death of John (Matt. 14:1–12; Mark 6:14–29); it comes instead from Josephus, *Antiquities* 18.136–37, although not in connection with the death of John, whose differing account comes from *Antiquities* 18.116–19. Here, too, the film draws extensively from later Christian traditions, including the portrayal of Salome as a voluptuous adolescent who provocatively claims that 'this beast [John the Baptist] amuses me'. Salome was a popular subject for Renaissance painters, such as Filippo Lippi (*The Feast of Herod,* 1460–64), or Bernardino Luini (*Salome,* 1527–31), who depict her as beautiful and full-breasted, but late nineteenth and early twentieth-century art and drama particularly sexualize her, as in Gustave Moreau's *The Apparition* (1876); Lovis Corinth's *Salome* (1899) or Gaston Bussière's *Dance of the Seven Veils* (1926), and most influentially, Oscar Wilde's 1893 play *Salome* and Richard Strauss' 1905 opera of the same name. In the film John advises Salome to shun the evil of her family and denounces Herodias for whoring with the 'captains of Assyria' and the 'young men of Egypt'. All this serves, in good midrashic form, to explain and elaborate on the antagonism between the women and John to which the gospels of Mark and Matthew, and the account in Josephus, only allude.

Although it was in some ways brilliantly constructed, if fairly transparent in its intentions, *King of Kings* was not a critical success. It was derided for being another 'overblown biblical epic', whose handsome young Jesus looked too much like a 1950s teen idol. But one might also wonder whether its claims about Jesus, Romans and Jews were in fact somewhat uncomfortable for an American audience, including film critics, still very much grappling with complicity in the Holocaust, with anti-Semitism, and with McCarthyism and anti-Communist sentiment, that some recent critics have seen as another of the film's subtexts (Williams 2009). It is perhaps a little too simple to say that *King of Kings* offered more of a 'Jewish–Hollywood' fantasy than Americans were prepared to buy, but it remains true that behind the epic veneer and the stilted acting of Jeffrey Hunter, *King of Kings* grappled with a wide array of difficult mid-century issues that seems both more telling and compelling in retrospect than its reception would suggest.

Ross S. Kraemer

Further reading

Stephenson Humphries-Brooks (2006) '"I Was a Teenage Jesus in Cold War America": *King of Kings, (1961)*' in his *Cinematic Saviour: Hollywood's Making of the American Christ*, Westport, CT: Praeger. pp. 23–37.

Adele Reinhartz (2007) *Jesus of Hollywood*. New York, NY: Oxford University Press.

Jane Schaberg (1992) 'How Mary Magdalene Became a Whore.' *Bible Review* 8(5): 30–37; 51–52.

Richard Stern, Clayton N. Jefford, and Geric Debona (1999) *Savior on the Silver Screen*. New York, NY: Paulist Press. pp. 61–92.

W. Barnes Tatum (2004) *Jesus at the Movies: A Guide to the First Hundred Years*. Revised and expanded. Santa Rosa, CA: Polebridge Press. pp. 77–88.

Tony Williams, 'Nicholas Ray's King of Kings', *CineAction*, 22 March 2009, available online at www.thefreelibrary.com/Nicholas+Ray%27s+King+of +Kings.-a0194486565

THE KING OF KINGS (1927)

[Production Company: Producers Distributing Corporation (PDC). Director: Cecil B. DeMille. Screenplay: Jeanie MacPherson. Cinematography: Peverell Marley. Cast: H. B. Warner (Jesus Christ), Dorothy Cummings (Mary the Mother), Ernest Torrence (Peter), Joseph Schildkraut (Judas), Jacqueline Logan (Mary Magdalene), Alan Brooks (Satan), Rudolph Schildkraut (Caiaphas), Victor Varconi (Pontius Pilate), Michael Moore (Mark), Muriel McCormac (Blind Girl).]

Few films have done more to define the Hollywood biblical epic than Cecil B. DeMille's *The King of Kings* (1927), or to embody the classic cinematic Christ than his leading actor, H. B. Warner. More famous, more expensive, and more ostentatious than the thirty-nine previous versions of the Christ story, the film has been described by one critic, Sheila Johnston, as 'an interesting blend of showmanship, eroticism, vulgarity, and a rather charmingly naive, or faux naive picture postcard piety' (Channel Four *Jesus Christ Movie-Star* 1992).

After some solemn music and a historical notice, the viewer's attention is immediately arrested by scenes, both lurid and lecherous, that take place in an upper class brothel, where (as the intertitle announces), 'The beautiful courtesan MARY OF MAGDALA, laughed alike at

God and Man.' Concerned to hear that her boyfriend, Judas, has fallen under the spell of the carpenter, Jesus of Nazareth, she decides to rescue him from Jesus' clutches. 'Harness my zebras – gift of the Nubian King! This Carpenter shall learn that He cannot hold a man from Mary Magdalene!'

Mary's encounter with H. B. Warner's Christ gives the first thirty minutes of the film a remarkable dramatic tension. This is resolved, first of all, by the audience's first poignant view of Jesus, whose face is seen in close-up through the eyes of a little blind girl whom he has healed, and, secondly, by the exorcism of Mary herself, when she is cleansed of the seven deadly sins, and becomes thereafter his chastened and now suitably modest follower.

The remainder of the film presents the familiar Gospel story as Jesus garners opposition from the Jewish authorities, as he teaches and heals, and as events move into Passion Week. Key biblical scenes are given the DeMille treatment: the High Priest's Plot to Kill Jesus, The Woman Taken in Adultery, The Cleansing of the Temple, the Temptation of Jesus by Satan (but here in the Temple rather than the Wilderness), the Raising of Lazarus, the Last Supper, the Betrayal of Jesus by Judas, Jesus Before the Crowd, the Crucifixion and the Resurrection.

A practicing Christian with part-Jewish origins, DeMille, like the audiences of his day, was steeped in the Bible and Judaeo-Christianity, and had already produced and directed *The Ten Commandments* in 1923. He would later go on to produce and direct the Roman-Christian epic, *The Sign of the Cross* (1932), thereby completing a trilogy of 'religious dramas' that it had been his ambition to make. '*The Ten Commandments* (1923)', he writes in his autobiography, 'had been the story of the Giving of the Law. *The King of Kings* was the story of the Interpretation of the Law. *The Sign of the Cross*, if I could make it, would tell of the Preservation of the Law' (Hayne 1960: 280).

The biblical source texts were the primary written foundation for screenwriter Jeanie MacPherson's script; the film is punctuated by scriptural intertitles in the King James Version, many of which had been wrested from their original context.

The first screenings – at the Gaiety Theatre in New York on 19 April, and Grauman's Chinese Theatre in Hollywood on 18 May 1927 – were entirely silent. A sonorized version of the film, in which snatches of familiar Christian hymns or music punctuated the film's key scenes, was released in 1931. This version includes 'Lead Kindly Light' at the healing of the little blind girl; 'Blessed are the Pure in Heart' at the exorcism of Mary Magdalene; 'The Hallelujah Chorus' from Handel's Messiah when the people fete Jesus; 'By Cool Siloam's Shady Rill' when Jesus embraces a lamb in the Temple; 'Holy, Holy, Holy' as he recites the Lord's Prayer; 'Abide with Me' at the Last Supper and at Jesus' final appearance; 'O Sacred Head sore wounded' in Gethsemane; 'Nearer my God to Thee' on the cross; 'Jesus Christ is Risen Today' at the resurrection; and 'Rock of Ages' in a last dramatic frame set against an American skyline.

If the Bible (however imaginatively reconfigured) constituted the textual basis for the film, and Christian hymns gave it its emotional tenor, Victorian religious painting, particularly its iconography of the Christ-figure as illustrated in the popular household bibles of the time, was the principal visual inspiration for *The King of Kings*. No less than 276 representations of religious paintings have been claimed for the film, among them a great many Renaissance ones, but it is the biblical illustrations of the French painter, Jacques Joseph Tissot (1836–1902), and the French engraver and illustrator, Paul Gustave Doré (1832–83), which provide the most striking parallels to Warner's Christ. Popularized in works such as Tissot's *The Life of our Saviour Jesus Christ: Three Hundred and Sixty-Five Compositions from the Four Gospels* (1899), whose biblical scenes were based on a four-year period spent in Palestine, or Doré's *English Bible* (1866), which appeared in lavish, costly editions in Britain and the United States, these images were a major component of the visual tradition inherited by DeMille and his audiences.

What DeMille did with these traditional images, however, was spectacular. Blending piety, sex and violence (a combination DeMille ascribed to the Bible itself) and employing some striking cinemato-graphy (e.g. the slow dissolve to the face of Jesus in the little blind girl scene, or the double exposures in the Magdalene's exorcism), he brought startling vitality to traditional biblical scenes (e.g. the fluttering dove over the illuminated chalice at the end of the Last Supper) and flesh and blood to familiar scriptural characters. While an objective Christ, a painterly style, a static camera and stylized religious expressionism gave the film an otherworldly aura, and elements of the film resembled religious tableaux, DeMille's use of medium close-up, close-ups and subjective point of view shots did much to humanize his characters (Higashi 1994: 186), as did the descriptive intertitles.

Embodying the patriarchal virility and gravitas that DeMille wanted of his Christ figure (Warner was just over 50 at the time of filming), combined with a paternal tenderness and compassion, the principal actor's on-screen presence was compelling. The fictional relationship between Mary Magdalene (Jacqueline Logan) and Judas (Joseph Schildkraut) also excited the attention of the audience, the former, with her audacious costume and luminous flesh, radiating arrogance and eroticism; the latter, with his dandified garb and clean-shaven, shifty appearance, exuding avarice and deceit. In contrast to the decadent lovers, audiences were presented with the chastely dressed, nun-like Mary, Mother of Jesus (Dorothy Cummings), seated at her loom and surrounded by doves, and Peter (Ernest Torrence), 'the Giant Disciple, a fisherman quick of temper but soft of heart', who takes the young, orphan Mark (Mickey Moore) under his wing. Ranged against Jesus, DeMille offers an obese, mordant and venal Caiaphas (Rudolph Schildkraut), who 'cared more for revenue than religion' and (like Judas) a clean-shaven, bejewelled and black-garbed supernatural opponent, Satan, who materializes in the Temple to tempt Jesus to conquer the world.

Revenue and conquest of the commercial world were, of course, what it was all about within DeMille's own institutional context in the developing Hollywood film industry, where the manufacture and distribution of epics such as *The Ten Commandments* (1923) or *The King of Kings* (1927) was a complicated and demanding enterprise. As Babington and Evans note: 'The paradigm of a Christian director working on a Christianized Jewish text for Jewish producers aiming at a predominantly Christian audience suggests the complications involved' (Babington and Evans 1993: 35). There were sound commercial, educational and religious reasons for spending $1.3 million filming the life of Christ in 1926 (Maltby 1990: 190), however, not least the considerable interest taken in the motion picture industry at that time by the American churches, especially liberal Protestants, who were undergoing something of an ideological crisis.

The nineteen-twenties were dominated by a business and consumerist ethos, with which the churches were in competition but by which they were also influenced, and they were not slow themselves to see the appeal of the new medium as an opportunity to pursue their own ends. It has often been pointed out that DeMille employed, as a consultant for *The King of Kings*, Bruce Barton, one of the founding figures of modern advertising, whose own best-selling book, *The Man Nobody Knows: A Discovery of the Real Jesus* (1925) had sought to give a fillip to the Protestant capitalist ethic by touting an executive-style Jesus, a tough, manly, entrepreneurial businessman who had 'picked up twelve men from the bottom ranks of business and forged them into an organization that conquered the world' (Maltby 1990: 199).

There is certainly something of Barton's Jesus in Warner's strong, decisive, real-world, hands-on Christ, as evidenced in the Cleansing of the Temple scene, but the Christ of DeMille's *The King of Kings*, who heals young Mark's lameness, and mends a little girl's doll, also demonstrates a paternal or even 'feminine' side, thereby appealing to Victorian and immediately post-Victorian ideals surrounding the home, the family, children and domesticity. Further, in exorcising Mary Magdalene's demons, and thereby domesticating her haughty independence and aggressive sexuality, DeMille offers a comment on the sexual mores of the twenties, and on the so-called 'new women' of that period.

This sexual conservatism is matched by the religious conservatism of the film, which unashamedly addresses itself to the skepticism engendered in liberal Protestantism by new critical approaches to the Bible, and non-historicist ways of interpreting tradition. The lame child who is present in almost every scene, and whom Peter adopts as his son, historicizes and sentimentalizes the Christian tradition that views 'John Mark' as the writer of the first Gospel, the recorder of Peter's reminiscences and the one referred to as 'my son' in 1 Peter 5:13.

Despite DeMille's claim that 'probably more people have been told the story of Jesus of Nazareth through *The King of Kings* than through any other single work, except the Bible itself' (Hayne 1960: 258), first box office returns indicate that it only just managed to break even (Maltby 1990: 208). 'There is evidence', on the other hand, 'that in its non-commercial format *The King of Kings* was one of the most viewed films of all time' (Babington and Evans 1993:5). Some members of the audience were overcome by the experience, like the American minister who later informed H. B. Warner: 'I saw you in *The King of Kings* when I was a child and now, every time I speak of Jesus, it is your face I see' (Hayne 1960: 253). Others, like the young Martin Scorsese, had a different reaction: 'I saw the silent *King of Kings*, the Cecil B. DeMille 1927 version, on re-release when I was fifteen or so in a small theatre in New York. I found it hard to concentrate on silent films having grown up in the sound era, and therefore some of the emotions were lost on me. Although I like DeMille's films, and particularly their design, I just found this one very boring' (Thompson and Christie 1989: 130).

DeMille had complied with American censorship guidelines on the treatment of religious subjects in 1927 (Tatum 1997: 54–5); British film censorship, which banned 'the materialized figure of Christ', required a special licence for the London screening of *The King of Kings* in 1928. DeMille had also taken care to respect religious sensitivities, especially in the filming process itself (Warner was kept in quasi-religious quarantine during the making of the film), and to avoid any charge of anti-Semitism in his retelling of the Jesus story. Caiaphas, for example, is made to accept sole responsibility for Jesus's death. There were Jewish protests, however, and he consequently made further alterations to the film as originally released.

'I knew,' he stated in his autobiography,

> that there would be in the audience religious people fearful of how a subject dear and sacred to them would be treated, and people who were sceptics and had come to scoff, and people who were cynics and had come to witness DeMille's disaster.
>
> (Hayne 1960: 252)

On the whole, however, the film was well received, and even today continues to be transmitted over the networks, where it still enchants, amuses, inspires, repels, entertains or bores those who watch it.

William R. Telford

Further reading

Bruce Babington and P. W. Evans (1993) *Biblical Epics: Sacred Narrative in the Hollywood Cinema*. Manchester: Manchester University Press.

Bruce Barton (1925) *The Man Nobody Knows. A Discovery of the Real Jesus*. Indianapolis, IN: Bobbs-Merrill Company.

Donald Hayne (ed.) (1960) *The Autobiography of Cecil B. DeMille*. London: Allen.

Sumiko Higashi (1994) *Cecil B. DeMille and American Culture. The Silent Era*. Berkeley, Los Angeles, CA and London: University of California Press.

Richard Maltby (1990) '*The King of Kings* and the Czar of All the Rushes: the Propriety of the Christ Story', *Screen*. 31(2): 188–213.

W. Barnes Tatum (1997) *Jesus at the Movies: A Guide to the First Hundred Years*. Santa Rosa, CA: Polebridge.

William R. Telford (1997) 'Jesus Christ Movie-Star: The Depiction of Jesus in the Cinema', in C. Marsh and G. Ortiz (eds) *Explorations in Theology and Film. Movies and Meaning*. Oxford: Blackwell. pp. 115–39.

David Thompson and Ian Christie (eds) (1989) *Scorsese on Scorsese*. London: Faber & Faber.

Further viewing

Channel Four (20 April 1992) *Jesus Christ Movie-Star*

THE LAST TEMPTATION OF CHRIST (1988)

[Director: Martin Scorsese. Producer: Barbara De Fina. Screenplay: Paul Schrader, based on the novel by Niko Kazantzakis: Editor: Thelma

Schoonmaker; Music: Peter Gabriel. Cast: Willem Dafoe (Jesus); Harvey Keitel (Judas); Verna Bloom (Mary, Mother of Jesus); Barbara Hershey (Mary Magdalene); Andre Gregory (John the Baptist); Juliette Caton (Girl Angel).]

> I was asked [by producers] why I wanted to make this picture, and I replied, 'So I can get to know Jesus better.'
>
> (Martin Scorsese)

Still under the influence of Pier Paulo Pasolini's gritty 1964 *The Gospel According to St. Matthew,* and burning with a desire to recreate the drama and iconography of the Passion that he had loved since his days as an altar boy, Martin Scorsese's interpretation of *The Last Temptation* aimed to involve a contemporary audience in the challenge posed by the mystery of Christ's incarnation. From the beginning of Scorsese's film, the audience understands this is not a traditional Gospel-interpreted account of the life of Jesus. The film opens with a dazed-looking Jesus working in his carpenter's shed, making giant crosses for the torturous punishments that the occupying Roman forces use to execute murderers, thieves, and political prisoners. While Jesus suspects that there is some purpose to his life, he fears God, and hopes that his collaboration with the enemy will turn God against him, silencing the mocking voices in his head. Immediately his friend, a political Jewish zealot, Judas dashes into the shed, breaks huge planks of wood, and castigates Jesus for his perfidy. 'You're a Jew killing Jews,' he shouts, in a decidedly Bronx accent. Dafoe shrugs and finishes his work, muttering to himself, trying to keep out of the way of the raging Judas. Finally his work completed, Jesus bends under the enormous weight of the cross, and carries the burdensome wood on his back up the hill to the waiting centurions.

As Jesus watches the prisoner lifted onto the cross and screaming in pain, five minutes into the film, the audience has the imprint of the Passion, as their burden to carry throughout the movie. This after-image, a theological footprint permeated with the sacramentality of close community and the intensity of grace, is trademark Scorsese. The actual setting and time period of the film are blotted out by the keen vision of the film-maker, who uses his neighbourhood cronies (Keitel, De Nero, Hershey, and even his parents in bit parts) as though his retelling of the Kazantzakis novel were taking place on a Sunday afternoon on Elizabeth Street in New York City. For Scorsese, brought up as a traditional Catholic, intrigued by the plaster statues and luxurious pageantry of the Church, the sacred is present in the profane things of the world. God works through specific people − Scorsese's favorite actors − and salvation depends on belonging to a community.

Harvey Keitel's Judas, shouting and waving his hands, wild-haired, spouting the 'New Yawk' dialect of the Scorsese neighbourhood, in a first-century village in the hills outside Jerusalem, reminds the viewer of a very young Keitel, caught in another neighborhood, an Italian peasant village dropped into urban Manhattan, the world of *Mean Streets* (1973). At the opening of *Mean Streets* Charlie (Harvey Keitel), explains to the Johnny Boy (De Niro) and the other guys,

> You don't make up for your sins in church. You do it in the streets. You do it at home. The rest is bullshit and you know it. It's all bullshit except the pain. The pain of hell. The burn from a lighted match increased a million times. Infinite.

In his films Scorsese continually recreates this neighbourhood where ethnicity and faith are wrapped tightly together. It is in Scorsese's neighbourhood that people are torn between their duty to God and their loyalty to the gang.

Like *The Last Temptation of Christ*, most of Scorsese's films, particularly *Taxi Driver* (1976), *Raging Bull* (1980), *Mean Streets*, *Goodfellas* (1990) and *Gangs of New York* (2002), are built around the tensions and devotions to the fellas in the neighbourhood, whether that neighbourhood is the brick and steel of the hard-scrabble streets of New York or the ancient-looking Moroccan villages. The afterimages created by these films are tinted with the sinful and the sacramental, in which the hood and the priest, the mistress and the wife, the gangster and the addict, swing between isolation and community. Through studying these films, it becomes clear that for Scorsese, Catholic sacramental sensibility is passed on through stories, rather than through doctrines and hierarchical structures.

What does Scorsese's neighbourhood have to do with Jesus in *The Last Temptation*? Clearly he is God, and we know his story before we see the sword and sandal Jesus films. In these earlier films Jesus does not struggle or fear his fate, except perhaps for that one heart-rending cry, 'Father, why have you forsaken me?' (Matt. 27:46 and Mark 15:34). But it is the fully human side of Jesus that attracts Scorsese. He wanted Jesus to be the kind of guy 'you could sit down with, have dinner or a drink with' (Scorsese 2003: 117). As the Letter to the Hebrews explains, 'we do not have a high priest who is unable to empathize with our weaknesses, but we have one who has been tempted in every way, just as we are − *yet he did not sin*'. (Heb. 4:15; emphasis added). That austere perfection, the Christ who is fully God, could not have lived a perfect, sinless life unless He *was* God.

But Scorsese's Jesus is not perfect. He shivers in fear of the whispering voices in his head. He is not certain whether it is God or Satan who is calling to him. As he walks along the empty shoreline of the Galilee, his cloak billowing in the wind, he seems vulnerable and uncertain of himself. He makes crosses for the Romans, he flirts with his childhood friend, Mary the Magdalene, and he stays away from the zealots like Judas who live in the village (filmed in a small uncharted Moroccan village that truly seems to be 2000 years old).

Gradually as the story unfolds, not in the Gospel narrative order, but in the order that highlights the developing tensions within Jesus's life, Jesus begs Judas to stay with him, to walk with him, accompany him, anything to stave off his fear and loneliness. Scorsese seems to be asking, 'What is sin?' Is it destroying the stalls of the moneychangers in the Temple, is it having fantasies about having sex with women, is it trying to run from God? Both film-maker and protagonist struggle with these questions. In the film Jesus confesses to Jeroboam, 'Lucifer's inside me. He says I am not the son of Mary and Joseph. I am the Son of God. I am God'. Dafoe delivers the line with a shrug, as though it is Lucifer jerking Jesus around, not a message from the Lord.

In his attempt to show Jesus as fully human, Scorsese emphasizes the confusion within Jesus as the film jump cuts from the villagers shouting at each other in the marketplace, to the bleak shore, where Jesus struggles alone with the whispering devil. Scorsese even uses colours to reflect Jesus' two taunting worlds. His skin is the texture of bleached wood; the sheep are the colour of the stones on the shore; the reeds in the lake the colour of the camels in the marketplace. Jesus tells Judas, 'I'm a liar. I'm afraid all the time. I cannot fight with God anymore.' Ever the earthy realist, Judas laughs. 'God's plan? Voices you hear are God's voice? The fainting spells, the visions, these are *God's* plan?' Finally, Judas asks Jesus and the audience, 'If I don't kill you, what happens?'

The question needs no answer because the audience knows the narrative. Scorsese lets the audience perceive the transformation of the man into the divine slowly and gradually, as Jesus himself experiences it. As we watch the spectacle of the miracles, we see that Jesus is not proud of his abilities; rather, he is terrified. Curing the blind man, mixing his saliva with herbs, was a trick that could be accomplished by many first-century magicians. But the learning curve sharpens; each miracle draws Jesus closer to the moment when the human will become God. One careless gesture finally combines the figure of Jesus with the figure of the Christ. Jesus eats an apple, an everyday human event, and then throws the core into a fire, which disappears! He is revealed: he is both human and divine. The Cross awaits. Jesus settles the question with the rabbis in the Temple. With a rare steely resolve, he tells the aged men wearing phylacteries and fringed prayer shawls, 'When I say I, rabbi, I mean God. You think God belongs only to you? God is not an Israelite. He belongs to everybody.' The rabbis stare at him. If they are to survive, this madman must die.

The lynchpin miracle, the one that leaves no question in Jesus' mind or in the mind of the audience that the Cross is near, occurs in a dark cave, where Jesus confronts death. As he raises Lazarus, he realizes that the voices were not false. He is God. While Lazarus's gnarled hand grasps his, pulling him into the dark of the tomb, it marks for the audience the moment that death begins to pull Jesus in, a death that he will have to experience as a man, although he is God.

It is the final 35 minutes of the film that drove the Church and the fundamentalist Christian media into a lather. Scorsese became a scourge. The fury swirled around the author's and film-maker's suggestion that Jesus jump down from the Cross, in the middle of his Agony, and walk off into his ideal world, the neighbourhood. (For detailed account of the controversy in getting *The Last Temptation* made and then getting audiences to see it, see Scorsese 2003, Appendix 273–79). Ironic that the fantasy on the Cross, the imagined narrative of Jesus marrying, having children, a home, in the familiar neighbourhood and a death from old age rather than torture on the Cross, is considered blasphemy; after all, marriage, baptism of children, and anointing of the sick and dying are sacraments of the Church.

When the Moral Majority heard about the film, the sexuality of Jesus, the desires that make him sinful, and therefore not God, who is without sin, they took action. Producers walked off the project, and studios wiggled out of their deals by cutting the budget, limiting locations. Finally when theater owners refused to book the film, a group of distinguished theologians met in New York City to give their views on the controversy. Episcopal Bishop of New York, Paul Moore, concluded that the film was in all ways 'Christologically correct'. Moore understood that in trying to tell the story from Jesus' point of view, as a carpenter who recognizes his destiny and struggles against it, Scorsese was continuing his lifelong exploration of the lure of evil. Theologically, this meant showing the concept of the incarnation, of Christ as fully human, rather than referring to it as a theoretical assumption, as so many of the other Jesus films had. Instead of a verbally defined incarnation, in *The Last Temptation* Scorsese made the word into cinematic flesh. Following his vision from earlier films, Scorsese presents in his work a spiritual essence that is always immanent in the material world, and the material always ready to split open to disclose its spiritual content.

Alice Bach

Further reading

Martin Scorsese (2003) *Scorsese on Scorsese*, ed. Ian Christie and D. Thompson. Rev. edition. London: Faber & Faber.

Further viewing

Mean Streets (Martin Scorsese, 1973)
Jesus of Nazareth (Franco Zefferelli, 1977)
Goodfellas (Martin Scorsese, 1990)

THE LIFE OF MOSES (1909–1910)

[Production Company: Vitagraph. Director: J. Stuart Blackton. Screenplay: Madison L. Peters. Cast: Pat Hartigan (Moses), Julia Arthur, William Humphrey, Charles Kent, Edith Storey (variety of roles).]

While Cecil B. DeMille's successive versions of *The Ten Commandments* (1923, 1956) have ensured Moses' status as a Hollywood icon, it is less widely known that Moses' first starring role in an American movie came much earlier, in Stuart Blackton's *The Life of Moses* (1909–10).

In the first decade of the twentieth century – before the fledgling American film industry took flight from the East coast for Hollywood – various civic and ecclesial authorities suspected that the films of Vitagraph and others were appealing to the baser desires of the nation, rather than contributing to the greater good. In response, Vitagraph began to release a variety of 'quality' films based on historical subjects (e.g. George Washington), the classical literary canon (e.g. Shakespeare's *Julius Caesar*), and the scriptures (Uricchio and Pearson 1993).

That Vitagraph's foray into biblical films was at least partly inspired by those of their European rival, Pathé, is suggested by Vitagraph's filming of some of the same stories, including *The Judgment of Solomon* (1909). At the same time, there was little in Vitagraph's other biblical films (e.g. *Salome* [1908], *Saul and David* [1909], and *Jephthah's Daughter: A Biblical Tragedy* [1909]) which would have prepared cinema-goers on either side of the Atlantic for *The Life of Moses* (1909–10), a film which established many of the interpretive and production trajectories which influenced DeMille's 'epic Moses' and indeed the genre of the 'biblical epic' generally.

Even in 1909, Moses was no stranger to the cinema, having featured already in Pathé's *La Vie de Moïse* (1905) – a film with a running time of just over five minutes (525 ft) in keeping with the footage of other Pathé 'biblical films'. While the trend toward longer running times on both sides of the Atlantic meant that Vitagraph's *Saul and David* (1909) consumed a full reel (1000 ft) and 'quality films' like *Julius Caesar* were even allowed two (2000 ft), Vitagraph's decision to devote a total of 5000 feet to *The Life of Moses,* released in five instalments between December 1909 and Feb 2010, was truly extraordinary. Alice Guy's *La Vie de Christ* (1906) and Ferdinand Zecca's *La Vie et Passion de Notre Seigneur Jesus Christ* (1907) had both stretched over multiple reels, but only the enduring popularity of the life of Christ had heretofore warranted such an inordinate investment in film footage. It is thus a measure of the scale of Vitagraph's ambitions and their confidence in the market for the film, that they were willing to fund a life of Moses which dwarfed even previous cinematic lives of Christ. Indeed, within two months of the release of the fifth and final reel in February 1910, *Moses* was already being viewed in its entirety (Uricchio and Pearson 1993: 163) and may thus lay claim to being the earliest biblical film of 'feature' length – 90 minutes.

The influence of this expansion of running time on 'epic' and specifically 'biblical films' may be seen in Kalem's better-known *From the Manger to the Cross* which was released in its entirety (rather than monthly instalments) in 1912, but did not surpass *Moses* in length. Subsequent association of epic subject matter with above average film length was assured by Griffith's *Intolerance* (1916) (163 min) and perpetuated by the biblical epics of the Fifties, including DeMille's 220 minute *Ten Commandments* (1956).

Also noteworthy alongside *Moses'* exceptional length, and not unrelated to it, is the promotional discourse surrounding the epic scale of the production's ambitions. A promotional poster trumpeted *Moses's* $10,000 scene of the Red Sea and total expenditure of $50,000, an enormous sum of money in an era where Biograph was spending $500–600 per reel on average (Uricchio and Pearson 1993: 170). Again, DeMille's later *Ten Commandments* (1956) illustrates the enduring association of the biblical epic with the discourse of unprecedented expenditure, as witnessed by this piece of thinly disguised pre-release publicity:

> Soon the longest, most costly, most monumental movie in all the history of moviemaking will begin unfolding its three hours and 41 minutes of biblical pageantry. ... This production of *The Ten Commandments* which costs $13.5 millon [a record at the time] cleaves to the Book of Exodus ... , filling its gaps from the writings of ancient historians and from present-day archaeological deduction.
>
> (*Life* 12 November 1956, pp. 115–22)

The discourse of literalism, that is, 'cleaving' to the biblical texts, reflects sensitivities surrounding the legitimacy of a particular filmic interpretation – sensitivities which were addressed for the first time in 1909 when Stuart Blackton, the Vitagraph film director, hired Rev. Madison Peters to offer his expertise and imprimatur. A well-known, interdenominational preacher, Peters was used by Vitagraph as screenwriter, consultant and guarantor of both the accuracy of the film's interpretation and, as may be seen below, the piety of its production: 'Those taking part in the making of the picture could be seen through the weeks in the study of the Bible in order that they might, in spirit, enter into what I had outlined in my manuscript story.' ('Bible Teaching by Pictures' *Film Index*, 4 December 1909).

This promotional discourse of the 'pious production' would later be deployed to good effect first in relation to Kalem's *From the Manger to the Cross* (1912) and then famously in DeMille's biblical epics – even as the latter filled the narrative 'gaps' with generous helpings of impiety. Indeed it could be argued that the cinematic filling of narrative gaps too finds its 'biblical epic' origins in Blackton's *The Life of Moses*.

So, for instance, Pathé's five-minute *La Vie de Moïse* (1905) begins with a scene well-known from Western art: 'Moses saved from the waters' (Exod. 2:3–10). Assuming the audience's knowledge of Exodus, the film then moves directly and without explanation to a 30 second scene of the 'Burning Bush' (Exod. 3:1–4:17). By contrast, Blackton's abundance of footage allows him to begin with graphic scenes of the Israelites at hard labour, a sequence which appears to have inspired DeMille's own opening to his *Ten Commandments* (1923) and perhaps also that of *The Prince of Egypt* (1998). Before eventually depicting the 'saving of Moses from the waters', Blackton lingers over the narrative of Moses' early life, about which the French film is silent. This narrative includes not only the hiding of Moses, but also the proclamation and implementation of Pharaoh's decree that the Hebrew male children be killed. Most significant for the subsequent development of the biblical epic, Blackton goes beyond the biblical text itself, foreshadowing the role of Pharaoh's daughter and her maids in Moses' deliverance by having them vainly beseech Pharaoh to repeal his murderous decree.

At this point the action cuts to the interior of the house of Amram and Jochebed, where Moses's mother asks Miriam to fetch some water from the well. The next cut introduces the scene at a well, where the sight of a woman pursued by a soldier and violently deprived of her child sends Miriam back to the house in a panic. Having warned her mother of the danger and joined her in praying for Moses's deliverance, Miriam then assists her mother as Moses is evacuated from the house. The action next moves to the banks of the Nile, clearly shot on location at a river rather than in a studio, as in the 1905 French film. As Jochebed hurriedly daubs pitch on the basket, Miriam is sent to search for a suitable place to deposit Moses along the water's edge. As she exits frame right, the action cuts to a studio scene of the riverbank which Miriam then enters from the left of the frame. Having spotted some steps down to the water and noticing Pharaoh's daughter approaching, Miriam retraces her steps and we cut back to the scene of her mother who has now finished preparing the basket. Matching cuts again bring them to the location spied by Miriam and having deposited the basket in the reeds, they both exit. From its focus on the water, the camera then tilts up to catch the entrance of Pharaoh's daughter and her retinue from the background. As they descend to the water's edge, Blackton cuts to parallel action – in this case, Jochebed's great grief and anguished prayers that her child may be spared – before cutting back to the Nile, where Moses is soon discovered. As Moses is being retrieved, the film cuts to a closer shot to afford a better view of the action before retreating to the earlier distance.

In comparison with the earlier *La Vie de Moïse* in 1905, Blackton's film more fully reflects the biblical narrative and indeed goes well beyond it by offering a plausible scenario to explain how Moses' parents learn of the threat to their child. Whereas the static, long-shot, autonomous-tableau style of *La Vie de Moïse* limits the development of narrative tension, Blackton's 1910 film reflects the growing appreciation of the impact of editing on filmic stories. Indeed the anxiety of Miriam, and eventually also Jochebed, on her return to the house is reflected not merely within the scenes themselves, but also in the progressively quicker pace of the editing. In addition to other editing advancements such as cross-cutting, Blackton's film also displays developments in camera work such as tilts and closer positioning which mark the evolution of American cinematic style and technique between 1905 and 1910 (Shepherd 2008).

When it arrived on European screens, Vitagraph's blockbuster *Moses* had an immediate impact on the renaissance of the biblical genre already underway in France. Unable to match Blackton's comprehensive coverage of the *Life of Moses* from birth to death, Andréani's *Moïse sauvé des eaux* (Pathé, 1911) chose instead to focus his much more limited footage on only one episode, 'the finding of Moses', in order to allow him to match and indeed exceed the level of detail offered by the American *Moses*. Likewise the focus of Louis Feuillade's *L'Exode* (Gaumont 1910) on 'The Passover', the 'Plague of the Firstborn', and the 'Departure from Egypt' seems to reflect an awareness that Blackton's film devoted a mere 10 minutes to a depiction of Exodus chapters 11–12. Such a suggestion is strengthened by the observation that even within these three episodes, it is at those narrative moments where Blackton most quickly moves on, that Feuillade tends to linger.

Perhaps showing Blackton's influence, Feuillade offers three shots in 'dramatizing' the Passover regulations (Exod. 12), portraying the preparation for the meal in the house of Moses – he functions in both films as the leader of the Passover Seder – the daubing of the doors with blood outside, and finally the celebration and meal back in the house. So too Feuillade's foregrounding of the melodramatic potential of the death of the firstborn, particularly Pharaoh's son, is likely to have been partially influenced by Blackton's treatment of this same episode. As in Blackton's film, in *L'Exode*, Pharaoh's son becomes the key witness and victim of his father's folly and hubris.

While DeMille's own interest in Pharaoh's son (*Ten Commandments*, 1923, 1956) would tend rather toward demonization, Blackton's elaboration on the biblical tradition at this point and elsewhere was crucial in the development of the biblical epic, as seen in the work of DeMille and others. For instance, Blackton's willingness to dwell on the courtship of Moses and Zipporah established a trajectory toward interpretive elaboration and innovation in the biblical epic, which find its echoes in Moses' romantic entanglements with Nefretiri (*Ten Commandments*, 1956) and indeed in the scene of Moses and Zipporah at the tent of Jethro in *The Prince of Egypt* (1998). By persuading Vitagraph to allow him 5000 feet of film for *The Life of Moses*, Stuart Blackton paved the way for the inclusion of such episodes and the expansion of subsequent versions of the Bible on film to truly epic proportions.

David Shepherd

Further reading

'Bible Teaching by Pictures,' *Film Index*, Dec. 4, 1909.

'DeMille's Greatest,' *Life*, Nov. 12, 1956. pp. 115–22.

David Shepherd (2008) 'Prolonging "The Life of Moses": Spectacle and Story in the Early Cinema' in: (ed.) D. Shepherd, *Images of the Word: Hollywood's Bible and Beyond*. Semeia Studies. Atlanta: Society of Biblical Literature. pp. 11–38.

Anthony Slide and Alan Grevinson (1987) *The Big V: A History of the Vitagraph Company*. Metuchen: Scarecrow Press.

William Uricchio and Roberta Pearson (1993) *Reframing Culture: The Case of the Vitagraph Quality Films*. Princeton: Princeton University Press.

MONTY PYTHON'S LIFE OF BRIAN (1979)

[Production Company: HandMade Films. Director: Terry Jones. Screenplay: Monty Python troupe (Graham Chapman, John Cleese, Terry Gilliam, Eric Idle, Terry Jones, and Michael Palin). Cinematography: Peter Biziou. Cast: Monty Python troupe in multiple roles, including Chapman (Brian, Wise Man #2, Biggus Dickus). Also Kenneth Colley (Jesus), Sue Jones-Davies (Judith).]

Like an epic Jesus film, the opening frames of *Life of Brian* portray an infancy scene (Matt. 2:9–11). The blessed child at the center of the action is not Jesus, however, but Brian Cohen, Jesus' unlucky doppelgänger. What follows is a comic, James Bond–style animated title sequence which underlines Brian's ordinariness and begins the mixture of film styles through which the film calls attention to itself and undercuts claims to truth, implicit in epic historical realism.

The film proper opens with Jesus' spectacular Sermon (compare that in *King of Kings* [1961]). The adult Brian and his mother Mandy are so far away that 'peacemakers' become 'cheese makers' (Matt. 5:9), those invested in the status quo become the blessed, and reverence becomes a querulous brawl. Losing interest, Brian and Mandy look for more exciting entertainment: a stoning. Because women are not permitted to attend stonings, Brian's mother Mandy, played by Terry Jones in drag, dresses as a man to attend. Surprisingly, it is the priest in charge who is stoned, by the crowd, on the grounds that he blasphemed. Afterwards, Brian and Mandy travel a road lined with skeletons on crosses – also found in *The Greatest Story Ever Told* (1965) – and meet an ex-leper beggar unhappy because Jesus' miracle has left him without vocation (e.g. Matt. 8:1–4).

At home, a Roman soldier awaits Mandy's sexual services. The humiliated Brian learns that he is a Roman soldier's bastard (compare the Talmud's comments on Jesus' ancestry, tractate Sanhedrin 104b; 67b). The epiphany inaugurates Brian's rebellious attempt to assert his Jewishness, a matter underlined with numerous ethnic slurs. This scene counters the trajectory found in Christian discourse, which moves from Jewish origins toward the universal (divine) Christ, but it echoes the path of historical criticism's discovery of a Jewish Jesus. The People's Front of Judea sends Brian to write anti-Roman graffiti, which leads to a pedantic Latin lesson from a centurion and to the first of Brian's many comic near escapes, a staple of comedies from the silent *The Gold Rush* (1925) or *City Lights* (1931) to the present. The revolutionary Judith stands in for Judas; she helps Brian back to PFJ headquarters. An attempt to kidnap Pilate's wife goes awry when the revolutionaries kill each other. Brian alone survives and escapes from his trial when Pilate's speech impediment renders the Roman guards helpless with laughter.

A passing UFO saves the fleeing Brian as he falls from a high tower (Matt. 4:5–7?). After the UFO crash lands, Brian hides again in PFJ headquarters. Falling from a rickety balcony into a marketplace of apocalyptic prophets, Brian attracts attention with a message echoing Jesus' teaching (e.g. Matt. 7:1; 6:28) far more clearly than the opening spectacular Sermon does. A crowd decides Brian is the messiah because he denies it; this may allude to the 'messianic secret', a concept developed by scholars to explain Mark's Jesus' avoidance of public messianic acclamations (e.g. Mark 1:44); the crowds chase Brian through the marketplace and into the wilderness. On the way, they squabble among themselves over whether the 'messiah's' definitive symbol is the sandal or the gourd; Brian had left both of these objects behind in his rush to escape the mob. When they find Brian, they acclaim him as a miracle-worker, based on their misunderstanding of some of Brian's comments, as well as of a hermit's complaint that Brian has caused him to break his vow of silence (cf. Matt. 9:32–33). As the followers storm off to kill the hermit as an unbelieving heretic, Brian departs with Judith.

After their sexual tryst, the nude Brian throws open the shutters of his mother's house to find the adoring throng below. Brian exhorts the people to think for themselves (compare Jesus' teaching in *Jesus Christ Vampire Hunter* [2001]), but they chant mindlessly after him, 'We're all individuals'; the exception is one wit who says he is not. When Judith acclaims – and thereby betrays – Brian, soldiers take him to Pilate who adds his name to the list of 139 other crucifixions scheduled for that day.

Failing to rouse the PFJ to save Brian, Judith convinces the crowd to ask for Brian's freedom (compare Matt. 27:11–16). As Pilate cannot pronounce Brian's name, comedy replaces the scene's typical blood lust. Comic misadventures, including the fact that several characters claim to be Brian (cf. *Spartacus*'s [1960] finale), lead to the release of a jokester, rather than Brian himself, who has been pardoned. At the crucifixions, the PFJ celebrates Brian's martyrdom by singing 'For He's a Jolly Good Fellow', the Judean People's Front commits suicide in protest, Judith confesses her undying admiration, and Brian's mother castigates him as a 'very naughty boy' (contrast the adoration, e.g. in John 19:17–30). In a final irreverence, the crucified sing 'Always Look on the Bright Side of Life (Death)', and a voiceover advertizes the sale of the record in the foyer (compare the successful music of *Jesus Christ Superstar* [1973] and *Godspell* [1973]).

In the context of Bible films, the question is whether *Life of Brian* is a Jesus film. Parallels with earlier Jesus films are obvious, as are the parodies of Gospel stories. Nonetheless, Brian is clearly not Jesus. Brian's replacement of Jesus opens a space for amusing riffs on the messianic secret, the development of sayings and miracle traditions, the making of messiahs, and the development of sectarian, rather than apostolic, Christianity. The troupe's comic title for their film during production, *Jesus Christ: Lust for Glory*, summarizes the point about the Jesus/Gospel tradition succinctly. That no glory attends Brian exposes the desire for glory in the Gospel tradition that obscures Judaism and the Jewish Jesus with spiritual, glorious *Christianity*. The film's comedy lays bare the semiotic incongruity between a Jewish nobody and the glorious Christ.

But the film is funny and comprehensible only if we perceive that in some sense that Brian is Jesus. Even if he is not *the* Jesus of the Gospels or of Hollywood, Brian takes on the style of a Jesus to comic effect. Another Jewish nobody reluctantly becomes a messiah cavalierly disposed of by the Roman Empire. The film's plurality of apocalyptic prophets, messiahs, and crucifixions, and the fact that the troupe plays multiple roles, further intensifiy the comic tropes of disguise and mistaken identity (see Mark 13:5–6, 21). Identities, even those of a messiah, become mere façades. Semiotics comes to the fore. Brian stands profanely beside a Jesus who is no longer unique.

The film, then, is more than a mere parody of followers. It may even be parabolic: 'There was a young Jewish bastard who became a crucified messiah … '. A parable exists alongside a dominant discourse and invites those inside that myth to explore their story's lineaments and absurdities. If myth calls for true belief, parable calls for reflection.

If myth uses comedy to mock and dismiss the outsider, parable uses comedy wryly to displace the insider. Parable does not say 'those fools'; it implies 'we Christians', 'we imperialists', 'we moderns', and so forth. While the film's comedy is often quite British, even to the use of a good Irish name for the nobody messiah, the send-up of Christianity, empire, and individualism extends the parable beyond local borders. The callous crucifixions, the soldiers who like following orders, and the incompetent administrators mock imperial excess, but such scenes stand alongside the PFJ's reluctant, amusing admission that the empire has provided some benefits, such as aqueducts, sanitation, safety, and roads. A crazy, right-wing prisoner even lauds crucifixion as the best thing the Romans ever did for the Jews. The absurdity – along with the claim that the crucified are lucky bastards and that crucifixion is a dawdle that gets one out in the open air – expresses a comic ambivalence toward empire, law and order ideologies, and revolutionaries. The tone differs dramatically from the brutal Roman defense of empire, the denial of empire's existence by the US, and postcolonial denunciation of empire. Comedy undercuts all these options by denying their seriousness and finality.

Similarly, while the film's messiah advocates individualism, the troupe laughs at it. The crowd's mindless chant that they are individuals reveals the fashion in which the litany of 'individualism' forms modern persons en masse more succinctly than does any Michel Foucault book (see, e.g. his *Discipline and Punish*). Incidentally, in addition to disenchanting the messiah's own teaching, the scene also undercuts the modern polarity that elevates Enlightenment individualism over benighted superstition – or faith.

The ambivalence created as one scene undercuts another resembles the style of Friedrich Nietzsche as described by Karl Jaspers: 'if one thinks one knows what Nietzsche says on a particular topic, one has not read enough Nietzsche' (see Kaufmann 1958: vii). One could say the same of the Bible or this film. Brian also resembles Nietzsche's famous idiot, who also is and is not Jesus (see his *Antichrist*). For Nietzsche, Jesus is but one of many idiots. As the idiot does not yet belong to a discourse system, ideology easily foists any role, even messiah, on such uncultured, semiotic blanks. One can compare the protagonists of *Being There* (1979), *Forest Gump* (1994), and Jesus films, which some critics disparage for failing to develop Jesus as a character (see Walsh 2003).

Like Nietzsche, the troupe speaks from a post-Christian perspective. Trained as children in Christianity, they have reached adult indifference. The UFO deliverance of Brian, like the comic misunderstandings of the Sermon, illustrates this distance well. The UFO parodies the Gospel *deus ex machina* pattern and Gospel exaltation of Jesus in the transfiguration (Matt. 17:1–9; Mark 9:2–10; Luke 9:23–27) and resurrection narratives (Matt. 28; Mark 16; Luke 24; John 20–21) and in the Johannine passion (John 18–19). By contrast, Brian is always falling down or out of something – a spaceship, a balcony. Nonetheless, along with Brian's marketplace acclamation, this 'lifting up' inaugurates the 'messianic' phase of Brian's career. That the alien UFO replaces the Gospel's authorizing divine voice is a transformation that befits a culture in which epics like *Star Wars* have replaced biblical epics in popularity.

Brian's crucifixion with 139 others similarly stands apart from Western Christianity's most basic symbol. The banality and plurality profane Jesus' cross. The focus on Brian's unlucky death reveals rather painfully that any meaning(s) arises only as various characters attach their own ideology to Brian's death or, for that matter, as Christians attach meaning(s) to Jesus' death. Message and media cohere eerily here because some of the theater complexes showing this film offered John Heyman's *The Jesus Film* (1979), with its ideology of Jesus' salvific death, at the same time. Twenty-five years later, at the height of the deadly, apocalyptic seriousness of *The Passion of the Christ* (2004), *Life of Brian* was re-released in theaters. For some audiences, the incongruities were salutary.

As the absurd, final song-and-dance routine suggests, salvation lies in comedy, which sits lightly and bemusedly in the face of death and dominant discourses. The jokester escapes and the crucified laugh at death, at life, and at themselves. If the film has a message, it is in the song 'Always Look on the Bright Side of Life'. As one laughs in disbelief at the absurdities, one may reflect on what makes a messiah, a Gospel, or a victorious sect. One may remember that messianic acclamations are wrong more often than not, if not always. At least one laughs at the incongruity of an ordinary, Jewish, bastard messiah. Of course (wink, wink) this is not the Gospel Jesus.

Richard Walsh

Further reading

James G. Crossley (2011) 'Life of Brian or Life of Jesus? Uses of Critical Biblical Scholarship and Non-Orthodox Views of Jesus in Monty Python's *Life of Brian.*' *Relegere: Studies in Religion and Reception* 1(1): 93–114.

Philip R. Davies (1998) 'Life of Brian Research', in J. Cheryl Exum and Stephen Moore (eds) *Biblical Studies/Cultural Studies: The Third Sheffield Colloquium*. Sheffield: Sheffield Academic Press. pp. 400–14.

Carl Dyke (2002) 'Learning from *The Life of Brian*: Saviors for Sinners', in George Aichele and Richard Walsh (eds) *Screening Scripture: Intertextual Connections Between Scripture and Film*. Harrisburg, PA: Trinity Press International. pp. 229–50.

Michel Foucault (1977) *Discipline and Punish: The Birth of the Prison*. Trans. Alan Sheridan. New York, NY: Random House.

Walter A. Kaufmann (1958) *Nietzsche: Philosopher, Psychologist, Antichrist*. New York, NY: Vintage.

Friedrich Nietzsche (1954) *The Antichrist*. In *The Portable Nietzsche*. Ed. and trans. Walter A. Kaufmann. New York, NY: Viking.

Richard C. Stern, Clayton N. Jefford, and Guerric DeBona, O.S.B., eds (1999) *Savior on the Silver Screen*. New York, NY: Paulist Press. pp. 233–63.

Richard Walsh (2003) *Reading the Gospels in the Dark Portrayals of Jesus in Film*. Harrisburg, PA: Trinity Press International.

THE NIGHT OF THE HUNTER (1955)

[Production Company: United Artists. Director: Charles Laughton. Screenplay: James Agee and Charles Laughton. Cinematography: Stanley Cortez. Cast: Robert Mitchum (Harry Powell), Shelley Winters (Willa Harper), Lillian Gish (Rachel Cooper).]

Set in rural America during the depression, *The Night of the Hunter* is a powerfully frightening story of children under threat, a wicked man and revivalist religion. Anyone, in any country, who experienced this rural, revivalist ambience before and after the Second World War, will recognize a great deal. Younger people may be horrified. The narrative derives its shape and momentum from the struggle for survival provoked by economic collapse and the people involved in that struggle, one despicable, many confused, and some admirable.

The plot is simple. Harry Powell, an itinerant preacher, is a ruthless exploiter of the fears and sufferings of others, a serial husband and murderer of wealthy widows. In jail for theft, he hears his condemned cellmate, Ben Harper, reveal in his sleep that a large sum of money is hidden somewhere in his house. The phrase ' … a child shall lead them' (Is. 11:6) gives the clue as to how it may be found. Following Ben's execution and his own release, Powell finds and marries Ben's widow, Willa, and sets to work on the children, John and Pearl. John, old enough to feel suspicious, defies him. Pearl, an infant, is less steadfast. After Willa disappears – murdered by Powell – John decides that he and Pearl must run away, taking the money with them. Powell goes in pursuit, but the children are rescued by Rachel, a beatific but tough elderly woman who keeps a houseful of children in distress, soothing them with her splendid repertoire of comforting utterances, some biblical, some folksy.

The King James Bible pervades this film both in actual quotation and as an influence behind the dialogue. The allusions are used in two ways. The film is top-and-tailed by the voice of Lillian Gish as Rachel, giving us the positive messages with which the film counteracts the evils that threaten innocent children: 'Blessed are the pure in heart ... King Solomon in all his glory ... ' (Matt. 5:8; 6:29) we hear at the beginning. But she also heralds Powell's first appearance with warnings about false prophets and evil trees. She concludes the film with a benediction: 'Lord, save little children. The wind blows and the rain's a-cold, yet they abide. They abide and they endure.'

Most of the other quotations from and allusions to the Bible are uttered by Powell. His mind judders between hypocrisy and delusion. He seems to believe in the God whom he ceaselessly addresses, but the gentler parts of the Bible become, in his mouth, mere ploys to entrap his victims. His God is a god of hatred. He has the words 'hate' and 'love' tattooed on his knuckles as an illustration for one of his set-piece sermons.

His biblical allusions give us the measure of his sensibility. Of the flick-knife he carries in his pocket, he says: 'I come not to bring peace but a sword' (Matt. 10:34). Driving alone, in a stolen car, he prays for guidance: 'What's it to be, Lord? You always send me money to preach your word ... ' and (referring to the string of widows he has married and murdered) ' ... you don't mind the killings. Your book is full of killings. There are things you do hate, Lord. Frilly things, lacy things, things with curly hair ... a strange woman is a narrow pit' (Prov. 23:27). On their wedding night he refuses Willa's offer of sex, giving her instead a sermon about lust. When John and Pearl parry his questions about the money, he snarls, 'A liar is an abomination before mine eyes' (Prov. 6:16–19).

In 1955, the film drew very dismissive reviews, as a result of which Charles Laughton never directed again. In the age of CinemaScope, surreal night-time effects in black and white and the old screen ratio provoked dismissive scorn. Some of the more expressionist moments in Mitchum's performance were thought risible, and the conclusion was derided as sentimental. The film was dismissed as melodrama; that it was an accurate and serious study of extremes in evangelical religiosity went unnoticed. This theme reaches a touching but also witty climax when Powell is lurking outside Rachel's house, singing his theme song, 'Leaning on the everlasting arms', and Rachel joins in with a descant: 'Leaning on Jesus'. For Powell, the everlasting arms are those of a vengeful God who, like Samson, smites his opponents hip and thigh. For Rachel they are those of a comforting, merciful saviour. Since Rachel intimidates Powell by carrying a shotgun at the ready, she also provides an interesting, witty footnote to the American constitutional right to bear arms: a film about redemption is finally resolved by a sweet old lady with a gun.

We might conclude that Rachel's life is a fulfillment of Bible Belt revivalist Christianity, while Powell's is a perversion of it. But we may also wonder whether Powell's religion is something more complex than a ploy to entrap wealthy widows. Powell is certainly a villain. But a hypocrite would not talk to God, as Powell does, when no gullible human is listening. Powell's misogyny and loathing of sex are an out-of-control, cracker-barrel version of the Manichaean heresy, according to which humans are physically formed by the rulers of darkness and procreation is demonic in origin. He has searched Christianity for something to support his neurosis and found it. But, at the same time, Christianity is not, for him, a statutory set of doctrines that he is bound to swallow whole. When, in their cell, Ben asked him what religion, exactly, he professed, he said it was one he and the Lord had worked out together. Catholic or Orthodox thinkers might regard the formula as a working definition of Protestantism.

Many early critics assumed that this murderous preacher was merely a criminal lunatic. But Powell, I think, half-believes what he preaches, that he is an instrument of divine wrath. Even given that this is a surrealist film, with a strong resemblance to *Mother Goose* and *Who's Afraid of the Big, Bad Wolf*, such naturalistic points of character are worthy of attention. The principal pointer to that surreality is Stanley Cortez' luminous black and white photography. Cortez, however, in spending time explaining cameras and lenses to Laughton, found that he could learn from his pupil. Between them they produced those stunning chiaroscuro effects, which, of course, are emblematic of light and dark, beauty and ugliness, good and evil.

The Night of the Hunter has been described by numerous recent critics as one of the most frightening thrillers ever made. Most of the time this intensity of fright derives from the relationship between Powell and the children. As a thriller it is cunningly organized. We know that the children are safe as long as Powell does not know where the money is, but the fate of an unspecified but large number of dead widows reminds us that their lives will be at risk as soon as he has found out. The 'child's nightmare' which Laughton was set on making is principally John's nightmare and it is through his eyes that we see most of the action. Until his mother disappears and he and his sister go on the run, John is trebly burdened: first, by his promise to his father to tell nobody of the money's whereabouts; secondly, by his awareness that his mother – who believes that the money has been destroyed – would pass the news straight to Powell if she discovered otherwise; thirdly, by Pearl's permanent eagerness to spill the beans because she loves Powell and does not understand the situation she and John are in. There is no-one to whom John can talk, and Powell hounds him at every opportunity.

During the course of the film, John is deprived of or let down by a series of previously reassuring presences. His father is executed for murder, his mother murdered by Powell. On the run, dragging the reluctant Pearl, he turns for help to a local widower, 'Uncle' Birdie, but 'Uncle' proves quite useless, having seen Willa's body in the river and drunk himself into a state of moral and physical collapse. Only at the end of the film does John learn once again to trust an adult.

Some aspects of *The Night of the Hunter* may instructively be compared with a film made in 1960, five years later: Alfred Hitchcock's *Psycho*. When Hitchcock became interested in doing a low budget, black-and-white thriller, he looked to *The Night of the Hunter*, among other films, for ideas. Three ways in which it may have influenced him are detectable. *Psycho,* like *The Night of the Hunter*, is a dark comedy. In both films, the question of whether the murderer is partly sane or wholly mad, is central. In *Psycho*, we see Norman Bates, the murderous motel keeper, having a long chat with Marion in his office. We notice his strangeness, but also many indications of self-awareness, in both speech and behaviour. Nonetheless, within moments, as we learn much later, it is he, in drag and clutching a large knife, who charges into Marion's shower, totally out of control. First time viewers might watch almost to the end of *Psycho* before realizing who the villain – if that is the word – actually is. Harry Powell, by contrast, seems very much in control of himself almost throughout. Sometimes, however, he appears to crack: when he watches the stripper; when he appears upside down from his top bunk in prison; on the two occasions when he shouts abusively at Pearl; and during the chase before the children escape in the skiff.

The stripping away of comforting presences which afflicts John in Laughton's film also occurs in *Psycho,* although Hitchcock inflicts this process of successive loss on the audience rather than on any of his characters. First Marion, the absconding secretary, then the amiable, shambling investigator Arbogast are stabbed to death by, apparently, an old woman wielding a huge knife. Well over halfway through the film, we are still in the dark, and two people for whom we have developed affection and a degree of trust have been taken from us.

Whether or not Hitchcock was in fact 'influenced' by *The Night of the Hunter*, the comparison between these two classic thrillers makes clear the very special quality of Laughton's film. In crude generic terms *Psycho* is a slasher movie, although that is by no means all it is. *The Night of the Hunter* is something quite different. Powell has a knife, it is true – a flick knife which when closed looks like a stunted crucifix – but we never see him use it, and since he does not find out where the money is until the moment when the children finally elude him, he can employ it only as a threat. This means that our reactions, from the time he insinuates himself into their home and starts hounding them, are governed by a complex amalgam of pity and terror on their behalf; of disgust and horror at his vicious pitilessness; and of powerful revulsion from the fear of what will happen if he gets his hands on the booty.

In its plot, characters and religious, historical and social contexts, *The Night of the Hunter* arouses pity and terror. It uses complex means to devastatingly simple ends. It is at once technically and professionally entirely competent and artistically daringly experimental.

Tom Aitken

Further reading

Simon Callow (1988) *Charles Laughton: A Difficult Actor*. London: Methuen.
Lillian Gish (1969) *The Movies, Mr Griffith and Me*. Englewood Cliffs, NJ: Prentice-Hall.
Charles Higham (1976) *Charles Laughton: An Intimate Biography*. Garden City, NY: Doubleday.
Christopher Tookey (1994) *The Critics' Film Guide*. London: Boxtree.

ONE FLEW OVER THE CUCKOO'S NEST (1975)

[Director: Miloš Forman. Producers: Michael Douglas and Saul Zaentz. Screenplay by Lawrence Hauben and Bo Goldman, from the novel by Ken Kesey. Cast: Jack Nicholson (Randle Patrick McMurphy), Louise Fletcher (Nurse Ratched), William Redfield (Dale Harding), Dean R. Brooks (Dr Spivey), William Sampson (Native American Chief Bromden), Brad Dourif (Billy Bibbit),

Sydney Lassick (Charlie Cheswick), Danny DeVito (Martini), Christopher Lloyd (Max Taber).]

> Vintery, mintery, cutery, corn,
> Apple seed and apple thorn,
> Wire, briar, limber lock
> Three geese in a flock
> One flew East
> One flew West
> And one flew over the Cuckoo's nest.
>
> (American children's folk rhyme)

The Merry Prankster Ken Kesey, who made dropping acid hip in the psychedelic San Francisco Sixties, wrote the book from which the film *One Flew Over the Cuckoo's Nest* was adapted. After graduating from Stanford's graduate creative-writing program in the early 1960s, Ken Kesey worked the night shift at a Veterans Affairs psychiatric hospital in nearby Menlo Park. While working as an attendant at the hospital and swallowing increasingly large doses of experimental psychedelic drugs for a US government-run program, Kesey wrote his first published novel, *One Flew Over the Cuckoo's Nest* (Viking 1962). Kesey and his Pranksters initiated what would become known as the hippie movement, characterized by face painting, prairie style clothing, and communal lifestyle, as well as psychedelic drugs, backyard and basement grown marijuana, and uppers and downers gleaned from medicine cabinets and doctor's 'scrip pads.' Another major voice documenting the movement was Tom Wolfe, who wrote a jazzy, loose-jointed book *The Electric Kool-Aid Acid Test* (1968) that captured the wild and turbulent years when the Merry Pranksters bumped across the country and back, hiding out in Mexico when the cops were too close on their trail, and romanticizing the lifestyle that had begun with the Summer of Love (1967).

A decade later, when popular culture was infused with hippie lore and music, Kesey's dazzling novel became a cinematic representative picture of life on the West Coast during the now-familiar hippie drug culture. Two counter-culture Hollywood figures, Czech director Miloš Forman, and film star, actor Jack Nicholson, were enthusiastic about the project. The challenge was to find an actress to play Nurse Ratched, someone who could stand up to Nicholson's braggadocio. Forman found such an actress in the person of Louise Fletcher. In hindsight, her casting was brilliant. Fletcher never doubts that she holds the winning hand, by simply never seeming intimidated by the larger-than-life Nicholson.

Fletcher's Nurse Ratched confidently rules her kingdom, a sorrowful place where defeated men shuffle by in paper slippers and dishevelled dress, and look out, whey-faced and wary, from rows of cots in rooms without front walls. With her army of orderlies and the consent of the doctors, she uses drugs and punishments to keep the patients compliant. And for the ones who do not bend to her will through her arsenal of pharmacology, she has electroshock treatments, and finally, the ultimate killing machine, the lobotomy that surgically steals the human spirit and turns a human being into a vegetable. Nurse Ratched has god-like power within her small universe. But in contrast to God, who creates humans with free will, her tyranny directly subverts the will of the humans under her care. She keeps the patients docile, medicated, dependent, and childlike. Whether intentional or not, the film reflects its post-Watergate era (1972), when the summers of love turned into an era of deception.

Understood by those in the hospital to be deaf and mute, Chief Bromden, a Native American actor of the Creek Nation, is both the narrator and a central character in the novel. To have a person who is described as deaf and without language himself as the narrator of a novel reflects the playfulness for which Kesey is known. Although the movie focuses on the chief's heroic actions at the end of the picture, until that point he is portrayed as an overgrown, semi-human lump, when not ignored completely. Like so many Native Americans, the Chief is seen and not heard, there but not there. He has been written off by everyone except McMurphy, to whom the Chief has revealed his true self. Of course it would have been practically impossible for the chief to have a part in the picture larger than that of the rambunctious, leering, cocky Nicholson. Indeed the silent man, close to a foot taller than Nicholson, is the perfect foil for the energetic con man. The chief becomes the muscle, Nicholson the brain.

Using an insane asylum as a metaphor for contemporary American society, Miloš Forman's 1975 film adaptation (filmed on location in a real mental hospital) is a comically sharp indictment of the Establishment's insistence on conformity. Set in 1963 Oregon, the story follows small-time criminal and convicted statutory-rapist Randle Patrick McMurphy (Jack Nicholson) as he is released from doing grunt work on a prison farm to undergo evaluation at a supposedly cushier psychiatric institution, where he hopes to serve out the rest of his short sentence. Insisting he is crazy, he charms the hospital's chief of psychiatry, or at least he thinks he does. The doctor agrees to evaluate Nicholson, and the conman smiles ingratiatingly. He has tricked the doc. He'll get his easy-going gig in the nuthouse. He is still in charge. Downstairs on the ward he encounters a motley crew of mostly voluntary inmates, including cowed mama's boy Billy (Brad Dourif); Native American Chief Bromden (Will Sampson), commonly believed to be deaf and dumb; Dale Harding (William Redfield), an intelligent but anxiety-ridden paranoid; and Martini (Danny De Vito) a young, giddy. retarded man with a frightened laugh and wild flailing arms. And then he meets the head nurse in charge, Mildred Ratched. Louise Fletcher, a slim blond with a quiet voice is the opposite of the novel's Big Nurse, who wrestles the patients to the floor, shouts, and indeed is the Big Nurse, the evil mother to them all. In the film the nurse does not touch the patients. Physical control is left to the orderlies, who stand around, awaiting her orders. She controls her world with words, as does God in Genesis 1. She does not interact directly with the population of her dark Eden. But there the similarity ends. The biblical text of Genesis 1 has no prohibitions, no sign of death. But the world of *Cuckoo's Nest*, as ruled by Nurse Ratched, is all prohibition, all death.

Ratched and McMurphy recognize immediately that each is the other's worst nightmare: an authority figure who equates sanity with correct behaviour, and a misfit who is charismatic enough to dismantle the system simply by evading its rules. But McMurphy is not worried. As played by Nicholson, he is a scamp, irresistible to women, who assumes he will seduce the virginal, stone-faced nurse before the week is out. Overplaying his hand, McMurphy instigates group insurrections large and small, ranging from a restorative basketball game to an unfettered afternoon boat trip and finally the climactic tragic after-hours party with hookers and booze. Nurse Ratched, however, remains unmoved. She is secure because she holds the machinery of power to ensure that McMurphy will not defeat her. Still, McMurphy's message to live free or die trying to overturn the world of pale death, overmedication, and canned music, is ultimately not lost on one inmate, revealing that a return to God's world is still possible.

When McMurphy steals a bright yellow hospital bus, the scene changes. From the white and dun-coloured walls of the institution to the glorious deep blue sky, green pine trees and the colourful harbour surrounding the lapis-tinted sea, the audience sees the difference between the bland world of negative control to the joyous world of nature and freedom. McMurphy herds his colleagues aboard a 'borrowed' deep-sea fishing boat, stops to pick up Candy (Marya Small) one of his many girlfriends, totally alive and the embodiment of sexuality, and tells the bewildered patients: 'You're not nuts, you're fishermen!' Gradually, with Nicholson's encouragement, they begin to feel stirrings of life and desire within them. With Jack's coaching and clowning, the men work together, hauling the slippery ropes, and actually catching a few fish. The men's excited voices, the hum of the boat's engine, the gorgeous white wake foaming over the deep blue sea stir the audience as well as the men. Maybe they're not nuts! Maybe they can break free of the oppressive hospital ward. Their triumph is short-lived. After being returned to the hushed world of white sheets, white uniforms and the powdered face of Nurse Ratched, McMurphy is informed that his stay at the mental hospital is not restricted to the terms of his original sentence; that, in fact, he could remain institutionalized for the rest of his life, as the institution sees fit. Meanwhile, Ratched cracks down on the patients in response to their increasing audacity, and when a brawl breaks out during one of her demeaning group sessions, she prescribes electroshock therapy for the insubordinate parties, including McMurphy and the Chief. While waiting for the treatment to begin, McMurphy discovers, through a softly uttered 'Thank you,' that Chief is neither deaf nor mute – he is only smart. He has outwitted the medications and bed straps. By staying silent, he avoids getting caught in the vise of power which destroys the minds of those who would question authority. After the devastating electroshock therapy, McMurphy returns to the ward, bent, weakened, slack-jawed, just like the guys on the ward who have no thought of ever leaving the hollowness of the ward. The other patients figure that McMurphy's fiery spirit has finally been 'cured.' Quickly the real McMurphy returns: the star of the ward, sly, tough, and electric.

Shortly thereafter, McMurphy sneaks in Candy and throws a clandestine, after-hours Christmas party for his fellow patients. This is McMurphy's last hurrah; with his sentence now indefinite and freedom no longer on the horizon, he is planning to escape. At the party, the repressed revelers go wild, guzzling stolen medications and swigging forbidden drinks, and audiences can only watch as the inmates unintentionally drop off one by one into sleep or oblivion. Even the ever-lively McMurphy and his loyal sidekick, the Chief, fall into the deep sleep of a fairy-tale spell. The chaos of Hell has entered into the world of sedated order. When Nurse Ratched arrives the next morning and surveys the scene, her face remains impassive. Her arms at her sides, her posture perfect, she picks her way through the party's messy aftermath, including unconscious patients littered about the room. She makes quick work of setting the hospital back in order, but when her orderlies find Billy and Candy, fresh from a night of sexual play, the other patients applaud. Overjoyed by his accomplishment Billy speaks for the first time without his devastating stutter. Cutting his triumph with the sharpness of her tongue, in her softest voice, with a faint smile, Nurse Ratched says she is going to tell Billy's mother what he has done. Billy's newfound confidence drains, and he loses control, punching himself repeatedly in the groin. Finally subdued and locked in the doctor's office, Billy slashes himself to death. McMurphy's fury bursts upon Nurse Ratched as he attempts to strangle her.

Before dawn the next morning, all is silent, mounds of sleeping patients casting gray shadows on the walls of the ward. The scene is disturbingly vague. One cannot tell whether the patients are in their nightly drugged sleep or dead. When Chief Bromden looks closely at McMurphy, only his face shows under a mound of white sheets and pillows. The Indian identifies the devastating scars of a lobotomy procedure on his comrade's forehead.

In a possible biblical allusion the film's ending offers the critical interpretive moment. Looking at the technocrat's surgical stigmata (the lobotomy scar) on the forehead of Nicholson, the Chief who has been a silent Suffering Servant throughout the film turns to action. Determined to preserve McMurphy's honour, the Indian snuffs out the remnants of life left in the man who would be saviour of the weak and oppressed men on the ward. The weapon of the Indian is ironic: not a sharp spear or knife, but a soft pillow is all that is needed to preserve the dignity of the Nicholson character. The chief understands that his duty is to assure that McMurphy will not remain helpless in the grip of the violent Ratched.

In keeping with his leader's spirit, the Chief follows through with McMurphy's original plan of escape, smashing a barred window with a hydrotherapy device and breaking through to the outside world. As the camera moves from inside the institution to outside into the natural world, Chief Bromden climbs through the jagged hole, and runs away, bearing with him the memory, and perhaps the spirit, of McMurphy. His huge body becomes a tiny figure blending in with the world that had been only memory to him in the half-life of the ward. Both men have been freed from the world of death into the world of life and freedom.

The audience is left with narrative disarray. Billy sought freedom and killed himself when he realized escape from Nurse Ratched and his mother was hopeless. McMurphy, who had promised them life in a colourful world, has been snuffed out; the Indian chief has escaped the death-dealing world of technology and slipped back into the living forests from which he came. Nurse Ratched presumably will be able to continue her iron-maiden control over those who are voluntarily in her care, but are too terrified to live in the outside world. The final scene is washed with the hopeful green of the forest and blue of the cloudless Oregon sky. Freedom is the promise at the end of the picture.

Alice Bach

Further reading

William K. Ferrell (2000) *Literature and Film as Modern Mythology*. London; Westport, CT: Praeger. pp. 75–84.

Ken Kesey (1962) *One Flew Over the Cuckoo's Nest*. New York, NY: Viking Press and Signet Books.

Charles B. Ketcham (1992) '*One Flew Over the Cuckoo's Nest:* A Salvation Drama of Liberation', in *Image and Likeness: Religious Visions in American Film Classics*, ed. John R. May. Knoxville, TN: University of Tennessee. pp. 145–52.

Tom Wolfe (1968) *The Electric Kool-Aid Acid Test*. New York, NY: Farrar Straus.

Further viewing

Chinatown (Roman Polanski, 1974)
Hair (Miloš Forman, 1979)
The Shining (Stanley Kubrick, 1980)
Amadeus (Miloš Forman, 1984)
The People vs. Larry Flynt (Miloš Forman, 1996)
The Departed (Martin Scorsese, 2006)

THE PASSION OF THE CHRIST (2004)

[Production company: Icon Productions. Director: Mel Gibson. Screen writer: Benedict Fitzgerald and Mel Gibson. Translated into Latin and Aramaic by William Fulco. Cinematography: Caleb Deschanel. Music: John Debney. Art directors: Pierfranco Luscrí, Daniela Pareschi, Nazzareno Piana. Major cast members: James Caviezel (Jesus Christ), Monica Bellucci (Mary Magdalene), Maia Morgenstern (Mary the mother of Jesus), Rosalinda Celentano (Satan).]

Mel Gibson's contribution to the Jesus movie genre covers the final twelve hours of Jesus' life, from Gethsemane to the crucifixion. The primary, relentless focus is on the brutal treatment Jesus endured from the hands of the soldiers, and the profuse amount of blood that he shed due to endless flogging and unlimited torture. A few flashback scenes are included, in order to help the audience connect the pain and suffering they are witnessing to the events of Jesus' life and his message. The brief resurrection scene at the film's conclusion, lasting less than two minutes, is more of an appendix than a culmination of his passion.

The Passion of the Christ opened in the US on Ash Wednesday, 25 February 2004. The date was carefully picked to signify the religious role the director wanted the movie to play. Gibson himself introduced his movie as a personal witness to his faith. He hoped that his violent portrayal of the passion of Jesus Christ would help the viewers 'see ... the enormity of that sacrifice – to see that someone could endure that and still come back with love and forgiveness, even through extreme pain and suffering and ridicule' (Webb 2004: 162). Due to its extreme violence, the movie was rated R. This rating did not stop people from taking their young children to see the movie, presumably on the assumption that no Jesus movie could be harmful viewing for the believer. Congregations planned trips to theaters, much as they might plan visits to neighbouring churches.

From the beginning of the cinema in the late nineteenth century the story of Jesus Christ has been a popular subject. Often the focus has been limited to his passion, along the lines of the medieval passion play, where the story about Jesus' suffering and death on the cross is dramatized, usually during holy week. Examples include *Jesus Christ Superstar* (1973) and *Jésus de Montréal* (1989). While the passion play is clearly an important prototype for Gibson, no less significant is the well-known tradition of the Stations of the Cross. Since the time of the early church, pilgrims have travelled to the Holy Land to walk the *via dolorosa* (the way of sorrow), through the city of Jerusalem and up to Golgotha. On their way the pilgrims stop and reflect on events from the passion story. This particular way of commemorating Christ's passion has continued to play a significant role in the observance of the Lent, especially within the Roman Catholic Church.

Gibson uses the Stations of the Cross as the structuring device for his passion story. Although the number and names of the stations have varied over the centuries, in the modern period there has emerged a pattern of fourteen stations, the first being the moment Jesus is sentenced to death and the last when he is laid to rest after being removed from the cross. Of the fourteen stations, five are based on extra-biblical sources, including the stations where Jesus meets his mother and a woman named Veronica, on his way to Golgotha. While the stations of the cross provide the framework for Gibson's Passion, the details come from a nineteenth-century mystic named Anne Catherine Emmerich (1774–1824). Emmerich's visions, printed in her book, *The Dolorous Passions of Our Lord Jesus Christ*, consist of descriptions of the violent treatment Christ suffered on his way to the cross. Emmerich's graphic accounts prove to be even bloodier than Gibson's.

When interviewed about his film, Gibson stated that his goal was to tell the passion story as it really happened. Gibson repeatedly referred to the Gospels as 'eyewitness reporting' and the movie as a 'literal' portrayal of those accounts (Fredriksen 2006: 31; Reinhartz 2007: 27). In order to lend an air of authenticity to his film, Gibson had the characters speak in Aramaic and Latin rather than English. Initially he had intended not to provide subtitles in English, but he reversed this decision before the premiere.

Regardless of Gibson's intentions, his movie is far removed from the Gospel accounts. This much is clear from his focus on the violent beatings endured by Jesus, which are only briefly mentioned by the gospel writers. But Gibson's understanding of the gospels, as being a literal account of what really happened, is also highly problematic. Gibson respects neither the 'preaching' nature of the gospels, nor the uniqueness of each gospel (Cunningham 2006: 49). He also seems unaware of the historical context in the late first century in which the Gospels were written, including Roman persecutions of Christians, which made it important to downplay the Roman role in Jesus' death and therefore to blame Christ's death on the Jews. For this same reason the Gospels suggest that Pilate executed Jesus against his own will (e.g. John 19:6–8). It is also important to keep in mind that the gospels were written after Herod's temple was destroyed in the course of the Jewish revolt, 66–73 CE. Christians considered the destruction of the temple to be God's punishment of the Jews for killing Christ. This sheds light on the crowd's response to Pilate's declaration of innocence: 'His blood be on us and on our children!' (Matt. 27:25). These words were later used to inflame anti-Semitic sentiments and actions (Fredriksen 2006: 43). Gibson responded to concerns about anti-Semitism by removing the subtitle for Matthew 27:25 (Reinhartz 2007: 248).

Gibson's depiction of the Jews as bloodthirsty and full of hate, and as posing a real threat to Pilate, was harshly criticized in the so-called *Ad Hoc Scholars Report*. Gibson received the Report in May of 2003, but it was not made public until after the premiere of the movie. The authors of the report warned Gibson not to repeat the mistake of classical passion plays, which often emphasized the role of the Jews as Christ's arch enemies (Ad Hoc 2006: 229). They also criticized Gibson's portrayal of Caiaphas as 'smug' and 'arrogant', and wearing the 'richest robes', while Pilate, contrary to his extra-biblical reputation as a ruthless and violent tyrant, is sympathetically depicted as well-meaning but apprehensive (Ad Hoc 2006: 244–45). Crucifixion was a common criminal, as well as political, punishment in antiquity. In the Roman empire, it was most often used for dangerous criminals and members of the lower class, and so it is plausible that it would have been used by Pilate as a tool to avoid uproar in Jerusalem during Jewish festivals like the Passover.

The gospels suggest that Jewish as well as Roman authorities believed Christ to be a real threat to the peace in Jerusalem during the Passover. The fact that Christ was arrested at night, and that Pilate even bothered to crucify him, suggests that Christ had significant support among the crowd. From Gibson's portrayal of the 'crowd', as belonging to the enemies of Christ, it is easy to assume that Gibson does not take those historical realities seriously (Fredriksen 2006: 39). Furthermore, the massive violence that precedes Christ's crucifixion in Gibson's film is not historically based. It was a custom to scourge those who had been sentenced to death on the cross. In his movie Gibson makes the most of this scourging, leaving hardly a dry spot on Jesus' body, while the other two men who are crucified with him receive only a few lashes. Gibson also stresses the uniqueness of Christ's crucifixion, relying on Emmerich for detailed descriptions of the procedure. According to contemporary sources, those who had been sentenced to death on the cross 'would carry only the cross-beams to the crucifixion site, where the upright beams would be permanently mounted' (Cunningham 2006: 62). In Gibson's movie those who were crucified with Christ carry the crossbeams, contrary to Christ who is made to carry a huge cross, with both beams, far too large for him to handle.

In many ways Gibson's passion movie has more in common with Gibson's own action movies than with previous Jesus films. Gibson knows that violence sells. While Gibson's focus on violence obscures the witness of the gospel writers, the main problem with his film lies in his interpretation of violence itself. For Gibson Christ's love is measured by the amount of suffering he endures, namely: *more pain, more gain*. By giving violence and abuse a spiritual significance,

> violence is not only justified as being the will of God, but it is also a necessary prerequisite for the good that is expected to come out of it. In other words, violence is desirable, and suffering is valuable in itself, regardless of its historical context.
>
> (Guðmundsdóttir 2008: 129)

This is a very dangerous message in our era, in which violence is evaluated according to its entertaining qualities and marketing value. By separating the last twelve hours of Jesus' life from the context of his message, his life, and his resurrection – the flashback scenes are not particularly meaningful to a viewer who does not know the story beforehand – Gibson's movie becomes simply a glorification of violence and abuse, nothing close to what the original gospel writers intended when they wrote their versions of the life and death of Jesus Christ.

Arnfríður Guðmundsdóttir

Further reading

Ad Hoc Scholars Report (2006) in Paula Fredriksen (ed.) *On the Passion of the Christ. Exploring the Issues Raised by the Controversial Movie.* Berkeley, CA: University of California Press. pp. 225–54. Available online at www.ccjr. us/images/stories/Passion_adhoc_report_2May.pdf

Philip Cunningham (2006) 'Much Will Be Required of the Person Entrusted with Much: Assembling a Passion Drama from the Four Gospels', in Paula Fredriksen (ed.) *On the Passion of the Christ. Exploring the Issues Raised by the Controversial Movie.* Berkeley, CA: University of California Press. pp. 49–64.

Paula Fredriksen (2006) 'Gospel Truths: Hollywood, History, and Christianity', in Paula Fredriksen (ed.) *On the Passion of the Christ. Exploring the Issues Raised by the Controversial Movie.* Berkeley, CA: University of California Press. pp. 31–47.

Arnfríður Guðmundsdóttir (2008) 'More Pain, More Gain! On Mel Gibson's Film, *The Passion of the Christ*' in Geert Hallbäck and Annika Hvithamar (eds) *Recent Releases. The Bible in Contemporary Cinema.* Sheffield: Sheffield Phoenix Press. pp. 115–32.

Adele Reinhartz (2007) *Jesus of Hollywood.* New York, NY: Oxford University Press.

Robert L. Webb (2004) '*The Passion* and the Influence of Emmerich's *The Dolorous Passion of Our Lord Jesus Christ*' in Kathleen E. Corley and Robert L. Webb (eds) *Jesus and Mel Gibson's The Passion of the Christ. The Film, The Gospels and the Claims of History.* New York, NY: Continuum. pp. 160–72.

Further viewing

Jesus Christ Superstar (Norman Jewison, 1973)
Jesus of Montreal (Denys Arcand, 1989)

THE PRINCE OF EGYPT (1998)

[Production Company: DreamWorks Animation. Producers: Penney Finkelman Cox, P. J. Hanke, Jeffrey Katzenberg, Linda Olszewski, Sandra Rabins, Ron Rocha, R. Don Smith. Directors: Brenda Chapman, Steve Hickner, Simon Wells. Screenplay: Philip LaZebnick. Art Production: Kathy Altieri, Richie Chavez. Cast (voices): Val Kilmer (Moses, God), Michele Pfeiffer (Tzipporah), Sandra Bullock (Miriam), Jeff Goldblum (Aaron), Ralph Fiennes

(Rameses), Danny Glover (Jethro), Patrick Stewart (Seti), Helen Mirren (The Queen), Martin Short (Huy), Steve Martin (Hotep).]

DreamWorks Animation's *The Prince of Egypt* bases its overall plot and most of its characters on the biblical book of Exodus. Nevertheless, the focus of this film differs significantly from that of Exodus. Except for its beginning, *The Prince of Egypt* tells a modern coming-of-age story, focusing on an individual (Moses). By contrast, Exodus presents a myth of social acculturation that focuses on a people (the Israelites). In both the book and the film the Israelites eventually gain their freedom. The film, however, concludes with Moses' heroism while Exodus concludes with Yahweh's presence over the tabernacle (40:36).

In *The Rites of Passage,* anthropologist Arnold van Gennep describes how young men in primitive societies socialize during the course of three stages (1960: 21): 1) separation – physical change, turmoil, etc.; 2) margin – journey, personal progress, removal from home and isolation, sense of dissimilarity, personal tragedy, romance, sexual initiation, overcoming obstacles, quest, etc.; and 3) aggregation – end of the journey, reconciliation with a group, new responsibility, career, etc. At the onset of a male's rite of passage, the community isolates the young man and tests him in order to establish the appropriate levels of independence and stability that are necessary for his success as an adult (1960: 80–81). A coming-of-age story models this socialization by portraying the ways in which an adolescent protagonist breaks taboos and experiences failures but ultimately passes his community's tests, returns home, receives acclaim, and embraces his new adult status. In these ways, a coming-of-age story depicts an individual's maturation.

A myth fosters a far less individualized agenda, creating what Branislow Malinowski calls 'a sociological charter' (1926: 121). It instructs its readers how to conform to social regulations of hospitality, funerals, careers, families, marriages, education, religious rituals, games, etc. In these ways, a myth depicts and reinforces a group's status quo.

These two genres, at the most basic level, fulfill essentially different functions. A coming-of-age story teaches how an adolescent becomes a successful, well-adjusted adult. Thus, a coming-of-age story privileges an individual. A myth, on the other hand, teaches how a group operates harmoniously, retrieves its lost power, and relieves its social tensions. As such, a myth privileges a group.

This essay follows *The Prince of Egypt* through the three coming-of-age stages: separation, margin, and aggregation. The movie is frequently compared to the biblical story of Exodus. These comparisons rely heavily on how a myth differs from a coming-of-age story. This essay highlights DreamWorks Animation's decision to privilege a modern, individual focus (on Moses) over a group focus (on the Israelites). Like other Moses films, such as *The Life of Moses* (1909–10) and *The Ten Commandments* (1956), *The Prince of Egypt* opens with a scene depicting the Egyptian oppression of the Israelite slaves. The song 'Deliver us', addressed to God, recalls Cecil B. DeMille's prologue to *The Ten Commandments* (1956):

> The theme of this picture is whether man ought to be ruled by God's law or whether they are to be ruled by the whims of a dictator like Ramses [sic]. Are men property of the State, or are they free souls under God? This same battle continues throughout the world today.

Similarly, the book of Exodus begins with an Israelite versus Egyptian agenda: after listing the names of the heads of the houses of Israel, Exodus establishes that characters represent nations – the elect and oppressed Israelites versus the idol-worshiping and oppressing Egyptians. DreamWorks interrupts its vilification of the Egyptians with a black screen, segregating its mythic beginning from its ensuing coming-of-age story.

The first rite of passage stage – segregation – begins with a solitary bobbing basket on the tumultuous Nile. Next, the film fast-forwards to the highly spirited and destructive chariot race between the 'brothers' Moses and Rameses. These competing chariot racers who indifferently destroy the slaves' labours recall the sibling rivalry of DeMille's 1956 film, as well as the iconic chariot race in *Ben-Hur* (1959). Rather than Rameses' minatory political jealousy as seen in Exodus, DreamWorks depicts a rollicking sports contest. This relocation of the siblings' competitive relationship from the political arena to the sports realm, preserves the innocence of a children's film and softens the biblical condemnation of the Egyptians. Thereafter, the film intensifies its coming-of-age focus on an individual, depicting Moses' sympathy for his scolded 'brother' Rameses. Their alliance shatters, however, after Moses discovers his Israelite identity and heritage, and subsequently kills an Egyptian guard who has been abusing a slave. That this killing is unintentional is another departure from, and softening of, the biblical Exodus story, in which Moses' act is purposeful, arising from his self-understanding as the protector of the Israelite slaves. It is only after this event that the DreamWorks Moses views Rameses as his enemy. Contrast Exodus, which expresses no sympathy for its nameless Pharaoh because its pro-Israelite social concern requires the story to vilify him. For both stories, murder becomes the catalyst for flight.

In *The Prince of Egypt* Moses enters van Gennep's second stage – margin – when he meets the daughters of Jethro and marries Tzipporah (cf. Exod. 2:15–21). The decisive point occurs when Moses encounters the burning bush (Exod. 3). Yahweh's voice teaches him what to say, instructs him how to act, provides him with a powerful staff, and discloses advantageous information. Unlike typical coming-of-age protagonists, DreamWorks' Moses is not merely guided toward success, but is guaranteed success. Because Moses knows that God secures his future, Moses experiences no insecurity. Despite slavery and the surrounding violence, Moses lives virtually worry-free, while his 'brother' Rameses suffers. While Exodus pits Yahweh against the Pharaoh for the sake of Israel, DreamWorks pits Moses against Rameses for the sake of personal triumph. After the burning bush scene, the movie cares less about the delivered and more about the deliverer – Moses – just as *Hamlet* cares less about Elsinore and more about Hamlet's image of divine scourge and minister. Moses does not face the significant trials, obstacles, confusion, insecurity, or taboos, that other young people endure at this stage in their development. In *The Prince of Egypt,* God singles out Moses as a typical modern hero whereas in Exodus, Yahweh singles out Moses to be his protector of the Israelites. Suiting its mythic functions, Exodus portrays Moses only as an extension of Yahweh's power. Limiting its coming-of-age motifs, DreamWorks portrays Moses as a young protagonist who somehow matures without erring and failing. In both stories, each plague and heart-hardening contributes to God's authority over the Israelites and Egyptians.

After the annihilation of the Egyptians, the film's Moses enters the final coming-of-age stage – aggregation. Tzipporah proclaims, 'Look, look at your people, Moses. They are free!' In the film, the Israelites have become the people of Moses while in Exodus, Moses has become Yahweh's emissary of divine law. *The Prince of Egypt*'s penultimate scene finalizes the sibling rivalry, opposing the two 'brothers' on opposite sides of the parted Red Sea where Rameses hopelessly rages, 'Moses! Moses!' in response to which Moses detachedly murmurs, 'Good-bye, brother'. One defeated, one victor. As the royally robed, staff-and-tablets-clasping Moses gazes at his people below, the opening song, 'Deliver us!' replays, but this time addressing Moses rather than God. This coming-of-age film ends with the exaltation of Moses, grown from a raucous teenager to the lone, heroic saviour of his people, whereas Exodus portrays Moses offered assistance in order to become Yahweh's emissary to the Israelites. While *The Prince of Egypt* ends with Moses' heroism, Exodus continues the story with the Israelites' transformation into the chosen people who journey to their land as Moses leads them. Additionally, Exodus benefits all Israelites through the first Passover (12:43–51), the consecration of the first born (13:1–2), Yahweh's cloud and fire (13:17–22), the manna as food in the desert (16), the water from a rock (17:1–7), the Ten Commandments (20), rest on the Sabbath (20:8), and an altar and a tabernacle (20:22–26). These events highlight Yahweh's divine plan, expectations, and protection. Repeated ventures to the mountain and back tax Moses' physical and emotional stamina. Once again, he finds himself listening to Yahweh's prohibitions – without conversation or explanation. As a mythic charter for Israel, Exodus catalogues Yahweh's guidelines for the Israelites' nourishment, legacy, and protection, in addition to charging Moses to correct those acting 'perversely' (32:30–34) and to threatening sinners with a plague (32:35). Paralleling the ancestral tributes of its beginning, Exodus concludes with Israelite empowerment. Because the Israelites are chosen, not entitled, they will survive and flourish only with Yahweh's assistance. Readers likely learn from this biblical myth to obey, praise, and trust the divine so that their community might be chosen to prosper. By contrast, *The Prince of Egypt's* portrayal of Moses as an emerging, modern hero adopts a far more individualistic religious identity.

As expected, DreamWorks consulted with many experts and invested large sums in research. In the production notes for *The Prince of Egypt*, Producer Penney Finkelman Cox recalls doing 'extensive research, reading the commentaries, histories and philosophical texts that deal with Moses and the Exodus story'. Jeffrey Katzenberg hired biblical scholars, theologians, archeologists, an attorney specializing in interfaith issues, and Egyptologists. Despite these attempts, *The Prince of Egypt* seriously departs from the mythic perspective of Exodus. One factor contributing to this departure may have been the desire to avoid privileging one community (the Israelites) and vilifying another (the Egyptians). However, in striving to avoid offense, DreamWorks created a lightweight coming–of–age story. Grossing over $128 million worldwide (www.BoxOfficeMojo.com), *The Prince of Egypt's* popularity indicates a cultural attraction toward a religion that guarantees personal success, rather than the social responsibility of Exodus. Every society needs its myths – to establish social charters in good times and bad. Exodus fulfills that need. Every society also needs responsible coming–of–age stories that guide adolescents past failures and rebellion toward a productive and rewarding adulthood. *The Prince of Egypt* falls short.

Comparisons between this ancient biblical story and the modern film highlight generic, cultural, and ethical differences. DreamWorks portrays an individual focus on heroic integrity while Exodus portrays a community focus on Yahweh's chosen people. As a coming-of-age story, *The Prince of Egypt* disappoints: the protagonist's development and future depend too heavily on his divine mentor and too little on challenges, taboos, and failures. By contrast, Exodus has long succeeded as a myth: its clear-cut prescriptions and proscriptions govern how a group's order is established and recovered.

Beyond its allure as a high-energy animated children's story, the film exerts an enormous attraction for modern audiences yearning to identify with a spiritual hero who could be seen as an icon for several religions. Further, despite complaints that DreamWorks divagated too severely from coming-of-age conventions during the margin stage, the studio aptly captured its audience's modern preference for a stress-free, heroic world. *The Prince of Egypt* stands as a powerful cinematic story of how one young male defeats a despotic emperor and becomes a divinely chosen hero. It provides a modern, individualistic version of a traditional myth. Both Exodus and *The Prince of Egypt* value identifying and acknowledging ancestry, keeping faith, protecting families, and standing against evil. While Exodus and *The Prince of Egypt* extol prudence, endurance, fidelity, and honour, they also license divinely ordained violence against the Other. Although both stories circumvent human participation in violence, they endorse dehumanizing binaries: humans quickly act to advance their privilege against an insolent Other. Just as Joshua's human violence follows immediately after Exodus' divine liberation (Josh. 10), *The Prince of Egypt* concludes by exalting human retribution – not the giving of the divine law. As *The Prince of Egypt,* like Exodus, acclaims a divine being who licenses violence against oppressors, it mirrors a world where aggression and religious rhetoric dangerously merge. Considering that, in DeMille's words the 'same battle continues throughout the world today', these stories help us examine the perception that any violence is divinely ordained.

P. Jennifer Rohrer-Walsh

Further reading

Arnold van Gennep (1960) *The Rites of Passage*. Chicago, IL: University of Chicago Press.

Bronislaw Malinowski (1926) *Myth and Primitive Psychology*. New York: W.W. Norton & Co.

Stephen Schwartz (1998) *Through Heaven's Eyes*. Boston: Dutton Juvenile.

Charles Solomon (1998) *The Prince of Egypt: A New Vision in Animation*. New York City: Henry N. Abrams.

THE ROBE (1953)

[Production Company: Twentieth Century-Fox. Producer: Frank Ross. Director: Henry Koster. Screenplay: Philip Dunne; (Albert Maltz – uncredited). Adaptation: Gina Kaus. Cinematography: Leon Shamroy. Editing: Barbara McLean. Music: Alfred Newman. Art Direction: George W. Davis, Lyle R. Wheeler. Set Decoration: Paul S. Fox, Walter M. Scott. Costume Design: Emile Santiago. Second Unit Director: Tom Connors, Jr. Sound: Bernard Freericks, Roger Heman Sr. Special Effects: James B. Gordon. Visual Effects: Ray Kellogg. Cast: Richard Burton (Marcellus Gallio), Jean Simmons (Diana), Victor Mature (Demetrius), Michael Rennie (Peter), Jay Robinson (Caligula), Dean Jagger (Justus), Torin Thatcher (Senator Gallio), Richard Boone (Pontius Pilate), Betta St. John (Miriam), Jeff Morrow (Paulus), Ernest Thesiger (Tiberius), Leon Askin (Abidor), Michael Ansara (Judas) (uncredited), Donald C. Klune (Jesus) (uncredited), Cameron Mitchell (voice of Jesus) (uncredited), Mae Marsh (Jerusalem woman aiding Demetrius) (uncredited), Harry Shearer (David) (uncredited).]

The Robe, published in 1942, was the penultimate novel written by Lloyd C. Douglas (1877–1951). The son of an Indiana pastor, Douglas became a much-traveled Lutheran minister working in Ohio, Indiana, Illinois, Washington DC, Los Angeles and Montreal, but ultimately converted to the more liberal Congregational Church. In 1933 he retired to write. He had already written many works offering advice to fellow ministers, but with *Magnificent Obsession* (1929) he established himself as a successful author of novels in modern settings. In the 1940s he wrote *The Robe* (1942) and *The Big Fisherman* (1949), both involving Biblical figures in first century Roman Judea, selling millions of copies, and reincarnated as films in the 1950s. Hazel McCann, an Ohio saleswoman who innocently wrote a letter to Douglas in October, 1940, to ask what had become of the man who won Jesus' 'coat', provided the immediate stimulus for the novel (Dawson and Wilson 1952: 323). Two years later Douglas dedicated the book to her.

The novel has been compared to the popular religious literary monuments of the late nineteenth century, *Ben-Hur* (1880) and *Quo Vadis?* (1895). But Douglas does not focus on the Passion of Christ or the early Christian community in Neronian Rome. His novel shifts between Rome and Judea, and concentrates on the robe Jesus wore at his crucifixion and the profound effect it has on Marcellus, the Roman tribune who took possession of it that fateful day by casting lots (Matt. 27:35). Contact with the robe eventually brings about Marcellus' conversion to Christianity, and at the conclusion of the novel he is martyred along with his love interest, Diana, another Roman patrician. Written during the first years of World War II, the novel reflects contemporary pessimism and harsh political realities. However, Marcellus finds comfort in Christian community, and the ultimate eschatological message of *The Robe* is that although evil may triumph in this world, the good will be rewarded in paradise. In its final page, Marcellus and Diana hand the robe over to a friend with instructions to take it to 'the big fisherman', as Christ's power is effectively transferred from the pagan Roman Empire to his disciple Peter.

In 1945 Douglas sold the film rights to the independent producer Frank Ross for $100,000. Ross had recently released *The House I Live In* (1945). Written by Albert Maltz, this short film preaches religious freedom and community, themes echoed in *The Robe*. Released through RKO, it won an Honourary Academy Award in the 'Tolerance Short Subject' category, so Ross hoped to release *The Robe* through the same studio, asking Maltz to adapt the novel. Adrian Scott, the intended associate producer, reported to Ross that Maltz's 272-page script portrayed Christianity 'not as a way of life but as a religion of miracles' (Dick 1989: 95). Maltz revised his script three times in 1946 and shortened it to 200 pages, but this was still a few years before Hollywood would begin to produce ancient biblical films on a regular basis.

The project languished in 1948 as Howard Hughes, who was not interested in biblical films, took control of RKO and the anti-Nazi, pro-socialist sentiments of Maltz – and nine other like-minded screen writers – exposed him to blacklisting under the shadow of the House Un-American Activities Committee. Darryl Zanuck at Twentieth Century-Fox agreed to provide the funding and assigned a reluctant Philip Dunne to rewrite the script. During those stormy years Dunne, too, appeared before the HUAC and even made a formal protest, testifying on behalf of Dalton Trumbo. But his service during World War II and executive positions in the Screen Writers Guild and the Motion Picture Academy seem to have shielded him from recrimination. Ross could not inform Dunne that Maltz had written the script, so Dunne assumed that Ross had written it and did not see the need to share credit with the producer. The truth was verified in 1997, and filmographies and DVD transfers now list Maltz as a co-author.

Dunne, who had received an Academy Award nomination for the biblical *David and Bathsheba* (1951), called the novel 'simple-minded' and many of Maltz' scenes 'trite and De Millish' (1992: 253–4). Eliminating Maltz' extraneous miracles, Dunne focused on the power of Christ's robe. Nonetheless, Dunne maintained much of Maltz's adaptation of the novel, which in turn supplements the accounts in the New Testament of Jesus' triumphal entry into Jerusalem and the crucifixion itself. In addition, Maltz created the scenes in which Marcellus' Greek slave, Demetrius, converts to Christianity and encounters Judas the night of Jesus' arrest. He also made more elaborate the purpose of the Christian meetings at Cana. Dunne in turn tightened some of the scenes in Rome so as to limit the historical period to the last five years of the Tiberius' reign and the accession of Caligula.

Zanuck assigned as director Henry Koster, a German-Jewish émigré who had been listed as an 'enemy alien' during the war and had been confined to his house at night. The complement of talents now included a blacklisted liberal communist, a non-blacklisted but outspoken anti-communist, and a German who rejected Fascism but was put under house arrest in the United States. Gina Kaus, credited with further adaptation of the script, was an Austrian-Jewish refugee. Some of these contemporary political strains surface in the scenes at imperial court. First there is the scene in which Tiberius sends Marcellus to collect the names of Jesus' followers:

> I give you an imperial commission ... For Rome, seek out the followers of this dead magician. I want names, Tribune, names of all the disciples, of every man and woman who subscribe to this treason. Names, Tribune, all of them, no matter how much it costs or how long it takes. You will report directly to me.

Then there is the final scene in the court of Caligula, where Marcellus confesses his Christianity but denies any plot against the state. There is an additional twist from the Nurnberg trials and a brilliant but insulting retort by Marcellus, who will die a martyr rather than swear a loyalty oath to the Roman state:

> Marcellus: It is not true that those of us who follow the teachings of Jesus are engaged in any plot against the state.
> Caligula: But isn't it a fact that you call this Jesus a king?
> Marcellus: Yes, sire, but his kingdom is not of this world. He seeks no earthly throne ... He forgave me for my crime against him.
> Caligula: Do you maintain that it is a crime for a Roman soldier to obey his orders?
> Marcellus: The empire is governed by men. Men sometimes make mistakes. And this, sire, was the greatest mistake ever made by Rome.

Caligula: So, the empire makes mistakes? And perhaps the emperor himself makes mistakes?

Marcellus: Sire, it is I who am on trial here, not you.

Important as this is, *The Robe*'s single most significant impact on the history of the cinema was its spectacular use of the anamorphic lens developed two decades earlier by Henri Chrétien. Responding to competition from television, 3D, and Cinerama, Zanuck promoted the system he marketed as CinemaScope, which compressed and then projected an image 2.66 times wider than the standard cinematic image. The enlarged screen could then mask three speakers designed for the four-track MagOptical stereophonic sound. Exhibiting a biblical spectacle like *The Robe* in this visually and aurally stunning process made it a ground-breaking production. This would require a number of theaters to refit their screens, so Koster shot two versions of the film, one in CinemaScope, one in standard format. *The Robe* would soon make the widescreen format preferable for all major films.

Unlike the novel, the film begins in a slave market in Rome, where Marcellus first encounters Demetrius, a Greek slave, and renews his childhood acquaintance with the patrician Diana, who is informally betrothed to Caligula. Caligula loses the sale of Demetrius to Marcellus. Though not yet emperor, Caligula expresses his anger by reassigning Marcellus to the Jerusalem garrison.

Marcellus and Demetrius arrive as Jesus is entering Jerusalem; Demetrius immediately believes in him. Soon after, Marcellus gives gold to the Roman centurion Paulus to ferret out the religious fanatics, but Demetrius takes offense and runs away, encountering that same night a morose Judas, who questions why humans must have their doubts. Pontius Pilate summons Marcellus, informs him that Tiberius has ordered him back to Capri, and adds that he must first perform one duty, 'a routine execution'. This turns out to be the crucifixion of Jesus, where Marcellus wins his homespun robe with a throw of the dice. As the thunder and lightning build, Jesus on the cross says, 'Father, forgive them, for they know not what they do' (Luke 23:34). Marcellus touches the cross and gets Christ's blood on his hand, and in the midst of the storm that follows, Marcellus covers his head with the robe and immediately screams in pain, demanding that Demetrius remove it. Demetrius does, curses Marcellus and the Roman Empire, and runs away with the robe.

Overcome by madness, Marcellus is haunted by the crucifixion and, like Macbeth, cannot rid himself of the image of his victim's blood on his hand. As a remedy, Tiberius gives him an imperial commission to return to Jerusalem to find the robe which 'bewitched' him and destroy it, but he also charges him to take the names of all those who follow this 'magician' and report back to him directly. After Marcellus and Diana reconfirm their love, Tiberius observes:

> This is how it will start – some obscure martyr in some forgotten province, then madness, infecting the legions, rotting the empire, then the finish of Rome. ... This is more dangerous than any spell. It is man's desire to be free.

Returning to Judea, Marcellus, now assisted by the Syrian Abidor, masquerades as a merchant buying homespun. He encounters several once disabled locals, some of them cured by Jesus, and Miriam, a disabled songstress who expresses her love for Jesus in melodic poetry. Through her and Justus, the community leader, Marcellus gradually learns about their world of faith and hope to replace his world of reason and military power. When Marcellus discovers the whereabouts of Demetrius and orders him to burn the robe, Demetrius explains that it is not the robe which has cast a spell but Marcellus' own conscience. Marcellus grabs the robe and tries to burn it himself, but instead he embraces it and regains his sanity.

Marcellus now joins a Christian gathering where Justus introduces Peter, the 'big fisherman', but Roman soldiers under the leadership of Paulus suddenly attack and kill Justus. Marcellus challenges Paulus, who informs him that Caligula has now succeeded Tiberius, and they fight a duel. Although Marcellus wins, he refuses to kill Paulus, instead humiliating the centurion. Peter admires Marcellus' courage and devotion and admits to Marcellus that he denied Jesus thrice, after which Marcellus admits that he was the one who crucified him. Marcellus pledges his 'sword, fortune, and life' to Christ.

Returning to Rome, Marcellus leads a raid to free Demetrius, whom Caligula has captured and put to torture, from the palace prison. The enraged Caligula orders the arrest of Marcellus. Attempting to escape in a speeding carriage, Marcellus bids farewell to Demetrius, sends the carriage on, and allows himself to be arrested.

In the imperial trial the next day, Marcellus, the robe in hand, defies Caligula by refusing his order to renounce 'this dead Jew'. Marcellus is sentenced to death. As in the novel, Diana volunteers to join him, and as they are led out in a procession, she hands the robe to a friend, saying: 'For the big fisherman!'

The Robe was a great success, costing some $4.5 million but earning $17.5 million in its initial release – more than any other film in 1953.

It earned another $8 million abroad, and doubled that amount subsequently. It was nominated for five Academy Awards, won two, and won several technical awards as well. With some foresight Zanuck prepared a sequel, *Demetrius and the Gladiators* (1954), although it was not nearly as successful. Dunne wrote the original script now with Demetrius deconverting from Christianity and reconverting by the end of the film.

Jon Solomon

Further reading

Irene Kahn Atkins (1987) *Henry Koster*. Metuchen NJ: The Directors Guild of America. pp. 127–33.

Monica Silveira Cyrino (2005) *Big Screen Rome*. Malden, MA: Blackwell. pp. 34–58.

Virginia Douglas Dawson and Betty Douglas Wilson (1952) *The Shape of Sunday: An Intimate Biography of Lloyd C. Douglas*. Boston, MA: Houghton Mifflin Company. pp. 323–49.

Bernard F. Dick (1989) *Radical Innocence: A Critical Study of the Hollywood Ten*. Lexington, KY: University Press of Kentucky. pp. 94–96.

Philip Dunne (1992) *Take Two: A Life in Movies and Politics*. New York, NY: Limelight Editions. pp. 253–56.

Allene Stuart Phy (1985) 'Retelling the Greatest Story Ever Told', in Allene Stuart Phy, ed., *The Bible and Popular Culture in America*. Philadelphia, PA: Fortress Press. pp. 56–59.

SALOME (1923, 1953)

[1923: Production Company: Nazimova Productions. Producer: Alla Nazimova. Director: Charles Bryant. Screenplay: Oscar Wilde (play); Natacha Rambova (scenario). Cinematography: Charles Van Enger. Cast: Mitchell Lewis (Herod, Tetrarch of Judea), Alla Nazimova (Salome, stepdaughter of Herod), Rose Dione (Herodias, wife of Herod), Earl Schenck (Narraboth, Captain of the Guard), Arthur Jasmine (Page of Herodias), Nigel De Brulier (Jokaanan, the Prophet). 1953: Production Company: Columbia. Producers: Buddy Adler, Rita Hayworth. Director: William Dieterle. Screenplay: Jesse Lasky Jr, Harry Kleiner. Cinematography: Charles Lang. Cast: Rita Hayworth (Princess Salome), Stewart Granger (Commander Claudius), Charles Laughton (King Herod), Judith Anderson (Queen Herodias), Sir Cedric Hardwicke (Tiberius Caesar), Alan Badel (John the Baptist), Basil Sydney (Pontius Pilate).]

In the accounts of the death of John the Baptist in the Gospels of Matthew (14:3–12) and Mark (6:17–29), King Herod's step-daughter makes a brief appearance. The king promises to give her anything if she will dance for him. The gospel writers do not state her name. Josephus identifies a young woman named Salome who has the lineage appropriate to this position, but he does not refer to this incident (*Antiquities* 18.136). Nevertheless, traditionally the name Salome has been attached to the anonymous woman who performs for Herod and then asks for the prophet's head on a silver platter. According to the Gospels of Matthew and Mark, Herod briefly resists, but then reluctantly agrees. Thus Salome has become symbolic of the evil female seductress. Centuries later, Salome also became the perfect model for the vamp, the sensual young woman who lured young men to their doom, spiritual, physical, or both. In 1918, Theda Bara starred in *Salome*, a film that is currently lost. This essay will focus on the 1923 adaptation which starred Alla Nazimova and conclude with some commentary on the 1953 version starring Rita Hayworth. Each of these films was also titled *Salome*, and each reveals how American films were able to redefine this biblical outcast as a feminist icon. The 1923 version is particularly fascinating due to Nazimova's control of the project, her daring aesthetic choices that were nevertheless representative of the times, and the film's presentation of feminist ideas that were not only relevant for the post-World War I era but remain so for ours.

For *Salome*, Nazimova selected the project, wrote the screenplay under her pseudonym of Peter M. Winters, directed (although screen credit goes to her long-term companion Charles Bryant), edited, and starred. She also provided her close friend, Natasha Rambova (nee Winifred Hudnut), with the opportunity to do the set and costume designs and cast most of the secondary roles.

Following her emigration from Russia, Nazimova achieved prominence in the United States in 1906 due to critical acclaim for her performances of Ibsen. In 1915, she began her screen career in the anti-war film *War Brides*. *War Brides* was the first in a series of films throughout her career in which she played a woman who suffers and dies when she attempts to defy a violent and oppressive masculine culture. In addition to *Salome*, such films include *Out of the Fog* (1918), *The Red Lantern* (1918) and *Camille* (1921). From 1915–20, Nazimova was a major star for Metro, after which her commercial success declined as the studio struggled to find appropriate vehicles for her. The studio finally gave her a three-picture contract with the freedom to select and guide her own productions. In fulfillment, she first produced *Camille*, *A Doll's House* (1922, now lost), and then invested all her personal savings of $300,000 plus an additional $100,000 loan in

Salome. This financial loss cost Nazimova her famous Hollywood home, The Garden of Allah, her influence in the film industry, and her star status. She never again had a major lead role. Yet, *Salome* was a logical choice for Nazimova's final attempt to maintain her status. Beginning with Oscar Wilde's 1887 theatrical version, from which Nazimova adapted her script, *Salome* captivated audiences in a variety of formats for the next thirty-five years. In addition to productions of the play and Theda Bara's film, there was also an operatic version by Richard Strauss (1905) and a ballet (1907). Each version perpetuated the greater Western cultural phenomenon defined by Edward Said (1978) as 'Orientalism', a system of beliefs about Arab, African, and Asian people and cultures based on stereotypes and prejudices rather than actual observation or research. As such, Orientalism helped Western societies maintain an understanding of 'the East' as mysterious and exotic, inferior to their own world, yet promising experiences unavailable elsewhere. As film and literature scholars have recently argued, Orientalism also provided a space for Western white women to express themselves through taking on roles as the marginalized women from these cultures. Nazimova did so in *Eye for Eye* (1918), *The Red Lantern* (1918) and *Salome*. Yet, in *Salome*, Nazimova did not merely try to cash in on popular trends. Instead, she took risks that challenged her audiences. Despite its commercial failure, the film provides a fascinating insight into the artistic trends and social issues of the era.

One trend was that of adult actresses playing children. Mary Pickford, the most popular actress of the 1920s, achieved fame and fortune through playing twelve to fourteen year-olds well into her twenties. Audiences fell in love with her spunky characters who overcame all obstacles through humour and determination. In *Salome*, Nazimova also played a fourteen year old. Yet, as she was forty-two at the time, she did not make it easy for audiences to accept her in the role. Furthermore, her character is far from lovable. Indeed, she is an impetuous child who will do whatever is necessary to fulfill her perverted desires. Ultimately, she is killed after achieving her wish of kissing Jokanaan's (John the Baptist) lips after receiving his severed head. Nazimova's highly stylized performance accentuates Salome's childish obstinance. In the opening scene, she sits with her back turned to King Herod, her step-father, looking disgusted and bored. She sneers and shakes her head broadly when Herod asks her to join his celebration. When she leaves the scene, she walks in small stiff-legged steps, as an angry child might, into the adjoining courtyard. In a later scene, she almost trips over the body of Narraboth, captain of the guard, who has committed suicide. Looking back, she kicks his corpse in annoyance. She shows no sympathy for anyone. Yet, when adoring the moon or gazing upon Jokanaan, Nazimova strikes balletic poses, her leg stretched back, her arms stiff and slightly out from her body, her face pressed forward. In these moments, her performance approaches a dance that emphasizes her lithe body and her character's immaturity.

Natasha Rambova's set and costume designs complemented the artificiality of Nazimova's performance. *Salome* was shot on a large sound stage with the two parts of the set, the banquet room and the terrace courtyard, separated only by a large scrim. The floor is completely smooth and there are no walls visible in the banquet room and no scenery outside the low terrace walls. Completing the set were large flowers painted on the walls between the banquet room and terrace, a large metal gate with similar metal flowers on it, and a strange birdcage style structure over the cistern in which Jokanaan is imprisoned. In addition to fitting the film's heavy self-referentiality, these choices also reveal influences from two important artistic trends of the era. The first was the art nouveau style, especially the fin-de-siècle work of Aubrey Beardsley, whose drawings had illustrated the published versions of Wilde's play. Art nouveau was characterized by swirling lines and a lack of depth, creating a sense of a hallucinatory ethereal space. The second was the use of mythic figures, a trend that may have influenced Rambova's costuming of the guards, court attendants, and Salome, whose appearance is suggestive of sprites and fawns.

For the costuming, Rambova again focused on the production's style rather than aiming for a faux historical realism as in the Bara and Hayworth productions. Nazimova wears a simple dark one-piece sleeveless shift with a very short bottom section and a large number of white baubles in her hair, that bounce around wildly whenever she shakes her head. Narraboth and his admiring companion, Queen Herodious's page, are both naked above the waist, wear thick matted wigs, a string of large beads, and heavy facial makeup. Narraboth also has decorated nipples. The page is terrified by Narraboth's lusting for Salome, and everyone is similarly frightened by Salome's desires for Jokanaan. In addition, the combination of Nazimova's boyish figure with the young guards' feminine appearance alludes to the themes of gender blending and sexual openness that also contribute to the film's confusing and sterile environment. Lust, death, and uncertainty dominate this world, within which Salome's demand to possess the beautiful prophet makes some sort of sense.

Jokanaan, like Salome, has a sleek build. But he is taller and wears even less than she, just an animal fur loin cloth that hangs down from his right hip and barely covers his genitals. When she first gazes at him down in the cistern, with a shaft of light casting the cage's shadows across him, he appears like a wounded bird. By contrast, when he is by her side in the courtyard, he stays phallicly rigid. Compared to the huge executioner, the terrified white guards, Salome's drunken and obese mother and step-father, and the troops of midgets and bizarrely costumed advisors who fill out the court retinue, Jokanaan is the most beautiful being present.

In the early twenties, flappers and working girls were becoming prominent and culturally influential. Some politicians, ministers, and columnists were expressing concern about the possible impact of women's new openness on social morality. As a result, Nazimova's stubborn and immature young protagonist, demanding both love and independence in a sexually ambiguous world, was touching on some very relevant issues. Salome was a forceful young woman attempting to assert herself within a decadent patriarchal world. Ultimately, she succeeds. But when she kisses Jokanaan's lifeless lips, Herod is outraged and orders her death. The heavy phallic imagery of spears piercing her body at the end is no accident. Nazimova did not attempt to reassure her audience. Instead, she depicted what happens to a strong female in a masculine world. Her feminist film and career received the same fate, which resulted in the silencing of an important artist's voice.

The 1953 *Salome*, directed by William Dieterlie, not surprisingly, relied much more on big-budget Hollywood elements: big-name stars, rich Technicolor, lavish sets, and large numbers of extras. These elements were de rigueur during the fifties as Hollywood used Biblical epics to combat the appeal of television. Thus, in addition to Hayworth in the title role, the cast included Charles Laughton as King Herod and Stuart Granger as Claudius, a fictional Roman soldier and secret follower of John the Baptist. From her first appearance to the last, Hayworth is given star treatment, displayed in a variety of beautiful v-neck gowns pinned at the shoulders to give them a slight resemblance to something that could conceivably have been worn in ancient Rome. Her hair and make-up are also constantly perfect and her final dance before Herod fully displays her face and body as she gradually discards her veils and lounges sensuously before the king. Yet, Hayworth is not simply an object of visual pleasure in the film. Rather, she is the strongest character, especially in contrast to the men.

Also unsurprising for a 1950s film is the obvious influence of cold war politics. *Salome* does not simplistically equate the oppressive Roman Empire with the Godless Soviets. Rather, the film promotes spiritual values over militaristic and materialistic ones, a message that was as relevant to America as to Russia. This message comes through Hayworth's performance; she repeatedly stands up to all the men she confronts throughout the film. Her goal is not luxury. Rather, the film concludes with Salome and Claudius, having rejected their positions and privileges, standing in the crowd listening to Christ deliver the Sermon on the Mount. Salome first rejects her Roman lover who refuses to choose her, a Judean, over a high position in the empire. She then repeatedly rejects Claudius's advances, turns back Herod's lustful offers, and finally defies her mother by going to hear the Baptist speak. In the end, she dances for Herod to try to save John the Baptist, but she is too late. Her mother has already asked for John's head, and it is brought in as Salome finishes her dance.

The film's ostentatious appeal and promotion of Hayworth's sensuality obviously contradict its ultimate promotion of spiritual values. Yet, Rita Hayworth makes Salome as much of a feminist as Nazimova did, and she shows that beauty and privilege should not always be equated with pampered and shallow.

Thomas Slater

Further reading

Bruce Babington and Peter William Evans (1993) *Biblical Epics: Sacred Narrative in the Hollywood Cinema*. Manchester: Manchester University Press.

Gavin Lambert (1997) *Nazimova: A Biography*. New York, NY: Knopf.

Michael Morris (1991) *Madam Valentino: The Many Lives of Natacha Rambova*. New York, NY: Abbeville Press.

Edward Said (1978) *Orientalism*. London; New York, NY: Penguin.

Gaylyn Studlar (1997) '"Out-Salomeing Salome": Dance, the New Woman, and Fan Magazine Orientalism', in Mathew Bernstein and Studlar (eds) *Visions of the East: Orientalism in Film*. New Brunswick, NJ: Rutgers University Press. pp. 99–129.

Kristin Thompson (1995) 'The Limits of Experimentation in Hollywood' in *Lovers of Cinema: The First American Film Avant-Garde, 1919–1945*. Madison, WI: University of Wisconsin Press. pp. 67–93.

Maureen Turim (1994) 'Seduction and Elegance: 'The New Woman of Fashion in Silent Cinema' in Shari Benstock and Suzanne Ferriss (eds) *On Fashion*. New Brunswick, NJ: Rutgers University Press. pp. 140–68.

Patricia White (2002) 'Nazimova's Veils: *Salome* at the Intersections of Film History' in Jennifer M. Bean and Diane Negra (eds) *A Feminist Reader in Early Cinema*. Durham, NC: Duke University Press. pp. 60–87.

SAMSON AND DELILAH (1949)

[Production Company: Paramount Pictures. Director: Cecil B. DeMille. Screen Writer: Jesse L. Lasky Jr, Frederic M. Frank and an uncredited Jeanie Macpherson from an original treatment by Harold Lamb derived from the Holy Bible, Judges 13–16 and the uncredited novel *Judge and Fool* (a.k.a. *Samson the Nazarite*) by Vladimir Jabotinsky. Cinematography: George Barnes (Director of Photography), Gordon Jennings (Director of Photographic Effects), Arthur Rosson and Ralph Jester (Unit Directors). Music: Victor Young. Art Director: Hans Dreier and Walter Tyler. Film Editor: Anne Bauchens. Main Cast: Hedy Lamarr (Delilah), Victor Mature (Samson), George Sanders (The Saran of Gaza), Angela Lansbury (Semadar), Henry Wilcoxon (Ahtur), Olive Deering (Miriam), Fay Holden (Hazeleponit), Julia Faye (Hisham), Russell Tamblyn (Saul), William Farnum (Tubal), Francis J. McDonald (Story Teller).]

Judges 13–16 (KJV and hereafter) recounted the divinely sanctioned rise and spectacular demise of the most famous judge of the Old Testament – Samson, the Danite. This Hebrew Hercules was the real Incredible Hulk who became a veritable Che Guevara of the Sinai Peninsula, warring against the Philistines when cheated out of a riddle prize (Judg. 14:12–18) and Philistine bride (Judg. 14:20–15:1–2). His name has entered the English language as a synonym for phenomenal physical strength, especially when the spirit of the Lord came upon him: he easily tore apart a young lion barehanded (Judg. 14:5–6), slayed thirty Ashkelon men for their garments (Judg. 14:19) and slaughtered a thousand Philistines with the jawbone of an ass (Judg. 15:15). Even when not acting as God's spirit-filled weapon, Samson easily broke his bonds (Judg. 16:7–9, 11–12, 13–14), captured three hundred foxes and attached firebrands between their tied tales (Judg. 15:4), slaughtered Philistines 'hip and thigh' (Judg. 15:8), and carried far uphill the door, posts and bar of the Gaza gates straight after a night of lovemaking (Judg. 16:3). He was a comical, trickster-figure of mythological proportions that challenged DeMille creatively to balance the mundane with the hyperbolic *without* causing audience incredulity, yet still jibe with scripture, theological trajectories and twentieth-century cultural expectations. DeMille was a master at this. 'For all its hokeyness *Samson and Delilah* is a brilliant film' (Exum 1996:13) and 'a masterpiece of biblical film-making (it gets better after repeated viewings); the 1949 film sparkles in spite of its age, with memorable dialogue and impressive overacting' (Exum 2002: 255).

Were it not for Samson's inclusion in the New Testament roll call of God's faithful (Heb. 11:32), he would have been easily dismissed as a biblical bad boy-loser *par excellence*, the last and also the least of the Old Testament judges. He was certainly no Israelite role model, having led no armies, conducted no religious services, and fathered no children; furthermore, he engaged in vendetta killings (Judg. 14:19; 15:8, 15), mistreated animals (Judg. 14:6; 15:4), violated his endogamy traditions (Judg. 14:1–3), disrespected and coerced his parents (Judg. 14:2) and deliberately compromised their religious purity (Judg. 14:8–9) and his own life-long Nazarite obligations (Judg. 13:5, 7; Num. 6:1–21). He was also an aggressive arsonist (Judg. 15:4–5), frequented harlots (Judg. 16:1), had romantic affairs with enemy women (Judg. 14:1–2; 16:4), lied repeatedly (Judg. 16:7, 11, 13), and very foolishly revealed the secret of his extraordinary strength – his uncut hair (Judg. 16:17).

Ironically, the strongest man in the world was twice defeated by physically weak women using persistent tears (Judg. 14:16–17) and vexatious nagging (Judg. 16:16) – the ideal womanly weapons against this weak-willed warrior. Once fatally betrayed, the now-shorn, God-abandoned and weakened Samson was quickly bound, blinded, imprisoned, and belittled (Judg. 16:21) before eventually committing suicide by toppling Dagon's temple upon himself and about 3,000 Philistines (Judg. 16:27, 30). Thus he fulfilled God's design to *begin* delivering the children of Israel from the domineering Philistines (Judg. 13:5) into whose hands he previously placed the evil-doing Israelites (Judg. 13:1). Overall, Samson's fate was Israel's history writ small; his blindness was a flesh-and-blood metaphor of a people who had lost sight of God, and his comeuppance was a case study of the squandering of God's gifts. All of this DeMille faithfully rendered visually and/or dialogically, if unevenly.

In addition to his strength, Samson is famous today as a he-man with a she-problem because of his turbulent romance with Delilah – the infamous sorceress of Sorek (Judg. 16:4–20) who has become a potent cultural symbol for temptation, deceit and betrayal. This paradigmatic case of woman's wickedness is the ancient forerunner of the libidinous Alex Forrest in *Fatal Attraction* (Adrian Lyne, 1987) and the manipulative Catherine Tramell in *Basic Instinct* (Paul Verhoeven, 1992). Technically, Delilah-the-spy is a Philistine national hero, but

DeMille continued the traditional theological and cultural trajectory of demonizing her, and subtextually constructed her as a Whore of Babylon-figure (Kozlovic 2002) and a Devil-figure (Kozlovic 2006b) by casting the notorious sex symbol of his day – Hedy Lamarr. Samson and Delilah's doomed dalliance was an archetypal depiction of disaster rooted in Samson's arrogant possessiveness and Delilah's scorned-woman rejection that thematically underpinned this sacred text-to-silver screen adaptation. DeMille had re-read the Book of Judges mid-rashically as a love story, that shifted the dehumanized biblical perspective of Israel's salvation history and replaced it with a counter-coherence featuring Delilah following her heart, changing allegiances (emotional, religious, political) and remaining true to Samson.

Employing the Bible, Jabotinsky's historical novel *Judge and Fool*, the artwork of numerous fine art masters, and the Bible illustrations of Gustave Doré, as source texts and pictorial imagery, DeMille rendered his Samson saga more thoughtfully, entertainingly and artistically than any film director before, deftly deploying interlocking sacred subtexts to buttress his 'good' versus 'evil' character construction. For dramatic and cost-cutting reasons, however, he avoided filming Judges 13 with its angelic annunciation and Nazarite prescription scenes. He also included a logical but weakly warranted backstory that posited Delilah as the fairer younger sister (Judg. 15:2) of Samson's duplicitous Timnite wife-to-be (DeMille's Semadar), to give greater dramatic power to this X-rated biblical tale of temptation, rivalry and control (both physical, sexual, political and religious).

DeMille's major film-making challenge was to induce audiences willingly to suspend their disbelief regarding Samson's superhuman feats with Victor Mature's body. He succeeded through film-making tactics ranging from power costuming to multiple onlooker astonish-ment, from suggestive dialogue to silent sound effects (Kozlovic 2007). Furthermore, given the narrative need to portray Samson's juvenile delinquent behaviours but still make this biblical brawler 'good', DeMille subtextually constructed his Samson as a Moses-figure (Kozlovic 2009) and as a Christ-figure (Kozlovic 2003), buttressed by the old Story Teller as a John the Baptist-figure (Kozlovic 2006a). This astute aesthetic tactic further propelled Samson into the holy realms, and conversely, the devilish Delilah deeper into the hellish realms by contrasting the moral distance between them.

DeMille also artfully engineered scripture in order to conform to traditional public expectations. For example, Delilah is popularly perceived as the barber who cut Samson's hair, but according to Judges 16:19, she 'called for a man, and she caused him to shave off the seven locks of his head'. This point is echoed delightfully in the caper comedy *Fitzwilly* (Delbert Mann, 1967) when its conman-protagonist, Claude R. Fitzwilliam, used it to scam gullible bar patrons out of their betting money. DeMille allowed his audiences to see what they wanted to see. His Delilah menacingly approached Samson's hair with a dagger before the camera quickly jump cuts to a sunrise scene and then again to the scene in which Samson awakens to find Delilah next to him, toying with a bowl of his cut curls. After betraying Samson, this female Judas suffered a textual death – she is absent from Judges 16:21 onwards – but evidently the popular cinema, opera, literature, song and modern-day scripture scholars cannot let go of her so abruptly. In DeMille's film, she attends Samson's public humiliation, repents of her treachery, rejects the Saran of Gaza and dies with her man.

Historically speaking, DeMille's Technicolor testament was a watershed film that reinvigorated the then-moribund biblical epic genre and triggered the 1950–60s rash of Bible films. Its commercial success filled Paramount's purse, earned DeMille public praise, and made his less successful peers envious, while his Samsonian destruction of the temple of Dagon became one of the most iconic Old Testament depictions in the twentieth century. In short, his romantic repackaging of Holy Writ via the Hollywood hermeneutic did what art and literature has always done: read the Bible and unpick its theological and historical consistencies, and, in this case, offer a modern melodramatic rendition that newly exposed the assumptions underlying the traditional readings of sacred texts.

To his stylistic credit, DeMille avoided the lure of distracting physical perfectionism. His Samson was not a gym-sculptured muscleman with perfectly symmetrical pectorals, abdominals and bulging biceps designed for competition posing; rather, he was crafted as a rustic strongman confidently secure in his divinely supported superiority. Victor Mature's beefy body and boyish charms won him the coveted role and he quickly became the loincloth king of his day, replacing Steve Reeves, who had refused to tone down his body builder physique for DeMille, but subsequently starred in *Hercules* (Pietro Francisci, 1958) and other Italian musclemen movies. Ironically, despite DeMille's repeated disgust, berating and beseeching, Mature insisted that stuntmen substitute for him during the dramatic lion-fighting and temple-toppling scenes due to his fear of injury.

Similarly, DeMille's Delilah was not a big-bosomed *Playboy* bimbo but a modestly endowed foreigner, Hedy Lamarr, who possessed an alluring Continental eroticism that reeked of the exotic and accompanied her notoriety as the neo-pornographic star of *Ecstasy* (Gustav

Machatý, 1933). This cunning casting choice generated valuable marketing buzz and erotic fantasies by viewers not normally interested in prayer-and-faith films. DeMille's showmanship succeeded brilliantly at the box-office by meeting audiences' spiritual *and* romantic demands firmly rooted in the scriptural Samson saga, 'the story of sexy stories ... always an entertaining and sacred scandal sheet' (Wurtzel 1998: 38). Interestingly, the worldly wise Saran of Gaza was modeled upon DeMille, while *Sunset Blvd.* (Billy Wilder, 1950) featured him directing *Samson and Delilah* at Paramount studios when interrupted by Norma Desmond eager to star in his supposedly forthcoming *Salome*. Overall, *Samson and Delilah* remains *the* definitive Samson film whose many cinematic construction secrets still await unearthing.

Anton Karl Kozlovic

Further reading

J. Cheryl Exum (1996) *Plotted, Shot, and Painted: Cultural Representations of Biblical Women.* Sheffield: Sheffield Academic Press.

——(2002) 'Lethal Woman 2: Reflections on Delilah and Her Incarnation as Liz Hurley', in Martin O'Kane (ed.), *Borders, Boundaries and the Bible.* London: Sheffield Academic Press. pp. 254–73.

Bruce Herzberg (2010) 'Samson's Moment of Truth', *Biblical Interpretation: A Journal of Contemporary Approaches* 18(3): 226–50.

Anton K. Kozlovic (2002) 'The Whore of Babylon, Suggestibility, and the Art of Sexless Sex in Cecil B. DeMille's *Samson and Delilah* (1949)', in Dane S. Claussen (ed.) *Sex, Religion, Media.* Lanham, MD: Rowman & Littlefield. pp. 21–31.

——(2003) 'Have Lamb will Martyr: Samson as a Rustic Christ-figure in Cecil B. DeMille's *Samson and Delilah* (1949)', *Reconstruction: Studies in Contemporary Culture* 3(1), available online at http://reconstruction.eserver. org/031/kozlovic.htm (accessed 24 August 2011).

——(2006a) 'The Old Story Teller as a John the Baptist-figure in DeMille's *Samson and Delilah*', *CLCWeb: Comparative Literature and Culture* 8(3), available online at http://docs.lib.purdue.edu/clcweb/vol8/iss3/2/ (accessed 24 August 2011).

——(2006b) 'Making a "Bad" Woman Wicked: The Devilish Construction of Delilah within Cecil B. DeMille's *Samson and Delilah* (1949)', *McMaster Journal of Theology and Ministry* 7: 70–102.

——(2007) 'Creating the Cinematic Illusion of Samson's Phenomenal Strength in Cecil B. DeMille's *Samson and Delilah* (1949)', *Belphegor: Popular Literature and Media Culture* 6(2), available online at http://etc.dal. ca/belphegor/vol6_no2/articles/06_02_kozl_creat_en.html (accessed 24 August 2011).

——(2009) 'Samson as a Moses-figure in Cecil B. DeMille's *Samson and Delilah* (1949)', *Americana: E-Journal of American Studies in Hungary* 5(1), available online at http://americanaejournal.hu/vol5no1/kozlovic (accessed 24 August 2011).

Lloyd Llewellyn-Jones (2005) 'The Fashioning of Delilah. Costume Design, Historicism and Fantasy in Cecil B. DeMille's *Samson and Delilah* (1949)', in Liza Cleland, Mary Harlow and Lloyd Llewellyn-Jones (eds) *The Clothed Body in the Ancient World*, Oxford: Oxbow Books. pp. 14–29.

Elizabeth Wurtzel (1998) *Bitch: In Praise of Difficult Women*. New York, NY: Doubleday.

Further viewing

Samson et Dalila (Ferdinand Zecca, 1902)
Samson (J. Farrell MacDonald, 1914)
Samson und Delila (Alexander Korda, 1922)
Samson and Delilah (Lee Philips, 1984)
Samson and Delilah (Nicolas Roeg, 1996)
Samson and Delilah (Corina Van Eijk, 2007)

A SERIOUS MAN (2009)

[Production Company: Relativity Media/Mike Zoss Prod./Studio Canal/Working Title Films. Director: Ethan Coen, Joel Coen. Screenplay: Ethan Coen, Joel Coen. Cinematography: Roger Deakins. Cast: Michael Stuhlbarg (Larry Gopnik), Richard Kind (Uncle Arthur), Fred Melamed (Sy Ableman), Sari Lennick (Judith Gopnik), Aaron Wolff (Danny Gopnik). Jessica McManus (Sarah Gopnik).]

Several films in recent years have been inspired by the biblical Book of Job or at least by some of its basic questions and narrative constellations. One recent film, Terrence Malick's *The Tree of Life*, which opens with an explicit quotation of Job 38:4 ('Where were you when I laid the foundation of the earth?'), is unique in that it lacks the (sometimes rather dark) humour that characterizes all of the other recent films that refer to Job – films such as *Drifting Clouds* (1996) by Finnish director Aki Kaurismäki (see Zwick 2001), *Bruce Almighty* (2003) and *Adam's Apples* (2005). With their comic, but not irreverent, approach to the problem of theodicy and the suffering of the innocent, these movies share a perspective on Job, also prominent in recent exegesis (cf. Whedbee 1976) that focuses mainly on the basic plot structure. The Book of Job's narrative is a story of epic loss that transforms into happiness in an almost fairy-tale-like manner. Despite its title, *A Serious Man* by the brothers Ethan and Joel Coen is not a serious drama in the sense that it is told with gravity and sternness. Rather, it is a comedy, but with the typical Coen-esque irony and black humour, and thus far different from light comedies such as *Bruce Almighty*.

A Serious Man is set in a Jewish community in the Minnesota of the late 1960s, a date established by the 1967 song 'Somebody to Love' by Grace Slick and Jefferson Airplane that is woven into the film. Of course the setting bares a strong resemblance to the place, time and atmosphere where the Jewish brothers Coen grew up (Minneapolis), and without doubt their memories and experiences have nurtured the film to a considerable degree. But it would be wrong to reduce *A Serious Man* to a humourous and satirical memoir of growing up in a narrow little world, with a smug middle-class sensibility and a conservative religious and moral climate. The film also offers a serious critique of the human capacity – not limited to religion or to Judaism – to cope with blows of fate and to hold on to the notion of a benevolent and almighty God in the face of suffering and evil.

Larry Gopnik teaches mathematical and theoretical physics at the local college and is cautiously optimistic that he will pass review and be granted tenure very soon. As the film opens, his world seems to be in balance, but cracks soon appear. Larry undergoes medical tests and waits anxiously for his final diagnosis. His son Danny, who is preparing half-heartedly for his bar-mitzvah, smokes marijuana regularly and complains incessantly about poor television reception. His daughter Sarah spends her evenings at a nightclub with the unsavoury name of 'The Hole'. His mentally challenged brother Arthur lives with him, and passes his time either in the bathroom or working out complex, and meaningless, theorems in his sketchbook. Larry's neighbour is quarreling with him about the boundary between their two properties. Thus the starting point of the film story differs significantly from the well-ordered, happy life of the biblical Job.

In addition to the ongoing irritations of his daily life, Larry, like Job, suffers a long streak of bad luck that throws him into a profound existential crisis. Larry's wife Judith unexpectedly reveals that she has fallen in love with the elderly and strange widower Sy Ableman and that she wants both a civil and a religious divorce. At the college, a Korean student, discontent with an examination mark, tries to bribe Larry with a large amount of money, and the student's father adds to the pressure by spreading rumours about Larry's corruption to Larry's colleagues, thereby jeopardizing his tenure application. Larry's financial situation becomes more and more strained as he has to engage very expensive but seemingly inefficient lawyers to cope with the divorce, as well as pay for the hotel room that he shares with his brother Arthur when he separates from his wife.

Although the crises that afflict Larry are not as substantial and grave as those that confronted Job, they are serious enough to provoke questions about the concept of a benevolent God. Whereas the afflicted Job is visited by his three wise friends to comfort him and then to give him answers regarding the reason of his suffering, in an inverted structural parallel Larry, looking for help and advice, himself contacts three reputed rabbis. But their advice – such as it is – is as dissatisfying for Larry as the advice of Eliphaz, Bildad and Zophar was for Job. The first rabbi is absent and his young, inexperienced deputy Rabbi Scott suggests only that Larry should meditate on the small things in life – the synagogue parking lot, for example – as a way of getting a grip on the mystery of God and the mystery of being. The second, Rabbi Nachtner, recounts – but fails to explain – a 'mystery tale' about Hebrew inscriptions on the inner side of the teeth of a 'goy' (non-Jew). The third and most renowned rabbi, old Rabbi Marshak, refuses to see Larry at all.

Although the first and the second rabbis both refer to mysteries, even if they are banal, their responses to Larry's existential questions differ substantially from the emphatic but fundamentally weak arguments put forward by Job's friends, who repeat the theme of reward and punishment that is so patently irrelevant to Job's own situation and is strongly critiqued by the books of both Job and Qohelet (Ecclesiastes). What the first two rabbis have to say looks more like a parody of the God speeches towards the end of the Book of Job. Like these rabbis, God does not directly answer or even address Job's questions, but instead points to the mysteries of his creation and the limits of human reason. And whereas the biblical Job finally and unexpectedly sets aside his critique of the notion of an omniscient and loving God, and surrenders to God's nebulous arguments, Larry, in a parody of Job, also relinquishes his critique of theodicy when he raises his student's examination score.

Thus while there are clear structural and narrative connections between the stories of Job and Larry, such as the series of catastrophes, the theological problem of unjust suffering, and the three incompetent advisers, these connections are often inverted or parodied. The ending is also inverted. As the film moves towards its conclusion, it seems that all will end happily, even miraculously, if not as abundantly as in the Book of Job: Sy Ableman dies in a car accident and Judith seems willing to return to Larry; Danny manages to read the Torah on the occasion of his bar-mitzvah, despite the fact that he is so stoned that he can barely walk to the podium or see the letters of the Torah scroll. But in the end, Larry's life spirals downwards again, even lower than before: Larry gets a call from his doctor who urgently wants to speak to him in person, despite the tornado that is set to hit the city at any moment. The final shots show the young students, among them Danny, standing outside their school and staring towards the darkness of the tornado-cloud, so paralyzed by this vision that they fail to seek shelter (the keys to the shelter in any case cannot be found). Our imaginations fill in what the screen does not show: the tornado hits, fulfilling Job 1:19: 'Suddenly a great wind came across the desert, struck the four corners of the house, and it fell on the young people, and they are dead.' In the Book of Job this cruel message *ends* the dark series of the proverbial Job's news; in *A Serious Man* it *opens up* a dark future beyond the ending of the film.

In the Bible it is the happy ending that saves the Book of Job from drowning in the darkness of unredeemed complaints about the absence of God. Like other features of the Book of Job this positive ending is inverted in the Coen brothers' film. This final inversion is the most serious attack on the biblical book's optimism regarding the presence of God and the notion that life and suffering have a deeper truth and sense that, while hidden and inconceivable for humankind, nevertheless exist and are guaranteed by God and his wisdom. In *A Serious Man* this optimism is shattered immediately before the ultimate ending, ironically just when it seems that everything will be all right after all. After his successful bar-mitzvah reading, Danny – not his father – is granted an audience with the very old and very wise Rabbi Marshak, whose office with all his books, objects and signs looks like the private chamber of an old fashioned scholar. Like all young men who have passed the bar-mitzvah initiation, Danny expects the rabbi to reveal some ultimate truth, or cliché, about life. But the rabbi – before handing Danny the transistor radio that had been confiscated by his Hebrew teacher at the beginning of the movie – recites the first verses of the Jefferson Airplane's song 'Somebody to Love' (faltering only slightly) followed by a list of the names of the band members (with the help of Danny), as if he is quoting the authors of the holy scriptures themselves. Rabbi Marshak recites as follows: 'When the truth is found to be lies / and all the hope within you dies.' This version represents only a slight modification of the original lyrics, which refer to 'joy' rather than 'hope'.

This is a truly bitter summary of the meaning of human existence, ascribed by the Coens not only to the rabbi but also to the religion and heritage he represents. Thus in the parodic and inverse – perhaps even perverse – hands of Ethan and Joel Coen, the bible, and within it the Book of Job, become tools for criticizing religion, or at least tools that a radical sceptic can use in order to discern what is true and what is illusion.

Indeed, the difference between reality and illusion would seem to be the basic issue that troubles the Coens in this film. The enigmatic prologue to the movie's story about Larry takes us to a Jewish *shtetl* in Poland, sometime in the distant past. Is the old man who visits a Jewish couple one night a *Dybbuk*, the ghost of a dead person clothed in a human body, or is he truly human? The woman's attempt to learn the truth by stabbing him is inconclusive: the old man stumbles out of the house, wounded, but still alive. The question about truth and illusion remains open, to be taken up again during Larry's math class, when he presents his students with the paradox of Schrödinger's cat, in which it is impossible to know whether the cat is alive or dead. The prologue, the paradox, and, indeed, the film as a whole, provide a vehicle through which the Coens can ask: Are there any trustworthy answers to the most basic questions of life and death?

Reinhold Zwick

Further reading

J. Cheryl Exum, (ed.) (1986) 'Tragedy and Comedy in the Bible', *Semeia* 32.
J. W. Whedbee (1976) 'The Comedy of Job.' *Semeia* 7: 1–39.
Reinhold Zwick (2001) 'Wolken ziehen herauf und vorüber: Strukturen des Komischen in der Bibel und bei Aki Kaurismäki', in Stefen Orth, Joachim Valentin and Reinhold Zwick (eds): *Göttliche Komödien. Religiöse Dimensionen des Komischen im Kino* (Film und Theologie, Bd. 2), Köln. pp. 69–95.

Further viewing

Drifting Clouds (Aki Kaurismäki, 1996)
Bruce Almighty (Tom Shadyac, 2003)
Adam's Apples (Anders Thomas Jensen, 2005)
The Tree of Life (Terrence Malick, 2011)

SHANE (1953)

[Production Company: Paramount Pictures. Producer: George Stevens. Director: George Stevens. Screenplay: A. B. Guthrie Jr. Cinematography: Loyal Griggs. Music: Victor Young. Art Direction: Hal Pereira, Walter Tyler. Cast: Alan Ladd (Shane), Jean Arthur (Marian Starrett), Van Heflin (Joe

Starrett), Brandon de Wilde (Joey Starrett), Jack Palance (Jack Wilson), Elisha Cook Jr (Stonewall Torrey).]

Shane is a classic western that contains virtually every cliché of its genre: big sky, open country, good guys, bad guys, and plenty of gun fighting. *Shane* was filmed in 1951 but was not released until 1953. Paramount nearly gave up on the project as George Stevens, the producer and director, spent a long time editing the film. For Stevens it was a period of transition from his lighter pre-war movies to his more sombre films with strong humanitarian themes after, and because of, the war. *Shane* was released the year after an equally iconic western, *High Noon,* directed by Fred Zinnemann, and shares with that film a gradual and slow build-up to a final climactic confrontation. Like *High Noon, Shane* exemplifies a strong humanitarian ethos and moral seriousness. Neither director returned to the genre after these films.

The Psalmist reminds us that help comes from the hills (Ps. 121) and at the start of the film Shane rides down into the valley of the shadow of death where the conflict between the beleaguered home-steaders and the bullying ranchers, exemplified by the Ryker brothers and their hired hands, unfolds. Shane, a gunfighter seeking to repent of his former ways, belongs to neither group. Indeed, in the first scene the Starrett family take him to be one of Ryker's hired men when he passes through their land. Later in the same scene as the Starretts are threatened by the ranchers, Shane is asked by one of the Ryker brothers 'Who are you, stranger?' and replies immediately: 'I am a friend of Starrett.' This reply puts Shane, the complete outsider, on the same side as the bullied and struggling homesteaders. This act of solidarity is underlined by the sharing of bread as he accepts their offer of supper and a job on the ranch.

Shane is often regarded as a Christ-figure, for, like Christ, he is prepared to die so that others may live. Shane comes into the com-munity determined to renounce violence and is branded a coward by the homesteaders for turning the other cheek during a confrontation in Grafton's bar. Although he is a gunfighter, Shane tries to choose another way: dressing differently to everyone else – buckskin fringe on his jacket and dress slacks and blue shirts – and by being passive, quiet and unassertive, an accomplished dancer, caring to children, and by ordering soda pop rather than whisky in the saloon. There is a physical difference to Shane as well as an ethical difference that sets him apart from uncouth rangers and careworn homesteaders alike.

Alan Ladd, who plays Shane, is a strange choice as western hero. He is a small, compact man without a commanding physical appearance.

Originally, Stevens had tried to cast Montgomery Clift who, had he been available, would have been a more conventional western hero. It is now hard to imagine anyone other than Ladd in this role. In many ways, Shane mirrors the Terence Stamp role as the visitor in Pier Paolo Pasolini's *Teorema* (1968), also often considered a Christ-figure. Like the visitor in Pasolini's film, Shane brings glimpses of 'salvation' to those who encounter him: Jean Arthur's unfulfilled wife longing for a better future; Brandon De Wilde's Joey looking for a role model; Van Heflin's Starrett, saved from his own futile self-destruction in a fight he could never win; Ben Johnson's Calloway, Ryker's hired hand, whose encounter with Shane changes his allegiances. The exceptions are the three men Shane kills: the two Ryker brothers with their feigned reasonableness, and Jack Wilson, the feared gunfighter hired by Ryker to clear out the homesteaders.

Jack Palance is magnificent as the sneering gunfighter, Jack Wilson. In Wilson, Stevens created a character that is the personification of evil. When Wilson enters Grafton's Saloon, even the dog slinks away in fear. The shootout with a homesteader is conducted according to the gunfighter's ritual, which includes a menacing five second pause before Wilson unnecessarily kills the innocent but hot-headed Torrey in one of the most heartrending gunfights in the western genre.

The careful drawing of Shane and Wilson's characters lead to their climactic confrontation, which represents the conflict between good and evil. Shane, who has tried throughout the film to renounce fighting and find another way, knows he has to face the evil and defeat it, so that the shadow of death can be banished and there can be peace in the valley. Stevens has Shane riding through the graveyard, with the symbol of the cross slowly dissolving as Shane enters the town to fight Wilson and the Rykers. He kills them but in the course of the fight he is shot in the back by one of the Ryker brothers. After speaking to Joey, 'commissioning' him to look after the ranch and his parents, he rides off through the churchyard and up into the hills. Is he wounded or is he dead? Stevens implies by the 'ascension' that Shane is dead.

As with most supposed Christ-figures in film, there is enough evidence to argue the case, but very often it is in the last resort the viewer who imposes that interpretation on the film. In favour of such an interpretation, one may point to Clint Eastwood's remake, *Pale Rider* (1985) which plays up the religious content to make the references explicit – presumably the Christ-figure imagery is something that the script writer and Eastwood himself must have seen in Stevens' *Shane*.

The role of Jean Arthur as Marian Starrett is interesting for the sexual chemistry between her and Shane. They do not act upon it, although Marian articulates it when she asks Shane if he is going to fight because of her. The same ambiguity can be read into the relationship between Jesus and Mary Magdalene. You almost expect Jean Arthur to start singing 'I don't know how to love him', like Mary Magdalene in Norman Jewison's *Jesus Christ Superstar* (1973).

Others would argue against the interpretation of Shane as a Christ-figure on the grounds that strapping a six-shooter to your waist and shooting three men is not exactly the way of the cross. Shane's belief in the gun – 'a gun is a tool, no better or worse than any other tool – an axe, a shovel or anything. A gun is as good or as bad as the man using it. Remember that' – is hardly a gospel idea.

In his pioneering book *Hero with a Thousand Faces* (1949) Joseph Campbell outlines the archetypal plot for heroic action in traditional mythologies. This monomyth has a significant contemporary American variation. Typically, the standard plot formula is this: a community in a harmonious paradise is threatened by evil; normal institutions fail to contend with this threat; a selfless superhero emerges to renounce temptations (women/money/fame) and carry out the redemptive task; aided by fate, his decisive victory restores the community to its paradisiacal condition; the superhero then recedes into obscurity.

This form of the monomyth certainly has echoes of the Christ-figure, the suffering, selfless servant who is prepared to give his or her life for others. It is the plot of virtually every western, science-fiction and super-hero film ever made. These are not Christ types; they have certainly jettisoned the inconvenience of the Sermon on the Mount. The redemptive violence of the American superhero negates any such identification even when the film-maker is eager to offer us a distinct 'Christ-trope' – a filmic riff that plays with Christian iconography but goes no deeper. This is the case with *Shane*.

The most important factor in the making of *Shane* is undoubtedly George Stevens' experience of World War II. Stevens was in charge of the US Signal Corps Special Motion Picture Unit. He took extensive colour footage of the Normandy landings, fierce fighting between the Allies and the Germans throughout France and into Germany, where his camera captured the horrific images of Dachau just after its liberation. The experience changed him. There is a shift from the fun loving, gag writing, director of Laurel and Hardy films or Fred Astaire's *Swing Time*, to the measured and much more sombre director of *A Place in the Sun* (1951), *Shane* (1953), *Giant* (1956), *The Diary of Anne Frank* (1959) and *The Greatest Story Ever Told* (1965).

Certainly, his post-war films were more significant in theme and garnered more awards than the early films and all carry the possibility of being life-changing experiences for the movie-goer. Stevens chose to use his craft to make the world a better place.

Having witnessed how men fell when shot, Stevens insisted in *Shane* that bodies should fall backwards with the force of the bullet. It is not too fanciful to regard his version of *Shane* and its long careful gestation as his meditation on American involvement in World War II: the false diplomacy of the Rykers in trying to avoid conflict with Starrett; the bullying and defeat of the weaker homesteaders; Shane's reluctance to get involved and yet his obvious sympathy for the homesteaders; Shane's final decisive action that finishes the conflict and allows peace to reign in the valley. All of this echoes, perhaps simplistically, American prevarication and then ultimately the decisive involvement in the War. What Stevens has witnessed with the Signal Corps and his 16mm camera has convinced him of the need to act to defeat evil. Undoubtedly, the Korean War which was taking place during the making and release of *Shane* made this message of the necessity of action to defeat evil even more urgent. It is in this sense that *Shane* is a profoundly theological film about the individual and national responses to evil in order to defend what is decent, honest and pure.

If that is the motive and the context of the film-maker, then the context of the story itself is also important. It is 1890s America, and the Indian wars as well as the Civil War are over. The background of the fight between Starrett and the homesteaders on the one side and the Rykers, the rangers and hired hands on the other is, in microcosm, the issue at the heart of the Johnson County War of 1892. *The Virginian* (1946), *The Ox-Bow Incident* (1943), *Heaven's Gate* (1980) as well as *Shane* all use this conflict as the historical context of the movie. Stevens clearly sees this period as a key transition in the history of America, and he cleverly captures this transitional moment in *Shane*. After the conflict, peace replaces violence, the family unit replaces the loner, the work-wear of denims replaces the buckskins of the untamed wild west.

This dynamic not only constitutes the arc of the story; it is also embodied in the character of Shane himself. Shane is a transitional figure who comes from the wilderness and becomes part of the domestic unit cultivating the land; his self-giving rids the valley of guns so that 'swords can be turned into ploughs and crops flourish … ' (Mic. 4). Even Shane's clothes emphasise this transition – his buckskins are not the same as the buckskins of Ryker's hired hands, they are somehow more domestic; Shane spends the times of violence in buckskin and times of farming and honest toil in denim with the six-shooter safely hidden away.

George Stevens' *Shane* certainly has a mythic quality. On one level it is simply a well-crafted classic of the Western film genre. On another, it is a moment of transition in American history, or even a cosmic story about the need to act to rid the world of evil. As a film about the dilemma of liberal interventionism, whether for nation-states or individuals, *Shane* is both contemporary and timeless.

Shane remains high on the American Institute list of greatest films (no. 47) and third on its list of great westerns. After Paramount's initial lukewarm attitude to the film before it was released, it received a good critical and box office response. It was nominated for six Academy Awards but won only for its stunning cinematography. In *Shane* and his later films, most notably *Giant* and *The Greatest Story Ever Told*, Stevens was concerned to animate great mythic tales amidst spectacular American scenery. It is noteworthy that although Van Heflin and Jack Palance were lauded for their work on the film, Alan Ladd received no award nominations for his role as Shane. In many ways, this oversight may be testimony to his success in the role, for the dilemmas facing Shane are the human dilemmas facing us all. It is not a showy piece of acting but a truthful performance that is pivotal to the success of the film. Stevens needed truthful performances, brilliant cinematography and careful editing so that *Shane* and his subsequent films could help the world live more humanely – a godly ambition indeed.

Peter Francis

Further reading

Joseph Campbell (1956) *Hero with a Thousand Faces*. New York: Meridian.
Philip French (2005) *Westerns*. Manchester: Carcanet.
John Shelton Lawrence and Robert Jewett (2002) *The Myth of the American Superhero*. Grand Rapids: Eerdmans.
Jack Schaefer (1984) *Shane: The Critical Edition*. James C. Work (ed.) Lincoln: University of Nebraska Press.

Further viewing

Swing-Time (George Stevens, 1936)
The Ox-Bow Incident (William Wellman, 1943)
High Noon (Fred Zinnemann, 1952)
Giant (George Stevens, 1956)
The Diary of Anne Frank (George Stevens, 1959)
The Greatest Story Ever Told (George Stevens, 1965)
Heaven's Gate (Michael Cimino, 1980)

SLING BLADE (1996)

[Production Company: Shooting Gallery. Director: Billy Bob Thornton. Screenwriter: Billy Bob Thornton. Cinematography: Barry Markowitz. Cast: Billy Bob Thornton (Karl Childers), Dwight Yoakam (Doyle Hargraves), Lucas Black (Frank Wheatley), Natalie Canerday (Linda Wheatley), John Ritter (Vaughan Cunningham), Robert Duvall (Mr. Childers).]

Sling Blade tells the story of Karl Childers, a slightly humped-over, mentally challenged man with a protruding lower lip who speaks in a grunty voice. As the film opens, Karl has just been released from a mental institution where he has been living for the past twenty-five years after murdering his mother and her illicit lover with a sling blade. Karl befriends young Frank Wheatley who lives with his single mother, Linda, and Linda's abusive, alcoholic boyfriend, Doyle Hargraves. In the climactic scene, Karl kills Doyle in an effort to protect and save the Wheatleys.

The film presents Karl as a Christ-figure whose complexities and ambiguities parallel the diverse images of Jesus found throughout the New Testament. Karl and Christ are paradoxical protagonists who are at once gentle and violent, weak and strong, saviours and avengers. The film offers space for reflection on several important issues: New Testament Christology (or christologies), the ideologically driven images of Jesus presented for our consumption today, and existential questions on the nature and construction of reality and truth.

Thornton's depiction of Karl Childers – note the resonance with Christ-child – is analogous to the portrayal of Jesus in the Gospels in the following major ways (more are in the details which cannot detain us here).

1   In his speech, gait, and dress, Karl is an outsider, a powerless 'fool' shunned by the establishment. Karl comes from lowly, humble beginnings, which are literally on the outside, namely, in the shed in his parents' backyard where he was forced to live as child (cf. the manger; Luke 2:7).
2   Those who accept Karl are themselves poor and socially ostracized – a struggling single mother and Vaughan, a homosexual in a conservative southern town (cf. the disciples of Jesus).
3   Karl is a teacher, mentor, and sage. Although he is a simpleton, he comes up with clever solutions to various problems (when the lawnmower won't start, he realizes it is out of gas). He becomes a

father-figure to Frank, helping the boy work through a host of difficult issues: why Karl murdered his mother and her lover, the murder of Karl's little brother, Frank's father's suicide, and how Frank should deal with Doyle.

4 Those who reject Karl refuse to participate in table fellowship with him – Doyle claims that Karl's presence makes him sick and asks: 'Who the hell could eat with him makin' all that goddamn racket with his throat?' By contrast, those who accept Karl do so by including him at table. He joins Linda and Frank for meals, Karl's co-workers include him in their lunches at the local burger shop, Vaughan treats Karl to lunch, and Karl joins in a dinner with Vaughan and his lover and another mentally challenged girl.

5 Karl is baptized as part of the preparation for his mission – saving the Wheatley family from Doyle.

6 Karl prepares for the climactic event – killing Doyle – by telling Frank that he is about to leave, a message met with resistance (cf. the disciples). He provides a word of comfort to Frank, saying that he will always be with him; he instructs the boy what to do in the final hours, and withdraws to a remote place to reflect and meditate (cf. Gethsemane; Matt. 26:36; Mark 14:32).

7 After the salvific event has occurred, Karl returns to the place from which he came (John 14:1–3), the mental hospital. Karl sacrifices his life, but does not lose it; instead he returns to a place more suitable for him, as he himself expressly notes.

The power of *Sling Blade*, however, does not derive simply from these parallels with the Jesus of the Gospels. Rather, it comes from the fact that Karl is also analogous to the image of Jesus in the book of Revelation – the apocalyptic, conquering Christ who leads the army of God on a white horse and with a sword in his mouth with which to strike down his enemies (cf. Rev. 1, 14, 19, 21). Reminiscent of the image of Jesus with a sickle in his hand (Rev. 14), Karl takes a lawn-mower blade, carefully sharpens it, and deliberately lays out a plan to hack Doyle to death. This is not the meek and mild Jesus of the Sermon on the Mount. This is not the passive Jesus who suffers on the cross for the salvation of others. This is violent, gruesome stuff.

Audiences reportedly often remained in the theater as the credits rolled, seemingly pondering the morally ambiguous conclusion of the film. Is Karl the hero or the villain? What is one to think and feel about the murder of Doyle? Would another solution have been better? There are scenes, after all, which do evoke some sympathy for

Doyle as a man who has himself had a hard life. Similar queries should be posed to the Bible's final book. Are readers supposed to be happy that Christ has saved the saints from the oppressive hand of the powers that be? Are they to be horrified at the blood of the destroyed enemies, which flows as high as the horse's bridle for miles around (Rev. 14:20). Should they wonder what happened to the noble ethics of many of Jesus' teachings in the Gospels? Are death and destruction necessary to bring salvation – or is there some other way?

It is important to note that the New Testament's diversity is not limited to a simple distinction between the Gospels and Revelation; for there are violent images of Jesus in the Gospels and elements of a gentle, suffering Jesus in Revelation. For instance, in Revelation 5, the 'Lion of the tribe of Judah' who 'has conquered' is also the 'Lamb standing as if it had been slaughtered'. Likewise, in the Gospels Jesus teaches a radical form of non-violence – turn the other cheek – and yet at the same time claims that the express purpose of his mission is to bring hostility: 'I have not come to bring peace, but a sword' and to turn family members against one another. His constant casting of aspersions at the Jewish leaders and others who oppose him, as well as his cleansing of the temple, also suggest a more malevolent Jesus. One particularly compelling Gospel text which juxtaposes these competing portrayals is the parable of the sheep and the goats in Matthew 25. In this passage, the Son of Man, that is, the apocalyptic Jesus, separates the righteous from the wicked based on how they treated the Son of Man when he was hungry, thirsty, naked, sick, or in prison: 'Just as you did to the least of these, so you have done to me'. The Son of Man is simultaneously the 'least of these' and the powerful ruler who rewards and punishes. He is both the weak, disenfranchised sufferer and the one who has authority to banish people into eternal torment. Likewise, Karl is both the marginalized simpleton to whom acts of charity should be shown and the almighty judge who saves some and condemns others. He is the weakling who wields the sling blade. The lamb is the lion.

Other texts could certainly be mentioned, but the point is that complex images of Jesus are interwoven throughout the entire New Testament. Jesus refuses to be classified, stamped once and for all with a simple label that neatly defines his identity. The power of *Sling Blade* derives from its presentation of Karl as one who mirrors the complexity of the New Testament's understanding of Jesus. This in turn prompts reflection on several issues.

First is the matter of Christology – or christologies. Interacting with the film calls attention to the ambiguous nature of Jesus Christ as a figure of love and judgement, peace and violence, humility and power, kindness and vengeance, creativity, and destruction. To be sure, the second elements in these binary sets represent, for many readers, the difficult features of Christ. Yet, they are undeniable components of the Bible and should be integrated into a deeper Christological understanding. As higher biblical criticism has shown, it is not enough to recognize that each of the four Gospels, as well as other New Testament books, presents its own story and picture of Jesus. Rather, as Karl's depiction suggests, one must grapple with the harsh and unpalatable images of Jesus found in the Bible.

Rather than ignore or jettison these violent aspects of Christ as postmodern sensibilities might dictate, one can appeal to Mikhail Bakhtin's ideas of 'polyphony' and a 'dialogic sense of truth' (1984: 81). Briefly, for Bakhtin, dialogic truth requires multiple perspectives, a 'plurality of consciousness' that cannot be contained or expressed in a single view. Dialogic truth exists at the point where unmerged voices intersect, that is, in conversation. A polyphonic text, such as the Bible, presents separate and distinct ideas that are genuinely independent of one another. In such a text, the dialogic interplay of these various consciousnesses calls the reader to join the 'conversation'. Truth, then, is not monologic; it cannot be contained in one perspective. Seen in this light, the various depictions of Jesus in the New Testament represent distinct and indispensible ideologies that participate in and contribute to the development of dialogic (and Christological) truth. At times the biblical polyphony might sound utterly cacophonous and leave one echoing Karl's sentiments: 'I've read the Bible. I reckon I understand a good deal of it … but I can't understand all of it … It wasn't what I expected in a lot of places.' It is these unexpected – or perhaps unacknowledged – aspects of the biblical tradition that contribute to its rich, mysterious tapestry of voices.

The second topic that emerges when the film and biblical text are brought into dialogue is the ideology which motivates and drives presentations of Jesus, offered for our consideration and consumption. This includes every last one of them – whether from academic or religious circles. There is, of course, no objective, neutral portrayal of Jesus. There is no 'real Jesus' against which all others can be measured. Every portrayal, starting with all the different ones in the New Testament itself, is generated by people who have certain ideas and perspectives which colour and shape their interpretation of Jesus. Everyone creates their own image of Jesus, one that is often a reflection of their particular historical, religious, social, and cultural location. The complex depiction of Karl cautions against accepting as final and authoritative a single perspective on Jesus, whether in the canonical tradition – John's Gnostic redeemer Jesus or Mark's enigmatic, mysterious parabler – or in the interpretive tradition – the 'conservative' Jesus who died to save people from hell, the 'liberal' social revolutionary, the 'intellectual' sage, or the apocalyptic Jesus. Naturally, then, the film also calls viewers to engage critically and self-consciously their own perspective on Jesus, and the ideologies and agendas that have molded and influenced it.

Finally, *Sling Blade* invites one to reflect more generally on the paradoxical nature of life itself – lived as it is amidst both weakness and strength, kindness and vengeance, humility, and arrogance. Truth and reality are messy. Our own individual identities and lives are messy. Our world is messy. Recognizing and contemplating the grayness of life can perhaps facilitate the development of one's moral and ethical dimensions. Learning to be sensitive, for example, to the ambiguities of characters in literature and film may create a sense of care and compassion in one's relationships to other complex people. As dynamic and ambiguous protagonists, Karl and Jesus are much more engaging, memorable, and meaningful mythic figures precisely because they embody the intricacies of human existence.

Mark Roncace

Further reading

Michael Bakhtin (1984) *Problems of Dostoevsky's Poetics.* Trans. Caryl Emerson. Minneapolis, MN: University of Minnesota Press.

Matthew McEver (1998) 'The Messianic Figure in Film: Christology Beyond the Biblical Epic', *The Journal of Religion and Film.* 2(2), available online at www.unomaha.edu/jrf/McEverMessiah.htm

Gary Saul Morson and Caryl Emerson (1990) *Mikhail Bakhtin: Creation of a Prosaics.* Stanford, CA: Stanford University Press.

Sara Anson Vaux (1998) 'Will You Ever Kill Again, Karl', *Christianity and the Arts.* 5: 20–22.

SON OF MAN (JEZILE) (2006)

[Production Company: Spear Films / Dimpho Di Kopane. Director: Mark Dornford-May. Screenplay: Mark Dornford-May, Andiswa Kedama; Pauline Malefane. Cinematography: Giulio Biccari. Cast: Andile Kosi (Jesus), Andries Mbali (Satan), James Anthony (Gabriel), Pauline Malefane (Mother Mary),

Joel Mthethwa (Joseph), Ruby Mthethwa (Mary Magdalene), Jim Ngxabaze (Judas), Sibulele Mjali (Peter), Mvuyisi Mjali (Cajaphas), Zorro Sidloyi (Annas), Zamile Gantana (General Pilate).]

Somewhere in Africa, militiamen comb through school grounds. Viewers familiar with news footage of the Rwanda genocide (1994) will recognize these men immediately as a killer-squad which will neither take hostages nor let anyone live to bear witness to the massacre. A panic-stricken young woman rushes from one locked classroom to another. Eventually she finds one unlocked room, but as she stumbles into the room she is taken aback with fear and horror: a heap of dead bodies, mostly children, lies in the corner of the classroom. Yet the woman knows that she will survive only if she lies down among them and pretends to be dead herself. She thereby eludes her pursuers, whose leader is a man wearing a long black coat and carrying a tall stick topped by a crooked cloven hoof. After the death squad has moved on, the atmosphere lightens, indeed, it almost seems to float. And as the woman raises her head, she perceives a young boy in a white loincloth standing in front of her with some small, white feathers attached to his body. With a brilliant smile on his face he proclaims: 'Hail Mary … !' Through bewilderment the Magnificat bursts from her in a resonant alto.

Before this contextualized and staged annunciation to Mary, the story of the South African feature film *Son of Man* opens with the temptation of the adult Jesus in the desert. This scene not only introduces the main character and his antagonist, Satan, the man with the cloven hoof stick, but also sets the tone for one of the film's main theological themes: the eternal conflict between God and the forces of evil and unholiness.

The magic realism of this scene soon gives way to a fast-moving narrative in a mixture of styles, including realistic and tense political drama, cheerfully naive mystery plays, and musical theatre. Yet despite this broad variety of styles, the film maintains its narrative and thematic unity. Indeed, the clash of the seemingly incongruous projects energy in abundance, a phenomenon rarely found in the cinema and even less in the Jesus film genre.

As he did with his adaptation of George Bizet's Carmen, *U-Carmen* – which won the 2005 'Golden Bear' at the Berlin International Film Festival – the director, English-born Mark Dornford-May, transposes a well-known story into the milieu of South Africa's Townships employing an entirely black cast. Jesus is a young African whose uniform is not a billowing white robe but blue jeans and colourful shirts; he is a 'Son of Man' in the everyday as well as the religious sense. He is energetic and

· filled with a deep empathy for those suffering from poverty and sub-jugation; at the same time he is a charismatic figure who performs miracles and, in the end, overcomes his own death.

In his passionate and intrepid dedication to a non-violent transfor-mation of society, this Jesus reminds us of his counterpart in Pier Paolo Pasolini's adaptation of Matthew's Gospel (1964). Like Pasolini, Dornford-May follows the path of the 'second naiveté' (Wallace, 1995), aiming for an integration of the paschal and post-paschal tra-ditions central to the theology of the gospels. These traditions include the resurrection as well as some exemplary miracles, most prominently the raising of Lazarus. 'Second naiveté' describes a directness that appears to be crude but in fact has profound meaning. In this case, the directness concerns the transcendental sphere, a dimension that usually eludes the representational film-medium. For example, instead of represent-ing the angels of the New Testament infancy narratives symbolically, by arrows of light or by off-screen voices from heaven, Dornford-May, like Pasolini, blithely presents human actors as angels, and even equips his child-angels with puffy white feathers denoting wings. This straightforward 'naive' approach dissolves all aspirations of realism in the case of transcendence and transposes many images to a level of signs and symbols. This also holds true for the miracles that are presented in a very direct and simple manner by both Pasolini and Dornford-May.

The film was shot entirely in Cape Town and its surroundings, including the Townships. This setting is not meant however to localize the story to a single African country but rather to represent the African continent as a whole, with particular focus on the regions that have been experiencing tribal, religious or other tensions arising from internal conflicts over power. Geographical and personal names are drawn from the gospel accounts, but the story itself takes place in the present, as indicated by the setting and costuming as well as by the repeated motif of the (fictional) television news broadcasts by 'Channel 7: Reporting from the Kingdom of Judea, Africa'. Channel 7 announces the death of Herod and the ensuing unrest and re-alignment of the state by a military government. Jesus is born right into this heated situation.

The first half of the film narrates Jesus' early life: the aforementioned Annunciation and Mary's Magnificat, the journey towards Bethlehem for the census, Jesus' birth in a stall, the proclamation to the (child) shepherds, the visit of the three 'magi' coming from afar – these are the staples of every traditional gospel harmonization. However, this film takes the crucial step of translating these elements to a present-day, realistic milieu and integrating them with African rituals and traditions. Jesus' temptation, for example, is situated in the context of a traditional African coming-of-age ritual. In addition, many episodes, such as the encounter between Jesus and a woman accused of adultery, draw a close connection to African Liberation Theology.

The vivid portrayal allows us to view these events with fresh eyes. A formative event in the life of young Jesus – a fictional 'neo-apocryphal' addition by Dornford-May – depicts him as an eyewitness to the massacre of infants whose original target was Jesus himself. The film implies that this event helped to shape Jesus' mission and his message of non-violent protest. In a wonderful montage after his initiation into adulthood according to African rites of passage (cf. Giere 2011; cf. Reinhartz, Staley, Walsh, eds) – a scene that substitutes for the baptism – Jesus gathers male as well as female disciples. With his socio-critical proclamation, and his abilities as a charismatic healer he is very well received by the people. Eventually, however, he falls victim to the criminal political 'elite' strongly concerned in preserving their power. Yet he does not die on the cross, but suffers the fate of many other anti-government and anti-apartheid activists: he is beaten to death. Steve Biko serves as the historical model for Jesus' 'passion'; Dornford-May not only draws parallels with regard to their mission and their death, but also has his 'Son of Man' use Biko's writings in his own speeches.

Jesus' adversaries bury him somewhere in the desert. His mother and followers find his body with the help of a defector, who plays the role of the Roman centurion who avows himself to Jesus under the cross (Mark 15:39; Matt. 27:54). Jesus' friends take his body to the city – striking the pieta pose on a pickup truck – and erect him on a cross high above the ground as a compelling protest against the terror of the regime. The public display of people murdered by the regime was an important political instrument during the anti-apartheid struggle. In the film, it must be noted, the enemies are not white but black; race is not at the center of the conflict but power. Jesus' followers, who were dejected by his death, regroup underneath the cross, among them the strong and courageous female disciples, who also belong to the circle of Jesus' apostles. Lead by Jesus' mother Mary and encouraged by the presence of the crucified, Jesus' followers defy the order of the military to disperse. Instead they dance with such self-confidence that the soldiers, who were under orders to dissolve this 'demonstration', did nothing to stop them. The viewer rejoices in this moment of triumph and transcendence, achieved through the tremendous spiritual power of the dance.

This powerful image, full of hope, resembles an immanent resurrection in the sense that 'Jesus' cause' lives on. Yet, in the end it is surpassed by a resurrection which symbolically takes up its transcendent dimension. Over the empty grave in the desert we see Jesus' shadow and then those of two angels. They vanish from this place and the resurrected 'Son of Man' in his pre-paschal form comes into view, together with a lively and cheerful host of angels. All together, they joyfully ascend the slope leading to the podium where he was displayed on the cross. Laughing and triumphant, the resurrected Jesus bids farewell, with the gesture of the fist raised towards heaven, thus sealing his victory over the unholy powers concretized in the film's Satan figure. The film then freezes and the end-titles begin to roll, accompanied by scenes from everyday life in African townships. Although poverty and misery are still clearly visible, these scenes are filled with the hope for liberation and justice, embodied by the Son of Man.

How does Mark Dornford-May – a formerly successful director with the 'Royal Shakespeare Company' – come to direct such a film with an entirely African cast? Dornford-May was born in Chester, a small English town close to the border of Wales. Chester is well known for, and proud of, its Mystery Play tradition dating back as far as the fourteenth century. Chester is one of only four English cities where this tradition was re-animated in the twentieth century after being banned for many years. As a child, Dornford-May acted the part of a child-angel and over the years he played various other roles, culminating in the star role of Jesus. He later became a theatre director. In 2000 he was invited to South Africa, where he founded the theatre company 'Dimpho Di Kopane' ('joined talents') which employs only black actors, singers and dancers. In the ensemble's search for its first project, the Jesus-story soon came into focus: crossing the immense tribal differences in language and culture this story proved to be a unifying tradition, given that about 90 per cent South Africans are Christian. The basic structure of the plot of the play was derived from the medieval mystery play of Chester. The stage production 'The Mysteries – Yiimimangaliso' received international critical acclaim and served as basis for *Son of Man*. Today, Mark Dornford-May manages and directs the production company 'Isango Portobello' in South Africa; he is married to the actress and singer Pauline Malefane, his 'Carmen' and 'Mother of Jesus'. In 2007 he was initiated into the South African Sotho-tribe in a traditional ceremony.

Son of Man and Michael Winterbottom's *The Road to Guantanamo* won the 2006 'Founders Prize' at the Traverse City Film Festival in

Michigan, one of America's most important independent festivals. In his commendation, Michael Moore, one of the 'founding fathers' of the festival, recognized *Son of Man* as 'one of the most beautiful and disturbing films of the decade'. In 2007 the film received the 'Grand Jury Prize' at the Sundance Film Festival and was enthusiastically received by the audience. Unfortunately, no company was found in the US to distribute this film; the director presumes that this is due to the concern that a film with an entirely coloured cast might not be profitable. In many other countries *Son of Man* still awaits distribution. The DVD edition became available in 2009.

Son of Man is an exceptionally rich, multi-faceted creation and arguably the most interesting and innovative Jesus film since *The Last Temptation of Christ* (1988) and *Jesus of Montreal* (1989). It is a film that crosses many genres, a film that uses many sources, a film with numerous new and inventive perspectives on the Jesus figure and his disciples. The film reveals anew the continuing relevance and inner force of the Gospel. One will rarely find a film which more authentically and powerfully confronts its audience with the fact that the Gospel still inherits 'a tremendous charge of vitality', as Pier Paolo Pasolini once said.

Reinhold Zwick

Further reading

Sam Giere (2011) '"This is my World!" *Son of Man (Jezile)* and Cross-Cultural Convergences of Bible and World', *Journal of Religion and Film*, 15(1), available online at www.unomaha.edu/jrf/Vol15.no1/Giere_MyWorld.html

Adele Reinhartz, Jeffrey L. Staley, and Richard Walsh (2013) *An African Son of Man: Essays on Mark Dornford-May's 2006 Film* [working title], Sheffield: Sheffield Phoenix Press.

Mark S. Wallace (1995) *The Second Naiveté: Barth, Ricoeur and the New Yale Theology*. Macon, GA: Mercer University Press (2nd edition).

Reinhold Zwick (2011) 'Between Chester and Capetown. Transformations of the Gospel in *Son of Man* by Mark Dornford-May', *Journal of Religion and Film*, 15(1), available online at www.unomaha.edu/jrf/Vol15.no1/Zwick Tranforms.html

Further viewing

The Mysteries – Yiimimangaliso (Mark Dornford-May, 2001)
U-Carmen e-Khayelitsha (Mark Dornford-May, 2005)

SUPERMAN (1978)

[Production Company: Warner Brothers. Director: Richard Donner. Writers: Jerry Siegel, Joe Shuster, Mario Puzo, Robert Benton, David Newman, Leslie Newman, and Tom Mankiewicz (uncredited). Music: John Williams. Cinematographer: Geoffrey Unsworth. Cast Members: Christopher Reeve (Superman/Clark Kent), Margo Kidder (Lois Lane), Gene Hackman (Lex Luthor), Jackie Cooper (Perry White), Ned Beatty (Otis), Marlon Brando (Jor-El).]

Superhero Superman just does not seem to go away; from the inception of his curious identity and story in Depression-era America, the tale has been with us in one form or another. First came the comic book – the very first of the superhero comics – in June, 1939; it runs still, after reaching its seven hundredth issue in 2010. In the 1950s Supe made it to television for a six-year run in *The Adventures of Superman*, starring George Reeves as the very mild-mannered reporter; that series plays still in cableland and in a 2006 DVD collection of all 104 episodes. In 1978 director Richard Donner delivered his classic treatment, a serio-comic biopic that featured the indelible performance by the late Christopher Reeve. Between 1980 and 1987 three sequels with Reeve followed, though Donner did not direct those, having lost control during the cutting of *Superman II*. Then in 2001 another television series arrived on the scene, named *Smallville*, for the town in which Clark Kent grew to superhood, or at least maturity. By the end of *Smallville*'s run of ten years and over two hundred episodes, it had become the television's longest-running comic book-based series and also its longest-running North American science fiction series. Meanwhile, in 2006 the cinematic Superman returned in noted director Bryan Singer's *Superman Returns*, a well-intentioned but flat and derivative extension of the mythology. Nor is that the end of the saga of the saga, for high-tech director Zack Snyder has marshaled an all-star cast (Russell Crowe and Amy Adams, among others) for *Man of Steel* (2013). All of this activity constitutes unusual, and altogether super perdurance for the super man.

Still, amid all these varieties of Superman, and countless other come-lately comic-book movie super heroes (Ironman, Spiderman, Batman, Captain America, the Hulk, the Green Hornet, Captain America, and Hellboy), the inimitable *Superman*, the jewel among fantasy flicks, is Richard Donner's 1978 version. Donner's treatment remains fresh, inventive, funny, exuberant, and, due perhaps to a measure of gentle irony, both deeply likeable *and* moving, especially when joined with *Superman II* (1980), a sequel shot simultaneously with the first. These two films were, and remain, fresh and lively, the remarkable product of a whole corps of scriptwriters that included such notables as Mario Puzo and Robert Benton. Nonetheless, when all is said and done, the narrative core and appeal of the story is not new but very old stuff, if marvelously freshened and ingeniously cloaked.

In all his incarnations, *Superman* offers a vital, fetching, and even revelatory rendition of the Christ story. Perhaps more than any Jesus movie ever, it is the one that comes closest to getting 'the joke', as Frederick Buechner puts it, that is at the heart of that wild, preposterous Christian assertion of an incarnation that resounds in love and is, again in Buechner's words, 'too good not to be true' (1977: 61, 71) At its release, a few critics had noted that the Jesus story was the likely source of the movie. That hunch was finally confirmed by the admission of producer Tom Mankiewicz that the film-makers did indeed from the start have the Jesus story in mind (see Mankiewicz's audio commentary in 2001 DVD edition).

The film's most obvious evidence of its Gospel origins appears in the arc of the story itself. On the doomed planet of Krypton, Superman's father, Jor-El, prepares to save the life of his infant son Kal-El by sending him through space to a distant planet where he will not only survive but have vastly superior physical strength, scientific knowledge, and, as events make clear, understanding, sympathy, and compassion. Of course, the names themselves suggest the characters' supra-human status, for 'El' in Hebrew means God. But an important innovation lies here. The comic book history of son Kal-El, alias Clark Kent and Superman, simply hurled the child randomly into space in the hope that he would land somewhere hospitable. In the film, Jor-El, clothed in white and glistening light, has selected a planet and civilization for his 'only son' that has the potential to be good if only they had a 'leader to show them the way'. And so he lands mysteriously in a blaze of light on earth in very rural America, the modern American equivalent of Galilee, an ignoble outback in the eyes of Jesus' contemporaries.

The humble and childless farm couple who find him, Martha Clark and Jonathan Kent, have names that could not be closer to Mary and Joseph without giving away the joke. With them, the adolescent Clark, masquerading as a nerd, keeps his supernatural powers a secret, as he is urged to do by his adoptive father, who assures him that for whatever reason he arrived on earth it 'was not to score touchdowns'.

Meanwhile he privately exults in kicking footballs into space and outrunning speeding locomotives. In late adolescence, he reluctantly leaves his widowed mother for an arctic 'fortress of solitude' where he is schooled by Jar-El via holograms in the ways of his earthly refuge. After roughly twelve years have passed, he ventures to Metropolis to assume his calling of servanthood. He is thirty years old, exactly the age at which it is traditionally thought that Jesus began his public life.

In *Superman*, Clark/Superman's chief struggle lies not primarily in defeating the evil, and the ridiculous, machinations of Lex Luthor but, in a marked parallel to the Lazarus story in John 11, in his choice to resurrect his true love Lois Lane. In *Superman II*, Kent struggles with the personal sacrifices of his calling – the choice to forego human intimacy, both sexual and relational – and so he remains celibate and very much alone, thereby echoing Jesus's chastity and solitude among uncomprehending, fickle followers.

The screenplay pointedly underscores the Christ motif in playful, humourous ways. The blustery Perry White, the editor-in-chief of the Metropolis newspaper *The Daily Planet* and Clark Kent's boss, announces that whichever reporter interviews the mysterious Superman will have the most important interview since 'God talked to Moses'. Jor-El sends his benedictory comments to 'my only son', a phrase he emphatically repeats in direct allusion to the famous phrase : 'For God so loved the world, he sent his only begotten son … ' (John 3:16). Before sealing Kal-El into the capsule that will carry him to earth, Jor-El sermonizes on the distinctly Johannine mystery of the co-indwelling of the Father and the Son (John 16:15, 28; 17:6–7, 10, 11, 21):

> All that I have, all that I have learned, everything that I feel, all this and more, I bequeath to you, my son. You'll carry me inside you all the days of your life. You will make my strength your own, see my life through your eyes, as your life will be seen through mine. From the son comes the father, and the father the son.

After Superman rescues Lois Lane from a serious helicopter accident, she asks haltingly, 'Who are you? The answer is simple, and also a fitting theological summation of the purposes of the Incarnation: simply put, 'A friend', says he. The question of Jesus' identity is a major theme in all of the Gospels – and is asked by the crowds, the disciples, and the authorities (Matt. 27:11, Mark 14:61–62, Luke 22:66–70, 23:3, and John 18:33–38).

This, though, is a movie, and words, no matter how fittingly scripted and placed, only go so far in accounting for audience enthusiasm. Indeed, the great achievement of the film lies in the crafting of narrative and character with an especially ingenious use of images and music, and in telling a story that has at its core profound human surprise and elation. To that end, the film-makers take a good while to deliver Clark Kent to Metropolis. His pre-history weighs heavily, imbuing him with considerable humanity, from his poignant departure from Krypton through his father's death and his tender farewell to his mother in response to the 'call' from the green crystal, a techno-version of the Holy Spirit. Throughout, viewers wonder what shape and guise this superman-in-the-making will finally assume. We get but a glimpse of the caped man as he leaves his hermitage in the Arctic.

At last, in the offices of *The Daily Planet*, arrives a clumsy, bumbling, inept clown, though as Perry White tells Lois, Clark Kent is a really good writer and 'the fastest typist I've ever seen'. Kent looks the nerd, or the clown, with hunched shoulders, over-sized eyeglasses that constantly slip, short pants, overlarge shirt, and greased-up hair. His voice squeaks, and he moves with the grace of an anxious penguin. Never has there been a less likely super man. The George Reeves of the 50s television serial was notable for his blandness; Donner's Clark Kent brandishes ineptitude in just about every sphere of ordinary life.

So it is with surprise and delight that this clumsy oaf transfigures into a creature of enormous grace, beauty, and power who does his wonder-filled work with finesse, gentleness, and humour. These qualities emerge in Superman's own relish for his tasks. He jokes with Lois Lane in the midst of saving her and is invariably polite, as when returning the tree-bound kitten to the little girl. This courtesy extends to his dealings with violent criminals, with whom he is always non-violent. He exults in his own ability to fly, especially when he takes Lois with him. Strangely, this is a Superman who is as interested in savouring the world as he is in saving it. Throughout, John Williams' score adds a resonant echo with its mix of majesty and lilting tenderness, especially in moments of revelatory surprise, as when the Kents' new son lifts the truck and when Supe dashes across the street tearing open his shirt to reveal the emblematic 'S'. Like the film's hero, the music self-consciously delights in its own tale.

The film's playfulness becomes even more apparent in its treatment of evil, in the person of Lux Luthor. If Clark Kent enjoys acting the clown, if only to make bystanders feel happy that they are not so inept as he is, the pompous Luthor takes his calling as 'the world's greatest criminal genius' entirely seriously, especially when dealing with his genuinely dense sidekicks, Otis and Miss Teschmaker. While he is insidious, his preposterous grand scheme of stealing a rocket to trigger an earthquake that will sink the California coast to turn his desert real estate into prime beachfront, is byzantine in the extreme. To be sure, he represents and intends evil but his buffoonish self-importance subverts his scariness, and contrasts with other movie villains such as the ominous Joker who opposes Batman in *The Dark Knight* (2008). Superman's job is to save the world from the darkness that Luthor represents. That job includes rescuing a school bus that is teetering from a bridge and saving Lois Lane from being swallowed up, whether by an earthquake or by self-concern. He comes to the rescue as a 'friend' who addresses the tragedies of both peril and lostness. He thus illustrates the proposition articulated in John 3:16, that divine love for humankind is so deep that it chooses to walk (or, in the case of Superman, fly) a wounded, tear-soaked earth. Jor-El sends his only son to earth for this very purpose. For those about him, then, and for viewers, no small part of the appeal of *Superman* lies in its re-telling of the central Christian narrative. Its high comedy, mystery, and adventure successfully cloak (or should we say 'cape'?) the source that gives the tale its power, cogency, and delight. Indeed, the great accomplishment of *Superman* is that it delivers the full thematic clout of what an Incarnation might look and feel like.

Roy M. Anker

Further reading

Roy M. Anker (2004) *Catching Light: Looking for God in the Movies.* Grand Rapids: Eerdmans.

Frederick Buechner (1977) *Telling the Truth: The Gospel as Tragedy, Comedy, and Fairy-Tale.* San Francisco: Harper.

Neil Hurley (1982) 'Cinematic Transfigurations of Jesus', in John R. May and Michael Bird (eds) *Religion in Film.* Nashville: University of Tennessee Press. pp. 61–78.

Adele Reinhartz (2007) *Jesus of Hollywood.* New York: Oxford University Press.

THE TEN COMMANDMENTS (1956)

[Production Company: Paramount Pictures. Director: Cecil B. DeMille. Screen Writer: Æneas MacKenzie, Jesse L. Lasky Jr, Jack Gariss, Fredric M. Frank derived from The Holy Scriptures, the ancient texts of Philo,

Josephus, Eusebius, The Midrash and the books *Prince of Egypt* by Dorothy Clarke Wilson, *Pillar of Fire* by Rev. J.H. Ingraham, *On Eagle's Wings* by Rev. A.E. Southon. Cinematography: Loyal Griggs (Director of Photography), J. Peverell Marley, John Warren, Wallace Kelley (Additional Photography), John P. Fulton (Special Photographic Effects). Music: Elmer Bernstein. Art Director: Hal Pereira, Walter Tyler, Albert Nozaki. Film Editor: Anne Bauchens. Costume: Edith Head, Ralph Jester, John Jensen, Dorothy Jeakins, Arnold Friberg. Major Cast: Charlton Heston (Moses/voice of God), Yul Brynner (Rameses), Anne Baxter (Nefretiri), Edward G. Robinson (Dathan), Yvonne De Carlo (Sephora), Debra Paget (Lilia), John Derek (Joshua), Sir Cedric Hardwicke (Sethi), Nina Foch (Bithiah), Martha Scott (Yochabel), Judith Anderson (Memnet), Vincent Price (Baka), John Carradine (Aaron), Olive Deering (Miriam), Douglass Dumbrille (Jannes), Frank DeKova (Abiram), Henry Wilcoxon (Pentaur), Eduard Franz (Jethro), Donald Curtis (Mered), Lawrence Dobkin (Hur Ben Caleb), H.B. Warner (Amminadab), Julia Faye (Elisheba), Lisa Mitchell (Jethro's daughter).]

Moses was the chosen of The Chosen, *the* heroic holy man of the Old Testament who presided over two watershed moments in Hebrew history – the Exodus from Egypt and the divine revelation at Sinai. His epic story is told within the books of Exodus to Deuteronomy and elsewhere (KJV and hereafter). Its narrative arc ranges from cast-out Hebrew baby (Exod. 2:3) to Egyptian prince (Exod. 2:10), from fleeing murderer (Exod. 2:12–15) to domesticated shepherd (Exod. 3:1), from divinely appointed leader (Exod. 3:2–10) to practicing miracle worker (Exod. 7:10; 14:21), from Egyptian plague-and-death bringer (Exod. 7–12) to national liberator (Exod. 13:17), from God's Decalogue lawgiver (Exod. 20:1–17) to burdened wanderer in the wilderness for forty years (Num. 14:33). Despite seeing God face to face (Exod. 33:11), overcoming incredible obstacles and successfully completing his arduous mission, Moses was himself denied entry into the Promised Land (Deut. 34:4) and then promptly died (Deut. 34:5).

Moses is a hero to three world faiths (Judaism, Christianity and Islam) whose sacred story was creatively reimagined by DeMille. He artfully employed sacred scripture, ancient history and religious novels to blend fact with fiction, and faith with fun, to save sinners' souls (Wright 1996). As he claimed near the end of his life: '*my* ministry was making religious movies and getting more people to read the Bible than anyone else ever has' (Orrison 1999: 108). This legendary Hollywood lay preacher crafted his Moses with human and holy qualities that cohered with scriptural prescriptions and public expectations, conditioned by two millennia of Church teachings and the narrative accretions of history, legend and art.

DeMille's Moses biopic traversed sexual temptation, moral virtue and the triumph of community. His major film-making challenge was to convey the weak, meek, mystical and monumental Moses in a logically meaningful, scripturally supported, and dramatically engaging fashion. Unfortunately, the Bible is silent about many of the factual details of Moses' biography. This practical difficulty prompted DeMille to employ strategies such as the deft deployment of creative scriptural extrapolation to fill in the narrative gaps (Kozlovic 2010) and thus make *explicit* what may only have been *implicit* within the scriptures.

To be a compelling film figure, DeMille's Moses had to balance solemnity with sagaciousness as the ambassador of God, the front man for the Sinai covenant and the possessor of great supernatural powers. He also had to cope with his own failings: he stammered and was fearful, passionate, emotional, violent and self-doubting when burdened by fickle followers and deadly denizens. Fortunately, DeMille's epic rendering of Holy Writ was a phenomenal commercial and cultural success that starred the relatively inexperienced Charlton Heston, chosen because of his likeness to Michelangelo's statue of Moses, and then closely coached on and off the set to ensure that DeMille's authorial vision prevailed.

DeMille also creatively merged archetypal imagery and epic effects with scriptural narrative. His Prince Moses was a conquering military general and an accomplished monumental architect, bringing to life Acts' description of Moses as 'learned in all the wisdom of the Egyptians' and 'mighty in words and in deeds' (Acts 7:22), as well as Exodus' comment that he was 'very great in the land of Egypt, in the sight of Pharaoh's servants, and in the sight of the people' (Exod. 11:3). In line with Deuteronomy's comment that at a 'hundred and twenty years old when he died: his eye was not dim, nor his natural force abated' (Deut. 34:7), DeMille's Moses was virile and monumental throughout his entire life. DeMille's true-believer stance was frequently at odds with less knowledgeable critics who decried his supposed filmic 'errors', but who did not know scripture as intimately as this life-long Bible student and lay scholar (Noerdlinger 1956).

DeMille had also cinematically enacted God's promise: 'I will be with thy mouth' (Exod. 4:12) and so he de-emphasized the Moses who was 'slow of speech' (Exod. 4:10) by crafting his prophet as the mouthpiece of God, and a holy warrior of few wasted words. DeMille-the-public-pleaser had decided that audiences could not tolerate a stammering Moses for very long. As a Christian apologist,

DeMille did not accentuate the scriptural Moses' unsavoury side involving sexual slavery (Num. 31:18), callously ordering the deaths of women and children (Num. 31:17), forcing people to drink powdered metal (Exod. 32:20), or mercilessly executing three thousand men (Exod. 32:28). DeMille chose instead to focus upon God's righteous wrath and to extend Moses' positive character trajectory by crafting him as a deeply layered Christ-figure to further enhance his heroic 'good guy' status and subtextual religious potency (Kozlovic 2006).

Historically speaking, *The Ten Commandments* had out-DeMilled DeMille's previous biblical blockbuster, *Samson and Delilah* (1949), to become the jewel in the crown of the religious movie genre, the epitome of the biblical epic and the apogee of DeMille's film-making career. Six decades later, it is still *the* definitive Moses biopic; it is regularly screened during Passover and Easter worldwide, and has earned numerous awards, prizes and nominations. In addition to being one of the most famous and financially successful Bible films of all time, it rightfully belongs to the 'They Don't Make'm Like That Anymore!' category because of its gargantuan, and, nowadays, financially unviable, production values. It is full of memorable dialogue and raw emotion, outstanding performances and stunning vistas shot in VistaVision, while its spectacular special effects and cast-of-thousands – DeMille's auteur signature – set the standard for the epic genre as a whole. The spectacular parting of the Red Sea, the green-misted Angel of Death, and the snake transmutation scenes among DeMille's other on-screen miracles still generate awe and unease today (Pardes 1996). DeMille originally planned to film all ten plagues of Egypt and had prepared many prop frogs (Exod. 8:2–14), but this segment, and others, never got filmed due to delay problems and cost cutting imperatives for his already exorbitantly priced production. Ironically, DeMille's dialogue and dramatic construction was far more powerful and engaging than the scriptures' account of events, which allegedly prompted James Thurber to quip: 'It makes you realize what God could have done if He'd had the money' (Fraser 1988: vii).

Not only did the film embody DeMille's true-believer biblical stance and pro-Christian biases, but it also provided a platform for his staunch pro-freedom, pro-America and rabid anti-Communist beliefs during the Cold War (DeMille 1956). These political views are explicitly articulated in the pre-prologue curtain address which opens the film (Nadel 1993). His film brought to attention 'the story of the birth of freedom, the story of Moses' and asked: 'Are men the property of the State, or are they free souls under God?' – a question which was fundamental for both Judeo-Christianity and Western civilization.

Indeed, it was DeMille's second page-to-projector attempt at telling the Moses-Exodus-freedom tale. In 1923, he first filmed a black-and-white triptych, also entitled *The Ten Commandments*, that featured Ancient Egypt, modern-day America, and a flash-back to Jesus in Ancient Israel. This film became a classic of the silent screen, a cinematic saviour of Hollywood threatened by moral vigilantes, and a partial template for his 1956 film (Higashi 1996).

DeMille sometimes factored in audience expectations that overruled historical accuracy. For example, the architecture of Ancient Egypt was garishly coloured, unlike the monochrome archaeological remnants seen today, and so DeMille deliberately de-coloured his on-screen architecture to cohere with this popular expectation and not to distract audiences from his storyline. And since DeMille's Moses was the epitome of ancient masculinity (and a mirror of DeMille-the-macho-man), he did not wear a feminine-like veil to cover his shining face as scripturally documented (Exod. 34:33–35).

Furthermore, as part of his symbolic system and multi-layered artfulness, DeMille used serpent imagery *overtly* to tag the snake-loving Egyptian empire, *covertly* to tag its serpent evilness from a Judeo-Christian perspective, and *subtextually* to suggest that the evil empire of 1950s Communism was as cunning as a serpent. Therefore, DeMille graphically depicted the confrontational rods-into-snakes transformation scene before Pharaoh (indicating God's one-upmanship over evil), and then subtly featured snakes everywhere else – upon the architect's scale (balancing evil), Bithiah's bead-making loom (weaving evil's fate), the Shur desert stone stele (marking evil's territory), the columns in Rameses' throne room (supported by evil), the royal snake balcony (guarded by evil), the harnesses of Pharaoh's charioteers (an army of evil), and the Golden Calf orgy scene (tagging evil). In addition, Rameses accused Nefretiri of having a 'serpent's tongue'; Nefretiri wore a snake-themed headdress (evil's woman) as did the Pharaohs (evil's earthly bosses) thus implying that their minds were under evil's domination. It was a significant part of DeMille's auteur trademark to repeatedly state the same message in as many ways as possible to ensure that it penetrated audiences' consciousness.

DeMille's film is a staple of American popular culture and a twentieth century cultural icon (Orrison 1999; Wright 2003); it is also a guilty pleasure for many people, including Martin Scorsese, who viewed it over forty times (Scorsese 1998: 46). It has been a target for comedy, as in *History of the World: Part I* (Mel Brooks, 1981), in which its DeMille-like Moses descended the holy mountain with God's fifteen commandments, only to drop a tablet and end up with the iconic ten of Judeo-Christianity, and in the cop comedy, *The Naked Gun 2½: The Smell of Fear* (David Zucker, 1991), in which the erection of Sethi's jubilee obelisk was shown just as Lieutenant Frank Drebin was having sex. A film clip of a lovelorn Nefretiri featured in *To Wong Foo, Thanks for Everything! Julie Newmar* (Beeban Kidron, 1995) when drag queens employed it as a style role model for a lovelorn Snydersville girl, and the parting of the Red Sea scene played on TV within the UFO classic *Close Encounters of the Third Kind* (Steven Spielberg, 1977) to signal another seminal moment of unfolding extra-terrestrial mysteries.

Of course, all subsequent Moses pictures have had to contend with DeMille's *magnum opus* in one way or another, to their inevitable credit or detriment (Britt 2004; Homan 2007). In 1999, *The Ten Commandments* was selected for preservation in the United States National Film Registry (Library of Congress) for being culturally, historically, or aesthetically significant. Overall, as Jon Solomon (2001: 158) succinctly summed it up: 'In terms of scope, inspiration, colour, and biblically (divinely?) inspired special effects, the film has still not met its equal.'

Anton Karl Kozlovic

Further reading

Brian Britt (2004) *Rewriting Moses: The Narrative Eclipse of the Text*. London: T&T Clark International.

Cecil B. DeMille (1956) *Why I Made The Ten Commandments: An Address by Cecil B. DeMille at a Luncheon at the Plaza Hotel Just Prior to the Opening of his Motion Picture Production at the Criterion Theatre in New York City*. USA: np.

George M. Fraser (1988) *The Hollywood History of the World*. London: Michael Joseph.

Sumiko Higashi (1996) 'Antimodernism as Historical Representation in a Consumer Culture: Cecil B. DeMille's *The Ten Commandments*, 1923, 1956, 1993', in Vivian Sobchack (ed.) *The Persistence of History: Cinema, Television, and the Modern Event*. New York, NY: Routledge. pp. 91–112.

Michael M. Homan (2007) 'The Good Book and the Bad Movies: Moses and the Failure of Biblical Cinema', in Sarah Malena and David Miano (eds) *Milk and Honey: Essays on Ancient Israel and the Bible in Appreciation of the Judaic Studies Program at the University of California, San Diego*. Winona Lake, IN: Eisenbrauns. pp. 87–112.

Anton K. Kozlovic (2006) 'The Construction of a Christ-figure within the 1956 and 1923 Versions of Cecil B. DeMille's *The Ten Commandments*'. *The Journal of Religion in Film* 10(1), available online at www.unomaha. edu/jrf/vollØno1/kozlovicMoses.htm.

——(2010) 'The Art of Creative Scriptural Extrapolation: Bithiah, Mered and 1 Chronicles 4:18 within Cecil B. DeMille's *The Ten Commandments*

(1956)', *Kinema: A Journal for Film and Audiovisual Media* 33 (Spring), available online at www.kinema.uwaterloo.ca/article.php?id=467&feature.

Alan Nadel (1993) 'God's Law and the Wide Screen: *The Ten Commandments* as Cold War "Epic"', *PMLA* 108(3): 415–30.

Henry S. Noerdlinger (1956) *Moses and Egypt: The Documentation to the Motion Picture The Ten Commandments*. Los Angeles, CA: University of Southern California Press.

Katherine Orrison (1999) *Written in Stone: Making Cecil B. DeMille's Epic, The Ten Commandments*. Lanham, MO: Vestal Press.

Ilana Pardes (1996) 'Moses Goes Down to Hollywood: Miracles and Special Effects', *Semeia* 74: 15–31.

Martin Scorsese (1998) 'Martin Scorsese's Guilty Pleasures', *Film Comment* 34(3): 46–8.

Jon Solomon (2001) *The Ancient World in the Cinema*. Rev. ed. New Haven, CT: Yale University Press.

Melanie J. Wright (1996) 'Dialogue or Dominance? Interfaith Encounter and Cecil B. DeMille's *The Ten Commandments*', *Discernment: An Ecumenical Journal of Inter-Religious Encounter* 3(1): 10–19.

——(2003) *Moses in America: The Cultural Uses of Biblical Narrative*. Oxford: Oxford University Press.

Further viewing

The Life of Moses (J. Stuart Blackton, 1909)
The Ten Commandments (Cecil B. DeMille, 1923)
Moon of Israel (Michael Curtiz, 1924)
Moses the Lawgiver (Gianfranco De Bosio, 1974)
Moses and Aaron (Danièle Huillet and Jean-Marie Straub, 1975)
Animated Stories from the Bible: Moses – From Birth to Burning Bush (Richard Rich, 1993)
Moses (Roger Young, 1995)
The Prince of Egypt (Brenda Chapman, Steve Hickner and Simon Wells, 1998)
The Ten Commandments (Robert Dornhelm, 2006)
The Ten Commandments: The Musical (Robert Iscove, 2006)
Exodus (Penny Woolcock, 2007)
The Ten Commandments (Bill Boyce and John Stronach, 2007)

FILM AND TELEVISION INDEX

FILMOGRAPHY

TELEVISION SERIES

INDEX TO ANCIENT SOURCES

SUBJECT INDEX